The Rule of Unwritten International Law

This book seeks to re-appreciate the concept of customary international law as a form of spontaneous societal self-organisation, and to develop the methodological consequences that ensue from this conception for the practice of its application. In pursuing this aim, the author draws from three different strands of scholarship that have not yet been considered in connection with one another: First, general jurisprudential theories of customary law; second, theories of customary international law, especially as they relate to international relations scholarship; and third, methodological approaches to the interpretation of international law. This expansive, philosophical layout of the book enables the author to put the conceptual enigmas of customary international law into a broader perspective.

Among the issues discussed in the book are the dichotomy of its traditional and modern forms and the respective benefits and disadvantages of inductive and deductive approaches to its ascertainment. In the course of this analysis, the author draws insights from Friedrich August Hayek's theory of law as a 'spontaneous order', an information-processing device which enables the participants of a legal system to make use of decentralised knowledge. The book argues that the major advantage of custom as a source of international law lies in the fact that it is the result of a gradual process of trial and error, rather than the product of deliberate planning. This makes it a particularly apposite source of law in a time of seismic shifts in the distribution of power within a vastly diverse community of States, when a new global order is expected to emerge, the contours of which are not yet clearly discernible.

This book applies general concepts of legal philosophy to explain the continuing relevance of custom as a source of international law while at the same time inferring from this theoretical framework concrete practical and methodological consequences, the most important of which is the special role that purposive interpretation plays with respect to rules of international custom. Given this broad approach, the book will be of interest to several groups of potential readers including academics interested in the philosophy of customary law in general, academic international lawyers and legal practitioners, especially judges, scholars of international relations and all those interested in how the international community of States organises itself.

Peter G. Staubach is a research fellow at Humboldt University in Berlin, Germany.

Routledge Research in International Law

For a full list of titles in this series, visit https://www.routledge.com/Routledge-Research-in-International-Law/book-series/INTNLLAW

Available:

Latin America and the International Court of Justice
Contributions to International Law
Edited by Paula Wojcikiewicz Almeida and Jean-Marc Sorel

Fragmentation vs the Constitutionalisation of International Law
A Practical Inquiry
Edited by Andrzej Jakubowski and Karolina Wierczyńska

Legal Accountability and Britain's Wars 2000–2015
Peter Rowe

Means of Transportation and Registration of Nationality
Transportation Registered by International Organizations
Vincent P. Cogliati-Bantz

Regionalism in International Law
Ján Klučka

The International Criminal Court and Nigeria
Implementing the Complementarity Principle Of The Rome Statute
Muyiwa Adigun

Armed Conflict and Forcible Displacement
Individual Rights under International Law
Elena Katselli Proukaki

The Rule of Unwritten International Law
Customary Law, General Principles, and World Order
Peter G. Staubach

State Interest and the Sources of International Law
Doctrine, Morality, and Non-Treaty Law
Markus P. Beham

The Rule of Unwritten International Law

Customary Law, General Principles, and World Order

Peter G. Staubach

Routledge
Taylor & Francis Group
LONDON AND NEW YORK

First published 2018
by Routledge

2 Park Square, Milton Park, Abingdon, Oxfordshire OX14 4RN
52 Vanderbilt Avenue, New York, NY 10017

Routledge is an imprint of the Taylor & Francis Group, an informa business

First issued in paperback 2020

Library of Congress Cataloging in Publication Data
Names: Staubach, Peter G., author.
Title: The rule of unwritten international law customary law, general principles, and world order / Peter G. Staubach.
Description: New York, NY : Routledge, 2018. | Series: Routledge research in international law | Includes bibliographical references and index.
Identifiers: LCCN 2017053226 | ISBN 9780815382911 (hardback) | ISBN 9781351207300 (web pdf) | ISBN 9781351207294 (epub) | ISBN 9781351207287 (mobipocket)
Subjects: LCSH: Customary law, International.
Classification: LCC KZ1277 .S73 2018 | DDC 341--dc23
LC record available at https://lccn.loc.gov/2017053226

ISBN: 978-0-8153-8291-1 (hbk)
ISBN: 978-0-367-59138-0 (pbk)

Typeset in Galliard
by Taylor & Francis Books

Contents

Preface

This book is a revised and updated version of my PhD thesis that I submitted in early 2015 and defended in March 2016 at Humboldt University Berlin. It began its life as something much narrower in focus: A comparative study of the doctrinal approaches of domestic courts in the application of rules of customary international law. As such, it was part of my work on the research project 'Domestic Courts and the Interpretation of International Law', conducted at Humboldt University and funded by the German Research Foundation. Very soon, however, I discovered that it is very difficult, and ultimately unsatisfying, simply to describe 'what the courts are doing in fact', without having a normative theory of what they should be doing, and why. This book is an attempt to answer this question. It seeks to explain both the nature and the continuing significance of customary international law, this strangely anachronistic source of law that has often been declared dead, yet that still permeates the international legal order and continues to perplex the law-appliers.

This book is a product of the extremely inspiring intellectual environment at Humboldt University Berlin. Special thanks are due to my supervisor, Professor Georg Nolte, who constantly encouraged and challenged me alike, while providing me with the academic freedom I needed in order to cut my own way through the jungle that is the theory of customary international law. Thanks are also due to my former colleagues at Professor Nolte's chair, especially to Helmut Aust, now Professor at Free University Berlin, and Alejandro Rodiles, Professor at the Instituto Tecnológico Autonomo de México (ITAM). With both, I spent long afternoons on stimulating discussions on intricate matters of the history and theory of international law, and both have been extremely generous in offering their good advice, especially at the many times when I felt my project was 'getting out of hand'.

I am also grateful to the anonymous reviewers for their thoughtful comments on my book proposal, as well as to Brianna Ascher and her wonderful team at Routledge, who have been extremely helpful during all stages of this book project.

Last, but not least, I would like to thank my parents for their support and encouragement. To them I dedicate this book.

Berlin, September 2017
Peter G. Staubach

I Introduction

A. The Rule of Unwritten International Law: A Pragmatic Ideal

In 1923, scarcely six years after the October Revolution, the Soviet legal scholar Evgeny Korovin published an influential book entitled *International Law of the Transition Period*.[1] His main argument was that the Soviet Union occupied a unique place among the states of the world, insofar as it was the first nation on earth in which a genuine proletarian revolution had been successfully completed. While world revolution was, according to Korovin, an inevitable historical necessity that would ultimately lead to the disappearance of sovereign states altogether, the Soviet Union had to maintain, for the time being, tolerable working relations with the remaining 'bourgeois' states. This excluded anything that would amount to a recognition of the political legitimacy of the 'imperialist nations', or contribute to their internal stabilisation, but included cooperation on non-political issues like disease control or other questions of a more technical or administrative nature.[2] Compared with traditional 'bourgeois' international law, Korovin's 'transitional international law' was characterised by an emphasis on bilateral treaties rather than customary international law as the primary source, as he regarded rules of international custom to be an anachronistic expression of the traditional relations between imperialist states, and thus not as a suitable instrument of progress towards a more just and equitable world order.[3]

History does not repeat itself, but sometimes it rhymes. And thus, a quarter of a century ago the world saw another historic upheaval, the downfall of the Socialist bloc in the years following 1989. These momentous events gave rise to the expectation that traditional international law based on the coexistence of

1 E Korovin, *Mezhdunarodnoe pravo perekhodnogo vremeni* (Moscow/Petrograd, Gosudarstvennoe Izdatel'stvo 1923); a German translation appeared in 1929 under the title *Das Völkerrecht der Übergangszeit: Grundlagen der völkerrechtlichen Beziehungen der Union der Sowjetrepubliken* (I Robinson-Kaunas tr, Berlin-Grunewald, Rothschild 1929).

2 Korovin, *Mezhdunarodnoe pravo perekhodnogo vremeni* (n 1) 15 et seqq.

3 For a more detailed analysis of Korovin's international law theory in this respect, see T Langström, *Transformation in Russia and International Law* (Leiden, Martinus Nijhoff 2003) 57–62.

sovereign states – a concept which the long stalemate of the Cold War had only reinforced – could be gradually replaced by a quantitatively and qualitatively new form of global law, a law that was no longer indifferent towards the internal political order of states. As Anne-Marie Slaughter put it in her seminal 1995 article *International Law in a World of Liberal States*, '[t]he most distinct aspect of Liberal international relations theory is that it permits, indeed mandates, a distinction among different types of States based on their domestic political structure and ideology'.[4]

The underlying assumption was that liberal democracies are less likely to resort to war, that the violation of human rights within a state has a direct negative impact on the stability of world order, and that it is therefore justified to exert influence on states to push them towards adopting liberal democratic forms of government.[5] This approach was most forcefully advocated by the philosopher John Rawls, who argued in his controversial[6] book *The Law of Peoples* that it was permissible for liberal democracies to engage in 'just wars' against what he referred to as 'outlaw states' (those which do not afford their citizens a minimum of human rights and democratic participation), as the latter should be conceived of as a threat to international peace and stability.[7] International lawyers who advocated the liberal political agenda were not prepared to go quite as far as Rawls in legitimising 'just war', but they, too, argued that the concept of 'sovereignty', with its clear distinction between internal and external affairs, was becoming obsolete,[8] and that a 'right to democratic governance'[9] was emerging in international law.

Korovin's approach and that of the liberal universalists of the early 1990s share some characteristics: Both believed that an epochal transition was taking place, as more and more states would ultimately adopt a more desirable political system. And both approaches were based on the assumption that these changes of internal political organisation would fundamentally alter the relations between states for the better. However, there was also a significant difference:

4 AM Slaughter, 'International Law in a World of Liberal States' (1995) 6 *European Journal of International Law* 503 (504).
5 For a positive assessment of this claim, see RL Schweller, 'Domestic Structure and Preventive War: Are Democracies more Pacific?' (1992) 44 *World Politics* 235; in a tone that is typical for this period, Schweller concludes that 'as long as the Soviet Union continues along the path of democratization and economic liberalization, it will not wage a preventive war against a reunified Germany' (ibid, 268).
6 For an overview of the debate, see G Brock, *Global Justice: A Cosmopolitan Approach* (Oxford, Oxford University Press 2009); see esp ibid, ch II: 'The Debate about Rawl's "Law of Peoples": Critics and Defences'.
7 J Rawls, *The Law of Peoples. With 'The Idea of Public Reason Revisited'* (Cambridge/MA, Harvard University Press 1999); for Rawl's 'just war' theory, see ibid, § 13 (89–94).
8 See for a prominent example of this approach L Henkin, 'That "S-Word": Sovereignty, and Globalization, and Human Rights, et cetera…' (1999) 68 *Fordham Law Review* 1.
9 T Franck, 'The Emerging Right to Democratic Governance' (1992) 86 *American Journal of International Law* 46.

Whereas early Soviet theorists, like Korovin, saw international law as a mere concomitant of a change that was precipitated by other forces, namely the inevitable pull towards a superior ideology, scholars like Slaughter, Franck or Henkin regarded international law as the mainspring of the alleged progress towards the universal victory of liberal democratic principles.[10] The perception of this time was that the end of the Cold War finally paved the way for the realisation of the ambitious goals enshrined in the UN Charter. With respect to the 1990s, it has been observed that 'a self-confident liberal conception of international law was the lodestar of the decade'.[11] Underlying this conception was, however, a peculiar vision of international law, one that emphasised collective action by international organisations, especially the UN Security Council, and global legislation through ambitious multilateral treaty regimes such as the WTO treaty, concluded in 1994, or the 1998 Rome Statute of the International Criminal Court. Already in 1987, W Michael Reisman had posed the (rhetorical) question of whether 'custom can really address the needs of global civilization in the late 20th century', arguing that 'purposive legislation' was even more indispensable on the international plane than it was on the domestic level in modern industrialised nations.[12]

Ultimately, the utopian ambitions present both in the early Soviet and in the liberal universalist approach to international relations were frustrated. Soviet scholars and politicians, for their part, increasingly realised since the early 1930s that proletarian world revolution was not as imminent as they had hoped, and that the Soviet Union still had to play for a longer time according to the established rules of international law and diplomacy.[13] After the Second World War, the transformation of the Soviet Union from a revolutionary power to an established major player in international relations had been completed, and its interest in the preservation of a system of international law based on common rules of general applicability and respect for state sovereignty had greatly increased: Thus, Grigory Tunkin claimed in 1962 that '[t]he Soviet

10 See esp AM Slaughter, 'A Liberal Theory of International Law' (2000) 94 *Proceedings of the American Society of International Law* 240.

11 See G Nolte, 'Persisting and Developing between Hope and Threat: International Law during the Past Two Decades and Beyond' in J Crawford/S Nouwen (eds), *Select Proceedings of the European Society of International Law: Third Volume* (Oxford, Hart 2012) 74 (76).

12 WM Reisman, 'The Cult of Custom in the Late 20th Century' (1987) 17 *California Western International Law Journal* 133 (134).

13 For a contemporary Western account of this shift, see T Taracouzio, *The Soviet Union and International Law: A Study Based on the Legislation, Treaties and Foreign Relations of the Union of Socialist Soviet Republics* (New York, Macmillan & Co 1935). A reviewer of Taracouzio's book aptly summarised the main result of its analysis of Soviet diplomatic practice: 'The general impression which most readers will doubtless obtain from Mr. Taracouzio's account is that the Soviet Government has conformed to a surprisingly large extent with the established practices of non-communist states as embodied in international law.' See F Sherwood Dunne, 'Book Review: The Soviet Union and International Law' (1936) 51 *Political Science Quarterly* 630 (631).

doctrine of international law proceeded and proceeds from the idea that general international law, the norms of which regulate relationships between all States independently from their social system, exists …'.[14]

It is perhaps premature to write off the flamboyant hopes of the early 1990s, but one can hardly fail to note a sense of despair and profound disillusionment among politicians and diplomats as well as academic international lawyers and international relations scholars: 'It may seem as if the world is falling apart', as then UN Secretary General Ban put it in his 2014 opening address to the General Assembly's sixty-ninth session, referring to the abundance of crises and calamities from Africa to the Middle East to Ukraine, and the concomitant streams of refugees.[15] In a similar tone, Richard N Haass has argued that world order is 'unraveling', and that 'the post-Cold War order, while imperfect, will be missed'.[16] Advising the US government to adopt a version of the 'Hippocratic oath' ('first, do no further harm') as a foreign policy maxim, he concluded, with a critical view on American engagement abroad, that '[t]he unfortunate reality is that democratic transformations of other societies are often beyond the means of outsiders to achieve'.[17] In Europe, the prospects for the liberal internationalist project do not look much brighter, especially since the 2016 decision of the majority of the British electorate to quit the European Union has dealt a heavy blow to this most ambitious project of supranational political integration through law. A significant number of international lawyers, too, have expressed concerns about a perceived instability of the international legal system, and the topic of an alleged 'crisis' of international law has repeatedly been made subject of conferences and workshops.[18]

There seems to be a certain perplexity with respect to the question of how to respond to the manifold symptoms of crises in international law and international relations, a perplexity that is unsurprising, given the fact that the events of the past 25 years amply illustrate that many ambitious projects to promote international stability and security by spreading the idea of liberal

14 English translation in L Malksöö, 'The History of International Legal Theory in Russia: a Civilizational Dialogue with Europe' (2008) 19 *European Journal of International Law* 211 (229).

15 UNGA, 'Address of the Secretary-General to the General Assembly: From Turmoil to Peace' (24 September 2014) UN Doc GA/11560.

16 RN Haass, 'The Unraveling: How to Respond to a Disordered World' (2014) 93 (6) *Foreign Affairs* 70.

17 Ibid, 77.

18 See eg W van Genugten/M Bultermann, 'Chapter 1: Crises – Concern and Fuel for International Lawyers' (2013) 44 *Netherlands Yearbook of International Law* 3 and the following chapters; MP Scharf/A Centner/K McClain, 'Foreword: Symposium International Law in Crisis' (2011) 44 *Case Western Reserve Journal of International Law* 1 and the following articles; see also JP Trachtman, *The Future of International Law: Global Government* (New York, Cambridge University Press 2012) ch 1: 'The Crisis of International Law'.

democracy have not only failed, but have often led to a deterioration of already fragile situations. The study of the concept of 'unintended consequences' has lately received considerable attention in international relations scholarship: Thus, it has been analysed how the 'regime change' in Iraq 2003 has strengthened the enemies of the West,[19] how the 'global war on terror' has severely exacerbated the plight of refugees,[20] and how even the well-meaning aid programs of international financial institutions, such as the World Bank, have sometimes backfired, for example by reinforcing the grip of authoritarian regimes.[21] Even the project of international criminal law, which is celebrated as 'a signal achievement in public international law since 1990 and the end of the Cold War',[22] has been argued to be inefficient or even counter-productive, both in deterring future atrocities[23] and in promoting reconciliation among different ethnic groups in the aftermath of civil wars.[24] Similarly, the 'precautionary principle' ('better safe than sorry'), often hailed as a cornerstone of contemporary international environmental law – unsurprisingly, given its intuitive accord with common sense – has been demonstrated to involve 'long-term consequences [which are] environmentally perverse'.[25]

Given the disappointment of the exuberant hopes that were put in what has been referred to as 'the process of legalisation after 1989',[26] it is hardly surprising that some scholars seem to seek salvation in a return to an ultra-realist, power-centred approach to international law and international relations: Thus, Walter Russell Mead has recently asked whether we are witnessing a 'return of geopolitics',[27] as instability in many troubled regions of the world is abundant, while the spectre of the Cold War seems to return from its grave. In international law, a common reaction to this nagging sense of uncertainty and

19 PW Galbraith, *Unintended Consequences: How War in Iraq strengthened America's Enemies* (New York, Simon & Schuster 2008).
20 S Aber et al, 'Unintended Consequences: Refugee Victims of the War on Terror' (2006) 37 *Georgetown Journal of International Law* 759.
21 See the case studies in C Daase/C Friesendorf, *Rethinking Security Governance: The Problem of Unintended Consequences* (Milton Park, Routledge 2010).
22 K Anderson, 'The Rise of International Criminal Law: Intended and Unintended Consequences' (2009) 20 *European Journal of International Law* 331.
23 See J Ku/J Nzelibe, 'Do International Criminal Tribunals Deter or Exacerbate Humanitarian Atrocities?' (2006) 84 *Washington University Law Review* 776; ML Smith, 'The International Criminal Court: An Effective Means of Deterrence?' (2001) 167 *Military Law Review* 156.
24 J Meerning, 'Justice and Peace? How the International Criminal Tribunal Affects Societal Peace in Bosnia' (2005) 42 *Journal of Peace Research* 271.
25 See FB Cross, 'Paradoxical Perils of the Precautionary Principle' (1996) 53 *Washington & Lee Law Review* 851 (920).
26 For a retrospective assessment of this process, see A Nollkaemper, 'The Process of Legalisation After 1989 and its Contribution to the International Rule of Law' in Crawford/Nouwen (n 11) 89.
27 W Russell Mead, 'The Return of Geopolitics: The Revenge of the Revisionist Powers' (2014) 93 (3) *Foreign Affairs* 69.

disorder is to look to rational choice models and game theory for guidance as to how effective, mutually beneficial rules of behaviour could look like.[28]

However, the application of rational choice theory to international law and international relations faces two significant challenges. The first stems from its focus on individual short-term self-interest: As Amartya Sen aptly put it: 'Since human beings can easily have good reason also to pay some attention to objectives other than the single-minded pursuit of self-interest, and can see arguments in favour of taking cognizance of broader values of normative rules of decent behaviour, RCT [rational choice theory] does reflect an extremely limited understanding of reason and rationality.'[29] This is especially true for the international sphere, where such a diversity of values and perceived self-interests exists that it is hardly conceivable to even reach an agreement on what choice among them would be 'rational'. An example of the effects of the narrow misconception of 'rationality' in rational choice theory is its failure to account for the fact that economic sanctions are so frequently ineffective.[30]

Yet there is a second, even more fundamental problem with rational choice analysis in regard to the international community, a problem that stems from the sheer complexity of interactions among almost 200 states and innumerable non-state actors on the international plane. This complexity is enhanced by the fact that the preferences of the actors are variable, and that they undergo constant processes of learning and adaptation to new circumstances.[31] The study of complex adaptive systems and their defining characteristics, such as non-linearity (the fact that they cannot be explained by simply adding up the properties of their individual components), emergence and self-organisation, is recently paid considerable attention to, both in biology and in the social sciences.[32] Although the discipline of international relations seems to be an apt field of reference for complexity theory, its analysis under the paradigm of 'complex adaptive systems' is but in its infancy, and is hitherto limited to the study of specific fields.[33] In international law, the evolving field of complexity

28 See eg JL Goldsmith/EA Posner, *The Limits of International Law* (New York, Oxford University Press 2006); for a more optimistic assessment of international law's performance, see AT Guzman, *How International Law Works: A Rational Choice Theory* (New York, Oxford University Press 2008).
29 A Sen, *The Idea of Justice* (London, Penguin 2010) 179.
30 See for an analysis of this problem eg WH Kaempfer/AD Lowenberg, 'The Theory of International Economic Sanctions: A Public Choice Approach' (1988) 78 *American Economic Review* 786.
31 For examples in this respect, see SE Page/A Jones-Rooy, 'The Complexities of Global Systems History' (2010) 10 *Journal of the Historical Society* 345.
32 For an introduction to the theory of complex adaptive systems, see eg JH Holland, *Complexity: A Very Short Introduction* (Oxford, Oxford University Press 2014) 24–36; see also id, *Hidden Order: How Adaptation Builds Complexity* (New York, Perseus 1995).
33 One of the few more comprehensive works is the edited volume NE Harrison (ed), *Complexity in World Politics: Concepts and Methods of a New Paradigm* (New York, State University of New York Press 2006); see also E Cudworth/S Hobden, *Posthuman International Relations: Complexity, Ecologism and Global Politics*

science has until recently hardly been noticed at all, although there are some tentative attempts to apply it to some particular areas. Thus, in a recent article, Joost Pauwelyn has analysed international investment law as a complex adaptive system, a system which 'was not rationally designed or entered into at one given point of time', but which 'gradually emerged from a series of small, historically contingent and at times accidental steps'.[34] Pauwelyn concludes that 'decentralized FIL [foreign investment law] is an organizational life form similar to species that have survived evolutionary biology', and argues that 'it is a model that other legal regimes can learn and copy from'.[35] Another area of international law that has been analysed through the lens of complexity theory is international environmental law.[36]

The main proposition of the present enquiry is that concepts derived from complexity theory are not only useful when it comes to the study of specific areas or regimes in international law, but that the fundamental idea behind the study of complex adaptive systems, that of self-organisation of a variety of different actors which individually command only limited knowledge and foresight, is at the heart of two of the classical sources of international law, namely those which are *unwritten*: Customary international law and the general principles of law. In a recent contribution, Daniel Bodansky argues in favour of a theory of 'non-treaty norms' that classifies them according to criteria which are different from those of traditional sources doctrine. Among these criteria or 'dimensions' he suggests is the category of 'non-purposive norms', which are, according to him, those which 'emerge through a decentralized, informal, often unconscious process of social interaction, in which it is difficult if not impossible to identify the "author" of a given rule'.[37]

In a similar fashion, Michel Virally has described customary international law:

> [T]he formation of a custom is a very complex process. It is not controlled by States individually; it is the result of a whole set of comportments by States, not necessarily planned and pursued. Custom has an aspect that I shall not term 'involuntary' (the term would be quite inexact), but nevertheless constitutes a process that largely escapes voluntary manipulation by States.[38]

(New York, Zed 2011), which focuses on the environmental aspects of international relations.

34 J Pauwelyn, 'At the Edge of Chaos? Foreign Investment Law as a Complex Adaptive System, How it Emerged and How it Can be Reformed' (2014) 29 *ICSID Review* 372 (374).

35 Ibid, 418.

36 See RE Kim/B Mackey, 'International Environmental Law as a Complex Adaptive System' (2014) 14 *International Environmental Agreements* 5.

37 D Bodansky, 'Prologue to a Theory of Non-Treaty Norms' in M Arsanjani et al (eds), *Looking to the Future: Essays on International Law in Honour of W Michael Reisman* (Leiden, Brill 2010) 119 (130).

38 M Virally, 'Contribution to the Discussion' in A Cassese/JHH Weiler (eds), *Change and Stability in International Lawmaking* (Berlin, Walter de Gruyter 1988) 110.

This understanding, which can also be found in the 1925 Hague Lectures of Charles de Visscher on the codification of international law,[39] seems strikingly similar to the concept of 'self-organised criticality'[40] used in complexity theory. It is, however, not the argument of the present study that one should adopt complexity theory as a fancy new paradigm for analysing the unwritten sources of international law, nor is it intended to design a completely novel theory of customary international law or the general principles of law. Rather, it shall be demonstrated that the classical understanding of the non-treaty sources of international law has embodied much of the character of a complex adaptive system, and that a recovery of this understanding can provide guidance in overcoming the present difficulties apparently attached to customary international law, such as its uncertainty, indeterminacy, and liability to political manipulation.

It may seem odd to choose the 'written-unwritten' divide as a basic criterion for analysing the sources of international law: Not only do we look back on more than a century of codification efforts, but even the very concept of custom in international law seems to be shifting away from the focus on 'deeds' to that on 'words', giving rise to a notion of 'modern' custom that is thought to be discernible largely from declarations and resolutions.[41] In a sense, all of international law is written down in one form or another today.[42] However, it shall be argued that unwritten rules of international law maintain some of their characteristic features even after they have been laid down in writing, a fact that poses a significant challenge to domestic judges, who are often not familiar with the intricacies of the process of customary international law.[43]

How is this conception of 'unwritten international law' to be reconciled with the demands of the rule of law? How can there be anything like a 'rule of unwritten international law', if certainty, predictability and security are seen as key elements of the concept of the rule of law? Does the rule of law therefore always have to be a 'law of rules',[44] in the sense of formal legislative enactments? And if the concept of 'rule of law' means just 'rule by formally enacted legislation', how is its other key demand, that no one shall be above the law, to be upheld, as even a tyrant can rule by formally promulgated edicts? If this

39 See C de Visscher, 'La codification de droit international' (1925-I) *Recueil des Cours* 325, 349–53; see on this point also J d'Aspremont, *Formalism and the Sources of International Law: A Theory of the Ascertainment of Legal Rules* (Oxford, Oxford University Press 2011) 100.

40 On this concept, see eg Holland, *Complexity: A Very Short Introduction* (n 32) 14.

41 On the concept of 'modern custom' see eg the comprehensive overview in A Roberts, 'Traditional and Modern Approaches to Customary International Law: A Reconciliation' (2001) 95 *American Journal of International Law* 757.

42 See R Bernhardt, 'Ungeschriebenes Völkerrecht' (1976) 36 *Zeitschrift für ausländisches öffentliches Recht und Völkerrecht* 50.

43 See eg M Mendelson, 'The Effect of Customary International Law on Domestic Law: An Overview' (2004) 4 *Non-State Actors and International Law* 75.

44 On this notion of the rule of law see A Scalia, 'The Rule of Law as a Law of Rules' (1989) 56 *University of Chicago Law Review* 1175.

understanding of the rule of law were the only possible one, the pessimism in the words of anthropologist Stanley Diamond might seem justified: 'Law arises in the breach of a prior customary order and increases in force with the conflicts that divide political societies internally and among themselves. Law *and* order is the historical illusion; law *versus* order is the historical reality.'[45] However, it shall be argued in the following chapters that the 'rule of law' and 'customary order' are indeed not an antinomy, but are mutually reinforcing. It is one of the main themes of the present book to illustrate how the core of the rule of law as a political ideal is to be sought neither in abstract natural law philosophy, nor in legal formalism, but in the innate capability of human beings and, by extrapolation, of their communities, to self-organisation by development of and adherence to common rules of behaviour. The fact that these rules have no discernible author means that they belong to no one in particular, and thus to all.[46] Only in this sense, it can truly be said that 'law, not men, rules', and it is no accident that the origin of concept of the 'rule of law' is inextricably linked with the common law legal culture.[47] In the words of the great Scottish Enlightenment philosopher Adam Ferguson, '[n]ations stumble upon establishments, which are indeed the result of human action, but not the execution of any deliberate human design'.[48]

From our existentially sceptical Postmodernist Western perspective, it is tempting to suspect behind such a view the belief in 'a world enchanted by the spontaneous dynamism of economic governance as a religion of immanence'.[49] And yet, in a world which is threatened by profound tendencies of disintegration, it may not be the worst idea to look at a tradition that stresses the human capacity to create, as it were, order from below. As Philip Allott says with respect to customary international law, 'society thereby makes law for itself through a tacit legislator which is society itself, universalizing its experience of self-ordering.'[50] The rule of unwritten international law, thus conceived, does not pretend to be an absolute, immutable yardstick of justice, nor is it confined

45 S Diamond, 'The Rule of Law versus the Order of Custom' (1971) 38 *Social Research* 42 (71).

46 Cf on this Hannah Arendt's description of the classical Greek ideal of 'polis' as 'a form of political organization in which the citizens lived together under a condition of no-rule, without a division between rulers and ruled.' H Arendt, *On Revolution* (London, Penguin, repr 1990) 30; for a discussion of this ideal of 'isonomy' in the context of international law, see T Franck, *The Structure of Impartiality: Examining the Riddle of Law in a Fragmented World* (New York, Macmillan 1968) 5.

47 See on this point JP Reid, *Rule of Law: The Jurisprudence of Liberty in the Seventeenth and Eighteenth Century* (DeKalb, Northern Illinois University Press 2004).

48 A Ferguson, *An Essay on the History of Civil Society* (Edinburgh, Millar and Caddel 1767) 187.

49 M Koskenniemi, 'Declaratory Legislation: Towards a Genealogy of Neoliberal Legalism' in R Liivoja/J Petman (eds), *International Law-making: Essays in Honour of Jan Klabbers* (London, Routledge 2014) 17 (38).

50 P Allott, 'The Concept of International Law' (1999) 110 *European Journal of International Law* 31 (38).

merely to prescribing a set of legalistic procedures; it is, to paraphrase Federalist No 51, part of 'the greatest reflection on human nature'.

B. Structure of the Book

In Chapter II, it will be demonstrated that the concept of unwritten law as a form of self-organisation of human beings is among the oldest notions of political philosophy, dating back to Aristotle's perception of man as a rational and social animal that is endowed with agency. The Aristotelian concepts of 'custom' and 'practice', situated at the heart of his normative anthropology, were directed against both Platonian utopianism and Sophistic nihilism. Through the medieval revival of Aristotelianism, these concepts had a profound influence on both the development of the common law and on the classical (pre-Enlightenment) concept of natural law. While natural law theory took an overly rationalistic (and unrealistic) turn during the Enlightenment, and thus ultimately provoked the reaction of 19th-century legal positivism, the Aristotelian conception of law as self-organisation continued to affect thinkers like Adam Smith and the German Historical School of Jurisprudence spearheaded by Savigny. Chapter II not only retraces the line of this tradition, but also assesses its relevance in the context of more recent debates about international law and international relations.

Chapter III looks at some of the most important theoretical and methodological approaches with respect to unwritten international law that have shaped the academic controversies of the 20th century: Starting with an exposition of the challenges of 20th-century legal realism, and the legacies which this movement left, it then discusses the somewhat difficult position that unwritten international law has been assigned in the major positivist theories of law, Kelsen's 'Pure Theory of Law' and HLA Hart's concept of law as a unity of primary and secondary rules. Analysing the basic methodological antinomy of 'deductive' and 'inductive' approaches to international law, the chapter proceeds to discuss the contributions of 'systems theory of law', and the virtues of FA Hayek's concept of law as a 'spontaneous order' as a descriptive device for the process in which unwritten rules of international law emerge and evolve. It concludes by analysing the role of the practitioner, whether international judge, diplomat or legal adviser, in the 'spontaneous order' of unwritten international law.

Chapter IV takes up the question of legal practice, and looks at the difficulties that judges face when they have to ascertain rules of customary international law. Arguing that neither international nor domestic courts have hitherto subscribed to an exclusively 'deductive' or 'inductive' approach, it goes on to analyse the problem of objectivity, especially from the perspective of domestic judges, in the face of the alleged indeterminacy of customary international law. The chapter finds that many, if not most, of the interpretative difficulties attached to customary international law stem from the ambiguity of the meaning of the concept of 'purpose' with respect to it.

Chapter V revolves around the problem of 'purposive interpretation'. It begins by outlining the ambivalence inherent in the notion of purpose as a legal concept, which is either understood as a subjective, authorial 'intent', or, in a more objective sense, as the 'function' that the law fulfils. The chapter argues that the 'purpose' of law always comprises both subjective and objective elements, and that the respective combination of the blend differs among the various sources of law. Thus, the 'purpose' of customary international law contains a greater objective element than that of treaties, a proposition which is illustrated by examples taken from the jurisprudence of international and domestic courts.

Chapter VI argues that purposive interpretation can do more than just elucidate the meaning of a particular norm: The concept of purpose also plays a significant role in analogical reasoning, in the construction of a legal system, and, on the supreme level of objectivity, in the recognition of the general principles of law.

The final Chapter VII rounds up the reasoning of the book and concludes that, despite arguments about the obsolescence of unwritten international law in our modern, rationalistic age, we should not underestimate the force of self-organisation as a source of order in an international society the evolution of which is becoming ever more complex, volatile and unpredictable.

II Unwritten Law as Self-Organisation

A Historical Perspective

A. Aristotle's Concept of Practice

When in the time of the ancient Greek 'Enlightenment'[1] around the middle of the 5th century BC it occurred to some philosophers that the identity of *kósmos, phýsis* and *nómos* – universal order, nature and law – hitherto taken for granted, might just have been a misperception, the idea arose that laws were the product of deliberate human action, that they could actually be *made*. Before, all order that existed had been regarded as resulting from divine providence: as Hesiod wrote in the 7th century BC, 'fish and beasts and winged birds devour each other, since there is no justice among them; but to human beings he [Zeus] has given justice'.[2] But during the 5th century, when it became more and more apparent that not only did the laws in the several *póleis* differ significantly from one another, but also that devastating wars between the Greek city states arose due to their respective rulers' *pleonexía*[3] (greed, acquisitiveness), it could no longer be maintained that human conduct was governed by an inborn sense for the perfectly just law of nature. This feeling of a breakdown of the traditional world order and a lack of new values provided the seedbed for one of the earliest and most long-living controversies in the history of legal philosophy.[4]

On one side stood the Sophists, who took a radically relativist position and rejected the possibility of any supra-individual epistemology of moral values. They introduced the distinction between things that were shaped by nature (*physei*) and others that originated from convention (*nomō*).[5] The only

1 On this period, which is also referred to as the 'Sophistic Enlightenment', see WKC Guthrie, *A History of Greek Philosophy, vol III: The Fifth Century Enlightenment* (Cambridge, Cambridge University Press 1969, 13th printing 2003).
2 Hesiod, *Erga kai hemérai*, 277 et seq.
3 For an extensive discussion of this and related concepts, and their relevance to classical Greek political thought, see RK Balot, *Greed and Injustice in Classical Athens* (Princeton, Princeton University Press 2001).
4 On the intellectual climate of this epoch see GT Menake, *Three Traditions of Greek Political Thought: Plato in Dialogue* (Lanham, University Press of America 2004) 113 et seq.
5 On the antithesis of 'nomos' and 'physis' see Guthrie (n 1) 55 et seqq.

intersubjective 'truth' they believed to be relevant for the assessment of the appropriateness of laws was *dóxa*, the public opinion.[6] As it was a natural attitude of the stronger individual to subjugate the weaker in order to enlarge his wealth and power, it was futile to promote the idea of a superior morality in order to restrain him from taking what by nature belonged to him – an early form of Social Darwinism, equating capability with right. Law was therefore conceived of as a deliberate human invention, created in order to enable human beings to live together in relatively peaceful coexistence, as a check against their natural antisocial inclinations.

The distinction thus established between the natural order on one side and the conventional or artificial one on the other, most clearly pronounced by Antiphon,[7] became the basis of the distinction between natural and positive law that haunts the debates of legal philosophy until the present day.[8] The attempts of the 20th-century's most eminent legal positivists, Hans Kelsen[9] and HLA Hart,[10] to discredit natural law doctrine, were therefore based on the axiomatic statement that *tertium non datur*, that a third way does not exist: that *ends* and *purposes* can only exist within the realm of rational human design, and that natural law is based on the anthropomorphic fallacy of presuming an independent, unchanging *télos* in nature, 'proceeding towards a definite optimum state which is the specific good appropriate for it'.[11] The positivist dualism between 'laws' of nature and positive laws, ie those made by convention, still permeates much of today's legal theory. Yet, as James Bernard Murphy has recently pointed out, 'it requires very Procrustean methods to force custom into the familiar dichotomy between nature and convention'.[12] Therefore, it seems justified to look at a distinct philosophical tradition which

6 Their alleged abuse of the concept of 'doxa' to manipulate Athenian citizens was a central charge in Plato's attack on the Sophists; see J Szaif, '*Doxa* and *Episteme* as Modes of Acquaintance in *Republic* V' (2007) 4 *Les Études Platoniciennes* 253.

7 See H Diels (ed), *Die Fragmente der Vorsokratiker, vol II* (Berlin, Weidmann, 3rd edn 1912) 298 (Fragment 44a); for a discussion of Antiphon's views see eg M Nill, *Morality and Self-Interest in Protagoras Antiphon and Democritus* (Leiden, Brill 1985) 53; for a recent discussion of fragment 44a, see D Riesbeck, 'Nature, Normativity, and Nomos in Antiphon, Fragment 44a' (2011) 65 *Phoenix* 268.

8 See on this problem JB Murphy, *The Philosophy of Customary Law* (Oxford, Oxford University Press 2014) 2–6; for the argument that the Sophists were the among the earliest precursors of modern legal positivism, see W Conklin, *The Invisible Origins of Legal Positivism: A Re-Reading of a Tradition* (Dordrecht, Kluwer Law 2001) 14–19.

9 Kelsen's refutation of natural law doctrine spreads throughout his works; for a concise restatement of his position see H Kelsen, 'The Natural Law Doctrine before the Tribunal of Science' (1949) 2 *The Western Political Quarterly* 481.

10 HLA Hart, *The Concept of Law* (Oxford, Oxford University Press, 2nd edn 1994) 185 et seqq; see esp 189 et seq, where Hart criticises the 'teleological conception of nature', which to him is at the basis of all classical natural law theories.

11 Ibid, 188–9.

12 Murphy (n 8) 3.

sought to transcend this seemingly irreconcilable antagonism between nature and convention: Aristotelianism.

The most interesting counter-position to the Sophists' approach was adopted by Aristotle in both his *Politics* and *Nikomachean Ethics*. In his political and legal theory, Aristotle was predominantly concerned with the concept of order – the central concept of most early political philosophy. Yet he proposed a distinctively more complex understanding of the sources of order than that suggested by the Sophists, and also than those presupposed in the theories of later political thinkers from Hobbes to Schmitt. For him, between the eternal realm of natural order (*phýsis*) and the temporary constructs of deliberate human reasoning (*lógos*), there existed a third source of order: the *éthos*, which was, according to Aristotle, formed by custom or habit and evolving over the course of time. 'In order to become good and wise, one requires three things: these are nature, habit, and reason.'[13]

These sources of order, however, were not regarded by Aristotle as mutually exclusive, but as complementary, their well-proportioned relationship being of crucial importance to the establishment of a proper social order. For him, there existed a hierarchy among these principles of order, with nature being the base, reason at the top and custom or habit positioned in between the two. Yet this implied that whereas the 'basal' principles, nature and custom, could exist without the higher, the opposite was not true: The legislator, when he conceives the law by using his reason, must know and respect both the exigencies of nature and the *ágraphoi nómoi*, the unwritten laws or social customs existing among his subjects.[14] This high value which Aristotle assigned to customary laws is pertinent throughout his *Politics*. In this context, he makes the following bold statement: 'Again, customary laws have more weight, and relate to more important matters, than written laws, and a man may be a safer ruler than the written law, but not safer than the customary law.'[15] What Aristotle refers to in this passage as being of superior value is not customary law in the technical sense of a precisely definable source of law with certain distinct prerequisites. From the juxtaposition of customary and written law it is apparent that he in fact referred to the *ágraphoi nómoi*, as opposed to rationally constructed written law imposed by a central authority.[16] To Aristotle, the specific value of these unwritten laws stems from the fact that they emerge from a slow, fragmentary process, through the practice of the community, whose totality is able to develop smarter answers to its needs than the wisest

13 Aristotle, *Politics* 1332a 38.
14 Ibid, 1332b 8 et seq.
15 Ibid, 1287b 9, quoted from the translation by B Jowett (Oxford, Clarendon 1885).
16 See on this concept M Oswald, 'Was there a Concept of "ágraphos nómos" in Classical Greece?' in EN Lee/APD Mourelatos/RM Rorty (eds), *Exegesis and Argument: Studies in Greek Philosophy Presented to Gregory Vlastos* (Assen, Humanities Press 1973) 70.

individual ruler could.[17] Here, Aristotle acknowledges the fact that it is impossible to preconceive all sorts of problems that the law might, at any given moment in time, be required to regulate, and stresses the importance of leaving to society the opportunity to develop spontaneous solutions. But his esteem for the unwritten laws does not only stem from motives of pragmatism: In Aristotle's theory, the *ágraphoi nómoi* serve as the link that connects the workings of human reason to the unchangeable world of nature, and constitute therefore an indispensable component of any well-ordered social system.

Aristotle did not apply his theory of governance to the field of international relations: he was not concerned with matters of international law, nor with the laws of a particular state, but he took the Greek ideal type of a *pólis* as an example for his philosophical exposition of the universal principles of good, 'virtuous' government of human communities.[18] The central concept of Aristotle's social theory is the notion of *praxis* (practice). Yet the Aristotelian *praxis* is not merely random (human) action, but action that is directed towards an end; and not towards any arbitrarily chosen end, but towards a specific end *inherent in the practice*, which is either determined by the natural propensities of the actor or by diligent use of his reason. Thus, the distinctive feature of Aristotle's concept of *praxis* is its innate teleology. And precisely through the force of this feature the socialisation of the individual becomes possible, since there are ends which the individual cannot reach alone, whether required by natural inclinations, such as procreation[19] or the need for the protection of one's well-being (*sōtería*), or the desire to attain higher cultural achievements. It is by this teleology of practice, this quest for ultimate well-being – in Greek: '*eudaimonía*' – that individuals, by engaging in certain practices, form *koinoníai*, communities of practice, thereby ascending from the individual ethical sphere to the collective, the social, and the political world. However, the Aristotelian concept of *praxis* differs significantly from most accounts of practice used in contemporary social sciences, in that Aristotle sees the benchmark for attainment of the practice's goal in the practice itself. Whereas the individual's reasoning does not usually extend beyond the circumstances immediately confronting him, the distinctively human property and function of *eupraxía* ('acting correctly'), a mixture of practical rationality and moral considerations, allows each individual to pursue his particular goals whilst at the same time fulfil his natural function as a *zōon politikón*, a 'social animal' forming communities with his peers; thus, the *póleis* emerged. Hence, Aristotle's vision of human nature is one that is much more harmonious and inclined to (spontaneous) order than the picture of a brutal state of nature that the sophists or later political philosophers such as Hobbes projected. Indeed, as the classical scholar Andrew Lang put it in 1886:

17 Cf Aristotle, *Politics* 1287b 10–13.

18 See JB Abramson, *Minerva's Owl: The Tradition of Western Political Thought* (Cambridge/MA, Harvard University Press 2009) 120–1.

19 Aristotle, *Politics* 1252a 28.

> In Aristotle's eyes, then, Nature is almost the unconscious action of the will of the world, bringing all things into uniformity with limit and right reason. … If we apply this doctrine [Aristotle's views on physics and metaphysics] to politics, we find that the *matter* is human character, and human circumstance, which *Nature* fashions into the forms of the family and the state. The *constant* tendencies in human character and circumstance make for good and for order.[20]

Although Aristotle did not specifically address in any depth the relationships among different *póleis*, much less matters one would regard as pertaining to 'international law' as understood today, some basic tenets of Aristotle's political theory are definitely worth considering in the context of this inquiry, as they provide a degree of both conceptual clarity and timeless insight rarely found in their later adaptations. In particular his concept of practice has recently gained relevance, since it was reintroduced into the debate by (legal) philosophers such as Alasdair MacIntyre[21] and Charles Taylor.[22] The fundamental source of philosophical disagreement between traditional scholarship and 'academic outsiders'[23] like Taylor and MacIntyre lies in the different standards of normativity they use in describing practice: Whereas the mainstream approach in philosophy and social sciences describes practices in terms of action undertaken 'in order to', to achieve a goal, to abide by the law or to satisfy other extraneous demands, the (Neo)-Aristotelian concept follows an innate standard of assessment, a rule of procedure.[24] What makes Aristotle's conception of practice particularly interesting in the context of international legal theory is the way in which he linked action to value; a kind of thought we are today inclined to dismiss as a rather primitive understanding misled by the 'naturalistic fallacy'. Yet this concept enabled Aristotle to explain how an individual actor, partaking in a community, contributes through his actions to the maintenance of order, regardless of the particular aims he may pursue.

Today, this teleological notion of practice seems very unfamiliar to many scholars working in the theory of international law – a state of affairs that is reflected in the fact that the concept of customary international law is still unclear and subject of vivid and controversial debate, especially since the challenge of the critical legal studies movement. As Anthony Carty categorically asserted, '[o]ne cannot simply study the practice of States as evidence of law because it

20 A Lang, *The Politics of Aristotle: Introductory Essays* (London, Longmans 1886) 9–10 (italics original).

21 Particularly in his book *After Virtue* (South Bend/IL, University of Notre Dame Press, 2nd edn 1984).

22 C Taylor, *Philosophical Arguments* (Cambridge/MA, Harvard University Press 1995) passim, in particular 230–247.

23 R Bubner, *Welche Rationalität bekommt der Gesellschaft? Vier Kapitel aus dem Naturrecht* (Frankfurt am Main, Suhrkamp 1996) 77.

24 See P Ricoeur, 'The Teleological and Deontological Structures of Action: Aristotle and/or Kant?' (1987) 21 *Royal Institute of Philosophy Lecture Series* 99 (99–100).

is logically inconceivable to study any evidence without *a priori* criteria of relevance and significance'.[25] For Martti Koskenniemi, the contemporary doctrine of customary international law is trapped inevitably between the equally unsatisfying extremes of 'materialism' and 'psychologism':

> Though international lawyers may sometimes have claimed to know the *normative Kraft der* [sic] *Faktischen*, it seems hardly likely that they should have smashed Hume's Guillotine without anyone working in political philosophy having heard about it – just as unlikely, in fact, as that they could have broken away from the hermeneutic circle to establish the meaning of human action without having to assume an essentially political position.[26]

The predominant view, according to which customary international law is constituted by the combination of an objective element – state practice – and the subjective belief that the particular practice is legally required (a notion usually referred to as *opinio juris*), is seen as fraught with epistemological difficulties: How is it possible to conceive a law that emerged from practice undertaken in the perception of following an existing rule? And how can such law change, since any practice in deviation from the existing standard must necessarily constitute a breach of the prior rule?[27] More important than these conceptual enigmas, however, are the practical intricacies that abound in the process of (judicial) ascertainment of customary international law: Thus, it has been said that '[b]oth constitutive elements evidently leave considerable room for differing assessments': 'How much is sufficient practice? How can sufficient *opinio juris* be shown?'[28] Whereas it is in principle easy to prove actual state action, the subjective element, the belief that the act carried out was legally warranted, is quite hard to aver. In practice, this element is frequently inferred by using the tautological argument that an act was carried out within a subject matter governed by international law, hence the *opinio juris* regarding its lawfulness could be presumed. Yet any attempt to formulate abstract criteria to distinguish legally relevant custom from other forms of social practice remained fruitless; the existing more or less uncontroversial rules of customary international law can hardly be analysed under a common generic principle, a 'rule of recognition' in Hartian terminology – which is not surprising, given the diversity of their historical origins. But since the reductionist understanding of

25 A Carty, *The Decay of International Law? A Reappraisal of the Limits of Legal Imagination in International Affairs* (Manchester, Manchester University Press 1986) 95.

26 M Koskenniemi, 'The Normative Force of Habit: International Custom and Social Theory' (1990) 1 *Finnish Yearbook of International Law* 77 (78).

27 Cf on these difficulties eg V Lowe, *International Law* (Oxford, Oxford University Press 2007) 38–9.

28 H Thirlway, *The Sources of International Law* (Oxford, Oxford University Press 2014) 58.

practice as a merely factual phenomenon seemed to be unable to explain how a normative standard can ever be inferred from a sheer behavioural regularity, and thus how something qualitatively different can emerge – namely values arising from facts – the proliferation of new (though not always original) theories on the nature and origin of customary international law still continues.[29] The spectrum of these approaches is wide, ranging from attempts to deny the intrinsic value of international custom by reducing its habitual observance by states to simplistic models of rational behaviour[30] to the outright rejection of state practice as a constitutive element, basing customary international law solely on *opinio juris* as a state of mind.[31]

The conceptual and practical difficulties of international custom and other unwritten sources of international law will be addressed in more detail in the subsequent chapters of this study; yet in the context of this historical sketch, it has become evident that the concept of practice prevalent in international legal theory today is very remote from that proposed by Aristotle: For him, practice was not merely a sociological fact, insurmountably separated from the normative sphere. Rather, he would have concurred with the theoretical biologist and complexity theorist Stuart A Kauffman, who recently noticed with respect to human behaviour:

> The reductionist world, where all that exist are the fundamental entities and their interactions, and there are only happenings, only facts, has no place for value. Yet we humans, who are presumably reducible to physics like everything else, are agents, able to act on our own behalf. But actions are 'doings', not mere happenings. Moreover, agency creates values: we want certain events to happen and others not to happen.[32]

Although the Aristotelian notion of practice has not yet received any discernible reception in the field of (contemporary)[33] international legal theory,

29 Eg BD Lepard, *Customary International Law: A New Theory With Practical Applications* (Cambridge, Cambridge University Press 2010); AT Guzman, *How International Law Works: A Rational Choice Theory* (New York, Oxford University Press 2008); EA Posner, *The Perils of Global Legalism* (Chicago, University of Chicago Press 2009); for a critical review of those three books by one of the leading scholars of customary international law see A D'Amato, 'New Approaches to Customary International Law' (2011) 105 *American Journal of International Law* 163.

30 EA Posner/JL Goldsmith, *The Limits of International Law* (New York, Oxford University Press 2006) 23–43; according to Goldsmith and Posner, the states' 'compliance' with norms of customary international law can be explained by four models in which they pursue their interests on the international plane, namely 'coincidence of interest', 'coercion', 'cooperation' and 'coordination'; under that theory, a state follows a rule of customary international law if (and only if) a benefit for its interests can be established under any of these models.

31 Cf Lepard (n 29) chapter 7.

32 SA Kauffman, *Reinventing the Sacred* (New York, Basic Books 2008) 11.

33 But see the discussion below.

the same is not true with respect to the situation in the social sciences. In particular the English School of international relations has embraced what has been called a 'telic' notion of practice:[34] A concept which perceives of practice not as something which is caused and controlled by any exogenous 'hidden motivator' or social structure, but guided by intrinsic rules and standards of excellence. Such a telic practice is, in the words of Stephen Turner, an activity seeking 'a goal which is conceived as a result of following certain general principles of procedure'.[35] In this sense, much of the custom thought to make up (unwritten) international law is *telic* practice: It provides procedures for appropriate action in certain situations; thus, it is in fact affording guidance, orientation for 'acting correctly' in the Aristotelian sense. As one scholar describes it, 'international law is a reasonably clear guide as to what is the done thing, and what is not, in any given set of circumstances, of what can be expected and what not, and what will be tolerated and what will likely be met with a disapproving, perhaps vociferous, response'.[36] Examples for this kind of prescriptive practice can be found in the laws of war, in diplomatic law, the law of the sea, and state immunity. All these subject areas have in common that they contain relatively precise directives of what to do in a certain situation. And they also have in common that they do not depend on their participants' agreement on lofty, abstract goals and aims such as 'peace' or 'human development', but are rather almost intuitively internalised by anyone actually *practicing* a certain activity. Though these 'rules' are certainly not always observed, their knowledge is by and large regarded a skill the mastery of which is required for the proper exercise of the respective function or profession – be it that of a soldier, a diplomat (respectively a foreign minister or other state official), a sailor or a judge.

Anne-Marie Slaughter's recent concept of a 'New World Order'[37] consisting of transgovernmental networks coordinating their efforts in particular areas in the absence of an effective overall institutional framework bears some resemblance to the Aristotelian communities of practice. In particular her discussion of the increasing dialogue among judges from various jurisdictions and their habit of quoting each other's decisions on certain matters of general relevance, not as binding, but as persuasive authority, seems to be a fruitful example of this.[38] What Slaughter's account lacks seems to be the understanding that the legal system in which the judges operate is but a part of the holistic system of human society; and that the judges, though they may share certain traits with

34 Cf C Navari, 'The Concept of Practice in the English School' (2010) 17 *European Journal of International Relations* 611.

35 S Turner, *The Social Theory of Practices* (Chicago, University of Chicago Press 2000) 28.

36 P Wilson, 'The English School's Approach to International Law' in C Navari (ed), *Theorising International Society: English School Methods* (Basingstoke, Palgrave Macmillan 2008) 167 (168).

37 AM Slaughter, *A New World Order* (Princeton, Princeton University Press 2004).

38 Ibid, 100–103.

their colleagues in other nations, are still part of a broader societal framework, whose problems and conflicts ultimately determine the nature of the cases the judges decide; and these concrete cases, decided with a view to finding the best possible way of maintaining the order of the society, will ultimately shape the law arising from the judgments – more than any theoretical considerations on the desirability of 'constructing a global legal system'.[39] Therefore, the global 'harmonisation' of jurisprudence depends more on the slow and piecemeal assimilation of wants and beliefs of the populations in the various countries; it seems doubtful whether the increasing number of transnational litigations alone, as Slaughter seems to suggest,[40] suffices to initiate this process.

In any event, it appears that international legal thought today by and large still follows the liberal internationalist paradigm, under which it is worthwhile to strive towards improvement and continuous harmonisation in the application of international law, whether through formal institutions or informal networks. The most popular alternative to this conception is to deny the legal relevance of international law altogether, reducing its observance to the logic of a tit-for-tat game – rules are only observed if and insofar as it is in the (short term) interest of the respective states.[41] In fact, this latter conception of (international) law had disciples throughout history: From the Sophists over Spinoza and Hobbes to Austin – without effective enforcement backed by sanctions, they alleged, there is no law 'properly so called'.

B. Medieval Receptions of Aristotelianism: Thomas Aquinas and the Common Law-Tradition

Yet for centuries there has been a view of the law that lies between the extremes of liberal internationalism and the 'realist' conception of an anomic state of nature where the most powerful will always prevail. Following Aristotle's trichotomy of human phenomena as natural, habitual and rationally conceived or artificial, the middle category occupied significant space in the politico-legal theories of the Middle Ages and the Early Modern Period. For medieval philosophers, it was perfectly natural to acknowledge the existence of a normative anthropology, of certain propensities of the human kind that limited the capability of lawgivers to modify or abolish certain institutions of human life. Yet this understanding did not imply anything like the later dichotomy of natural versus positive law. In fact, the term natural law (*jus naturale*) denoted the same thing as Aristotle's intermediate category of *éthos*, namely custom or habit. Thomas Aquinas, the greatest medieval Aristotelian, adopted Aristotle's categories, modifying them to bring them in accordance with his Christian

39 Ibid, 65.
40 Ibid, 100.
41 For a critical assessment of this trend, see O Hathaway/AN Lavinbuck, 'Rationalism and Revisionism in International Law: Book Review of JL Goldsmith/EA Posner, *The Limits of International Law*' (2006) 119 *Harvard Law Review* 1404.

faith. The category of *phýsis* he replaced by the eternal law, the unchangeable will of God. The human law, equivalent with Aristotle's *nómos*, was the law that a ruler had volitionally enacted; here, Aquinas warned against placing too many expectations in the force of arbitrarily drafted law:

> [H]uman Law cannot punish or forbid all evil deeds: since while aiming at doing away with all evils, it would do away with many good things, and would hinder the advance of the common good, which is necessary for human intercourse. In order, therefore, that no evil might remain unforbidden and unpunished, it was necessary for the Divine Law to supervene, whereby all sins are forbidden.[42]

Aquinas also confirmed that natural law, although derived from every human being's innate ability to partake in the eternal law of God, and therefore immanent in the reason with which humans manage their affairs, was a custom (or habit) and thus potentially subject to change. As regards the relationship between written law and natural law, he stated:

> The written law is said to be given for the correction of the natural law, either because it supplies what was wanting to the natural law; or because the natural law was perverted in the hearts of some men, as to certain matters, so that they esteemed those things good which are naturally evil; which perversion stood in need of correction.[43]

Today, Aquinas' particular version of the Aristotelian trichotomy of *phýsis, éthos* and *nómos* may seem as a quintessentially medieval mixture of legal theory and theology, and thus as being of interest only to the historian of philosophy. However, it has been argued that 'Aquinas offers us several viewpoints that open *postmodern* possibilities for understanding problems left unsolved and unexplained by the modern political philosophy'.[44] How so? Because it may allow us to take a fresh look at the problem of practical reasoning, and especially at the modern antinomy of 'will' and 'reason': 'That reason and will are not a dichotomy at potential opposition but an integrated whole is an expression of the holistic nature of Thomasian ethics. This is perhaps his most significant challenge to modernity.'[45] But how did Aquinas transcend this dichotomy of 'reason' and 'will'? By stressing the human capacity of practical reasoning, he ultimately relied on the powers of the intellect, not as a *source* of law (as the

42 Thomas Aquinas, *Summa Theologica*, Pars Prima Secundae, Q 91 Art 4, quoted from the translation by the Fathers of the English Dominican Province (New York, Benzinger Brothers 1915).

43 Ibid, Q 94 Art 5.

44 JP Rentto, 'Postmodern Aquinas: A Fresh Start' in DW Hudson/D Moran (eds), *The Future of Thomism* (South Bend, University of Notre Dame Press 1992) 149 (150).

45 Ibid, 154.

rationalistic natural law thinkers of the Enlightenment did), but as a *means* of discovering it.[46] In contradistinction to the 18th-century *jusnaturalism*, Aquinas' natural law is discovered inductively, not deductively. Yet given the relative imperfection of the human intellect, and the differences among people's characters and inclinations, the law thus discerned can always only be an approximation, and it can only be discovered gradually and discursively. As Juha-Pekka Rentto aptly describes Aquinas approach:

> It is in fact a theory of contextuality in human affairs which does not overlook that the different levels of law properly reflect a descending contextual universality and an ascending contextual specificity. For that reason men have different ordering principles for organizing their lives into reasonable wholes. Some things organize themselves by nature, others are naturally organized by sound human reason, while further others require that man take their nature in their own hands and choose between different possible ways of organizing them.[47]

The aim of this exercise of practical reasoning is thus not to create a utopian new world order of perfect justice, but to reach a common conclusion about the normative evaluation of certain state of affairs, an incremental progress towards agreement based on arguments which, as Thomas Scanlon has put it, 'others cannot reasonably reject'.[48]

Aquinas' conception of law had a significant impact not only on theology but also on legal practice. An important yet little known influence of Thomistic legal thought can be seen in the history of English common law. The great medieval jurists of the common law tradition, like Henry de Bracton[49] and John Fortescue,[50] were intimately familiar with the scholastic punditry at Oxford.[51] And in fact, there seems to be no legal tradition which is more intimately related to scholastic philosophy than the common law.[52] Its peculiar

46 See on this important difference L Schaller, *Der Rechtsformalismus Kelsens und die thomistische Rechtsphilosophie: Vergleich zweier Systeme des Rechtsdenkens* (Fribourg, Kanisius 1949) 58 et seq.

47 JP Rentto, '*Ius Gentium*: A Lesson from Aquinas' (1992) 3 *Finnish Yearbook of International Law* 103 (119).

48 T Scanlon, *What We Owe to Each Other* (Cambridge/MA, Belknap 1998) 5: 'Thinking about right and wrong is, at the most basic level, thinking about what could be justified to others on grounds that they, if appropriately motivated, could not reasonably reject.'

49 H de Bracton, *De Legibus et Consuetudinibus Angliae* (G Woodbine ed, New Haven, Yale University Press 1922).

50 J Fortescue, *De Laudibus Legum Angliae* (A Amos tr, Cambridge, Cambridge University Press 1825).

51 For the continuing influence of scholastic political and legal philosophy in Tudor England even after the Reformation, see eg SA Chavura, *Tudor Protestant Political Thought 1547–1603* (Leiden, Brill 2011) 89 et seqq.

52 For an exposition of some of these links, see P Goodrich, 'Ars Bablativa: Ramism, Rhetoric, and the Genealogy of English Jurisprudence' in G Leyh (ed), *Legal*

nature, as Roscoe Pound noted, stems from two of its main principles, the *supremacy of law* and the *doctrine of precedent.* According to Pound,

> [t]he same spirit is behind each [of these principles]. The doctrine of precedents means that causes are to be judged by principles reached inductively from the judicial experience of the past, not by deduction from rules established arbitrarily by the sovereign will. [The] doctrine of the supremacy of law is reducible to the same idea. It is a doctrine that the sovereign and all its agencies are bound to act upon principles, not according to arbitrary will; are obliged to follow reason instead of being free to follow caprice. Both represent the Germanic idea of law as a quest for the justice and truth of the Creator. The common-law doctrine is one of reason applied to experience.[53]

The main feature of the common law is thus its unique combination of practical reason, derived from long-time experience, and the firm belief in the 'rule of law' as a shield against capricious, abusive exercises of raw sovereign power. Nevertheless, it may seem puzzling how Pound describes the doctrine of precedent as an incarnation of reason: What about highly unreasonable precedents which are nevertheless regarded as binding under the rule of *stare decisis*, in particular when authored by higher courts? This feature of the common law (and of other case law systems) has historically often been a source of mockery and contempt, chiefly but not exclusively from continental jurists who firmly believed in the superiority of rationally conceived, comprehensive codifications.[54] In *Gulliver's Travels*, Jonathan Swift ironically portrayed the attitude of the English legal profession:

> It is a maxim among these lawyers that whatever has been done before, may legally be done again: and therefore they take special care to record all the decisions formerly made against common justice, and the general reason of mankind. These, under the name of precedents, they produce as authorities to justify the most iniquitous opinions; and the judges never fail of directing accordingly.[55]

Hermeneutics: History, Theory and Practice (Berkeley, University of California Press 1992) 43; for an analysis of the continuing relevance of Aquinas' thought to the common law tradition, see also D Van Drunen, *Law and Custom: The Thought of Thomas Aquinas and the Future of the Common Law* (New York, Peter Lang 2003).

53 R Pound, *The Spirit of the Common Law* (Boston, Marshall Jones 1921) 182–183.

54 A good example in this respect is Max Weber's discussion of the common law system; on this issue see IP Sahni, 'Max Weber's Sociology of Law: The Judge as Mediator' (2009) 9 *Journal of Classical Sociology* 209.

55 J Swift, *Gulliver's Travels into Several Remote Nations of the World* (London, A Moore 1726) part IV, ch V at the end.

Although Swift's quip may have some historical merit, and by looking at the development of the common law one can easily point to some 'most iniquitous opinions', it should not be forgotten that case law systems provide particular opportunities for the correction of such 'errors'. The application of precedents is not a mechanical process like the application of statutes. Rather, it involves the perpetual review of the principles of prior decisions. Thus, it is unlikely that decisions with devastating consequences for the well-being of a society may prevail for too long – unlike, as history shows, in the case of legislation. One of the most original historians of the common law in the past century, Carlton Kemp Allen, stated this in a manner that is worth being quoted in full:

> It must never be forgotten that the Judge has to review every precedent cited to him, not as a precise formulation of a general, abstract rule of law (like an article of a code), but as a concrete application of, or as an argument in favour of, some real or supposed rule of law. We say that he is bound by the decisions of higher Courts; and so he undoubtedly is. But the superior Court does not impose fetters upon him; he places the fetters on his own hands. He has to decide whether the case cited to him is truly apposite to the circumstances in question and whether it accurately embodies the principle which he is seeking. The humblest judicial officer has to decide for himself whether he is or is not bound, in the particular circumstances, by any given decision of the House of Lords.[56]

This technique of *distinguishing* prior cases whose *ratio decidendi* the judge views as inapposite to the particular case he is called upon to decide provides a tool for the critical reassessment of tradition, while at the same time limiting the individual judge's discretion as to the question on what considerations he can appropriately base his decision. Underlying the common law methodology, we see a phenomenon that could be described as the determinant force of prior decisions: this force stems not only from the earlier judgment's convincingness, but also from the permanent need to solve problems without sufficient authoritative guidance. The practice of using precedents is therefore a paradigmatic example of what Martin Heidegger called the *One* or the *They-Self*,[57] an average way of acting that forms the primordial basis of the positive ontological constitution of being.[58] Yet tradition is no absolute value in the common law: the rules of decision provided by precedent cases are always subject to revision in each case where they apply (or are found not to be applicable), and even their apparently unmodified application can in fact in the future lead to a certain 'drift', a gentle modification of the existing law, as no particular case and thus

56 CK Allen, *Law in the Making* (Oxford, Clarendon, 7th ed 1964) 290.

57 In the German original 'Das Man'; see for a discussion of the importance of this concept Martin Heidegger, *Sein und Zeit* (Tübingen, Mohr Siebeck, 10th ed 1963) 126–30.

58 Ibid.

no instance of application is absolutely identical to the prior; and since the rule or principle that is thought to form the connection between the individual instances of its application is nowhere authoritatively positivised, such adaption to changed circumstances still retains the imprint of authority derived from longstanding tradition. The way in which the common law 'ripens' and 'hardens' over the course of time obviously bears some resemblance to the development of unwritten international law, in that it does not emanate from a single source, but that it in fact has its existence in the process of its practical application. This is an obvious reason for the unease scholars of international legal positivism have always felt when confronted with customary international law and the general principles: that it is impossible to discern a precise moment in time when a certain 'rule' transcends the realm of mere social practices and becomes binding law; or, in the case of the general principles, when an alleged principle has received such widespread acceptance among domestic legal systems that it seems justified to 'elevate' it to the elysian fields of international law. Hedley Bull, in his classical treatise *The Anarchical Society*, described the complexities in the emergence of international rules thus:

> These rules [of the international society] may have the status of international law, of moral rules, of custom or established practice, or they may be merely operational rules or 'rules of the game', worked out without formal agreement or even without verbal communication. It is not uncommon for a rule to emerge first as an operational rule, then to become established practice, then to attain the status of a moral principle and finally to be incorporated in a legal convention; this appears to have been the genesis, for example, of many of the rules now embodied in multilateral treaties or conventions concerning the laws of war, diplomatic and consular relations, and the law of the sea.[59]

It is tempting to describe the common law methodology as radical empiricism, as it commences with the particular decision and thence proceeds towards the generalisations; as Justice Oliver W Holmes famously observed in his very first law review article, written in 1870: 'It is the merit of the common law that it decides the case first and determines the principle afterwards'.[60] This aphorism, although not entirely mistaken, is nevertheless profoundly misleading. It is certainly not true that common law judges at any time in any country have generally rendered more subjective and unprincipled decisions than those operating under a legal system where written law dominated. And it bears emphasising that the very idea of the rule of law, perhaps Britain's greatest jurisprudential gift to the world, has a meaning that is substantially different

59 H Bull, *The Anarchical Society* (Basingstoke, Palgrave Macmillan, 4th ed 2012) 64–5.

60 OW Holmes, 'Codes, and the Arrangement of the Law' (1870) 5 *American Law Review* 1.

from the continental notion of *Rechtsstaat* or *état de droit*, 'state of law' or 'statutory state', concepts that were essentially products of 19th-century legal positivism, denoting that public officials had to be authorised by written statutes when encroaching upon individual rights. Contrariwise, the term *rule of law* was derived from the historically powerful position of the legal profession, which functioned as a form of corporative non-state entity rooted in society and was thus not a structural part of the state (to the extent that one may properly speak of statehood with reference to the late medieval and early modern era), but stood to a certain degree in opposition to it.[61] To be sure, the much revered unwritten English constitution, 'the most rational, as well as the most antient in Europe,'[62] was in part a fiction, used as a strategy to justify the dominant position of judges and advocates and as a shield against 'arbitrary' legislative intrusions. But it was in fact not only the legal profession which shaped the formation of the common law, but the process also received significant impulses from the scientific exploration of roman law, pursued chiefly at the Regius Chair of Civil Law at Oxford, which, after its foundation by Henry VIII in 1540, was held by two of the most eminent scholars of international law of their epochs: Alberico Gentili (appointed 1587) and Richard Zouch (1620). The benefit of this recourse to the ancient sources was not only due to the authority of their venerable age or the perceived practical wisdom of their legal maxims, but also to the fact that they provided procedures for the solution of real life conflicts, whether domestically or internationally in reach. Moreover, they formed the foundation of a real common European legal heritage, a heritage that persisted for centuries despite the many petty skirmishes and larger wars among the various realms and principalities that suffused the European landscape.

Carl Schmitt, in a remarkable lecture[63] delivered at several European universities during the years of 1943 and 1944, praised this 'truly European common law', developed by the legal profession and academia, and called for its revival as an alternative to the deplorable ideology of 'state-centred positivism'; an ideology that, according to Schmitt, gave rise to the fatal conception of a sharp distinction between 'internal' and 'external' affairs, as pronounced by Heinrich Triepel in 1899 in his *Völkerrecht und Landesrecht*.[64] Schmitt

61 Cf JP Reid, 'The Jurisprudence of Liberty: The Ancient Constitution in the Legal Historiography of the Seventeenth and Eighteenth Centuries' in E Sandoz (ed), *The Roots of Liberty: Magna Charta, Ancient Constitution, and the Anglo-American Tradition of the Rule of Law* (Columbia/MO, University of Missouri Press 1993) 147.

62 F Gregor, 'Preface' to J Fortescue, *De Laudibus Legum Angliae* (new ed, Cambridge, Cambridge University Press 1775) iv–v.

63 C Schmitt, 'Die Lage der europäischen Rechtswissenschaft' in id, *Verfassungsrechtliche Aufsätze aus den Jahren 1924–1954* (Berlin, Duncker & Humblot, 4th ed 2003) 386–429.

64 H Triepel, *Völkerrecht und Landesrecht* (Leipzig, Hirschfeld 1899).

condemned Triepel for his alleged legal parochialism[65] and described positivism as *legalité qui tue*, 'legality that kills'.[66]

Today, the idea of refashioning international law as a new *jus commune* or *jus gentium*, developed and administered through the interactions of courts all over the world, continues to exert considerable attraction, as recent contributions, such as Jeremy Waldron's *Partly Laws Common to All Mankind* and Anne-Marie Slaughter's essay *A Global Community of Courts* demonstrate. Yet it is not to be expected that the 'good old days' of a 'Jus Publicum Europaeum' will simply return, this time on a global level: As Schmitt was perfectly aware of, and recent contributors sometimes tend to forget, its historical possibility depended upon the existence of similarities in terms of views, personal background, experiences and (legal) education that the members of the legal profession, but also more generally of the 'ruling class' shared with their equals across Europe; similarities that, on a global level, certainly do not exist to the same extent. Nevertheless, the historical development of the common law methodology provides interesting insights into the dynamics of a legal system based on the principle of decentralised self-organisation, insights that are crucial to the understanding of the nature and process of unwritten international law: As common law judges were (and to a certain degree still are) not bound by a single source of authority when it comes to determining the normative principles and considerations that may legitimately be taken into account when deciding a case, the dichotomy of *internal* and *external*, or domestic and international, has historically not played such a great role.

This general understanding of international law as being not exhaustively reducible to any particular 'source' of authority prevailed in the US Supreme Court until well into the 20th century, as demonstrated in a famous 1934 dispute between Delaware and New Jersey over a riparian border, which was, as it antedated the constitution, to be decided in accordance with the principles of international law on the matter. Justice Benjamin Cardozo forcefully

65 Schmitt (n 63) says about Triepel (at 388): 'Die von Heinrich Triepel in dem eben genannten Buch des Jahres 1899 entwickelte dualistische Lehre der Beziehungslosigkeit zwischen Innen und Außen ist durchaus herrschend geworden. Für unser Thema "Europäische Rechtswissenschaft" bedeutet sie eine glatte Verneinung seines juristischen Vorhandenseins, selbst in völkerrechtlicher Hinsicht. Denn entweder befasst sich der Jurist mit dem innerstaatlichen Recht eines Landes, dann ist sein staatsbezogener Blick ausschließlich nach innen gerichtet und kann unmöglich den Abgrund überwinden, der Innen und Außen dualistisch trennt; oder er hat es mit dem Völkerrecht, genauer: mit den Normen des Rechts zwischenstaatlicher Beziehungen zu tun, dann sind es immer wieder nur einzelne Staaten, deren Willen durch gegenseitige Verträge, Vereinbarungen oder Gewohnheiten die Normen des positiven zwischenstaatlichen Rechts schafft. Niemals kommt es zu einer konkreten Ordnung.'

66 Cf ibid, 423: 'Das Wort von der todbringenden Gesetzlichkeit, von der "légalité qui tue", spricht die Gefahren dieser Zersetzung des Rechts in dem Netz immer neu "gesetzter" Sollensvorschriften aus. So bleibt uns wirklich nur der Aufruf zur Rechtswissenschaft als der letzten Hüterin der absichtlosen Entstehung und Entwicklung des Rechts.'

embraced the role of a common law judge in determining equitable solutions to the circumstances of the case:[67] 'In these circumstances, the capacity of the law to develop and apply a formula consonant with justice and with the political and social needs of the international legal system is not lessened by the fact that, at the creation of the boundary, the formula of the *thalweg* had only a germinal existence.'[68] Thus, according to Cardozo, it was well within the power of the court to apply the principle of boundary delimitation it deemed adequate, regardless of whether it was temporally applicable to the case: 'The gap is not so great that adjudication may not fill it.' He concluded with a famous, assertive statement on the role of domestic judges in the process of international law: 'International law, or the law that governs between states, has at times, like the common law within states, a twilight existence during which it is hardly distinguishable from morality or justice, till at length the imprimatur of a court attests its jural quality.'[69] In one of his major contributions to jurisprudence, *The Nature of the Judicial Process*, Cardozo distilled his legal philosophy on the role of the judge in a common law system down to an elegantly framed conclusion:

> The work of a judge is in one sense enduring and in another sense ephemeral. What is good in it endures. What is erroneous is pretty sure to perish. The good remains the foundation on which new structures will be built. The bad will be rejected and cast off in the laboratory of the years. Little by little the old doctrine is undermined. Often the encroachments are so gradual that their significance is at first obscured. Finally we discover that the contour of the landscape has been changed, that the old maps must be cast aside, and the ground charted anew.[70]

Here it becomes evident how the Aristotelian-Thomistic idea of practical reason, preferring gradual modification over radical upheavals and stressing the importance of respecting the innate rationality of things, has survived in the common law legal tradition; a tradition which in turn influenced leading minds of the 18th and early 19th century, giving rise to the so-called 'Scottish Enlightenment', a second stream of Enlightenment legal and moral philosophy that is frequently concealed by the rationalist hubris of Diderot and Voltaire, symbolised in the latter's famous aphorism: '*Voulez-vous avoir de bonnes lois? Brûlez les vôtres, et faites-en de nouvelles!*'[71] Thus, the common law tradition remained largely immune to these iconoclasms.

67 *New Jersey v Delaware* [1934] 291 US 361.
68 Ibid, 383.
69 Ibid.
70 B Cardozo, *The Nature of the Judicial Process* (New Haven, Yale University Press 1921) 178.
71 Voltaire, *Dictionnaire Philosophique*, sv 'loi'.

C. Kant, Adam Smith and Savigny: Unlikely Allies on Self-Organisation

In the field of international law, a similar approach exerted considerable influence as well, sometimes in unlikely contexts: Kant's contribution to the theory of international law, for example, is often reduced in contemporary academic perception to the utopian vision of a world order based on contractual relations between republican states that he suggested in his 1795 essay *Perpetual Peace*.[72] Yet, at the end of its 'First Supplement', Kant seems to accept the reality of decentralised self-organisation among nations, not based on morality, but on self-interest, namely on the desire for commerce:

> The commercial spirit cannot co-exist with war, and sooner or later it takes possession of every nation. For, of all the forces which lie at the command of the state, the power of money is probably the most reliable. Hence states find themselves compelled – not, it is true, exactly from motives of morality – to further the noble end of peace and avert war, by means of mediation, wherever it threatens to break out, just as if they had made a permanent league for that purpose.... In this way, nature guarantees the coming of perpetual peace, through the natural course of human propensities.[73]

This little piece illustrates how deeply Kant's thought was influenced by another eminent moral philosopher and political economist of the 18th century, one who is most notably associated in public perception with the concept of an 'invisible hand' guiding the actions of market participants: Adam Smith,[74] whose *Wealth of Nations* is frequently (and to some extent unfairly)[75] cited as the founding document of *rational choice theory*, was actually endowed with a much more complex and comprehensive understanding of human behaviour than those modern rational choice economists and legal theorists, who conceive of human beings merely as pieces in their simplistic 'games', tend to believe.[76] To be sure, Smith also used a game metaphor, although in a different and more sophisticated way: he compared the relationship between a lawgiver and his subjects to that of a chess player to the pawns on a chequerboard. Yet in the game he conceived, the figures had a distinct individual will:

72 I Kant, *Perpetual Peace: A Philosophical Essay* (Campbell Smith tr, London, Swan Sunshine 1903).
73 Ibid, 157.
74 Marcus Herz, a student and friend of Kant in Königsberg, referred to Smith in a letter as Kant's '*Liebling*' (favourite); see I Kant, *Akademie-Ausgabe, vol X: Briefwechsel aus den Jahren 1747–1787* (Berlin, Walter de Gruyter 1996) 126.
75 For a more differentiated account see N Ashraf et al, 'Adam Smith: Behavioural Economist' (2005) 19 *Journal of Economic Perspectives* 131.
76 For a sharp, witty criticism of the shortcomings of rational choice economic theory see A Sen, 'Rational Fools: A Critique of the Behavioral Foundations of Economic Theory' (1977) 6 *Philosophy & Public Affairs* 317.

> The man of system seems to imagine that he can arrange the different members of a great society with as much ease as the hand arranges the different pieces upon a chessboard. He does not consider that the pieces upon the chessboard have no other principle of motion besides that which the hand impresses upon them; but that, in the great chessboard of human society, every single piece has a principle of motion of its own, altogether different from that which the legislature may choose to impress on it.[77]

In fact, the significant contributions of Smith to legal theory have not yet received due consideration from legal scholars,[78] whereas economists of such different schools of thought as Friedrich A Hayek[79] on one side and Kenneth Arrow and Amartya Sen[80] on the other were willing to take a holistic view on Smith's achievements. Particularly Smith's second most important work, the *Theory of Moral Sentiments*, can be described as a counterweight to the self-centred vision of the individual purported in the *Wealth of Nations*; here, Smith argues that an innate feeling of sympathy towards other human beings is part of the human condition and enables us to serve as 'impartial spectators' who feel pity and disgust when seeing a fellow human mistreated by a reckless and violent aggressor. This sense of right, according to Smith, enables us to keep our selfish interests in check and thus ensures the very basis of our living in societies, which would otherwise be destroyed by our antisocial impulses in an instant.

It is not possible here to adequately summarise Smith's elegant and well-wrought theory; it may suffice to say that his concept of sympathy and sociality appears not so idealistic and unscientific any more at a time like ours, when leading evolutional biologists, such as Edward O Wilson, suggest the notion of 'eusociality'[81] as a fundamental principle of evolution – a theory that, though still controversial, has the potential to disprove much of the post-Darwinian concept of the 'selfish gene', and particularly to refute the degenerate forms of reception that Darwin's theory of evolution has received in social science and economics. These insights, should they stand the test of further empiric inquiry, could indeed provide a fascinating source of inspiration for legal philosophy, because they would effectively undermine the vision of human society as something that is kept together by a rationally conceived bond, a *magna*

77 A Smith, *Theory of Moral Sentiments* (London, A Millar, 6th ed 1790) part 6, ch 2.

78 But see the recent contribution by J Petersen, *Adam Smith als Rechtstheoretiker* (Berlin, Walther de Gruyter 2012) in particular 51–65.

79 Cf on Smith and Hayek L Infantino, *Individualism in Modern Thought: From Adam Smith to Hayek* (London, Routledge 1998).

80 Most notably in *The Idea of Justice* (London, Penguin 2010), where Sen adopts Smith's concept of the 'impartial spectator' to project a pluralist theory of justice for the diverse world community that is unable to agree on universal values or transcendental goals.

81 For a current overview see MN Novak et al, 'The Evolution of Eusociality' *Nature* 466, 1057–62; for a popular yet fascinating account of this theory see EO Wilson, *The Social Conquest of Earth* (New York, Liveright 2012).

persona or *Leviathan*, that was forged to control the violence caused by the exercise of unlimited selfishness by its individuals.

Although the concept of a 'social contract' has probably never been understood literally to refer to an actual historical event, even modern contractarian theories of international relations, like those by John Rawls, Charles Beitz and Michael Walzer,[82] presuppose at least the *hypothetical* consent of the subjects governed by law, arguing that humans are 'by their nature' free and ought to be restrained only if and insofar as they themselves surrender their freedom to certain reasonable limits. As it is in practice hardly ever possible to actually conduct the fair and equal negotiations required to achieve such kind of reasonable consensus on the very foundations of any given community, modern contractarianists tend to substitute the procedural justification of law with a substantive theory about what the participants would reasonably have agreed upon. When one compares the three major contractarian theories[83] of law and justice, all published during the 1970s, it becomes obvious that their substantive content differs so significantly that the (common) theoretical framework of a hypothetical contract served merely as an excuse in which the authors cloaked their own subjective, prejudicial preferences and ideas as to how law and society ought to be organised properly.

The 19th century, although commonly (and by and large correctly) depicted as the foundational period of modern legal positivism, nevertheless brought significant new impulses to the understanding of law as an organic, emerging entity, arising from the intercourse of human beings in accordance with their natural propensities and inclinations and, as such not being a suitable object of either wholesale rationalistic design or of whatever arbitrary manipulations individual rulers might wish to undertake.

A major contribution to this understanding was provided in the works of the German Historical School of Jurisprudence, led by Friedrich Carl von Savigny. The core of his legal philosophy is presented in his pamphlet *Of the Vocation of Our Age for Legislation and Jurisprudence* of 1814, wherein he argued against the plan of creating a uniform codification of German civil law. The essence of Savigny's approach is aptly summarised in his famous statement that the laws, like the language and manners of a people, 'have no separate existence, they

82 J Rawls, *The Law of Peoples* (Cambridge/MA, Harvard University Press, 4th pr 2002); C Beitz, *Political Theory and International Relations* (Princeton/NJ, Princeton University Press 1979); M Walzer, 'The Moral Standing of States: A Response to Four Critiques' (1980) 9 *Philosophy & Public Affairs* 209.

83 Referring to: 1. J Rawls, *A Theory of Justice* (Cambridge/MA, Harvard University Press 1971); 2. R Nozick, *Anarchy, State and Utopia* (Oxford, Blackwell 1974); 3. J Buchanan, *The Limits of Liberty: Between Anarchy and Leviathan* (Chicago, University of Chicago Press 1975). This comparison may seem somewhat unfair, as the scope of the three works is not quite identical. However, the point made here is that a philosophical analysis of what is in the (properly understood) interest of the participants of any hypothetical social contract cannot be isolated from the philosopher's personal *a priori* conception of what should reasonably be agreed upon.

are but the particular faculties and tendencies of an individual people, inseparably united in nature, and only wearing the semblance of distinct attributes to our view'.[84] Savigny's approach was thus not only anti-universalistic, since he stressed the *particularity* of the laws among different peoples, indivisibly interwoven with their culture and circumstances: he also emphasised the laws' *historicity*, namely the fact that they necessarily reflected a certain stage in the development of a society, or, put differently, its individuals' inclinations towards certain doings and thoughts.

Of course, this was a blatant strike against the Enlightenment philosophical vision of an objective natural law, of a law that could be construed *more geometrico* through the application of human reason, that could be deduced from certain first principles and that was consequently, as emanating from human nature, one and the same for all times, under all circumstances and among all nations. Yet Savigny did not fall into the relativistic trap that often menaces approaches based on highlighting the varieties and inconsistencies between different legal systems, nor did his theory lead him to become a formalistic positivist who avoids the uncertainties inevitably accompanying evolutional conceptions of law by limiting his field of inquiry to the study of legislation formally enacted by any axiomatically prescribed 'authority'. Rather, he still adhered to a form of natural law, but to one based on the novel anthropological understanding of historicism, according to which human 'nature' was a variable the content of which depended on an accumulation of circumstances such as the individuality, the natural surroundings, the 'destiny', the temporal progress and material conditions – in short, on the *history* – of a given population.[85]

It was this understanding of law as a cultural mechanism of collective action, a mode of self-organisation of a society, that nourished Savigny's fundamental scepticism towards legislation as the product of an arbitrary sovereign will, indeed, his critical attitude towards the desirability of attempts to codify the existing (unwritten) law. For Savigny, the (only) true repository of the law lay in the 'common consciousness of the people'.[86] He identified numerous perils associated with the attempt to create a uniform civil code for the various principalities of which Germany consisted at that time: First, he doubted that it was possible to frame a comprehensive code anticipating all particular cases that might arise in the future; this, however, would be the expectation against which a codification would be measured, as the discussed proposals were intended to serve as the only law-authority henceforth.[87] Rather, he feared that the dominating spirit of a codification would be essentially derived from the ephemeral views and subjective sentiments and beliefs of the particular age,

84 FC Savigny, *Of the Vocation of Our Time for Legislation and Jurisprudence* (Abraham Hayward tr, London, Littlewood & Co 1831) 23.
85 Cf F Stahl, *Die Philosophie des Rechts, vol I* (Tübingen, Mohr, 5th ed 1878) 570 et seqq.
86 Savigny (n 84) 28.
87 Ibid, 38.

and that these would hinder the progress of the law towards its 'natural' direction determined by the emerging challenges and conditions under which the people lived. His second objection regarded the fitness of his age, and particularly the aptitude of its legal science, to undertake so vast and challenging a project (hence the title of his pamphlet: *Of the Vocation of Our Age*...). He described a legal system as inwrought with 'leading axioms', principles that enabled the expert of legal science to deduce the particular rules and notions in cases when no controlling authority can be found otherwise, just as, in geometry, it is sufficient to know 'two sides and the included angle, and the whole triangle is given'.[88] These axioms would have to be discerned and formulated with the utmost precision in order not to distort the existing functionality of law – a task that Savigny did not think his contemporaries were capable of performing adequately. Rather, codification of law would most likely lead to a situation where the administration of justice is ostensibly regulated by a code, yet in effect still guided and informed in all doubtful cases by the power of the 'true governing source of law', namely the *Volksgeist* or legal consciousness, a source that Savigny identified with concepts hitherto known by names such as 'natural law', 'jurisprudence' or 'axiological law'.[89] Above all, Savigny saw a great virtue in the diversity of substantive civil laws among the various German states:

> It is, therefore, an error to believe that the common weal would gain new life by the annihilation of all individual relations [in the German original *Verhältnisse*, denoting both (interpersonal) *relationships* and *circumstances*]. Were it possible to generate a corporate spirit in every class, every town, nay, every village, the common weal would gain new strength from this heightened and multiplied individuality. When, therefore, the influence of law on love of country is the question, the particular laws of particular provinces and states are not to be regarded as obstacles. In this point of view, the law merits praise if it falls within, or is adapted to fall within, the feelings and consciousness of the people; and blame, if, like an uncongenial or arbitrary thing, it leaves the people without participation.[90]

In these lines, Savigny did not only perform an early praise of legal pluralism *avant la lettre*, he also presented a remarkable restatement of Aristotelian political theory, as he stressed the importance of the participation of individuals in their communities and their identification therewith as the basis of 'good law', which he saw as a form of sound social (self-) ordering. Moreover, he acknowledged the fact that a legal system embodies a hierarchy of norms, and that certain norms are of peculiar importance because they function as pillars that sustain the whole construction of law; these norms that he called 'legal axioms' allow the jurist to 'triangulate' (to use Savigny's metaphor) the

88 Ibid, 38–9.
89 Ibid, 40.
90 Ibid, 58–9.

adequate rule of decision in cases where ostensibly no norm or precedent applies or (more frequently) where the existing rules are contradictory – an argument that remarkably resembles Ronald Dworkin's theory of jurisprudence, particularly his concept of deciding 'hard cases' by resort to 'General Principles of Law'.[91]

For Savigny, the great virtue of the existing legal order of Germany was its combination of regional legislation addressing the particular needs of a certain local population with the common law that was applied in all German states, and that thus formed a bond like the German language or certain mores. The Common Law Savigny referred to was, of course, derived from the sources of Roman law, pronounced in the works of leading scholars, like Savigny himself, as it was adapted to the need of 19th-century Germany by the force of the *Volksgeist*. The almost mythical concept of *Volksgeist* (literally 'spirit of the people' or 'national genius') has earned Savigny much sneer from later legal theorists, but he was certainly not a fantasist who literally believed in the people as a metaphysical entity with its own distinct reason and will. In fact, this term was just supposed as a metaphor of self-organisation, just as Adam Smith's 'invisible hand of the market' or the modern concept of 'wisdom of crowds'; and Savigny, just as Smith before and Hayek and Popper after him, was deeply sceptical about the possibility of artificially constructing a framework of order for an entity as complex and organic as human society – a difficulty that he, like his intellectual fellows, attributed to the inevitable want of sufficient information on the side of any central planning authority.[92]

Although Savigny did not explicitly deal with (public) international law, he deserves credit for being one of the founding fathers of private international law – or 'conflict of laws', in Anglo-American parlance – a field that he approached from his belief that a human relationship should be judged under the law most befitting its nature.[93] Yet of more interest here are the implications of his general legal theory with respect to the importance of unwritten law and the pitfalls of its codification. The significance of the issues he discussed for international law is obvious, yet his arguments have received relatively little attention by international lawyers. One notable exception to this, however, is a remarkable article by Julius Stone, written in 1957, entitled *On the Vocation of the International Law Commission*.[94] As the title already indicates, Stone drew from Savigny's 1814 text to criticise the increasing efforts to codify unwritten international law, and in particular the construction of the United Nations' International Law Commission (ILC) for that purpose, an organ that had

91 See in particular R Dworkin, *Law's Empire* (Cambridge/MA, Belknap 1986) 239 et seqq and passim.

92 For Savigny's place in this tradition, see Murphy (n 8) 89–91.

93 FC Savigny, *System des heutigen römischen Rechts, vol VIII* (Berlin, Veit u Co 1849) passim; see on Savigny's contribution in this respect H Battifol, *Aspects Philosophiques du Droit International Privé* (Paris, Dalloz 1956) 166–7.

94 J Stone, 'On the Vocation of the International Law Commission' (1957) 57 *Columbia Law Review* 16.

existed for scarcely a decade at that time. Firstly, he argued that the very ailment of unwritten international law that codification sought to redress, namely its uncertainty, was in fact, properly understood, an asset:

> [T]his very state of affairs [the uncertainty of unwritten international law] leaves a vast scope for juristic and judicial manipulation by way of interpretation; and since each generation of interpreters inevitably approaches its task with the outlook and interests of its own contemporary world, the chronic uncertainties of the law provide channels through which changing conditions can to a degree influence the contents of international law. Within the modest limits involved, this dialectical process permits changes to take place under the cover of a mantle of stability and continuity of traditional doctrine. It is to be observed, moreover, that even an unclear rule constitutes a *certain* means of social control, moderating the claims of States to the extent of keeping them within the range of debated alternatives.[95]

This function of social control, Stone argued, would be put at risk by uncritical codification efforts, since new written rules of absolute clarity, certainty and neatness could lack State acceptance, as they would presumably enclose areas in which the States hitherto had enjoyed certain discretion due to the ambiguity of customary rules. Hence his warning: 'While not glorifying the present deficiencies of international law, we must thus always remember that particular offered remedies may only aggravate the ills.'[96]

Secondly, Stone followed Savigny in suggesting that the spirit of the age was just not ripe for codification of international law. Since the contemporary international community was deficient with respect to the required 'political element', the basis of common convictions or '*Volksgeist*' which he regarded as essential to the formulation of a sustainable code of law, premature codification could terminate the sound development and growth of the law:

> This leads us immediately to the relevance to the international field of the classical themes of Savigny on the theory of codification. … It follows that would-be codifiers of international law have a particularly heavy responsibility (analogous to that of the framers of municipal codes and constitutions) not to encumber future generations with the limited foresights of the present but rather to invest their formulations, as Savigny would have put it, with the delicate balance of precision and vagueness, detailed prescription and general principle, which will permit adequate growth as new problems emerge which are as yet scarcely conceived in the womb of time.[97]

95 Ibid, 18.
96 Ibid.
97 Ibid, 21.

This is not the place to exhaustively assess the accurateness of these predictions. Rather, the aim of quoting them is to demonstrate the continuing relevance of Savigny's jurisprudential thought to the field of international law, a relevance which was eloquently and wittily asserted by Stone. Of course, considering the ILC's achievements over the past 50 years, it can certainly be argued that Stone's exhortations about the perils immanent in codification efforts were hugely exaggerated, given the fact that most of the important major multilateral treaties adopted during the past half century have in one way or another received preparatory treatment at the hands of the ILC, and it does not appear that, for example, the Vienna Convention on the Law of Treaties 'encumbers' the present generation with the 'limited foresight' of its drafters.

In fact, the ILC already has become something like a 'laboratory' of international law, delimitating positions on which a consensus could possibly be reached on the larger scene of a diplomatic conference. A certain difficulty is posed by the dual mandate of the commission under its Statute, authorising both the 'codification' and the 'progressive development' of international law.[98] Thus, it was almost inevitable that discussions arose as to whether a particular norm drafted by the ILC represented the former (and was thus binding anyway as a matter of customary law) or the latter (and as such only binding on the parties of a particular treaty). In fact, it has been stated that 'the Commission has proceeded on the basis of a composite idea of codification and progressive development'.[99]

This pragmatic approach, however, recently became the target of increasing criticism.[100] At a time when major breakthroughs in the field of multilateral treaty-making seem more difficult to achieve than ever, in a world that is much more diverse and fragmented than anytime during the Cold War, the ILC is struggling to retain its relevance as an organ contributing effectively to the strengthening of the rule of international law. And it is unclear where the Commission will position itself in the future within the wide range of suggestions made for the improvement of the quality of its work.[101] Yet a widely held perception seems to be, as ILC member Sean D Murphy argues, that it is desirable for the ILC to focus more clearly on the study and accurate representation of existing norms, rather than creating an undistinguishable medley of codification and progressively developed norms packaged rather innocuously as 'report', 'practice guide' or 'draft articles', ultimately lacking acceptance

98 Cf Art 15 of the Statute of the International Law Commission, UNGA Res 174 (II) (21 November 1947).

99 United Nations, *The Work of the International Law Commission* (New York, United Nations, 7th ed 2007) 45.

100 See eg F Berman, 'The ILC within the UN's Legal Framework: Its Relationship with the Sixth Committee' (2006) 49 *German Yearbook of International Law* 107 (127).

101 See for the discussion Y Chen, 'Structural Limitations and Possible Future of the Work of the International Law Commission' (2010) 9 *Chinese Journal of International Law* 473.

by the states.[102] Should Murphy's prediction prove to be accurate, the ILC would in fact turn into something that Savigny and his follower Stone would have embraced: '[T]o convert the International Law Commission from a body of learned lawyers preparing draft codes for Governments, which either do not want any code or want a code with different provisions, into an International Law Research Centre for the basic problems arising in the more dynamic, changeful, and disrupted segments of international law.'[103] In any event, it seems that the ILC is increasingly aware of the risks posed by overzealous codification attempts: As its member Xue Hanqin argued in a 2009 presentation,

> [i]n promoting the rule of law, we should constantly bear in mind that the international legal system is not built upon a constitutional framework as domestic legal systems, but upon international relations. Currently when international relations are undergoing fundamental change, it is not surprising that existing legal mechanisms can no longer meet their objectives and purposes ... Supposedly good law does not necessarily lead to its designed goals.[104]

Savigny, though universally acknowledged as a great jurist and legal historian, is not always given his due as a legal philosopher, since he sometimes lost himself in the adoration of ancient sources, whereas his critical analysis of them often remained rather shallow. However, his immensely influential *evolutionary theory of law* has been critical to overcoming the rather naïve Enlightenment conception of an immutable law of reason, while at the same time evading the pitfalls of legal positivism. This third way, sometimes aptly referred to as *legal naturalism*[105] (to distinguish it from the somewhat tainted concept of natural law, which at that time denoted something eternal, super-human) soon gained popularity beyond the borders of German academic jurisprudence, substantially influencing eminent figures like Sir Henry Maine and Paul Vinogradoff; this historical school of jurisprudence is often seen as the legal pendant to Darwin's theory of evolution. While Savigny had won the battle with his forceful argument against codification, and thus was able to delay the creation of a uniform German civil code for almost a century (it was only in 1900 that the *Bürgerliches Gesetzbuch*, the civil code for the whole of Germany, finally took effect),

102 SD Murphy, 'Codification, Progressive Development, or Scholarly Analysis? The Art of Packaging the ILC's Work Product', in M Ragazzi (ed), *The Responsibility of International Organizations: Essays in Memory of Sir Ian Brownlie* (Leiden, Martinus Nijhoff 2013) 29.

103 Stone (n 94) at 48.

104 H Xue, 'The Role of the ILC's Work in Promoting Peace and Security' in G Nolte (ed), *Peace through International Law: The Role of the International Law Commission* (Heidelberg, Springer 2009) 183 (185).

105 See eg R Barnett, 'Toward a Theory of Legal Naturalism' (1978) 2 *Journal of Libertarian Studies* 97.

ultimately his opponents won the war, and today it seems rather preposterous even to think of governing a modern, economically advanced nation state without a plethora of minute statutory regulation. What has become clear, however, is that Savigny's scepticism towards codification still poses valuable intellectual challenges in the field of international law, where not only a central legislative authority is lacking, but where in fact even the fundamental agreement on general common aims and goals is often quite fragile.

With Savigny and his legacy, our brief *tour d'horizon* through the history of the idea of law as an intelligent, self-organising system ends. The common theme among the thinkers we dealt with has been their conception of a kind of law that can only be *discerned*, not deliberately *made*. It is the aim of this study to demonstrate that even in the contemporary international order such kind of law exists, and that it is precisely what I have proposed to call by the name of *unwritten international law*. This law, which arises by way of self-organisation of the international community, whether of its totality or of parts of it, contributes significantly to the promotion of order and stability in international relations; yet it aggregates without formal enactment and, more importantly, without centralised rationalistic design. In the chapters to follow, I shall attempt to establish the written/unwritten divide as a fundamental conceptual distinction not only of international law, but of law in general. However, I do not intend to unravel the firmly established sources doctrine, but rather to clarify and enrich it in some aspects: It is, as Karl Marx remarked, insufficient to navigate only on the source and ignore the stream.[106] The importance of such a view is more and more recognised in international legal theory and practice. A particularly interesting example in this regard is presented by the recent study undertaken by the International Law Commission on the issue of 'Treaties over Time':[107] The question of how treaties evolve through the process of their application and how the practice of the states who are parties to them shapes the meaning of their terms. This undertaking exemplifies the initial assumption, namely that unwritten international law as a concept does not only relate to the unwritten sources of international law, but that it in fact presents a mode in which international law aggregates and evolves beyond the narrow boundaries of the process of formal international law-making. It was this same perception of law being endowed – metaphorically speaking – with a life of its own, developing beyond the limited foresight of its original authors, that led the great Argentinean legal philosopher Sebastián Soler to declare: 'La

106 Cf K Marx, 'Das Philosophische Manifest der Historischen Rechtsschule' in *Rheinische Zeitung* Nr 221 (9 August 1842): 'Die historische Rechtsschule … hat ihre Quellenliebhaberei bis zu dem Extrem gesteigert, dass sie dem Schiffer anmutet, nicht auf dem Strome, sondern auf seiner Quelle zu fahren…'

107 For an overview by the ILC's Special Rapporteur on 'Treaties over Time/Subsequent Agreement and Subsequent Practice in Relation to Interpretation of Treaties', see G Nolte, 'Introduction' in id (ed), *Treaties and Subsequent Practice* (Oxford, Oxford University Press 2013) 1.

ley es mas sabia que el legislador'.[108] But wherein consists that wisdom of the law which is claimed to be greater than that of the legislator?

In the following chapter, it is intended to identify factors which contribute to the formation of unwritten international law as a normative system. To this end, I will analyse some of the dominant strands of legal theory that have evolved over the course of the 20th century, and assess their aptitude to advance the understanding of the concept of unwritten international law and to improve the methodology for its ascertainment.

108 S Soler, *La Interpretación de la Ley* (Barcelona, Aries 1962) 117.

III Theoretical Problems and Methodological Approaches

A. The Legacies of Legal Realism

It may be a commonplace that 'we are all realists now', but the meaning of this assertion is considerably more difficult to fathom.[1] This is because the term 'realism' means many different things to many different people. The plurality of meanings of the concept of 'realism' is particularly visible in international law, which is positioned, as it were, at the point where general legal theory and the theory of international relations intersect. Perhaps the most frequent use of the term 'realism' with respect to international law is derived from the eponymous bundle of theories of international relations, the common denominator of which is their profoundly anti-utopian and ultimately 'tragic' vision of human nature.[2] Although there are considerable differences between the so-called 'classical realist' and 'structural-' or 'neo-realist' schools of international relations,[3] their common trait is their focus on power as the driving force behind the conduct of states, and the fact that they ascribe a relatively marginal role to legal rules as independent factors motivating state behaviour.[4]

More interesting for the present inquiry into the theoretical and methodological difficulties associated with the evolution and ascertainment of rules of unwritten international law are, however, other forms of realism, those which are generally summarised under the broad category of *legal* realism. The view of the process of legal interpretation as a form of logical inference, of syllogistic reasoning, which had dominated in 19th-century legal positivism, was

1 See for a general overview H Dagan, 'The Realist Conception of Law' (2005) *Tel Aviv University Law School Paper* 21; available at <http://papers.ssrn.com/sol3/papers.cfm?abstract_id=608383>accessed 20 August 2017.

2 For an exposition of this tradition of classical realism, see RN Lebow, *The Tragic Vision of Politics: Ethics, Interests and Orders* (Cambridge, Cambridge University Press 2003).

3 For a comparative overview, see T Dunne/M Kurki/S Smith (eds), *International Relations Theories: Discipline and Diversity* (Oxford, Oxford University Press, 2nd ed 2010) 58–76 (classical realism) and 77–94 (structural realism).

4 Therefore, realist international relations theory has also been described as 'legal nihilism'; see A Buchanan, *Justice, Legitimacy and Self-Determination. Moral Foundations for International Law* (Oxford, Oxford University Press 2007) 45.

fundamentally challenged by various sociologically oriented schools of jurisprudence that flourished in many countries during the early decades of the 20th century.[5] Whereas the different responses to 19th-century formalism are often indiscriminately referred to as *legal realism*, there are three major distinctive schools discernible within this movement: The American legal realist movement, the 'free law movement' in Germany and Austria, and, beginning somewhat later, the Scandinavian legal realist school. Although these three schools of thought share the same general impetus, namely to bridge the gap between 'law' and 'life', each had a distinct focus.

The American legal realist movement, whose leading exponents, such as Roscoe Pound and Benjamin Cardozo, attained highest ranks in the judiciary and in legal academia,[6] was primarily concerned with institutional reform in order to adapt the legal system to the needs of a modern industrial society. They considered many of the rules of the common law as being antiquated and failing to provide answers to the social problems of a nation that constantly grew more diverse and divided. In their view, it was part of the task of the judicial system to actively redress these deficiencies by attending to the social concerns of the emerging 20th-century mass society, instead of sticking to the idea that a case could be resolved by way of logical inference from the *ratio decidendi* of some venerable 18th-century precedent. The conflict of aims between continuity and change in the legal process was particularly bothersome to Cardozo, who knew from first-hand experience the dilemma faced by judges who had to deal with rules and precedents they perceived as outdated.[7]

Another school of sociological jurisprudence which rejected the syllogistic conception of legal interpretation was the German *Freirechtsbewegung* ('free law movement'), spearheaded by Hermann Kantorowicz. This movement stressed the fact that the law is necessarily incomplete, that 'there are as many gaps as words' in it.[8] From this finding they inferred that judges do not only have the right but the duty to fill these gaps – not by logical deduction from any superior 'principle', but rather through an act of free choice, by drawing from the principally infinite set of available information those they deemed relevant to the decision of the specific case at hand. A particularly interesting figure associated with this school of thought was Eugen Ehrlich, a professor of

5 A very concise, yet somewhat dated overview of the various approaches in the US, Latin America and Europe can be found in L Recaséns Siches, *Nueva Filosofía de la Interpretación del Derecho* (Mexico and Buenos Aires, Fondo de Cultura Economica 1958) 38–127.
6 Pound, as Dean of Harvard Law School, and Cardozo, as an Associate Justice of the US Supreme Court as well as a prolific writer on legal theory, heavily influenced the legal discourse in the United States until the present day.
7 He devoted a series of lectures to the problem of continuity and change in the development of the law: see B Cardozo, *The Nature of the Judicial Process* (New Haven, Yale University Press 1921); id, *The Growth of the Law* (New Haven, Yale University Press 1924); id, *The Paradoxes of Legal Science* (New York, Columbia University Press 1928).
8 H Kantorowicz, *Der Kampf um die Rechtswissenschaft* (Heidelberg, Winter 1906) 15.

legal sociology at the University of Czernowitz in what was then the Austro-Hungarian province of Bukovina (in modern-day Ukraine). Ehrlich, who is today counted among the founding fathers of sociology of law as an academic discipline, stressed the importance of studying what he referred to as 'the living law', as opposed to 'the law in the books'.[9]

Unsurprisingly for a legal sociologist, he developed a keen interest in the study of customary law, which he chose as the topic of a lecture he delivered on the occasion of becoming rector of Czernowitz University in 1906.[10] In this lecture, entitled *Die Tatsachen des Gewohnheitsrechts* ('The Facts of Customary Law'), Ehrlich argued that in order to truly grasp the essence of customary law as a phenomenon, one has to broaden the focus of inquiry, including social institutions and relationships that are not yet – or no longer – regarded as legally relevant. For him, the core question of the doctrine of sources was this: 'How do factual interactions turn into legal rights and legal relationships?'[11]

According to Ehrlich, the transition from mere customs to customary *law* historically occurred when human beings began to gradually assemble in larger groups. Inborn feelings of compassion and sympathy had been sufficient to 'cement the ties of a family or a clan',[12] but in larger tribes these purely personal emotional attachments were insufficient to guarantee a minimum of social peace and stability. However, as the ability to live together in groups of increasing numbers provided a vital evolutionary advantage to those having the capacity to do so, the rules became detached from their original emotional basis and assumed a separate existence, backed by mutual feelings of dependency and often under the protection of powerful sacred taboos.[13] What is interesting about Ehrlich's treatment of customary law is not so much the – admittedly speculative – historical analysis (which, nevertheless, bears interesting resemblances to much more recent sociobiological theories),[14] but the consequences he drew from his study for the investigation of modern legal phenomena: He argued that social institutions and traditions are the primary element of customary law, an element which is, however, mediated and to a certain extent obfuscated by the intercession of rules created for the purpose of deciding among conflicting rights and claims. Yet important to him was that one should not lose sight of the fact that such rules of decision, and generally

9 For a recent evaluation of his work and its lasting influence on legal sociology, see the various contributions collected in M Hertogh (ed), *Living Law: Reconsidering Eugen Ehrlich* (Oxford, Hart 2009).

10 See E Ehrlich, *Die Tatsachen des Gewohnheitsrechts: Inaugurationsrede, gehalten am 2. Dezember 1906* (Leipzig and Wien, Deuticke 1907).

11 Ibid, 9.

12 Ibid, 10.

13 Ibid, 19 et seq.

14 Cf eg EO Wilson, *The Social Conquest of Earth* (New York, Liveright 2012) 57 et seqq; see also W Fikentscher, *Law and Anthropology* (München, Verlag der Bayerischen Akademie der Wissenschaften 2009) esp ch 7.

all of the well-known institutions of the law, such as courts, legislative bodies and administrative agencies, are only a small part of the true 'living law', which is independent of and often untouched by such formal establishments.

Neither the American legal realists, who were primarily occupied with reforming domestic institutions to adjust them to the perceived realities of modern life, nor Kantorowicz and Ehrlich, whose principal interest was historical sociology of law, spent much time applying their theories to the field of international law. This was different, however, with the third stream of early 20th-century legal realism, which originated in Scandinavia. This brand of legal realism, associated most notably with the names of Karl Olivecrona, Axel Hägerström, Alf Ross and Max Sørensen, differed from the American and the Austro-German schools in that its primary goal was not so much a practical or historical, but an epistemological one: The Scandinavian realists wanted to 'purge' law of 'metaphysical' connotations.[15] They attempted to deconstruct fundamental legal concepts like 'right', 'duty', 'source of law', 'legal validity' or 'unlawfulness' by demonstrating that these notions were inextricably interwoven with the 'mythical and irrational ideologies of natural law', a heritage that they believed still attached to those concepts even in their modern positivist disguise.[16] A typical example of how the Scandinavian legal realists viewed international law is Alf Ross' major textbook on the subject.[17] In this treatise, Ross began by challenging fundamentally the concept of 'sovereignty', which he regarded as a pre-Enlightenment remnant, the mystical idea that a collective entity can somehow be conceived of as a personification endowed with a unified will: 'Sovereignty here refers to the invisible, mystical power or ability to create valid law'.[18] Together with the notion of sovereignty, Ross also attempted to do away with the concept of 'legal validity' as hitherto used by international lawyers: Instead of considering 'validity' to be a metaphysical quality attached to legal rules, he proposed that one should be satisfied with the explanation that the 'bindingness' of a rule is a purely psychological phenomenon, in the sense of being a factor motivating behaviour, and thus belongs exclusively to the factual realm.[19] Therefore, Ross proposed to give up the – allegedly failed – attempts to justify the 'bindingness' of law by reference to the own will of the person to be bound, or by alluding to 'objective' theories of rightness

15 Hägerström's motto was: 'Praeterea censeo metaphysicam esse delendam!'; see A Hägerström, *Die Philosophie der Gegenwart in Selbstdarstellungen, vol VII* (Leipzig, Felix Meiner 1929) 158.

16 This program was formulated in particular clarity by Alf Ross in his *Kritik der sogenannten Praktischen Erkenntnis: Zugleich Prolegomena zu einer Kritik der Rechtswissenschaft* (Copenhagen, Munksgaard 1933) ch 1.

17 A Ross, *Lehrbuch des Völkerrechts* (M Brakas tr, Stuttgart, Kohlhammer 1951); for a recent thorough analysis of Alf Ross' approach to international law, see AL Escorihuela, 'Alf Ross: Towards a Realist Critique and Reconstruction of International Law' (2003) 14 *European Journal of International Law* 703.

18 Ross (n 17) 39.

19 Ibid, 47–50.

and justness, and to simply accept the motivating power of legal rules on the human consciousness as an empirical fact of social psychology.[20]

Is there any relevance to contemporary international law of the three classical strands of legal realism described above? Although none of these schools gained widespread acceptance among practical international lawyers, it is not difficult to see the legacies that they left in some of the great theoretical debates of the past few decades. The influence that is perhaps easiest to retrace is that which the American legal realist movement exerted on the New Haven School of international law, whose protagonist Myres S McDougal explicitly embraced the activist goals of American legal realism as part of his mission statement: Citing Roscoe Pound, he argued that the New Haven School's purpose was to develop 'a functional critique of international law in terms of social ends'.[21] Less obvious to discern is the lasting influence of Ehrlich, whose focus was much more theoretical than that of the American legal realists, and whose reception was impeded by the utter destruction by two World Wars of the academic environment in which his ideas had flourished. However, Gunther Teubner has endorsed Ehrlich and his notions of *Juristenrecht* and 'living law' as a source of inspiration for his theory of 'legal pluralism', the increasingly popular[22] conception that transnational law is centred on and rooted in society, an approach which allows for the coexistence of different and even conflicting normative orders.[23] The Scandinavian brand of realism, with its sceptical and anti-metaphysical impetus, seems to have exerted considerable influence on the development of the so-called 'critical legal studies' movement and related approaches to international law. This has been explicitly acknowledged by Anthony Carty, one of the movements earliest proponents,[24] who appreciated the deconstructivist attitude of Ross ('Scandinavian realism … has effectively swept away this whole formalistic apparatus as illusory'), but argued that the Scandinavian realists had not gone far enough.[25] Martti Koskenniemi, while being slightly less enthusiastic about Alf Ross than Carty, readily

20 Ibid, 49.

21 See MS McDougal, 'International Law, Power, and Policy: A Contemporary Conception' (1954) 82 *Recueil des Cours* 137 (137); on the New Haven School's connection with American legal realism, see HH Koh, 'Is there a "New" New Haven School of International Law?' (2007) 32 *Yale Journal of International Law* 559.

22 See eg N Krisch, *Beyond Constitutionalism: The Pluralist Structure of Postnational Law* (Oxford, Oxford University Press 2010); J Klabbers/T Piiparinen (eds), *Normative Pluralism in International Law: Exploring Global Governance* (Cambridge, Cambridge University Press 2013).

23 See G Teubner, 'Global Bukowina: Legal Pluralism in the World Society' in id (ed), *Global Law Without a State* (Dartmouth, Aldershot 1997) 3

24 See eg his seminal treatise *The Decay of International Law* (Manchester, University of Manchester Press 1986).

25 See A Carty, 'Scandinavian Realism and Phenomenological Approaches to Statehood and General Custom in International Law' (2003) 14 *European Journal of International Law* 817 (841).

admitted that one of Ross' books had 'struck me as an eye-opener' when he read it as a postgraduate student of international law.[26]

The most important legacy of the legal realist approaches described for the understanding of the unwritten sources of international law is perhaps less their respective specific content, but the fact that they really served as 'eye-openers', in that they permitted jurists to take a broader view on normative and sociological phenomena than classical formalist positivism had seen fit. To a certain extent, the mission of 20th-century legal realism has been fulfilled by modifying the direction of mainstream scholarship: Indeed, as one author remarks, today '[o]ne can easily imagine a new generation of international legal scholarship in which the distinctions between realism and positivism become unimportant compared to the enormous overlap in perspective among scholars who see themselves as working in the two supposedly divergent traditions'.[27]

However, the fact that contemporary proponents of legal realism in international law are facing less opposition from 'mainstream' scholarship (wherever this 'mainstream' may flow at a given time) does not mean that all is well in the world of international legal realism. On the contrary, the more attempts to (re-)introduce empiricism to the methodology of law succeed, the more obvious becomes their fundamental dilemma in terms of legal philosophy: In order for the law to be effective, its content has to be sufficiently resonating with the realities of the factual world; whereas, in order to retain its normativity, it must stay clear of the murky swamps of political realism. In the field of international law, this dilemma has been most famously depicted by Koskenniemi, who described the international legal discourse as alternating between the two equally undesirable extremes of being either too apologetic with respect to actual state behaviour, will and interest, or engaging in an idealistic pursuit of a utopian world order, thereby losing touch with the complex and contradictory realities of world politics.[28]

B. Kelsen and the *Grundnorm* of Customary International Law

This conflict has explicitly been acknowledged by the most philosophically distinguished theorist of legal positivism of the 20th century, Hans Kelsen. Surely, it was Kelsen's desire to frame a theory of law based on his neo-Kantian creed according to which the spheres of 'Is' and 'Ought', or of facts and norms, had to be conceived as being strictly separated; a theory under which a norm could derive its validity only from a higher norm, all the way up to the – hypothetical – *Grundnorm* (basic or fundamental norm), but could never be

26 M Koskenniemi, 'Alf Ross and Life Beyond Realism' (2003) 14 *European Journal of International Law* 653 (653).

27 DAJ Telman, 'International Legal Positivism and Legal Realism' in J Kammerhofer/J d'Aspremont (eds), *International Legal Positivism in a Post-Modern World* (Cambridge, Cambridge University Press 2014) 241 (262).

28 M Koskenniemi, *From Apology to Utopia: The Structure of International Legal Argument* (Cambridge, Cambridge University Press, reissue 2005).

inferred from a merely factual state of affairs. Nevertheless, he readmitted the world of facts into his concept of law by making one significant concession. According to Kelsen, it was the precondition, though not the source, of the validity of a norm that the legal order to which it belonged was overall *effective*:

> The efficacy of the total legal order is a condition, not the reason for the validity of its constituent norms. These norms are valid not because the total order is efficacious, but because they are created in a constitutional way. They are valid, however, only on the condition that the total order is efficacious; they cease to be valid, not only when they are annulled in a constitutional way, but also when the total order ceases to be efficacious. It cannot be maintained that, legally, men have to behave in conformity with a certain norm, if the total legal order, of which that norm is an integral part, has lost its efficacy.[29]

In other words, Kelsen regarded a legal system's overall efficacy as a necessary (yet not sufficient) condition of the legal validity of its individual norms.

But apart from that concession, Kelsen maintained the operative closure of the legal system, by stressing that any particular norm could only derive its validity from a superior norm that authorised and regulated the lower norm's creation. With respect to the process of interpretation, this implied the existence of a fundamental difference between a norm's authoritative interpretation by a body legally authorised to concretise the law and interpretation as an exercise of jurisprudence: Whereas the latter, resembling a kind of scientific inquiry, could merely determine a certain range of possible interpretations, the former comprised a creative act, an exercise of discretion, predetermined insofar as a competent authority was named in the superior norm that was to be concretised.[30]

Thus, Kelsen conceived the legal process as being essentially governed by delegations of power, granting the respective authorities the competence to concretise the higher, more abstract norm and, consequently, to produce a lower, more concrete one. The Kelsenian theory of interpretation as law-creation, with the hypothetical basic norm being at the top and the judicial or administrative decision at the bottom of the pyramid of legal norms, is certainly a model of striking simplicity and elegance. Nonetheless, it can hardly conceal its origin from a theory of domestic constitutional law. Whereas the concept of a hierarchy of legal norms certainly makes sense in the context of the national legal order, where substantive provisions are usually accompanied

29 H Kelsen, *General Theory of Law and State* (Cambridge/MA, Harvard University Press 1945) 118–19.

30 A concise statement of the Kelsenian theory of interpretation with respect to international law can be found in the 'Preface On Interpretation' to his treatise on *The Law of the United Nations* (London, Stevens & Sons 1950) xiii–xvii.

by authorisations for their enforcement, the international legal system, apart from certain treaty regimes, does not generally provide mechanisms for the authoritative interpretation of its norms. And more fundamentally, it seems unclear what any conceivable basic norm of the international legal system could possibly look like, since such a norm would either be vague to the degree of being meaningless, or unable to cover the totality of legal norms that are acknowledged as being part of international law today and are by and large efficacious. Kelsen himself, in his *General Theory of Law and State*, framed his idea of the basic norm of international law thus: 'The States ought to behave as they have customarily behaved.'[31] Assuming the correctness of this formulation, the basic norm of international law would be a premise that allows regarding certain human actions, ie facts, as norm-creating. This is at first surprising, given Kelsen's meticulously guarded separation wall between 'Is' and 'Ought', between facts and norms; yet the basic norm itself is normative in nature, and it regulates the creation of customary law by the states (in other words, it delegates the power of customary norm-creation to them).

This also implies that norms of customary international law derive their validity immediately from the basic norm, whereas treaties – in the Kelsenian view – are based on the intermediate customary principle of *pacta sunt servanda*. And another important consequence is implicated in this conception: since the emergence of customary international law is primordial, no delegation of norm-concretising power is possible or required for its production:

> Law is always created by an act that deliberately aims at creating law, except in the case when law has its origin in custom, that is to say, in a generally observed course of conduct, during which the acting individuals do not consciously aim at creating law; but they must regard their acts as in conformity with a binding norm and not as a matter of arbitrary choice.[32]

This means, however, that Kelsen's hierarchy of norms collapses when it comes to customary (international) law. As the Argentinean legal philosopher Jorge A Bacqué has put it, '[t]he metaphor of the "legal pyramid" is only applicable to codified domestic law and international treaty law.'[33]

Another consequence of Kelsen's theory is that the other form of unwritten international law, which is usually referred to as the general principles of law, has only a subordinate place in the theory of legal sources. The reference made in Article 38 (1) (c) of the Statute of the International Court of Justice to the 'general principles of law recognized by civilized nations' is interpreted by Kelsen not to denote an independent source of international law, but rather as

31 Kelsen (n 29) 369.
32 Ibid, 114.
33 JA Bacqué, 'Stufenbau der Rechtsordnung' in E Bulygin/EG Valdez (eds), *Argentinische Rechtstheorie und Rechtsphilosophie heute* (Berlin, Duncker und Humblot 1987) 111 (115) (my transl).

a grant of authority to the ICJ to fill 'gaps' in the law where no specific treaty or customary provision is applicable. These gaps, though, are not logical gaps, as international law either regulates a certain state behaviour or is silent on it, but 'gaps' which occur when the solution arrived at through application of the existing positive norms of international law are regarded as unsatisfactory. 'There can be no doubt that such a power may be conferred upon a law-applying organ by a treaty.'[34] Thus, under Kelsen's theory the general principles are at the bottom end of a chain of delegation of decision-making authority: Since he regarded the sentence 'custom is a law-creating fact' as the basic norm, the ability to make legally valid treaties derived from the customary norm *pacta sunt servanda*; and a treaty provision, namely Article 38 ICJ Statute, delegated to the International Court the power to concretise the law – with recourse to the general principles – when decisions of particular cases required it to fill *lacunae*, ie redressing moral or political grievances arising from the application of the higher norms of international custom and treaty law. Here, it becomes evident that the theoretical purity of Kelsen's theory comes at a price: it deprives the science of international law of all its material logic – in fact, of any specific content. Yet the theory provides a valuable starting point for our exposition of the process of unwritten international law, since it directs the eye to some of the conceptual difficulties and misunderstandings that still impede the development in international law of a more coherent and rational legal methodology, which today still ranks far below the degree of sophistication this discipline has attained in many domestic legal systems.

The Kelsenian kind of formalistic positivism has never exerted a dominant influence on the practice of international law.[35] But it cannot be denied that formalist arguments are a perpetual temptation to scholars and practitioners of international law alike, an understandable trait for a profession that is continually struggling to create and preserve structure in an unstructured and disintegrated environment. This is reflected in the tendency, influential among many international lawyers, to emphasise the importance of institutions, a tendency that is rooted in both the liberal theory of international relations and the ongoing debate about 'global constitutionalism'. While early scholars who advocated a constitutionalist understanding of international law, such as Alfred Verdross,[36] Hugo Krabbe,[37] Léon Duguit and Georges

34 H Kelsen, *Principles of International Law* (New York, Rinehart 1952) 307.

35 Cf D Kennedy, 'Kelsen als Pragmatist des Völkerrechts – Die Oliver Wendell Holmes Lectures des Jahres 1941' in A Carrino/G Winker, *Rechtserfahrung und Reine Rechtslehre* (Wien/New York, Springer 1995) 95; but see J Kammerhofer, 'Hans Kelsen's Place in International Legal Theory' in A Orakhelashvili (ed), *Research Handbook on the Theory and History of International Law* (Cheltenham/Northampton, Edward Elgar 2011) 143 (166).

36 A Verdross, *Die Verfassung der Völkerrechtsgemeinschaft* (Wien/Berlin, Springer 1926).

37 H Krabbe, *The Modern Idea of the State* (GH Sabine and WJ Shepard tr, Leiden, Martinus Nijhoff 1921) Chapter X.

Scelle,[38] tried to establish the superiority of certain material values (such as solidarity or the tenets of Christian natural law), modern proponents of a constitutional theory of international law more frequently focus on a formal hierarchisation[39] of norms in the international legal system, with the UN Charter being posited at the apex.[40] Nevertheless, these attempts to designate the Charter as the 'constitution of the international community' cannot claim support from Kelsen's theory, as he regarded Article 103 UN Charter merely as a partial exception to the *lex posterior* rule, not as a norm depriving inconsistent international obligations on the parts of the members of their legal validity.[41]

The absence of a genuine hierarchy of norms (apart from the concept of *jus cogens*, whose preconditions and legal consequences are still not entirely understood), combined with the lack of institutional arrangements for the law's authoritative interpretation, creates a serious impediment for the application of formalist theories of legal interpretation in international law. This means that the correctness of a certain interpretation can often neither be determined by its consistency with a norm of higher legal validity, nor by the fact that it has been rendered by a competent authority. Given this state of affairs, it appears as if the science of international law cannot be successful in addressing the pressing needs of the international community without developing a *material* or *substantive* theory of the ascertainment and interpretation of international norms. Such a theory would have to be distinguishable from both major methodological tendencies in legal theory, namely formalism and realism. More precisely, it would have to combine the valuable insights of both without stepping into the pitfalls of each:[42] Whereas formalism rightfully stresses the importance of logical consistency of the law and of the systematisation of legal sentences, it frequently neglects or devalues the empirical realities and overemphasises the role of deductive reasoning. Realism or empiricism, on the other hand, tends to reduce the legal process to a collection of factual problems and to undervalue the virtues of systematisation.

C. Deduction, Induction, and the Search for a 'Rule of Recognition'

The juxtaposition of legal realism and Kelsenian formalist positivism has illustrated that these two approaches, at least in their ideal-typical forms, are

38 Cf eg G Scelle, 'Le Droit constitutionnel international' in *Mélanges R. Carré de Malberg* (Paris, Recueil Sirey 1933) 502–15.

39 See generally T Kleinlein, *Konstitutionalisierung im Völkerrecht* (Heidelberg/New York, Springer 2011) 315–423.

40 Cf B Fassbender, 'The United Nations Charter as the Constitution of the International Community' (1998) 36 *Columbia Journal of Transnational Law* 529.

41 Kelsen (n 30) 111–21; see on this question J Kammerhofer (n 35) 158.

42 On this point see C Alchuorron/E Bulygin, *Normative Systems* (Wien/New York, Springer 1971) 65–7.

essentially incompatible with one another not only from a philosophical, but also from a methodological point of view: Whereas Kelsen's approach is based on the premise that the validity of a legal rule is derived from the fact that it has been created in accordance with a superior rule, and thus on a *deductive* line of reasoning, legal realism, regardless of its particular kind, is based on empirical, and thus predominantly *inductive* reasoning. More precisely, this methodological antagonism is the *result* of the philosophical antagonism between these two theoretical models, in that inductive statements about facts, such as the actual behaviour of states, can as such never be the cause of validity for a legal rule in the Kelsenian world characterised by a strict 'Is-Ought' dichotomy.

The most vigorous proponent of a strictly *inductive* approach to international law in the 20th century was Georg Schwarzenberger.[43] For Schwarzenberger, the motivating force was his profound disillusionment with what he regarded as 'the arbitrary eclecticism with which so-called positivists have practiced – and still practice – their method, and which makes them indistinguishable from the voluntarists of the Grotian school'.[44] His charge was, in other words, that the dominant positivist approaches during his time were still rationalistic natural law theories in disguise, in that they attempted to deduce rules of international law from 'first principles', such as the purported 'fundamental rights of states' or the doctrine of 'abuse of rights'.[45] Instead, he proposed a methodology which was based on the scrupulous inquiry into actual state practice. In the field of customary international law, this meant that 'the most urgent task is the systematic analysis, country by country, of the attitudes of the subjects of international law'.[46] With respect to the general principles of law, Schwarzenberger's inductive approach implied that such principles could only be regarded as approximations, or, as it were, working hypotheses:

> The essential point is that every one of such principles is an abstraction and generalisation from individual cases or legal rules … If this mental process is recognised as what it is, it is a helpful systematic and didactic technique. Whether any particular generalisation is justified depends on whether it takes place on its optimal level, that is to say, on neither too high nor too low a level of abstraction.[47]

In a nice quip, Schwarzenberger compared the deduction of legal rules from 'first principles' to the 'magician's hat trick': 'As we learn when we grow up, this mysterious gentleman is actually able to produce from his hat only as many rabbits as he had previously concealed in it.'[48] Rather, he suggested, one

43 See esp his book *The Inductive Approach to International Law* (London, Stevens & Sons 1965).
44 Ibid, 13.
45 Ibid, 14.
46 Ibid, 35.
47 Ibid, 73.
48 Ibid, 51.

should conceptualise a legal principle as an 'electronic brain' (Schwarzenberger was writing in 1965): 'It is able to give reliable answers only to the extent to which it has been fed with sufficient data.'

At a time like our present, when it is often argued that a deductive approach to customary international law is more 'modern' than the inductive one,[49] Schwarzenberger's acerbic critique of the naïve belief in deduction as a 'magician's hat trick' seems worth remembering. However, one should not underestimate the shortcomings of Schwarzenberger's approach as well. Certainly it would be too easy to dismiss the 'inductive approach to international law' simply by remarking that the validity of the inductive method itself cannot be established through induction.[50] More problematic than this philosophical inconsistency, however, are the practical uncertainties and contradictions arising from an exclusively or predominantly inductive approach, in particular where no sound understanding of the value as well as the limits of that methodology exists: for the inductive method, in law as well as in the sciences, suffers the deficit of not being able to provide logically valid inferences, but only probabilities, approximations – at least unless one includes each and every particular case in the basis of induction, which is, of course, impossible.[51] Nevertheless, a purely inductive analysis of state practice may theoretically lead to the discernment of a number of rules by way of extracting the underlying 'principle' from a number of precedents, ie diplomatic practice, utterances of state officials, or domestic judicial decisions, although it is highly doubtful whether such an analysis can ever avoid the accusation of bias with respect to its selection of materials.

Yet the more important problem with such an approach seems to be that in this way, only individual rules can be conceived, but never a 'legal system', or a 'normative order'. One may ask whether this really poses a problem, since the incompleteness of international law may just mirror the contradictory and tension-filled reality of international relations. It has even been alleged that any possible attempts to reconcile contradicting norms by way of the method of 'systemic integration' could weaken international law's effectiveness, by making it appear more complete and coherent than it actually is.[52] However, the

49 For a recent overview of this debate, see eg WT Worster, 'The Inductive and the Deductive Approach to Customary International Law Analysis: Traditional and Modern Approaches' (2014) 45 *Georgetown International Law Journal* 445.

50 On this classical objection against induction, see eg B Russell, *The Problems of Philosophy* (Oxford, Oxford University Press, reissue 2001) 33–8.

51 For a different view with respect to the 'juristic induction' see Sebastián Soler, *La Interpretación de la Ley* (Barcelona, Aries 1962) 178: 'La diferencia fundamental entre la inducción jurídica y la induccíon por enumeración consiste en que la primera se funda sobre series completas, lo cual deriva de uno de los caracteres específicos de la estructura jurídica: su finitud. Las series jurídicas de conceptos no pueden ser llevadas al infinito; tienen un tope, porque lo regulado siempre es limitado.'

52 See J d'Aspremont, 'The Systemic Integration of International Law by Domestic Courts' in A Nollkaemper/ O Fauchald (eds), *The Practice of International and*

greater danger to a stable and just international order arguably consists in the acceptance of a shape of international law that lacks unifying principles, thus allowing its subjects to cherry-pick rules as ad-hoc justifications of their behaviour.

A famous attempt to combine the virtues of empirical analysis with the rigour and certainty of legal formalism has been undertaken by HLA Hart in his *Concept of Law*.[53] Hart concurred with Kelsen insofar as he stressed that the validity of the rules of a legal system can only be derived from a rule, not from mere facts, such as sheer superior power. The solution to the problem of distinguishing law from 'gunman's order' he proposed consisted in the distinction 'between two different, though related kinds of rules':

> Under rules of the one type, which may well be considered the basic or primary type, human beings are required to do or abstain from certain actions, whether they wish to or not. Rules of the other type are in a sense parasitic upon or secondary to the first; for they provide that human beings may by doing or saying certain things introduce new rules of the primary type, extinguish or modify old ones, or in various ways determine their incidence or control their operations.[54]

HLA Hart described international law as made up entirely of primary rules of obligation,[55] ie rules that declare a certain conduct admissible or prohibited, but lacking secondary rules pertaining to questions of change and adjudication of positive law, as well as a unifying 'rule of recognition'. As a 'rule of recognition' Hart describes 'a criterion for identifying primary norms of obligation'.[56] This absence of secondary rules is, according to Hart, indicative of a legal system at a relatively primitive or rudimentary stage of its development. In the past five decades since the first publication of *The Concept of Law*, however, the development of international law advanced significantly towards the identification and positivisation of secondary rules. To name but two examples, the rules of treaty interpretation have been codified in Articles 31–33 of the 1969 Vienna Convention on the Law of Treaties, and the question of the consequences entailed by a breach of primary obligations is meticulously detailed in the ILC's Draft Articles on State Responsibility of 2001. Here, it must be said that the concept of secondary rules, as suggested by Hart and well received in the academic community, suffers from a significant ambiguity, as well as an oversimplification, both of which limit its value as an analytical tool for the assortment of different kinds of legal norms. Take the 'rule of recognition' as an example: it appears that it can be read as either an epistemological

National Courts and the (De-)Fragmentation of International Law (Oxford, Hart 2012) 141–65.

53 HLA Hart, *The Concept of Law* (Oxford, Clarendon, 2nd ed 1994).

54 Ibid, 81.

55 Ibid, 214.

56 Ibid, 100.

rule, a procedural rule for law-determination or a grant of authority to law-creating agencies.

Hart recognises the plurality of possible 'rules of recognition', but he seems to beg the question of their nature by saying that a 'variety of criteria' for the identification of legally valid rules may be accepted in social practice, and that there can be distinct 'rules of recognition' with respect to legislation, customary law and judicial decisions;[57] but why then bother with using this concept at all, if it is no more sensitive or expedient than the traditional sources doctrine? And is it plausible to assume that society always accepts a 'rule of recognition' first, or does it rather conceive rules of obligation, from which, when compared, a common denominator can be discerned, which might subsequently be applied as a criterion of law-ascertainment? In fact, the idea of a 'rule of recognition' as the basic criterion for the ascertainment of valid legal rules seems much like Kelsen's basic norm turned upside down (or rather, downside up): One can either conclude deductively, ie downwards from a postulated basic norm, or inductively and upwards from the judgments and to another fundamental norm.[58] As Frede Castberg put it: 'In the former case, the irregular judgments will become – if not invalid – at least contrary to the law. In the latter case, the postulated fundamental norm must be subjected to revision.'[59]

Jean d'Aspremont has recently used the Hartian approach as a basis for his formalist theory of the ascertainment of international law.[60] He suggests that one should adopt Hart's 'social thesis' (as opposed to the 'source-thesis' of classical formalism, which used a rule's pedigree as the sole criterion for ascertaining its legal validity). Put simply, the criterion of legal validity, in d'Aspremont's interpretation of Hartian positivism, should be sought in the practice of the law-applying authorities of international law. Unsurprisingly, the most important law-applying authority which d'Aspremont identifies is the International Court of Justice,[61] but he acknowledges the increasing role played by other international courts and arbitral tribunals, and concedes that 'certain non-State actors also provide interesting insights as to the meaning of law-ascertainment criteria' (here, d'Aspremont explicitly refers to the work of the International Committee of the Red Cross in the field of international humanitarian law).[62]

It cannot be denied that the concept of secondary rules, especially a 'rule of recognition', is quite helpful in characterising both the achievements and the continuing shortcomings of international law compared to other legal orders.

57 Ibid, 101.
58 For a critical comparison of Kelsen's and Hart's legal theory, see generally M Pawlik, *Die Reine Rechtslehre und die Rechtstheorie H.L.A. Hart: Ein kritischer Vergleich* (Berlin, Duncker & Humblot 1993).
59 F Castberg, *Problems of Legal Philosophy* (London, Allen & Unwin 1957) 46.
60 See J d'Aspremont, *Formalism and the Sources of International Law: A Theory of the Ascertainment of Legal Rules* (Oxford, Oxford University Press 2011).
61 Ibid, 205.
62 Ibid, 207.

Nevertheless, the positivist attempt to deprive international law (or law in general) of any ontological foundation by dissolving it into an accumulation of particular rules, whose production and mutual relationship is governed merely by a separate set of rules belonging to the same general category, appears particularly challenging when it comes to unwritten international law.[63]

A rather heroic attempt to face these difficulties involved in the formulation of such 'rule of recognition' is recently being undertaken by the International Law Commission (ILC) in the context of its project 'Identification of Customary International Law'. The Commission has decided to include the topic in its working programme in 2012, appointing the former British Foreign Office's legal advisor, Sir Michael Wood, as Special Rapporteur.[64] The development of this project over the past five years reflects the difficulties of coming to terms with a subject that is laden with both theoretical enigmas and practical intricacies. The Special Rapporteur had been aware of these difficulties from the outset: In a first, brief note submitted to the commission,[65] he pointed to the perceived difficulty of clearly delimiting the topic,[66] and stressed that the aim of the project should be to provide practitioners, such as judges, with certain guidelines for the ascertainment of customary norms, rather than to frame a conclusive vision of the nature and origin of customary international law.[67] Concerning the methodology to be applied to achieve this aim, the Special Rapporteur opined that 'the most reliable guidance to the topic is likely to be found in the case law of international courts and tribunals', adding that 'guidance may also be found in the case law of national courts, codification efforts by non-governmental organizations and the writing of publicists'.[68]

During the discussion of the note in the International Law Commission, the general sentiment was against making the ambit of the project too broad and theoretical; rather, the need for a thorough analysis of contemporary – mostly judicial – practice to be undertaken as the basis for any conclusions to be reached about the process of identifying international custom was repeatedly emphasised.[69] In his concluding remarks, the Special Rapporteur again stated it to be the aim of the project to discern 'systemic' or 'secondary' rules of law identification from the material considered, and to put these in an accessible

63 For a discussion from a positivist perspective of some of the difficulties involved in ascertaining customary international law, see J Kammerhofer, 'Uncertainty in the Formal Sources of International Law: Customary International Law and Some of Its Problems' (2004) 15 *European Journal of International Law* 523.

64 ILC, 'Report of the International Law Commission on the Work of its 64th Session' (6 May to 7 June and 1 July to 2 August 2012) UN Doc A/67/12, paras 156 et seq.

65 ILC, 'Formation and Evidence of Customary International Law: Note by Michael Wood, Special Rapporteur' (30 May 2012) UN Doc A/CN.4/653.

66 Ibid, paras 20–2.

67 Ibid, para 24.

68 Ibid, para 18.

69 ILC, 'Report of the International Law Commission on the Work of its 64th Session' (n 64) paras 173–7.

form so as to aid practising judges and other officials charged with the application of customary international law.[70] Given this more practice-oriented focus, it seems to have been a wise move made by the ILC in 2013 to change the topic from 'Formation and Evidence of Customary International Law' to 'Identification of Customary International Law', indicating that the aim of the project was to 'produce a practical outcome that would be useful to practitioners and judges', without, however, 'prejudicing the flexibility of the customary process or future developments concerning the formation and evidence of customary international law'.[71]

As of today (2017), the topic is still pending, but substantial progress has been made: During the ILC's 2016 session, a set of sixteen 'Draft Conclusions'[72] has been provisionally adopted, which are recently being considered and commented on by the governments. At its present state, the ILC draft largely consists of a restatement of well-established doctrine concerning customary international law, the like of which could be found in any standard textbook on international law. As concerns some of the more hotly debated issues involved, such as the importance of proving both of the traditional elements, state practice and *opinio juris* (Draft Conclusion 2), or the central role of states in the emergence of rules of customary international law (Draft Conclusion 4), the ILC's approach may disappoint some of the more progressively minded scholars – this is not the place to assess the virtues and vices of the ongoing ILC project (some specific questions will be dealt with at later stages of this study). However, what is interesting in the current context is that the ILC, after so many years of codification activity, has finally decided to seriously and explicitly consider the appropriate methodology for determining the existence and content of rules of international custom, and to formulate what could be called 'rules of recognition' in this respect.

The prospect of having a set of principles relating to the identification of international customary law, endowed with a considerable authority due to their proclamation by the ILC, may seem rather promising to practising international lawyers. Indeed, any such practical guidelines pertaining to the recognition of customary international law, provided they be widely made known, will be of considerable value in promoting the rule of law in the international society:[73] First, because they provide judges, especially those on domestic courts which are often perplexed by the intricate problems of the process of customary international law,[74] with a guide as to which materials they should

70 Ibid, paras 193–9.

71 ILC, 'Report of the International Law Commission on the Work of its 65th Session' (6 May to 7 June and 8 July to 9 August 2013) UN Doc A/68/10, para 98.

72 UN Doc A/CN.4/L.871.

73 On the importance of a 'rule of recognition' for strengthening the international rule of law, see S Besson, 'Theorizing the Sources of International Law' in id/J Tasioulas (eds), *The Philosophy of International Law* (Oxford, Oxford University Press 2010) 163 (180 et seqq).

74 On the present difficulties which domestic courts are facing in the ascertainment of rules of customary international law, see below Ch 4 D–F.

take into account when ascertaining the existence of a rule; and second, because they allow government officials, especially legal advisers, to assess more easily the potential implications of state behaviour for the international law-making process.[75]

It should be noted, however, that the drafting of a set of principles or guidelines on how to identify customary law international law is only one step towards a better understanding of this source. Just as the rules on treaty interpretation incorporated in the Vienna Convention on the Law of Treaties, the ILC's 'Draft Conclusions on the Identification of Customary International Law' will be but a tool – a very useful tool for that matter, but nonetheless one which requires, as it were, the hands of a skilled craftsman to use it. Applying such tools requires a sound understanding of the process of customary international law. It may seem convenient to avoid the theoretical controversies pertaining to customary international law by focusing on judicial practice, on 'what the courts are actually doing'; however, the first dispute to arise about the interpretation of such practice will most likely lead back to the very issues the ILC had intended to exclude from the ambit of its project. On the other hand, the limited scope of the ILC's project on customary international law should be seen as an opportunity: Thus, it is not in danger of becoming the 'ultimate political appropriation of an ultimate idea', despite the fact that 'the Commission will, as always, seek the views of governments and other holders of international public power, on this interesting problem of legal philosophy'[76] (after all, why shouldn't the Commission listen to those who are, for better or worse, still the most important actors involved in the production of customary international law?). In fact, it will be the task of legal philosophy to (critically) accompany the project, and to provide the deeper understanding of the role of customary international law in the international society which is inevitable to guide those applying the ILC's 'Draft Conclusions' in their practical legal reasoning.

D. Unwritten International Law as a 'System'

Anyone who undertakes to frame guidelines for the practical application of international custom needs to ask herself one question: whether it is proper to

75 For the 'special onus' placed on legal advisers by the peculiar nature of customary international law, see eg M Wood, 'Legal Advisers' in R Wolfrum (ed) *The Max Planck Encyclopedia of Public International Law* (Oxford, Oxford University Press 2012) para 19 et seq; see also C Parry, *The Sources and Evidences of International Law* (Manchester, University of Manchester Press 1965) 67: 'It requires also to be borne in mind that States, in relation to customary international law no less than treaties, are essentially laymen. What they do and say, to become explicable, must always, therefore, be subjected to a certain amount of professional interpretation.'

76 As has been predicted by P Allott; see his 'Comment on Jean d'Aspremont, Formalism and the Sources of International Law' (EJIL Talk!, 12 December 2012) <http://www.ejiltalk.org/comments-on-jean-daspremont-formalism-and-the-sources-of-international-law-a-theory-of-the-ascertainment-of-legal-rules/> accessed 20 August 2017.

regard customary international law as an incongruent assortment of rules, emerged from the arbitrary, sometimes erratic behaviour of states; or whether it is more appropriate to conceive of its rules as being parts of a true *legal system*, ie a unity that is more than the sum of its particulars, an international objectivity placed above the subjective wills of the individual states. What may at first seem like a rather abstract, theoretical question of jurisprudence is in fact a matter of great consequence when it comes to the practical problem of ascertaining the content of concrete norms, and particularly to the question of how to deal with *lacunae*, with gaps in the fabric of law. This is actually not a novel question to scholars or to practitioners of international law, as is reflected in a controversy between Kelsen and his student Hersch Lauterpacht. Kelsen maintained that 'gaps' in international law are logically impossible:

> If there is no norm of conventional or customary international law imposing upon the state (or another subject of international law) the obligation to behave in a certain way, the subject is under international law legally free to behave as it pleases; and by a decision to this effect existing international law is applied to the case.[77]

Kelsen thus restated the doctrine pronounced by the Permanent Court of International Justice in the *Lotus Case*, according to which, absent an explicit prohibitive norm, there is no presumption in international law for any restriction on a sovereign state's freedom to act as it pleases.[78] From a Kelsenian point of view, rules of international law form enclaves of order in a vast wilderness governed by the law of the jungle. Lauterpacht, on the other hand, devoted significant efforts to the question of how a situation of *non liquet* could be avoided in concrete legal disputes arising between states that were to be decided by international tribunals. Lauterpacht identifies several methods in which a court could proceed in cases when existing law (written or unwritten) did not provide for an unambiguous standard of assessment with respect to the opposing claims involved. Specifically, he elaborates four ways to address the problem of *lacunae*: By way of analogy with rules of international law, by application of general principles of law and principles of private law, by judicial reconciliation of conflicting legal claims and by reference to the needs of the international community and the effectiveness of treaty obligations.[79]

Clearly these methods or approaches are heuristic in nature, intended to be understood as guidelines for perplexed judges faced with unprecedented situations rather than as philosophically sound rules of inference; epistemologically, even some of the principles summarised by Lauterpacht within the same general method are posited on different logical levels, as, for example, in

77 Kelsen (n 34) 305.

78 *The Case of the S.S. Lotus* (France v Turkey) [1927] PCIJ (ser. A) no 10 (Sept 7).

79 H Lauterpacht, *The Function of Law in the International Community* (Oxford, Oxford University Press 1933) §§ 25–8.

his fourth method: 'Effectiveness of treaty obligations' is a relatively concrete consideration in the process of treaty interpretation, whereas recourse to the 'needs of the international community', formally also a teleological consideration, leaves to judges broad discretion to include in their reasoning arguments that are not strictly jurisprudential in nature – it is, certainly, much easier to determine the purpose of a concrete treaty than to ascertain what the 'needs of the international community' are. Nevertheless, Lauterpacht's attempt at addressing the problem of *lacunae* poses precisely the questions that a methodology of unwritten international law has to answer, especially if the term is understood, as in this study, to refer to norms that emerged through the practice of (informal) social self-organisation, without direction by a central authority.

In a sense, the concept of 'order' is at the very foundation of law. Without a certain amount of regularity it would be impossible to speak of 'law'; in fact, in the wider, non-juristic sense of the term, 'law' is even synonymous with 'regularity'. Thus, one of the meanings ascribed to the term 'law' in the Oxford English Dictionary is 'a generalization based on a fact or event perceived to be recurrent'. Of course, it is absolutely necessary and correct to emphasise the fundamental distinction that exists between descriptive and normative 'laws', between the laws of nature and the rules of human conduct. All naturalistic theories of jurisprudence are subject to the inevitable objection that it makes a huge difference whether it is said that a stone 'must' fall down to earth according to Newton's law of universal gravitation, or whether a human being 'must' abide by the law in order to avoid negative sanctions imposed on the lawbreaker by the community.[80] But as appropriate as the insistence on the distinction between norms and facts may be philosophically, it can never be more than an epistemological axiom the validity of which must necessarily stand or fall with the meaning that one assigns to the terms 'fact' and, in particular, 'norm'. Not very many of the particular rules of international law do in fact consist exclusively in abstract, *a priori* value judgments; at most, they are based on rather distant embodiments of such values. Quite often, there exists a plurality of purported reasons for the existence and acceptance of a norm or complex of norms in international law. For example, many rules of international humanitarian law cannot be described *exclusively* as *either* serving the self-interest of the warring parties, enforced by reciprocity, *or* being founded upon the moral conscience of the world community: for the protection of the own soldiers against reprisals may well be a 'moral' consideration *and* a tactical one; and, conversely, the media age in which we live, and the democratic decision-making processes in many countries of the world do not permit to exclude 'moral' obligations from the ambit of factors to be taken into account when designing a strategy. Other norms, such as those regulating the use of shared waterways or the processing of international

80 See eg H Kelsen, 'A "Dynamic" Theory of Natural Law' (1956) 16 *Louisiana Law Review* 597, attempting to refute the contemporary natural law theory proposed in J Wild, *Plato's Modern Enemies and the Theory of Natural Law* (Chicago, University of Chicago Press 1953).

commercial aviation, are primarily coordinative in nature, and are thus mainly self-enforcing – oftentimes, their evolution and continuous application can be explained through a rather simple 'zero-sum-game' or 'prisoner's dilemma'.

It is perhaps no exaggeration that most of the problems and weaknesses ascribed to contemporary international law stem from the fact that it is impossible to generate an abstract hierarchy of goals or values, a finite set of preferences that would allow it to determine the relative weight of any conceivable (legal) argument compared to its counterargument. This impossibility is often attributed either to the selfishness of states, which are not willing to accept for themselves what they demand from others, or to the great cultural, political and religious diversity of the international community, which does not favour such hierarchisations, as they could potentially be incompatible with domestic value systems. These and similar critical views, common as they are, do in fact not go far enough. They base their understanding of international law on the same (false) premise as their opponents, namely that the very notion of 'law' presupposes the existence of a prior, abstract consensus on certain goals or purposes. From this point of view, it is easy to stress the shortcomings of international law, and to deride the hypocrisy of those who pretend to believe in liberal international institutionalism, knowing fully well that fundamental agreement about the future design of anything like the so-called 'international community' is not likely to be reached any time soon.

In an unfortunate, self-deprecating manner, scholars as well as practitioners sometimes contribute to upholding a certain public image of international law, according to which it does not have much impact on the actual decisions states make, at least not in areas vital to their national interests, but that they behave so as to prove the truth of the proverbial maxim that 'big fish eat little fish'. International lawyers inadvertently contribute to this perception of international decision-making processes by overemphasising the independence of the legal system, maintaining that legal arguments are capable of standing on their own: that they differ fundamentally from considerations of practical reason and political wisdom and need neither confirmation nor revision by any of the latter. International legal argument, thus conceived, is probably the only technique of (purportedly) rational decision-making that *by definition* consists in *not* taking into account a great number of potentially relevant criteria of assessment.[81]

The most extreme emanation of this conception of the nature of law is perhaps to be found in systems theory. Proponents of this theory, such as Niklas Luhmann[82] and Gunter Teubner,[83] describe the alleged self-referentiality

81 Of course, every method of decision-making consists ultimately in the elimination of irrelevant alternative arguments; the point here is that the legal system, according to this widespread conception, dismisses a great amount of potentially relevant information by purely formal criteria, without considering its material content.

82 See in particular N Luhmann, *Das Recht der Gesellschaft* (Frankfurt, Suhrkamp 1993).

83 Eg G Teubner, *Recht als autopoietisches System* (Frankfurt, Suhrkamp 1989); id (ed), *Autopoietic Law. A New Approach to Law and Society* (Berlin, de Gruyter 1988).

and operational closure of the legal system as strength rather than weakness; in their view, the principal feature of law is the fact that it is capable of regulating its own production. In this view, the legal system allows for external influx only to the extent that this 'input' is adaptable to the system's pre-existing framework of reasoning, which centres on the legal/illegal distinction. Law thus conceived as a system is described as a form of organic, almost living entity, which has its own life cycle and, perhaps the most controversial allegation of systems theory, a paramount, unifying 'will' or 'purpose' of its own: self-preservation and perpetuation of the system. In the meantime, systems theory of law has received considerable interest from scholars of international law. Anthony D'Amato, for example, has attempted to construct a theory of international law as an autopoietic system the distinctive features of which are recursiveness and emergence.[84] According to D'Amato, the international legal system is able to achieve its self-perpetuation through the application of a number of 'filters', by which incoming claims are assessed as to their admissibility. These filters or rules of preference are *self-preservation* (of the system), *equality* (does the claim allow for its equal application to all states?), *reciprocity* (no special privilege for one side of the dispute) and *interdependence* (preference is given to interdependence-producing over independence-producing claims).[85] These 'bias-filters', as D'Amato calls them, are thought to create 'rebuttable presumptions' in favour of those claims that contribute to the stability, and, foremost, to the self-sustenance of the international legal system.

Systems theory of (international) law unquestionably provides valuable models for analysing the institutional self-interests of the legal profession in general, and of specific organs, like courts, but also attorneys, in particular; thus, as a sociology of the legal profession it is beyond any doubt the most adequate theory yet invented, as it can, for example, retrace certain biases and (hidden) motivations influencing the reasoning of judges. Yet it seems that one ventures into dangerously metaphysical terrain if one accepts the notion that 'The Legal System' forms some sort of independent, organic entity, endowed with an autonomous will and serving primarily its own interest, which incidentally happens to coincide with the promotion of order and stability in the world. Such an approach wantonly neglects the diversity of interests among the subjects of international law, and the fact that individuals from various cultures and communities, even if all trained in the legal profession, differ too much in character, convictions and education that they are unlikely to ever form anything like eager agents of the interest of the 'international legal system'. Yet the biologist metaphor underlying systems theory of law, describing law as a living, autonomous entity, is perhaps a typical example of the way in which legal scholars often attempt to draw concepts from other fields, be it the

84 A D'Amato, 'International Law as an Autopoietic System' in R Wolfrum/V Röben (eds), *Developments of International Law in Treaty Making* (Heidelberg, Springer 2005) 335.

85 Ibid, 365–78.

sciences or even the arts, in order to make visible the somewhat transcendental, elusive, nature of law. As one scholar remarked, using a zoological analogy himself: 'Law is a scavenger. It grows by feeding on ideas from outside, not by inventing new ones of its own.'[86]

These 'metaphors', however, not infrequently become detached from the field in which they originated and turn into a self-fulfilling prophecy, even at a time when they have long been disproved in their original context. This surely happened to the concept of so-called 'Social Darwinism', which was developed through a misapplication of Darwin's concept of evolution as 'the survival of the fittest' to the social sciences, from where it finally influenced the jurisprudence of such legal luminaries as Justice Holmes. The tendency of lawyers to seek solid ground in other disciplines is perfectly understandable, given that jurisprudence has ever since the emergence and diversification of social sciences in the second half of the 19th century struggled to find its place in the world of knowledge, a struggle that has clearly been exacerbated by the attempts of so-called Postmodernist philosophy to 'deconstruct' the law, ie to destroy the 'illusion' of law as a rational, coherent decision making procedure.[87] The responses to these threats have either consisted of trying to integrate law into a social science 'proper', most often sociology, but also economy, political science or international relations, or in attempts to separate law from other fields by 'purifying' it from both moral considerations and sociological empiricism; the latter tradition, of course, became known as 'positivism'. A particular form of this 'isolationism' is the so-called 'systems theory of law', which is apparently taking pride from the law's aloofness, its being almost indifferent towards the goals and convictions of the actors outside the 'system'.

How does all this relate to the interpretation of unwritten international law? Firstly, it demonstrates that contemporary legal theory is not particularly helpful in this respect. As we have seen, theories that attempt both to explain law's normativity *and* provide a finite, predetermined set of rules for its ascertainment and interpretation, must either limit their scope to a relatively small part of what is regularly referred to as (international) law, or presume the existence of widespread violations of law (ie, law according to their theory) on the part of the actors applying it – particularly the courts. This is by no means a novel insight; for example, the perceived 'paradox' that – theoretically – a rule of customary international law can only be changed by acting contrary to it, thereby sowing the seed of a new practice, has become a *cause célèbre* in the literature of international law, still exerts a seemingly irresistible temptation on every new generation of writers, enticing them to come up with new theories allegedly 'resolving' it. Another, yet more serious and practically relevant difficulty is the problem of how ethical considerations and moral precepts can be

86 ED Elliott, 'The Evolutionary Tradition in Jurisprudence' (1985) 85 *Columbia Law Review* 38.
87 R Cotterell, *The Politics of Jurisprudence* (Oxford, Oxford University Press, 2nd ed 2003) Chapter IX.

integrated into the positivist sources doctrine, the problem here being that certain values, although widely paid lip-service to, cannot be traced to any specific instances of state practice. Nevertheless, scholars and attorneys alike do not cease to quote customary international law as the source of certain obligations not contained in a binding treaty, particular human rights norms;[88] a habit that provoked Sir Robert Jennings to remark caustically: 'Most of what we perversely persist in calling customary international law is not only *not* customary law: it does not even faintly resemble a customary law.'[89] The difference between proponents and opponents of the inclusion of human rights law and other norms pertaining to individual rights in the canon of customary international law is just a symptom of a greater divide about whether or not it is necessary to substantially enlarge the scope of materials considered for customary law's determination. Although contemporary textbooks still contain rather tedious enumerations of which acts and utterances of which state bureaucrats may be taken into account as evidence of 'constant and uniform usage, accepted as law', it is meanwhile a well-observed phenomenon that the traditional approach to the identification of customary international law does no longer reflect the increased normative needs of an ever more interconnected world society. As Christian Tomuschat remarks with respect to international human rights law:

> Whereas relations between states can be observed by empirical means, the way in which states behave in their dealing with individual citizens escapes such methods. On the global plane, millions of contacts occur every second. Not even the most sophisticated electronic mechanism would be able to register the human rights-specific features of all of these relationships. … This list of rights and/or forbidden acts and activities is not so much based on actual stocktaking of the relevant state practice but rather on deductive reasoning: if human life and physical integrity were not protected, the entire idea of a legal order would collapse.[90]

This deductive, so-called 'modern'[91] approach to customary international law, which emphasises the importance of the element of *opinio juris* over actual state practice, and derives this *opinio* from official statements, preferably from

88 Cf on this ongoing debate: K Kedian, 'Customary International Law and International Human Rights Litigation in United States Courts: Revitalizing the Legacy of The Paquete Habana' (1995) 40 *William & Mary Law Review* 1395; V Dimitrijevic, *Customary Law as an Instrument for the Protection of Human Rights*, Istituto per gli Studi di Politica Internazionale (ISPI) Milano, Working Paper 7 (2006).

89 RY Jennings, 'The Identification of International Law' in B Cheng (ed), *International Law: Teaching and Practice* (London, Stevens & Sons 1982) 3 (5).

90 C Tomuschat, *Human Rights: Between Idealism and Realism* (Oxford, Oxford University Press, 2nd ed 2008) 39.

91 Cf on this A Roberts, 'Traditional and Modern Approaches to Customary International Law' (2001) 95 *American Journal of International Law* 757.

UN General Assembly resolutions and the like, comes with its own pitfalls. First, it risks distancing the 'official' law, as pronounced in solemn declarations, from the 'living' law that is actually practised on the ground. This might not even be all bad, if it meant to hold notorious human rights abusers by the standards they hypocritically avowed to uphold. Yet in fact, the result is likely to be a further weakening of trust in and credibility of international human rights, as the gap between preaching and practice increasingly widens. What is called for seems rather to be a comprehensive approach which combines the virtues of formalism and realism, while not neglecting the actual impact of moral ideas on the behaviour of human beings – and, by extension, states; in other words, an understanding similar to the approach characterised by one scholar as 'informed pragmatism between morality and form'.[92] But how can a theory of unwritten international law further this goal?

It has been argued in Chapter II above that the particular virtue of unwritten (international) law was historically believed to be due to the fact that it arises as the product of a process of complex, decentralised self-organisation. But is this really a virtue, or rather a weakness, given the fact that this process might lead to a rather inchoate form of law, compared to a systematically drafted multilateral treaty regime? In the view of the present author, the main benefit of unwritten law, which also makes this form of law particularly adequate for the purposes of organising the international community, is its *superior information content.*

E. A 'Spontaneous Order'

In every system or order with a minimum degree of complexity, individuals must rely in their actions and decisions to a large extent on knowledge which they did not learn from their own first-hand experience, but rather acquired from other actors through the course of their mutual interactions with one another. This is so because the total amount of information potentially relevant to a particular decision, even if theoretically available to the respective actor (eg by means of advanced information technology), is simply too great to be always individually assessed prior to making the decision. Nevertheless, everyone whose actions are to be successful must necessarily follow a certain pattern of behaviour adapted to one's environment: the kind of world we live in. The adoption of such patterns or habits does not necessarily ensue from purely strategic considerations. It is rather by living in the company of other individuals, and by witnessing some fail and others succeed, that one orientates towards the pattern of behaviour of the successful actors, which are successful in this particular instance because they possess a comparative advantage in terms of relevant information.

92 See G Nolte, 'Between Informed Pragmatism, Morality and Form' in E Jouannet/ H Ruiz-Fabri/JM Sorel (eds), *Regards d'une génération sur le droit international* (Paris, Pedone 2008) 277 (283).

It is by this relatively simple concept that Friedrich August Hayek, in his *Law, Legislation and Liberty*, seeks to explain the development of law and society. According to him, it is the law, in the form of abstract rules of behaviour, that creates society – not the other way around. The law, he argues, must be first, because it is only by following certain rules of conduct that the degree of order indispensable to the development of a society can be achieved.[93] The type of order that ensues from this kind of only half-conscious rule following-behaviour Hayek calls *spontaneous*; he links it to the Greek concept of *kósmos*, denoting a natural order, as opposed to *táxis*, a man-made order, such as that of an army arrayed for a battle. He asserted that such a grown or natural order of human conduct necessarily comprised certain distinct properties not usually found in law arising from legislation:

First, it does not have a 'purpose' of its own, but rather works to the effect of protecting the expectations that individual actors within the order have formed, enabling them to pursue their particular (and often conflicting) goals within a common framework of abstract rules and principles.[94] These principles, then, provide a certain level of stability and predictability, only thus allowing the individual to enjoy a certain freedom of action without continually being disturbed by the unpredictable and potentially destructive behaviour of her fellows.

Secondly, Hayek alleged that law that grew from custom and precedent is characterised by its *higher* rather than lower *degree of abstraction*.[95] This proposition seems highly counterintuitive at first, because it is the natural assumption about case law-systems that they abound with a plethora of particularities derived from the details of historical cases, whereas jurisdictions in which written legislation dominates are thought to be characterised by law of a more systematic and coherent nature. Yet to Hayek, there are good reasons to assume the contrary to be true: As jurists in a case law-jurisdiction are well-trained in distinguishing the essentials from the accidentals of a potentially applicable precedent, they are apt to gradually develop a system of general rules and abstract principles from the particular instances of their application, enabling them subsequently to extend and adapt the 'essence' of prior decisions to newly arising issues and thereby to create a realistic image of the existing 'spontaneous order of actions'.

According to Hayek, the role of a judge in such a spontaneous order is 'to maintain the ongoing order of actions'.[96] This aim is achieved by articulating the – unwritten – rules of behaviour, on the observance of which the existence of the order depends, and which must continue to be followed if the order is to persist. The result of the formation of such an order is that the individual

93 FA Hayek, *Law, Legislation and Liberty* (London, Routledge, reissue 2013) 34 et seq.
94 Ibid, 10–79.
95 Ibid, 37–8 and 81–4.
96 Ibid, 94–6.

actors, despite the fact that they may differ considerably regarding the particular goals or interests they choose to pursue, are nevertheless able to form certain expectations with respect to the behaviour of other individuals and groups of individuals in situations with which they may often be unacquainted yet. Such coordination of expectations is possible due to the very existence of an *order*, which Hayek defines as 'a state of affairs in which a multiplicity of elements of various kinds are so related to each other that we may learn from our acquaintance with some spatial or temporal part of the whole to form correct expectations concerning the rest, or at least expectations which have a good chance of proving correct'.[97] Here, a difference becomes evident between Hayek's concept of spontaneous order and the positivistic notion of a legal system as an order of norms, unified by a common criterion of legal validity: According to Hayek, the element that unifies the various *abstract* norms is the concrete 'order of actions'; for positivism, on the other hand, law consists of *concrete*, potentially highly specific norms, unified by an abstract, purely formal principle, namely the criterion of validity or (in Hartian terms) the 'rule of recognition'.

It is easy to criticise Hayek for what might be perceived today as an example of a somewhat naïve overreliance on the self-ordering powers of community, a concept that is widely regarded – particularly since the 2008 financial crisis – as being discredited by the shortcomings of liberal economic theory in addressing important regulatory demands. Yet Hayek was clearly no laissez-faire liberal, but rather stressed the importance of abstract rules and principles of behaviour, acknowledging that the very existence of human coexistence rests upon their being upheld.[98] And with respect to international relations, Hayek's concept of 'spontaneous order' is perhaps even more convincing, as a descriptive device, rather than, as in the context of domestic legal orders, an ideal of political liberalism to which it is desirable to aspire. Conceiving unwritten international law as such a kind of 'spontaneous order' has two significant implications for its interpretation: First, it is principally possible by studying the part of the order which is known to discern the rules that produced it, and thence to extrapolate the structure of the parts of the order that are yet unknown. Secondly, it follows that the more the order is understood, the more it is possible to consciously interfere with it when this becomes necessary to preserve its existence, eg by adjusting it to rapidly changing circumstances which leave no time for gradual assimilation; on the other hand, however, this also implies that the less is known about the inner workings of a spontaneous order, the more difficult any attempt to deliberately alter it is going to be, and the more pernicious are the consequences that will ensue from hastily and improvidently conceived modifications of the overall order.

Because Hayek's language is often ambiguous, he has frequently been misinterpreted, particularly by admirers. This is especially the case where it has

97 Ibid, 35.
98 Ibid, 54–7.

been attempted to apply his theory to international relations. To take but two examples: Edwin van de Haar recently applied the Hayekian concept of 'spontaneous order' to the idea of an international balance of power, implicitly making him an intellectual ally of a Nixon-Kissinger style of foreign policy.[99] Adrián Osvaldo Ravier, on the other hand, argued that from an alleged 'Hayekian perspective', the levelling, dedifferentiating influence of globalisation, especially global economic integration, and the ensuing meaninglessness of national borders would necessarily lead to a better, more stable and peaceful world.[100] Whereas the former approach can claim a certain consistency with Hayekian theory, although van de Haar creates an overly static image of the concept of spontaneous orders,[101] the latter, I think, is contradicted by Hayek's own words: In *The Road to Serfdom*, he explicitly acknowledges that 'there was more beauty and decency to be found in the life of small peoples', and goes on to stress the importance of local self-government; also, he warns against the creation of international economic institutions, which, he says, 'would mean a more or less conscious endeavour to secure the dominance of the white man, and would rightly be so regarded by all other races'.[102]

For Hayek, the rule of law, whether on the international or the domestic plane, meant the submission of all actors to a set of abstractly formulated, outcome-neutral, predetermined rules of behaviour. Or, as he put it himself, of rules which 'are general not only in the sense of applying equally to all people, but also in the sense that they do not refer to particulars but apply whenever certain abstractly defined conditions are satisfied'.[103] It might seem as if this Hayekian ideal of the primacy of abstract rules – something he called *nómos*, ie law proper or 'the law of liberty' – is even more elusive in international law than in domestic legal orders, given the fact that states differ much more among themselves than individuals within a state, which makes the formulation of general rules applying equally to all of them far more complex.[104]

In any event, a view like Hayek's is opposed to the image of international relations fostered by (self-proclaimed) 'realists', according to which, beyond the nation-state, there exists only a quasi-anomic state of nature, as the international community lacks a central authority, so that states do not follow general rules of behaviour, but make their decisions on a case-by-case basis

99 E van de Haar, 'Hayekian Spontaneous Orders and the International Balance of Power' (2011) 16 *The Independent Review* 101.

100 AO Ravier, 'Globalization and Peace: A Hayekian Perspective' (2009) 1 *Libertarian Papers* No 10.

101 For an interesting argument about the destabilising effects of classical balance-of-power doctrine see H Kipp, *Völkerordnung und Völkerrecht im Mittelalter* (Cologne, Deutsche Glocke 1950) 150–4.

102 FA Hayek, *The Road to Serfdom* (London, Routledge, repr 2004) 241.

103 FA Hayek, *The Political Ideal of the Rule of Law* (Cairo, National Bank of Egypt 1955) 35.

104 This argument is forcefully stated in JL Brierly, 'Vital Interests and the Law' (1944) 21 *British Yearbook of International Law* 56.

according to their perceived temporary interests.[105] But the model of unwritten international law as a spontaneous order does account quite well for the fact that in international relations a remarkable stability exists in many fields of action, allowing states with fundamentally different or even diametrically opposed ideologies to pursue their particular goals while observing outcome-neutral rules of general application. A similar conception of the legal order was embraced by Rudolf von Jhering when he described (Roman) law as a deposit of the reason of thousands of individuals, a treasure trove of knowledge that allows the jurist to transcend the limitations of his own weak mind by making use of the intellectual force of all preceding generations combined.[106]

Yet the vision of a spontaneous order seems so remote from the contemporary understanding of law as a social tool that it is not surprising that Hayek's theory encountered a considerable amount of criticism, even among economic liberals. Richard A Posner,[107] for example, presented a rather one-sided restatement of Hayek's legal theory; he (incorrectly) asserted that Hayek had ignored the necessity of adapting the law to rapidly changing circumstances[108] and accused him of doctrinarily limiting the role of judges to the enforcement of existing customs.[109] In fact, there is nothing doctrinaire or even 'anti-intellectual' about Hayek's deep-rooted scepticism towards overly

105 Cf eg JL Goldsmith/EA Posner, *The Limits of International Law* (New York, Oxford University Press 2006) passim, in particular 3–17; Goldsmith and Posner do not, in their own words, 'think that international law is irrelevant or unimportant or in some sense unreal. … But under our theory, international law does not pull states towards compliance contrary to their interests, and the possibilities for what international law can achieve are limited by the configurations of state interests and the distribution of state power.'; ibid, 13. In the view of the present author, the persuasiveness of this statement turns on how narrow a meaning one ascribes to the term 'state interests'. In the sense in which it is used by Goldsmith and Posner, i.e. as 'a state's preferences about outcomes' (ibid, 6), it is considerably to narrow to account for all motivations, including unarticulated ones, that may underlie a state's actions on the international level.

106 R v Jhering, *Geist des römischen Rechts auf den verschiedenen Stufen seiner Entwicklung. Zweiter Theil, Zweite Abteilung* (Leipzig, Breitkopf & Härtel 1858) 331–2.

107 RA Posner, 'Hayek, Law and Cognition' (2005) 1 *New York University Journal of Law and Liberty* 147.

108 In fact, Hayek explicitly acknowledged this as one of the reasons why 'grown law' requires correction by legislation; cf Hayek (n 93) 84.

109 The function of the judge, according to Hayek, extends far beyond mere enforcement of pre-existing customs: rather, (s)he is regarded as an 'institution' of the spontaneous order, whose task it is to preserve the 'ongoing order of actions' by articulating such rules of behaviour as are conducive to it; by doing so, the judge essentially transforms the unarticulated, sometimes even unconsciously followed rules of behaviour into a coherent system of order, allowing individuals to form expectations that have a reasonable chance of being met. The main difference between Hayek and Posner seems to be that Hayek doubts the desirability of judges trying to implement particular theories or economic models of 'efficiency' through their decisions.

confident attempts at reshaping human society undertaken in order to achieve particular aims temporarily regarded as desirable under the prevailing social and economic theories of the moment.[110]

This bears emphasising especially with regard to international law, as it stands today 20 years after the end of the Cold War. As no single ideology has enough power and exerts enough attraction globally to achieve the status of a model for a new, comprehensive world order, and as it is widely perceived that we are entering into an age in which 'no single country or durable alliance of countries can meet the challenges of global leadership',[111] a general system of abstract rules of behaviour, as Hayek suggested, seems to be as much as one can possibly hope for in order that a relatively stable system of international relations be maintained. He cautions against placing too high hopes into the creation of huge, transnational institutions, and encourages taking the concepts of subsidiarity and localism seriously. He would probably have decisively approved of ideas such as microloans, which empower local populations to small-scale entrepreneurship, or, as he might have said it, allow them to decide for themselves how to best make use of their specific knowledge of the circumstances immediately surrounding them, as they are the ones most familiar with them, in order to efficiently improve their situation.

On the other hand, Hayek reminds us starkly not to underestimate the vital importance of the rule of law as a means of coordinating the diverse interests and expectations of any particular member of a great society, a goal that can only be achieved by having predetermined, abstract rules of behaviour of general application. Thus, he would have seen rather critically the recent rise of concepts like 'adhocracy'[112] and 'coalitions of the willing',[113] as these phenomena bring a disruptive force into the already volatile, unstable web of international relations. His use of the term 'spontaneous order' should thus not be mistaken as advocating for the currently fashionable concept of 'informal international law'.[114] Unwritten international law, conceived as a Hayekian spontaneous order, is no void abstraction, nor a purely metaphysical speculation about *a priori* principles of justice. It is as outcome-neutral as it needs to be to accommodate the increasing multitude of seemingly irreconcilable value systems confronting one another in an ever closer world community, while at the

110 For a spirited defence of Hayek's legal theory along these lines, see recently J Petersen, *Freiheit unter dem Gesetz: Friedrich August von Hayeks Rechtsdenken* (Tübingen, Mohr Siebeck 2014).

111 I Bremmer, *Every Nation for Itself: Winners and Losers in the G-Zero World* (London & New York, Penguin 2012) 1; cf also F Zakaria, *The Post-American World* (New York, Norton & Co 2009) passim.

112 On this concept and its relevance, see eg A Etzioni, 'The Domestic Sources of Global Adhocracy' (2012) 10 *Social Change Review* 99.

113 For a good (and rather critical) overview of the concept, see eg A Rodiles Breton, 'Coalitions of the Willing: Coyuntura, Contexto y Propiedades. Un Primer Esbozo' (2007) 7 *Annuario Mexicano de Derecho International* 675.

114 On this see eg the various contributions to J Pauwelyn/J Wouters (ed), *Informal International Lawmaking* (Oxford, Oxford University Press 2012).

same time being principled enough to avoid the pitfalls that inevitably ensue from the reckless pursuit of political expediency, or from a myopic form of 'realism' that prefers to make decisions on an ad-hoc basis, thereby disappointing legitimate expectations and increasing international disorder and instability.

F. The Task of the Practitioner

Having argued above, albeit rather sketchily, that unwritten international law can be conceptualised as a form of spontaneous order of human behaviour, the question remains what consequences can be drawn from this conception for the practice of its application. In the following chapter (IV) of this study, the function of the judge shall be used as a paradigm for expounding in more detail the methodological exigencies of the process in which unwritten international law is continually ascertained and adapted to the ever-changing circumstances and exigencies of international life. This choice of paradigm may seem, at first glance, curious or even awkward, because it is a common perception that international law displays great resistance against all attempts to its 'juridification', and still lacks, in large part, any compulsory adjudication. This objection is certainly justified; however, it seems that there are at least three reasons why the approach adopted here is not illegitimate.

The first and most obvious reason is that the observation of a lack of *fora* for adjudication at the international level is not as true anymore as it was a few decades ago. The proliferation of specialised international tribunals, be it in the field of criminal law, investment arbitration, the law of the sea, or human rights law, rather gives rise to (legitimate) concerns about further fragmentation of international law to ensue from this plurality of new voices. These concerns, however, are mitigated by the fact that the International Court of Justice still plays a vital role as the centre of the international judicial machinery. Its workload certainly did not skyrocket after the end of the long stalemate caused by the ideological antinomies of the Cold War; but it also cannot be said to have stagnated, given the decent number of decisions the court renders each year. Of course, many of these are not exactly the high-profile cases involving major issues of world public policy, and hence do not attract great media coverage; and as many countries still have not submitted to the court's compulsory jurisdiction, these 'grand' issues are unlikely to be addressed regularly in its decisions, save when they take the form of advisory opinions; and some of the hopes that were placed in a stronger function of international adjudication by optimists like Kelsen,[115] Lauterpacht[116] and Jessup,[117] both before and after World War II, proved unrealistic in hindsight. Nevertheless, it is quite

115 H Kelsen, *Peace Through Law* (Chapel Hill, University of North Carolina Press 1944); see in particular 'Part I: Peace Guaranteed by Compulsory Adjudication of International Disputes'; ibid, 3–67.

116 Cf Lauterpacht, *The Function of Law in the International Community* (n 79).

117 See P Jessup, *A Modern Law of Nations* (Hamden/CT, Archon 1948, repr 1968).

impressive to observe how states increasingly submit even issues of vital national importance, such as border disputes or divergences about trade routes, to the International Court for decision. Moreover, one should not forget the famous phrase coined by Justice Holmes that 'great cases make bad law';[118] thus, the fact that the court is usually spared from getting involved in many of the most contentious issues of war and peace may even have a beneficial effect on its ability to exert a lasting influence on the fundamental tenets of international law.

This last consideration is arguably also relevant in the context of the second reason why it seems appropriate to study the process of unwritten international law from the judicial perspective – an issue already addressed briefly in the above: The fact that domestic courts in recent years are getting increasingly involved in the application and enforcement of international law. This growing eagerness of courts to apply norms of international law in municipal judicial proceedings, sometimes doubtlessly motivated by institutional self-interest,[119] yet perhaps more often sparked simply by the massive increase in international regulation seen these days, is met with mixed reactions by observers, depending upon their particular standpoint: Whereas 'progressive' lawyers, especially those working in the field of international human rights, praise this tendency as a potential major breakthrough for attempts to strengthen the international rule of law,[120] the foreign policy establishment remains at best ambivalent in its attitude towards these developments,[121] exhorting about potential threats to the executive's 'natural' foreign policy prerogative or invoking concerns about the democratic legitimacy[122] of the judiciary's use of international law.

118 Cf *Northern Securities Co v United States* (Holmes J dissenting) [1904] 193 US 197, 400–1: 'Great cases like hard cases make bad law. For great cases are called great, not by reason of their real importance in shaping the law of the future, but because of some accident of immediate overwhelming interest which appeals to the feelings and distorts the judgment. These immediate interests exercise a kind of hydraulic pressure which makes what previously was clear seem doubtful, and before which even well settled principles of law will bend.'; for a critical reconsideration of this statement in the context of Holmes' general judicial philosophy, see F Schauer, 'Do Cases Make Bad Law?' (2006) 73 *University of Chicago Law Review* 882.

119 Cf E Benvenisti, 'Reclaiming Democracy: The Strategic Uses of Foreign and International Law by Domestic Courts' (2008) 102 *American Journal of International Law* 241.

120 Cf eg Dimitrijevic (n 88); Kedian (n 88); for a generally positive perspective on the impact of domestic courts on the progressive development of international law see also A Roberts, 'Comparative International Law? The Role of National Courts in Creating and Enforcing International Law' (2011) 60 *International & Comparative Law Quarterly* 57.

121 For a (moderately) sceptical account see RY Jennings, 'The Judiciary, International and National, and the Development of International Law' (1996) 45 *International and Comparative Law Quarterly* 1.

122 Cf J Yoo/J Ku, *Taming Globalization: International Law, the US Constitution, and New World Order* (Oxford and New York, Oxford University Press 2012) passim; for the alleged 'democratic deficit' of international law see also J

Regardless of where one posits oneself in this ongoing debate, it seems that the objective trend provides another reason to scrutinise the judicial role with respect to unwritten international law.

The third reason why it seems appropriate to adopt the judicial perspective is more general, as well as more complex in nature, and thus it warrants some further explanation. Even assuming that the role of courts under (unwritten) international law is still not quite as prominent as in the context of domestic legal systems, there is something unique to the nature of the judicial activity that makes it appear as the most adequate paradigm for a study such as the present. It seems that everybody who, in her professional activities, regularly touches upon matters related to the legal profession, whether as advocate, politician, diplomat or businessman, must necessarily at times put herself in the position of a disinterested judge, trying to arrive at an objective conclusion about the legality or illegality of certain conduct. This is obvious in the case of an attorney who must, besides making the case of her client appear as strong as possible, provide a reasonable assessment of the objective state of the law in order to anticipate for her client foreseeable reactions and consequences that might ensue from a certain devised conduct. Thus, for example, a foreign office's legal counsel would be ill-advising her government if she represented to it only the conception of international law most favourable to its freedom of action, as this would not permit the responsible actors to devise the most effective and safe strategy. But there is another reason why even a government attorney should not deviate too far from the acceptable standards of the law, and should resist the temptation of regarding international law as a mere form of a 'debating contest', a witty, stimulating exercise of intellectual hair-splitting; a reason that was aptly formulated by Jeremy Waldron in his essay on *The Rule of International Law*:

> These lawyers should remember that they are acting for and advising an entity that is not just limited by law but governed by law in its very essence – a nation of laws, not men, in all its operations. Their advice should be given with the integrity of the international legal order in mind. Legal advice given in this spirit should not be grudging about legality, treating the rule of law in the international arena as an inconvenience or an envelope to be pushed. Legal advice should certainly not be given in a spirit of studied recklessness or deliberately cultivated obtuseness about the nature and extent of the obligations of international law. Instead, legal advice should be given in a spirit that embraces the importance of the international legal order and the obligatory character of its provisions.[123]

McGinnis/I Somin, 'Should International Law Be Part of Our Law' (2007) 57 *Stanford Law Review* 1175; J Rubenfeld, 'Unilateralism and Constitutionalism' (2004) 79 *New York University Law Review* 1971; C Bradley, *International Law in the US Legal System* (Oxford and New York, Oxford University Press 2013) xii.

123 J Waldron, 'The Rule of International Law' (2006) 30 *Harvard Journal of Law & Public Policy* 15 (26).

This responsibility of attorneys for the preservation of the integrity of the legal order and the maintenance of the rule of (international) law has meanwhile found several external manifestations. It is, for example, no longer to be taken for granted that lawyers do not incur (criminal) responsibility for their advice, if this advice eventually leads to the commission of international crimes; thus, the old Roman adage that *nemo ex consilio tenetur* no longer unconditionally applies. Ever since the 1946 conviction of leading jurists of the former Nazi German 'Reichs Ministry of Justice',[124] a case famously epitomised in Stanley Kramer's 1961 motion picture 'Judgment at Nuremberg', the prospect of being held responsible is not but a very remote possibility for legal advisors working on highly controversial issues, although in the more recent case of the US government lawyers responsible for drafting the (in-)famous 'torture memos',[125] a verdict of professional misconduct was the gravest sanction they had to fear.[126]

Having thus established (or rather, attempted to establish) the importance of the judicial perspective on international law, the question arises of what are the main demands that a judge facing a problem concerning the application of an unwritten norm of the international legal order has to address. Here, a key fact about the nature of unwritten international law bears repetition first: Although it may appear from distant observation that the development of the law is a process of slow and steady movement, a closer look reveals that progress often comes *per saltum*, by leaps and bounds, stimulated by the immediate necessities of a situation.[127] Michael P Scharf has recently popularised the concept of 'Grotian moment', 'a term that denotes a paradigm-shifting

124 In the case of *United States v Josef Alstötter and other defendants*; see the acts of the Nuremberg Military Tribunal, vol III, 3–1199.

125 See on this P Sands, *Torture Team: Rumsfeld's Memo and the Betrayal of American Values* (New York, Palgrave Macmillan 2008).

126 As happened to John Yoo, now a professor at UC Berkeley School of Law, who worked for the US Department of Justice's Office of Legal Counsel (OLA); the Department of Justice's Office of Professional misconduct concluded in 2009 that Yoo was guilty of 'intentional professional misconduct', because he 'knowingly failed to provide a thorough, objective and candid interpretation of the law', see the Office of Professional Responsibility's Report of July 29, 2009, 'Investigation into the Office of Legal Counsel's Memoranda Concerning Issues Relating to the Central Intelligence Agency's Use of "Enhanced Interrogation Techniques" on Suspected Terrorists', at 251, available at <https://www.thetorturedatabase.org/document/doj-office-professional-responsibility-report-investigation-olcs-memoranda-concerning-0> accessed 20 August 2017.

127 Cf the expression of a similar insight in B Cardozo, *The Paradoxes of Legal Science* (New York, Columbia University Press 1928) 253–4, who compares the progress of law to the false impression of continuous motion produced in a cinema: 'Is it possible that in rationalizing the development of law, in measuring the radiating energy of principle and precedent, we have been hampered by a like illusion? We have sought for a formula consistent with steady advance through a continuum. The continuum does not exist. Instead there are leaps from point to point. We have been beguiled by the ideal of harmonious progression. Centres of energy exist, of attraction and repulsion. A landing-place is found between them. We

development in which new rules and doctrines of customary international law emerge with unusual rapidity and acceptance'.[128]

Such a 'leap' in the law's development is often occasioned by a momentous historical event (an example being the terrorist attacks of September 11, 2001) after which the need for reconsideration of the old rules and precedents is perceived as a seemingly irresistible demand. However, the inducement for change is not always such an outwardly observable incident: maybe it is even more often the case that a massive accumulation of smaller events and incidents occurs almost unnoticed by the observer, until at some point the pressure becomes so great and imminent that the old order is fundamentally shaken – an event which frequently results in a certain confusion or puzzling about how a seemingly trivial cause can exert such a tremendous effect. What is neglected is of course the huge weight of incidents that amassed before the moment in which many quantitative changes turn into a qualitative one. An example of this latter paradigm would be the process of decolonialisation, during which a growing frustration and feeling of injustice about the domination of large parts of the world by European powers was fuelled by daily incidents of discrimination and humiliation.

In the realm of law, such trends are present in the form of the great antinomy between stability and change, between rest and motion, between well-tried experience and progress. As Roscoe Pound put it, 'Law must be stable, and yet it cannot stand still'.[129] In the words of Benjamin Cardozo:

> Rest and motion, unrelieved and unchecked, are equally destructive. The law, like human kind, if life is to continue, must find some path of compromise. Two distinct tendencies, pulling in different directions, must be harnessed together and made to work in unison. All depends on the wisdom with which the joinder is effected.[130]

Or, as one international lawyer argued more recently, but in a similar vein: 'Most rules of international law are not set in stone, but it is equally not acceptable to push them lightly aside by merely invoking their age or the different context in which they came about.'[131] Yet this antinomy between stability and progress is just one of the two great demands facing the judge under unwritten international law. The other is the task of generalising, the formulation of abstract rules and principles from the individual instances of their application. What appears in theory to be a relatively easy task for a trained lawyer, is enwrought with complications in practice, as the distinction

make these landing places for ourselves through the methods of the judicial process. How shall they be wrought? Where shall they be found?'

128 MP Scharf, 'Seizing the Grotian Moment' (2010) 43 *Cornell International Law Journal* 440 (441).

129 R Pound, *Interpretations of Legal History* (New York, Macmillan 1923) 1.

130 B Cardozo, *The Growth of the Law* (New York, Columbia University Press 1924) 2.

131 Nolte (n 92) 183.

of the essential from the accidental in any given precedent, be it a judicial decision or an incident of interaction of states with one another, is among the most difficult problems in analytical jurisprudence; and even more complex it becomes when a number of such 'instances' or precedents, of which all custom ultimately consists, are to be compared in order to discern a common underlying precept guiding the actions of the participants. Here, it seems that the individual instances of application of any purported norm of unwritten international law often differ so profoundly, and sometimes even facially contradict each other, that a purely quantitative analysis could never lead to the articulation of a principle with the required clarity and unambiguity.[132] Hence, a normative analysis is required, based on comparison with the existing principles of international law, a process in which ideally the contradictory facts can be reconciled on a higher level of abstraction, for example by formulating an exception to a rule. But even where these problems of generalisation can be solved, one fundamental antinomy also remains here. Whereas existing principles have a tendency of extension, by way of analogy, unto their logical extremes, a method of limitation is needed: First, because existing principles, once extended, necessarily must collide with each other at one point. And second, because the need for new principles to be articulated may arise, and room is to be made for them in the system of existing ones.

Given these antinomies inherent in the complex, decentralised process in which unwritten international law emerges and develops, can it really be maintained that its rules can be ascertained in a manner that has some modest claim to objectivity? And how do courts, whether domestic and international, deal with them? Their strategies as well as their shortcomings in this judicial 'quest for objectivity' shall be analysed in the next chapter.

132 See on this problem A Bleckmann, 'Völkergewohnheitsrecht trotz widersprüchlicher Praxis?' (1976) 36 *Zeitschrift für ausländisches öffentliches Recht und Völkerrecht* 374.

IV The Quest for Objectivity

A. Two Concepts of Objectivity

Before answering the question whether unwritten international law can be described as 'objective', one first needs to specify what is meant by the 'objectivity' of law in general and that of international law in particular. In order to discern possible meanings of this rather general, abstract concept, it seems helpful to look at some of its more specific antonyms:

First, the term 'objectivism' in international law can denote the conceptual opposite of 'voluntarism', the view that international law depends for its existence on the will of the individual states.[1] Despite the prediction of a 'decay of consent'[2] in international law, it is still argued that the assent of states to be bound by the rules of customary international law plays a pivotal role in their formation and even in their remaining in force.[3] The increasing frequency with which such arguments are recently brought forward is perhaps to be viewed in

1 On this conceptual pair, its meaning and its implications, see eg O Corten, *Méthodologie du droit international public* (Bruxelles, Editions de l'Université de Bruxelles 2009) 46–55.

2 See N Krisch, 'The Decay of Consent: International Law in an Age of Global Public Goods' (2014) 108 *American Journal of International Law* 1.

3 A paradigmatic example of the renewed attraction of this approach is the influential article by CA Bradley & M Gulati, 'Withdrawing from International Custom' (2010) 120 *Yale Law Journal* 202, wherein the authors argue against what they call the 'mandatory view' of customary international law and propose a view according to which states are free under certain circumstances to 'opt out' of customary obligations, just as they can withdraw their consent to be bound by a treaty. Another recent plea in favour of a voluntarist understanding of customary international law can be found in A Orakhelashvili, *The Interpretation of Acts and Rules in Public International Law* (Oxford, Oxford University Press 2008) esp ch 4; Orakhelashvili summarises his position as follows: 'It was concluded above that the process of the emergence of customary rules is in principle dependent on processes that can only be explained by consensual positivism. The factor which allegedly limits the relevance of positivism is that once rules are established, they are deemed to acquire their own existence and pursue their own rationale.' (ibid, 496); thus, Orakhelashvili goes not quite as far as Bradley and Gulati, in that he does not explicitly endorse the possibility of withdrawing consent once a rule of customary international law has emerged.

the context of a more general shift towards 'neo-voluntarism',[4] a tendency that seems to fit squarely into the larger trend of a revived interest in positivism and formalism in international law.[5]

Yet there is a second, more practical level on which the unwritten norms of the international legal order are frequently described as lacking objectivity: The level of law-ascertainment and application.[6] In that context, 'objective' is not meant as an antonym of 'subjective' or 'volitional', but rather as the opposite of terms such as 'indeterminate' or 'arbitrary'.[7] Put differently, a legal system would be fully objective in the sense of being determinate if it provided a concise, unambiguous answer to every conceivable question about the legality of every act that falls within its purview. In such a system, the act of law-application would be entirely free of discretion on the part of the law-applying authority, reducing the inherent arbitrariness of its decision to zero. Or, put differently again, 'the standard of a determinate answer is, roughly, what virtually all lawyers and other intelligent persons familiar with the legal system would believe, after careful study, the law provides'.[8]

To be sure, it is widely acknowledged today that such absolute certainty, or determinacy, does not exist in the realm of either domestic or international law: although in the latter a traditionally held position has been that everything which is not explicitly prohibited by international law is allowed, and consequently the possibility of a *non liquet* does not exist,[9] the question remains

4 For the argument that such a trend is observable in the field of international human rights law see T Christakis, 'Human Rights from a Neo-Voluntarist Perspective' in J Kammerhofer/J d'Aspremont (eds), *International Legal Positivism in a Post-Modern World* (Cambridge, Cambridge University Press 2014) 421; for a similar trend in the context of European integration see W Streck, 'Neo-Voluntarism: A New European Social Policy Regime?' (1995) 1 *European Law Journal* 31, whose predictions about a renewed emphasis on state sovereignty seem to have at least partly materialised in the aftermath of the recent crisis of the European Union.

5 Although, of course, positivistic and formalistic approaches do not necessarily imply a voluntarist conception of international law. A recent representative of the renewed interest in international legal positivism – and also of the discipline's 'historical turn' – is the book by M García-Salmones Rovira, *The Project of Positivism in International Law* (Oxford, Oxford University Press 2014); see also the various essays in Kammerhofer/d'Aspremont (n 4).

6 For a recent example of this line of argumentation see eg J Kammerhofer, 'Uncertainty in the Formal Sources of International Law: Customary International Law and Some of its Problems' (2004) 15 *European Journal of International Law* 523.

7 See on this notion of objectivity K Greenawalt, *Law and Objectivity* (New York and Oxford, Oxford University Press 1992) 3–4 and passim.

8 Ibid, at 3.

9 An argument forcefully stated by H Kelsen, *Principles of International Law* (New York, Rinehart & Co 1952) 304–7; see on this problem also IF Dekker/ WG Werner, 'The Completeness of International Law and Hamlet's Dilemma: *Non Liquet*, the *Nuclear Weapons* Case, and Legal Theory' in IF Dekker/HG Post (eds), *On the Foundation and Sources of International Law: Dedicated to the Memory of Professor Herman Meijers* (The Hague, TMC Asser Press 2003) 3.

whether such 'explicit' prohibition exists with respect to a particular conduct, and how far its scope extends. The frequency of legal disputes under international law demonstrates that despite the alleged existence of a 'closing rule', namely the principle of state sovereignty, the determinacy of its rules is generally not greater than that of their domestic counterparts, although the fact that large areas of international law are still rarely litigated over or challenged in court may convey a feeling of false certainty. Conventional wisdom asserts that the international *lex scripta*, both as a codification of unwritten norms and as the result of the negotiation and drafting of new treaty rules, possesses a comparative advantage over unwritten international law. As Oscar Schachter put it,

> [i]t is easy to see the advantages of this process [of codification and progressive development]. In place of the uncertain and slow process of custom, built upon instances that are necessarily contingent and limited, governments negotiate and collaborate in formulating rules and principles to meet perceived needs of the entire community of States. The texts bring clarity and precision where there had been obscurity and doubt. Moreover, all governments have the opportunity to take part in the legislative process and to express their consent or objection in accordance with their constitutional procedures. Neither of these opportunities was clearly available to all States in the creation of customary law.[10]

Similarly, and with explicit reference to the problem of interpretation, the French scholar Serge Sur asserted that in the application of unwritten international law, the political element is far more dominating than in the interpretation of written conventions: 'L'imprécision des méthodes d'interprétation du droit non écrit, et spécialement du droit coutumier, maintient la liberté politique des interprètes.'[11] The merit of this abstract, philosophical belief in the superiority of rationalistic, deliberately designed written laws has already been called into question in the preceding, more theoretical chapters of this study. Here, we shall consider the closely related, but more specific assertion that unwritten norms offer less guidance, provide less certainty and are thus less capable of pacifying disputes than written norms in a treaty. This argument has been so widely accepted, it seems, that one scarcely notices the fact that it is based on a rather counterintuitive assumption: Is it not displaying a characteristically naïve overreliance on the power of linguistics to assign more weight to the words of a written text, than to the force of repeated practical example?[12] And with

10 O Schachter, *International Law in Theory and Practice* (Dordrecht, Martinus Nijhoff 1991) 66.

11 S Sur, *L'interprétation en droit international publique* (Paris, Pichon 1975) 286; the quoted passage forms the heading of a chapter dedicated to the problems of interpreting unwritten international law.

12 For a similar argument see D Bederman, *Custom as a Source of Law* (Cambridge, Cambridge University Press 2010) passim, in particular the concluding section 'How and Why Custom Endures' (ibid, 168–82).

respect to Schachter's optimistic belief that 'the text brings clarity and precision where there had been obscurity and doubt': Does anyone with a minimum of insight in the way international diplomatic conferences proceed really believe that the paramount consideration of the participating actors is to adopt a text of the lowest possible degree of inherent ambiguity? One feels instantly reminded of the (in-) famous diplomatic adage, frequently attributed to Talleyrand, that 'la parole a été donnée à l'homme pour déguiser sa pensée'.[13]

B. The Case Method and the Concretisation of Abstract Rules and Principles

There exists, however, a perfectly intelligible reason for the perplexity, widespread among both scholars and practitioners, about customary international law: For while a written norm can be drafted, at least in theory, so as to attain an infinite degree of specificity, even in the form of one single command issued to only one particular person and applying to only one particular instance, rules discerned from practical example – whether deliberately given or not – rarely reach this level of concreteness and specificity. The reason for this lies in the fact that each instance or case in which a particular rule is applied varies from all others with respect to an almost infinite set of contingencies, whereas the essentials (ie the facts or circumstances pertaining to the manifestation of the rule in question) are often not only difficult to ascertain, but also inchoate and fragmentary. The difficulties of distinguishing the accidentals from the essentials of a precedent case is certainly most familiar to lawyers operating under common law systems, as demonstrated by a quip frequently cited in introductory lectures on the 'case method': 'That other case involved a red car, and this car is green.' And it seems that determining the content of a rule of customary (international) law is often even more difficult and tedious than discerning the essentials of a judicial precedent: after all, the latter constitutes at least a deliberate utterance, however doubtful its precise meaning and its place within the chain of precedents may be.[14]

The widespread impression that customary law, whether domestic or international, is lacking certainty, seems to stem from a misunderstanding of its proper nature and its function within a legal system, resulting in unreasonable expectations as to its degree of specificity. Such misconceptions about the

13 A similar, yet more elaborate remark was made by Voltaire, who wrote in his *Dialogue du Chapon et de la Poularde* of 1763: 'Ils ne se servent de la pensée que pour autoriser leurs injustices, et n'emploient les paroles que pour déguiser leurs pensées.'

14 Nevertheless, both forms, customary law stricto sensu, ie non-judicial practice, and judicial precedents, fall within the broader ambit of 'unwritten law' as the term is used here, because in both instances the actual rule is not fully developed at once, but emerges as the result of a series of instances in which it is applied. On the relationship between judicial precedent and custom see generally HF Jolowicz, *Lectures on Jurisprudence* (London, Athlone 1963) 218–9.

nature and force of customary law permeate even the works of history's most eminent scholars of jurisprudence; Blackstone, for instance, attempted to establish a requirement of 'certainty' as a precondition of judicial enforceability of any given custom by using the following example: 'A custom, to pay two pence an acre in lieu of tithes, is good; but to pay sometimes two pence and sometimes three pence, as the occupier of the land pleases, is bad for its uncertainty.'[15] It is indeed hard to conceive how a court could possibly enforce the latter custom; however, it seems that Blackstone's examples, involving specific amounts of money, are a kind of rule that will hardly ever arise as custom: First, because the value of money is (and always has been) subject to significant changes, so that the continuity of the individual instances essential to the formation of a customary rule is unlikely to exist. Second, and more fundamentally, norms of customary law are *abstractions*, derived from a number of individual cases that may differ in all respects save the one that allows for generalisation, and thus gives rise to the rule. Therefore customs, as specific as they may be, are unlikely to ever contain precise numerical values.[16]

It appears that in international law, generally speaking, the lack of certainty with respect to the particular contents of its unwritten norms is even more marked than in domestic legal orders. Quite often agreement as to the existence of a norm can be found only on the most abstract level; thus, textbooks and introductory courses tend to convey a feeling of false certainty and exactitude by referring to a huge number of 'principles' and 'generally accepted customs' as the unshakeable cornerstones upon which the whole edifice of the international legal order rests. This portrayal must in turn inevitably lead to growing unease or frustration on the side of the observer, who will quickly realise that even the most fundamental tenets of international law are subjected to contest and dispute in any case touching upon any state's vital interests. And, yet more startling, once one attempts to look behind the façade of even the most venerable legal principle and to scrutinise the individual instances of practice cited in support of it, it is surprising to see how much discrepancy and contradiction exists among them, so that the abstract principle, almost like a picture puzzle, seemingly vanishes upon close inspection. Not even the greatest luminaries of international law have been immune to this sobering discovery; Sir Hersch Lauterpacht, upon becoming a member of the International Court of Justice in 1955, described it thus:

15 W Blackstone, *Commentaries on the Laws of England* (Oxford, Clarendon, 8th ed 1768) I, 78.

16 Although this is certainly not impossible: one may, for example, think of the precise delimitation of the territorial waters in the international law of the sea, which, however, has changed over the course of history, and is now *contractually* limited to 12 nautical miles, cf Article 3 of the 1982 UN Convention on the Law of the Sea. Another example given by Blackstone is much more realistic in this respect: '[A] custom, to pay a year's improved value for a fine on a copyhold estate, is good, though the value is a thing uncertain: for the value may at any time be ascertained'; see Blackstone (n 15) 78.

> Once we approach at close quarters practically any branch of international law we are driven, amidst some feeling of incredulity, to the conclusion that although there is as a rule consensus of opinion on one broad principle – even this may be an overestimate in some cases – there is no semblance of agreement in relation to specific rules and problems.[17]

Although this general problem is widely recognised, the views as to the consequences to be drawn from it vary considerably, depending on a person's general philosophy, professional occupation, and – arguably – his or her temper.

The two most common contemporary responses to the difficulty described above are pragmatism and the so-called 'critical legal studies' movement. Whereas the latter aims at deconstructing the belief in the neutrality of the legal system by demonstrating the fundamental power relations that are claimed to be purposefully masked by pseudo-objective legalism, the pragmatic approach (often adopted by practitioners) acknowledges the ultimately fictional character of the idea of absolute legal determinacy, yet regards it as a useful fiction that enables the legal system to exert a mediating influence on the tempers of its subjects.[18]

Obviously neither of these two common explanations for the persistence of law throughout the history of human societies is completely satisfactory: Whether one regards the law as a tool of oppression or a benevolent lie, had its objectivity really been a fiction from the very beginning, it is difficult to conceive of reasons for the failure of every attempt to replace it by anything else, whether it be religious morality, raw power, or political and economic ideology.[19] In the view of the present author, the fundamental misconception underlying both the critical and the pragmatic approach is that they uncritically accept the positivistic notion of law as a system of rules. And indeed, if one reduces the notion of law to rules, norms, or standards of behaviour, devoid of any ontological foundation, the discovery that those rules are often indeterminate must fundamentally shake one's belief in the very concept of law: for if a rule is ambiguous and incapable of providing a definite answer to a particular question, especially when it is seen as isolated from the solid – biological or sociological – grounds on which empirical study is possible, it must appear as

17 H Lauterpacht, 'Codification and Development of International Law' (1955) 49 *American Journal of International Law* 16 (17).

18 For a pointed defence of the pragmatic approach to law see S Fish, 'The Law Wishes to Have a Formal Existence' in id, *There's No Such Thing As Free Speech (And It's a Good Thing, Too)* (Durham, Duke University Press 1993) 141.

19 One of the more recent examples of this development is the fact that the Marxist theory of the 'withering away' of law fell quickly into disrepute in each society that actually adopted a Socialist political system; for the development of the Soviet approach to international law from denial to active participation, see eg WW Kulski, 'The Soviet Interpretation of International Law' (1955) 49 *American Journal of International Law* 518; K Grzybowski, 'Soviet Theory of International Law for the Seventies' (1983) 77 *American Journal of International Law* 862.

an empty shell that can be filled by astute attorneys with whatever content they desire. Thus, it seems that the very concept of the 'rule of law', today often abused as a catchphrase and expanded beyond recognition, can be meaningful only if the 'law' it refers to is regarded as more than a mere arbitrary collection of – sometimes deliberately ambiguous – rules.

C. The Problem of Objectivity in Practice – Domestic and International

The problem of objectivity is best explained by reference to practical examples. As often in the study of unwritten international law, the law of state immunity provides an excellent field of reference, given the bulk of cases constantly arising in domestic courts around the world that raise intricate issues related to the legal status of foreign sovereign entities and their agents and personnel. It is a characteristic of this vast and diverse field of international law that differences between states hardly ever exist when it comes to the recognition of an abstract rule, for example, that *some* state officials enjoy immunity before domestic courts in *some* situations; rather, the crucial questions are, which officials can resort to the plea of immunity, whether their immunity is absolute or limited to 'official' duties, infinite or ending with their term of office, and whether certain behaviour, however 'official' in nature, is so outrageous as to merit depriving the individual perpetrator of the benefit of an immunity otherwise enjoyed by him or her.

A recent case illustrating this point is the 2011 decision of the UK's Administrative Court in the case of *Khurts Bat v Investigating Judge of the Federal Court of Germany*.[20] In this case, the court had to determine whether Mr Khurts Bat, Head of the Office of National Security of Mongolia, who at the time of his arrest in London allegedly stayed on a 'special mission' in the United Kingdom, enjoyed immunity and thus could not be extradited to Germany, where an European Arrest Warrant had been issued against him for his involvement in the abduction of a Mongolian national from France to Germany some time earlier. In arguing that customary international law did provide him with such immunity, the Mongolian government relied on the fact that it had informed, via its London ambassador and other diplomatic channels, the British authorities in advance of the visit of this high-ranking government official, and that the British side had in no way objected to it. More precisely, the Mongolian government claimed three sources of Mr Bat's alleged immunity: Personal immunity as an envoy on a special mission, personal immunity as a high government official, and immunity *ratione materiae*, namely 'by virtue of his actions on behalf of that State as opposed to his status, ie, *ratione personae*',[21] as the court defined the third alternative.

20 *Khurts Bat v Investigating Judge of the Federal Court of Germany and ors* [2011] EWCH 2029 (Admin).

21 Ibid, para 63.

The first two alternatives, which would have provided Khurts Bat with personal immunity, were rejected by the court in relative brevity: Concerning his alleged status as a diplomatic envoy on a 'special mission', the court held that the United Kingdom, represented by its Foreign and Commonwealth Office, had not given the explicit and prior consent required by customary law[22] for the establishment of a special mission.[23] Concerning the argument that Bat as Head of the Office of National Security, and thus as a high government official comparable to heads of states and foreign ministers was entitled to personal immunity regardless of Britain's consent, the court had few difficulties to refute it: Interpreting the International Court of Justice's decision in the *Arrest Warrant*[24] case, the British court held that the position of the Head of the Office of National Security was not comparable to that of a head of state, prime minister or foreign secretary, whose immunity the ICJ found to be necessitated by the demand of maintaining a state's capacity to conduct international relations:

> It is clear to me that Mr Khurts Bat falls outwith that narrow circle. In British terms he is a civil servant whose counterparts, so the United Kingdom contends, would be someone of director level, at a mid-rank in the FCO. The documents showing his job description and his authority, shown to the court by the Government of Mongolia, underline his status as an administrator far removed from the narrow circle of those who hold the high-ranking office to be equated with the State they personify and with those identified by the International Court of Justice.[25]

Thus, the court was now left to determine the validity of the third argument invoked by Mongolia in support of Mr Bat's immunity, namely, that the acts for his alleged involvement in which he had been indicted in Germany were official in nature, conducted on behalf of the Mongolian state, and therefore were covered by immunity *ratione materiae* under customary international law; thus, the Mongolian government argued, the European Arrest Warrant was unlawful and could not legally be acted upon by the British authorities. The manner in which the court dealt with this argument is of particular interest for the topic discussed here: It provides an illustrative example of how the

22 For the requirement of the receiving state's prior and explicit consent to a special mission the court relied in particular on Articles 1(a) and 2 of the *Convention on Special Missions of 8 December 1969 ('New York Convention')* 1400 UNTS 231, which was not applicable between the parties, but was apparently regarded by the court as reflecting customary international law. For an overview of the (customary and conventional) international law of special missions see I Roberts/E Denza, 'Special Missions' in I Roberts (ed), *Satow's Diplomatic Practice* (Oxford, Oxford University Press, 6th ed 2009) 187.

23 *Khurts Bat* (n 20) paras 22–46.

24 *Arrest Warrant of 11 April 2000 (Democratic Republic of the Congo v Belgium)* [2002] ICJ Rep 3.

25 *Khurts Bat* (n 20), para 61.

concretisation of a relatively abstract, generally recognised norm of unwritten international law in order to facilitate its application to a particular legal controversy is approached by a domestic court.

In its analysis of the question of whether Khurts Bat enjoyed immunity *ratione materiae* for his abduction of a Mongolian national committed (partially) on German soil, the court began by noting that '[n]otwithstanding the wealth of written commentary, there is a dearth of cases which have decided that an official acting on behalf of a State is entitled to immunity from criminal prosecution in respect of an offence committed in the forum state.'[26] The only situation of this type the court unearthed in which a state had actually invoked immunity on behalf of one of its agents in such a situation dated back to 1841, when the British government had (unsuccessfully) raised this argument in support of a Canadian sheriff implicated by the American authorities in the notorious *Caroline* incident.[27] More recent cases, including the *Rainbow Warrior* affair, did not provide the court with any example of a state having invoked immunity for one of its agents suspected of having committed a crime on the territory of the forum state; most often, the responsible state either said nothing (especially when one of its citizens was engaged in spying), or just defended them in general terms, without reference to immunity. Equating cases in which a state failed to invoke immunity on behalf of its agents with those where immunity had been invoked but rejected by the forum state, the court concluded that state practice did not support Mongolia's assertion that Khurts Bat enjoyed immunity *ratione materiae* for criminal acts committed on German soil:

> It seems to me the fact that, in recent years, States have not claimed immunity is just as much evidence of the absence of State practice as those cases where immunity is claimed but denied by the forum state. I am particularly persuaded by Dr Franey's analysis of *The Rainbow Warrior* case and the difficulty of identifying State practice by reference to events which occurred, in relation to the loss of *The Caroline*, between 1838 and 1841. That seems to me to be a poor guide to modern State practice.[28]

It is not my purpose here to discuss the substantive correctness of the court's analysis. Rather, the discussion of the *Khurts Bat* case was intended to demonstrate the difficulties that a purely inductive, seemingly 'objective' approach to the ascertainment of international norms, as proposed most notably by Schwarzenberger,[29] faces when confronted with the task of concretising

26 Ibid, para 70.

27 The British subject, Sheriff Macleod, was nevertheless tried in a New York court, but released due to a lack of evidence proving his involvement in the blowing up of the American vessel *The Caroline* by Canadian rebels.

28 Ibid, para 99.

29 On his theory see above Ch 3 C.

even a seemingly well-established rule such as the granting of immunity *ratione materiae* to state officials.

The particular difficulty in the *cas d'espèce* consisted in delimiting the scope of an alleged exception (a crime had been committed on the territory of the forum state) to a rule (state agents enjoy immunity *ratione materiae* with respect to their official acts), which itself can be described as kind of an exception to the jurisdiction of a state otherwise competent to adjudicate a certain matter. The court tried to solve this dilemma by the assumption that the scarcity of claims to immunity *ratione materiae* raised by states on behalf of their agents is, in terms of state practice, equally conclusive as explicitly raised, yet rejected claims to immunity; an assumption that, though fictitious, has some *prima facie* plausibility, although states may have chosen to remain silent for a number of reasons – as the court itself acknowledged.[30] Arguably, though, the court should have taken into account another possible form of 'silence' as well: How many similar cases may have arisen where it was the forum state that chose to remain silent, ie not to prosecute a foreign state's agents for crimes committed on its territory? And if such instances were to be discovered, how would this affect the validity of the court's reasoning?

The purely inductive approach to the concretisation of rules of customary international law is especially problematic in cases where it is unclear what, in fact, is the general rule, and what the exception: On this question it often depends which side of a controversy has to present state practice in support of its position, and which side is favoured by the conspicuous absence of precedents. This problem is illustrated in Judge ad hoc van den Wyngaert's dissenting opinion in the *Arrest Warrant* case: In that case, the ICJ's majority had held that an acting foreign minister enjoyed the same absolute personal immunity as an acting head of state, and that, as it could not find conclusive state practice supporting an exception in cases where grave human rights violations were involved, a Belgian court had violated international law in issuing an arrest warrant against the Congolese foreign minister. Van den Wyngaert, however, asserted that the court had failed to prove conclusive state practice supporting its allegation that a foreign minister was covered by head-of-state immunity in the first place, and had thus mistakenly shifted the burden of proof on Belgium.[31] This accusation contains some truth at least in one respect: The majority did not reach their conclusion that incumbent foreign ministers enjoy absolute personal immunity by way of an extensive analysis of actual state practice; rather, it likened the position of a foreign minister in the conduct of international relations with that of other officials who undisputedly enjoyed immunity, such as heads of states, heads of governments and diplomats. Noting the important functions fulfilled by foreign ministers in international relations, the

30 *Khurts Bat* case (n 20) para 95.

31 *Arrest Warrant* case (n 24) (Dissenting Opinion of Judge ad hoc van den Wyngaert) [2002] ICJ Rep 137, paras 11–23.

court deemed it necessary to accord to them the same status of inviolability as granted to the other functionaries:

> In the performance of these functions, he or she [the foreign minister] is frequently required to travel internationally, and thus must be in a position freely to do so whenever the need should arise. He or she must also be in constant communication with the Government, and with its diplomatic missions around the world, and be capable at any time of communicating with representatives of other States.[32]

Some commentators have described this 'functionalist' methodology of the majority in the *Arrest Warrant* case as a departure from the ICJ's traditional approach to the ascertainment of customary international law, which allegedly had focused more stringently on the inductive analysis of state practice.[33] However, even a cursory review of the case law of the ICJ and its predecessor, the Permanent Court of International Justice, reveals that there has never been a period during which a purely inductive approach to the identification of customary law persistently dominated. Especially in cases when the court found that no generally accepted rule of customary international law pertaining to the *cas d'espèce* existed, it occasionally ventured relatively far into considerations of necessity and utilitarianism. The *Anglo-Norwegian Fisheries* case provides an apt example of this: After having rejected the British assertion that international law contained a rule strictly limiting the territorial waters of a state to a certain distance from its natural coast line, the court nevertheless attempted to formulate legal principles governing the issue of delimitation of the territorial sea:

> It does not at all follow that, in the absence of rules having the technically precise character alleged by the United Kingdom Government, the delimitation undertaken by the Norwegian Government in 1935 is not subject to certain principles which make it possible to judge as to its validity under international law.... In this connection, certain basic considerations inherent in the nature of the territorial sea bring to light certain criteria which, though not entirely precise, can provide courts with an adequate basis for their decisions, which can be adapted to the diverse facts in question.[34]

32 *Arrest Warrant* case (n 24) para 53.

33 See eg HW Jung, *Rechtserkenntnis und Rechtsfortbildung im Völkergewohnheitsrecht* (Göttingen, vr unipress 2012) 34; for an opposite analysis, according to which the *Arrest Warrant* case marks a shift back to the traditional strictly inductive approach, see A Alvarez-Jimenez, 'Methods for the Identification of Customary International Law in the International Court of Justice's Jurisprudence 2000–2009' (2011) 60 *International and Comparative Law Quarterly* 681 (694); it seems that both arguments are partially correct: In proving the existence of personal immunity with respect to foreign ministers, the court indeed followed a purposive, 'functionalist' approach; with respect to the alleged exception from that rule, it demanded a full proof of relevant state practice.

34 *Anglo-Norwegian Fisheries* case [1951] ICJ Rep 116 (133).

This is a fascinating passage, because in it the court performs a volte-face of some kind: After having required an improbably high level of consistency and density of state practice for a norm of customary international law to arise, one might have expected it to end the matter here with a reference to the *Lotus* principle, according to which, in the absence of a specific prohibition, states are free to do whatever they want. Instead, the court enters a completely new field of inquiry, pondering over what 'some basic considerations inherent in the nature of the territorial sea' might reveal as to the subject matter of the dispute.

One could describe this approach as a form of natural law-reasoning, as it is aimed at discerning the legal rules applicable to a certain area by examining *the nature of the things.* More fitting, however, seems the comparison with the tenets of legal realism which have been described above.[35] This similarity becomes particularly apparent as the court went on to discuss the 'economic interests' involved in the dispute, which merited looking 'beyond purely geographical factors'.[36] True, the court did not go so far in this case as to design a system of rules based purely on a balancing of the competing interests involved, but returns to an inquiry of the historical development of Norway's approach to the delimitation of its territorial waters, finding that other states, including the United Kingdom itself, never explicitly objected to it. But even in this rather traditional analysis of the constitutive elements of customary international law, ie *opinio juris* and state practice, the court laid particular emphasis on the specificities of the situation and the competing interests of the parties to the dispute.[37] This flexibility in the court's approach to the ascertainment of unwritten rules of international law is visible in a number of its early decisions and advisory opinions,[38] for example in the advisory opinion concerning *Reservations to the Genocide Convention*,[39] an opinion whose rationale was aptly assessed by Lauterpacht as follows:

> [T]he Opinion of the Court in this case, far from being based exclusively – or mainly – on the denial of what hitherto had been thought to constitute the customary rule on the subject, was in fact based on wider and more persuasive considerations. In the interests of justice and the necessities of international intercourse it is legitimate to attach decisive importance to

35 See above, Ch 3 A.

36 *Anglo-Norwegian Fisheries* case (n 34) 133.

37 See eg ibid, at 139: 'The notoriety of the facts, the general toleration of the international community, Great Britain's position in the North Sea, her own interest in the question, and her prolonged abstention would in any case warrant Norway's enforcement of her system against the United Kingdom.'

38 See eg H Lauterpacht, *The Development of International Law by the International Court* (London, Stevens and Sons 1958), in particular Ch 28: 'State Sovereignty and Customary International Law', where Lauterpacht discusses a number of these decisions.

39 *Reservations to the Genocide Convention* (Advisory Opinion) [1951] ICJ Rep 25.

> the particularities of a given situation – as already noted, such peculiarities did exist in the case of the Genocide Convention – and, in reliance upon more general principles forming part of the existing law, to distinguish that situation from that subject to the normal and accepted rule and to adjudge accordingly.[40]

Whereas the ICJ's majority in the two aforementioned cases had stressed the need to take into account the specificities of a particular situation when ascertaining the applicable rule of customary international law, in other cases the court did just the opposite: It extended the scope of application of an established rule or concept of international law so as to cover a subject that had before not usually been subsumed under it. An early example of this approach to a rule of unwritten international law is the ICJ's decision in the *Nottebohm* case.[41] Here, the court picked up the criterion of 'effectiveness' of a citizenship, developed by domestic and international tribunals to decide whether individuals with a dual nationality could rely on the one most favourable to them. Applying this criterion of effectiveness to assess the validity *between states* of the act of naturalisation itself, even where an individual possessed the citizenship of one state only, the court essentially placed a new restriction on the freedom of states to decide on the conditions under which they might validly award their citizenship.[42] Although the court denied that it did anything but apply pre-existing law, its reasoning in this case has been aptly described as 'extension by analogy'.[43] Thus, it resembles the court's methodology in the *Arrest Warrant* case that we discussed earlier, where the court used analogical reasoning to establish a rule providing absolute personal immunity to incumbent foreign ministers. In other cases, the International Court specifically rejected the possibility of drawing an analogy, based on its finding that the reason of a certain rule was not applicable to the situation at hand; early examples of this are the advisory opinions on *Reparation for Injuries suffered in the Service of the United Nations*, where the court rejected the proposed application of the rules of diplomatic protection on actions taken by international organisations on behalf of its agents,[44] and on the *International Status of South-West Africa*:

40 Lauterpacht (n 38) 373.
41 *Nottebohm* case (second phase) [1955] ICJ Rep 4.
42 For a highly critical contemporary analysis of the court's reasoning see AN Makarov, 'Das Urteil des IGH im Fall Nottebohm' (1955) 16 *Zeitschrift für ausländisches öffentliches Recht und Völkerrecht* 407.
43 Eg by Ch de Visscher, *Problèmes d'Interprétation Judiciaire en Droit International Public* (Paris, Pedone 1963) 42: 'L'arrêt rendu par la Cour internationale de Justice en l'affaire *Nottebohm* fournit un exemple caractéristique de l'extension par analogie d'une règle coutumière.'
44 See *Reparation for Injuries suffered in the Service of the United Nations* (Advisory Opinion) [1949] ICJ Rep 174 (182): 'Nor does the analogy of the traditional rule of diplomatic protection of nationals abroad justify in itself an affirmative reply [to the question presented to the court, i.e. whether the UN could claim reparation on behalf of its agents]. It is not possible, by a strained use of the concept of

In the latter case, the somewhat different question arose whether the concept of 'mandate' in international law had to be construed analogically to its twin concept under domestic law.[45]

The brief discussion of some – admittedly rather arbitrarily selected[46] – classical cases of the International Court served a twofold purpose. First, it illustrated the relevance of one of the two antinomies we have identified at the end of the previous chapter as underlying themes for the further inquiry: The tension-filled relationship between the demand of generality, ie the extension of established concepts unto their logical extremes, and of that of specificity, or of the suitability of legal rules to address particular situations and interests; this antinomy, together with that between the demands of stability and progress, will play a significant role in the following chapters dealing with the practice of unwritten international law.

Second, the examples given above served to demonstrate that even the International Court of Justice, which throughout its decisions and opinions continuously stressed the overarching importance of an inductive approach to the ascertainment of unwritten norms of international law,[47] acknowledges the need to supplement this purely empirical analysis of actual state practice and the official statements accompanying it with different modes of reasoning, which are not necessarily exclusive, but at least peculiar to the judicial function. And it is precisely this additional step, going beyond the pure assembly of precedents, in and through which the concept of 'interpretation' in relation to unwritten norms of international law obtains a meaningful content. Indeed, it has recently been argued that the term 'interpretation' with respect to customary international law should *only* be used for the process by which an *already recognised* rule of customary law is applied to a specific situation, as distinct from the (logically prior) *discernment* of a rule from instances of state

allegiance, to assimilate the legal bond which exists, under Article 100 of the Charter, between the Organization on the one hand, and the Secretary-General and the staff on the other, to the bond of nationality existing between a State and its nationals.'

45 See *International Status of South-West Africa* (Advisory Opinion) [1950] ICJ Rep 128 (132): 'The object of the Mandate regulated by international rules far exceeded that of contractual relations regulated by national law. It is therefore not possible to draw any conclusion by analogy from the notions of mandate in national law or from any other legal conception of that law.'

46 In a more complete discussion of the ICJ's approach to the ascertainment of customary international law, a huge number of additional cases would have to be included, most notably, of course, the *North Sea Continental Shelf* case and the *Armed Activities (Nicaragua v USA)* case; those and other cases will be discussed in the subsequent chapters dealing with more specific issues of the application of unwritten international law.

47 Although it has been argued that the ICJ did not always follow this premise; for a recent analysis, see S Talmon, 'Determining Customary International Law: The ICJ's Methodology between Induction, Deduction and Assertion' (2014) 4 *Bonn Research Papers on Public International Law*.

practice and *opinio juris*.[48] According to this view, the process of ascertainment of custom is a predominantly *inductive* operation, while the application of rules that have already been widely recognised would be a mainly *deductive* process, not dissimilar to the construction of the text of a treaty.[49] While this distinction seems clear enough in theory, one should not forget that a customary rule does not exist as a Kantian 'thing in itself': Any attempt to formulate even the most well-established rule of customary international law, for example in a textbook of international law, is necessarily but an approximation, while the rule *as such* is visible only in the individual instances in which it has been acted upon or invoked by the states. Therefore, anyone who applies it has to counter-check her interpretation against the existing state practice in order not to delegitimise the result as pure wishful thinking.

In their attempt to make the application of customary international law more objective and predictable, some domestic courts have long used a technique that has recently gained new interest and popularity in legal academia: Judicial Dialogue.

D. Objectivity through Judicial Dialogue?

One can hardly say that the practice of courts to engage in a judicial dialogue about rules of customary international law is a new phenomenon. In fact, the mutual cross-citation of domestic courts from various nations, and their discussion and careful analysis of the decisions rendered by their peers in other jurisdictions, predates the recognition of the modern positivistic concept of customary international law and even the Benthamite invention of the very term 'international law'. It dates back to a time when the rather broad umbrella term 'law of nations', denoting a collection of rules and precepts largely based on natural law, was used instead; a term which, by the way, in particular Anglo-American courts continued to use long into the 20th century. It would be an intriguing task to study the origins of the practice of judicial dialogue in the field of this 'law of nations'. For our purposes, it may suffice to cite an exemplary passage from an 1812 decision written by the great first Chief Justice of the United States, John Marshall:

> This law [of nations] is in part unwritten, and in part conventional. To ascertain that which is unwritten, we resort to the great principles of reason and justice. But, as these principles will be differently understood by different nations under different circumstances, we consider them as being, in some degree, fixed and rendered stable by a series of judicial decisions. The decisions of the Courts of every country, as far as they are founded upon a law that is common to every country, will be received, not

48 See P Merkouris, 'Interpreting the Customary Rules of Interpretation' (2017) 19 *International Community Law Review* 126.
49 Ibid, at 136.

> as authority, but with respect. The decisions of the Courts of every country show how the law of nations, in a given case, is understood in that country, and will be considered in adopting the rule which is to prevail in this.[50]

This passage is fascinating for two reasons:

First, it marks a shift of paradigms in the history of international law: From the conception of the law of nations as an abstract, ahistorical natural law construed *more geometrico* ('the great principles of reason and justice') to the insight that all law, including the 'law of nations', is a historically and culturally contingent product of human society. Second, and more importantly, it presents us with one of the first explicit justifications of the practice today known as 'judicial dialogue': Namely, that it helps to overcome the vagueness and contingency of the unwritten sources of international law, to safeguard against legal parochialism and cultural biases, and thereby to make the ascertainment of international law more objective and predictable.

Today, the aims and aspirations of the proponents of judicial dialogues have become considerably loftier. Thus, Anne-Marie Slaughter expressed hopes that through it there might arise a 'world in which courts perceive themselves independent of, although linked to, their fellow political institutions, open to persuasive authority, and engaged in a common enterprise of interpreting and applying national and international law, protecting individual rights, and ensuring that power is corralled by law'.[51] Especially in the field of customary international law, the role of judicial dialogue among domestic courts is increasingly described as contributing to the progressive development of the rules of international law, rather than being a mere tool in ascertaining their content.[52] Richard Falk had already claimed that much in 1964, at a time when the influx of newly independent states into the international order and the peaceful coexistence of two fundamentally opposed political and economic systems were the pressing issues of international law: 'Domestic courts in the older states can help adapt international law to the modern world by developing principles that express tolerance for diverse social and economic systems.'[53] The demand for a shift in the role of domestic courts from enforcers to creators or 'creative developers' of customary international law is supported by the argument that their decisions play a unique double role in the sources of international law, being both state practice under Art 38 (1) (b) and 'subsidiary means for the determination of rules of law' under Art 38 (1) (d) of the

50 *Thirty Hogsheads of Sugar v Boyle* [1815] 13 US 191 (198).

51 AM Slaughter, 'A Typology of Transjudicial Communication' (1994) 29 *University of Richmond Law Review* 99 (132).

52 See A Roberts, 'Comparative International Law: The Role of Domestic Courts in Creating and Enforcing International Law' (2011) *International and Comparative Law Quarterly* 57.

53 R Falk, *The Role of Domestic Courts in the International Legal Order* (Syracuse, Syracuse University Press 1964) xxi–xxii.

Statute of the International Court of Justice,[54] an argument that was already raised by Hersch Lauterpacht[55] in 1929. The crucial role of domestic courts in the formation of customary international law was confirmed by the International Court of Justice in the *Jurisdictional Immunities* case, where it was stated that their decisions can be regarded both as state practice and *opinio juris*:

> In the Court's opinion, State practice in the form of judicial decisions supports the proposition that State immunity for *acta jure imperii* continues to extend to civil proceedings for acts occasioning death … This practice is accompanied by *opinio juris*, as demonstrated by the positions taken by States and the jurisprudence of a number of national courts …[56]

The possibility that domestic judges may be acting as agents of progress is anticipated with particularly high aspirations in the field of customary international human rights law, where it is hoped that they might achieve the implementation of rules that the political branches of government of their states, responsible for the negotiation and ratification of treaties, are unwilling to subscribe to.[57] Some authors argue in favour of abandoning altogether the positivist distinctions between comparative domestic law and international law, and between the sources of international law, and express the hope that, through the process of judicial dialogue, a new *Jus Gentium*, or 'common law of mankind', might arise.[58]

In these and other glowing appraisals of the role that domestic courts have played and continue to play in the development of customary international law, it is often neglected that this source of law poses a unique host of difficulties and challenges to national judges. These challenges are partly contingent, in which case they can be expected to be overcome by serious efforts, and partly essential, depending on the very nature of the relationship of domestic judges to the international legal order.

When discussing the application of international law by domestic courts, and the obstacles which they are facing in this process, the first thing one always has to bear in mind is the particular situation in which they are placed by the fact that they are subject to legal constraints emanating from two independent,

54 Roberts (n 52).

55 H Lauterpacht, 'Decisions of Municipal Courts as a Source of International Law' (1929) 10 *British Yearbook of International Law* 65.

56 *Jurisdictional Immunities of the State (Germany v Italy, Greece Intervening)* (Merits) [2012] ICJ Rep 99, para 77.

57 See eg KM Kedian, 'Customary International Law and International Human Rights Law in United States Courts' (1999) 40 *William & Mary Law Review* 1395.

58 See in particular the forceful argument by J Waldron, *"Partly Laws Common To All Mankind": Foreign Law in American Courts* (New Haven, Yale University Press 2012); see also CG Weeramantry, 'Custom: The Growing Role of Customary International Law' in id, *Universalising International Law* (Leiden, Martinus Nijhoff 2004) 219.

and possibly contradicting, sources: Whereas the norms they apply are international in origin, their powers and competencies, in short their status, is still determined by their own domestic constitutional environment. In this respect, the classical words of Anzilotti still hold true – if not as a matter of legal doctrine, than at least as a sociological description: 'The limits within which freedom is left to [domestic] judges to interpret international law … depend on the internal law of the individual states, as they are a matter pertaining substantially to the competence of the judiciary vis-à-vis the other functions of the sovereign power.'[59] This observation is still valid more than a century later, as is attested to in the First Report of the International Law Commission's Special Rapporteur on *Formation and Evidence of Customary International Law/Identification of Customary International Law*:

> While there may be much to learn from the approach of domestic courts, it should be borne in mind that each domestic court operates within the particular confines of its own domestic (constitutional) position. The extent and manner in which customary international law may be applied by the domestic courts is a function of internal law.[60]

In this context it should be noted that the traditional distinction between the concepts of *monism* and *dualism*, pertaining to the doctrinal controversy about whether or not international and domestic law form part of one and the same legal order, is of relatively little relevance to the practical difficulties discussed here, because such a crude classification does not reflect adequately the specificities of the relationship between international and domestic law in any given country. Indeed, one can say – with a grain of salt – that 'every nation is dualistic, in that one must consult the nation's domestic law in order to determine international law's status within that system'.[61] Moreover, the mere fact that a domestic legal system is based on a monist understanding says nothing about the rank accorded in it to international law.[62] Therefore, a more nuanced analysis seems preferable, looking at the different ways to incorporate customary international law into domestic legal orders, and the rank accorded to it.

59 D Anzilotti, *Il Diritto Internazionale Nei Giudizi Interni* (Bologna, Zanetti 1905) 195 et seq; translation of the quoted passage by the present author.

60 ILC, 'First Report on Formation and Evidence of Customary International Law by Michael Wood' (17 May 2013) UN Doc A/CN.4/663, para 84.

61 CA Bradley, *International Law in the US Legal System* (Oxford, Oxford University Press 2013) xii.

62 Since monism can be logically conceived either as the primacy of international or the primacy of national law, as is even acknowledged by some of the staunchest supporters of a monist understanding of the relationship between international and domestic law; see eg H Kelsen, 'Die Einheit von Völkerrecht und staatlichem Recht' (1958) *Zeitschrift für ausländisches öffentliches Recht und Völkerrecht* 234 (248): 'Beide Systeme sind gleich korrekt und gleich berechtigt.… Die Entscheidung selbst liegt außerhalb der Rechtswissenschaft.'

As far as the manner of incorporation is concerned, it seems that there are three fundamentally different ways: *First*, customary international law can be regarded as automatically being 'part of the law of the land', without any specific rule of incorporation; this model is being followed, at least in theory, by legal doctrine and practice in many common law countries since the time of Blackstone and Mansfield. *Second*, there can be a specific constitutional provision incorporating it, which is the case in countries like Austria,[63] Germany, , Italy,[64] Russia[65] and many others; often, though, the wording of these provisions is rather imprecise, as they refer to 'the general rules' or 'the general principles' of international law, instead of explicitly mentioning customary international law. *Third*, there is neither a constitutional provision, nor a generally accepted doctrine of automatic incorporation, such as in the Netherlands,[66] in Spain[67] or in Luxemburg.[68] In theory, then, application of customary international law by domestic courts is severely restricted, and is possible only when it has been specifically incorporated by the legislative branch into domestic law. However, courts in those countries do refer to customary international law, especially in the field of state immunity, but also in connection with questions of statehood, international personality, or rules of customary international law on matters pertaining to the provisional application of treaties.[69] In practice, the status of customary international law in the legal orders of the third category of countries is determined on the basis of case law of the highest courts.[70] Sometimes, there are also general clauses authorising courts to apply rules of customary international law in certain fields: Thus, for example Article 36 (2) (a) of the Spanish Civil Procedure Act refers to the 'rules of Public International Law' on immunity as a limitation on the jurisdiction of the Spanish courts.

The rather simple threefold framework described above becomes considerably more difficult when one looks at the specificities of each country, and the practice of its courts. The most important point here, with significant potential to disenfranchise courts from the process of judicial dialogue on customary international law, is the question of the *rank* accorded to the rules of

63 Art. 9 (1) Federal Constitutional Law.
64 Art. 10 (1) Constitution.
65 Art. 15 (4) (First Alternative) of the Constitution of the Russian Federation.
66 See EA Alkema, 'Netherlands' in D Shelton (ed), *International Law and Domestic Legal Systems* (Oxford, Oxford University Press 2011) 407 (419–21).
67 See S Stirling-Zanda, 'The Determination of Customary International Law in European Courts' (2004) 4 *Non-State Actors and International Law* 3 (18).
68 P Kirsch, 'Luxemburg' in Shelton (n 67) 385 (398–400).
69 See eg the examples given in Stirling-Zanda (n 68).
70 With respect to the Netherlands, it has been noted that '… [i]n the absence of a constitutional provision which makes other, notably customary rules of international law, part of the national legal order, it is assumed that international custom or general principles become partof domestic law only after having been applied by the Supreme Court.'; see CM Brölmann/EW Vierdag, 'Netherlands' in PM Eisemann (ed), *The Integration of International and European Community Law in the National Legal Order* (Alphen aan den Rijn, Kluwer Law 1996) 433 (456).

customary international law in the respective domestic legal order. In many common law countries, where customary international law is thought as automatically incorporated as part of the common law ('law of the land'), it can be overridden by acts of legislation like ordinary domestic common law; such is the case for example in the United Kingdom,[71] where 'it yields to statutes',[72], although there exists a 'presumption of compatibility'.[73] In the US, the situation is similar, although complicated by the increasing academic discussion on whether customary international law forms part of *federal* common law or state law.[74] Although the traditional view, according to which customary international law is federal common law and thus trumps state law, is still adhered to by the Supreme Court and the majority of scholars, signs are not wanting that the opposite, so-called 'revisionist' view is gaining ground[75] – a development with the potential to wreak havoc on the consistent and effective implementation of customary international law in US courts. In any event, in the 2014 case of *Argentina v NML Capital*,[76] the Supreme Court's majority opinion, written by the late Justice Antonin Scalia, contained a categorical assertion of the predominance of statutory law over (possibly contradicting) customary international law: 'Any sort of immunity defense made by a foreign sovereign in an American court must stand on the [Foreign Sovereign Immunities] Act's text', Scalia wrote. 'Or it must fall.'

In those countries where customary international law is incorporated en bloc by a specific constitutional provision, the rank accorded to it in the hierarchy of sources varies considerably. To name but a few examples: Whereas in Italy, customary international law is incorporated by Art 10 (1) of the Constitution at the same rank as constitutional law (although, according to the Italian Constitutional Court, below the '*principi supremi*' of the Constitution),[77] in

71 See SC Neff, 'United Kingdom' in Shelton (n 67) 620 (626–8).
72 *Cheney v Conn (Inspector of Taxes)* [1968] 1 WLR 242 (ChD), 245 D–E.
73 See the cases cited in S Fatima, *Using International Law in Domestic Courts* (Oxford, Hart 2005) 13.16.1.
74 The most influential article in this respect was CA Bradley/JL Goldsmith, 'Customary International Law as Law of the United States' (1989) 10 *Michigan Journal of International Law* 450.
75 See PR Dubinsky, 'United States' in Shelton (n 67) 630 (644–7).
76 The slip opinion is available at <http://www.supremecourt.gov/opinions/13pdf/12-842_g3bi.pdf>accessed 27 August 2017.
77 See eg the recent decision by the Italian Constitutional Court, 22 October 2014, Decision No 238, where the Court struck down a law implementing the ICJ's judgment in the case concerning *Jurisdictional Immunities of the State (Germany v Italy, Greece Intervening)* (n 56), because it held that the granting of immunity even for crimes against humanity would be contrary to the 'supreme principle' of access to court under Art 24 of the Italian Constitution: 'Come si è già osservato, il totale sacrificio che si richiede ad uno dei principi supremi dell'ordinamento italiano, quale senza dubbio è il diritto al giudice a tutela di diritti inviolabili, sancito dalla combinazione degli artt. 2 e 24 della Costituzione repubblicana, riconoscendo l'immunità dello Stato straniero dalla giurisdizione italiana, non può giustificarsi ed essere tollerato quando ciò che si protegge è l'esercizio illegittimo

Germany, according to Art 25 Basic Law, it prevails only over statutory law, and thus ranks below the constitution. In Austria, customary international law forms part of Federal Law,[78] as seems to be the case in the Czech Republic.[79] In China, on the other hand, customary international law – or, as Art 142 of the 'General Principles of Civil Law' prefers to call it, 'international practice' (*Guoji Guanli*) – only *may* be applied where there is neither a statutory nor treaty provision applicable.

A particular problem appears in legal orders based on Islamic (*sharī'a*) law, such as the Islamic Republic of Iran: Not only have the rules of customary international law to be specifically incorporated to become domestically binding, but this incorporation is only valid as far as the rules do not contradict precepts of the *sharī'a* (as interpreted, in the case of Iran, in accordance with the Shiite *Ja'farī* school of jurisprudence).[80]

The huge differences in terms of the rank accorded to international law in the various states cannot remain without impact on the capacity of judges to engage in an open dialogue on customary international law, and, ultimately, on the value of their decisions as a source of international law. In countries where customary international law is applied mostly in mediated form, potentially distorted by the statutes implementing it, or where it is even relegated to the rank of a subsidiary source of law, courts have no incentive to conduct a thorough review of international practice, or to engage in the tedious task of developing a method of ascertaining customary international law in a manner consistent with international law doctrine.

E. A Diversity of Methods: The Example of State Immunity

This brings us to what is perhaps *the* most important challenge faced by domestic courts charged with the application of customary international law: The lack of a generally accepted methodological framework for its ascertainment. Although domestic courts, if they at all bother to discuss the necessary preconditions of a rule of customary international law, refer in some form to the two elements of practice and *opinio juris*, there is not nearly a methodological consensus among them as to how customary international law is proved. In particular, there seems to be little reflection on the appropriate relationship between inductive and deductive elements in judicial reasoning on customary international law, and on the range of materials and the geographical distribution of evidence to be taken into account. To demonstrate

della potestà di governo dello Stato straniero, quale è in particolare quello espresso attraverso atti ritenuti crimini di guerra e contro l'umanità, lesivi di diritti inviolabili della persona.' (ibid, at para 5.1).

78 According to Art. 9 (1) Federal Constitutional Law.

79 See AJ Belohlavek, 'Czech Republic' in Shelton (n 67) 195 (202–3).

80 See eg R Moschtaghi, 'The Relation between International Law, Islamic Law and Constitutional Law of the Islamic Republic of Iran – A Multilayer System of Conflict?' (2009) 13 *Max Planck UN Yearbook* 376 (388 et seq).

the diversity of approaches, it seems useful to briefly recall a few cases, older and newer ones, from the field of state immunity – an area which has long been shaped to a significant degree by domestic case law.[81]

1. Germany: The Empire of Iran Case

An example of a court discussing a broad variety of materials in ascertaining a rule of customary international law can be found in the classical *Empire of Iran Case*,[82] decided by the German Federal Constitutional Court in 1963.[83] In this case, one of the first in which a German court adopted the doctrine of restrictive immunity, the Federal Constitutional Court had to rule on the admissibility of a claim by a plumbing company for payment for repairs conducted in the Iranian embassy in Germany. The court began by acknowledging that the traditional rule of absolute immunity, which had unquestionably been applied in German courts until 1945, was increasingly being challenged by courts in a number of states.

Looking at foreign case law, the court discerned three groups of countries: Courts in Belgium, Italy, Austria, France, Greece, Egypt and Jordan had adopted the doctrine of restrictive immunity, granting it only for *acta jure imperii*. Courts in a number of other countries, such as the Netherlands and Sweden, were divided on this matter, whereas courts in a third group of countries, consisting of the UK, the United States and most Eastern European states, still adhered to the doctrine of absolute immunity. Noting that a consensus on absolute immunity among domestic courts did no longer exist, it went on to support this conclusion with references to several bilateral and multilateral treaties providing immunity only for *acta jure imperii*. Additionally, the court bolstered its reasoning by quoting codification efforts by the League of Nations and the ILC, studies conducted by the International Law Association and the Institut de Droit International, and the opinions of learned writers.

Two things are interesting in this case: First, the wide range of materials the court took into account did not lead to a clear picture, as both the courts and the publicists were divided (although the court claimed that there was a slight majority in favour of restricted immunity). And second, the conclusion the

81 As X Yang aptly describes it in his comprehensive study on *State Immunity in International Law* (Cambridge, Cambridge University Press 2012) 28: 'As far as State immunity is concerned, however, judicial decisions are now not a *subsidiary* but a *principal* means for the determination of rules of law; one might even say that judicial decisions constitute the very *source* of international law on State immunity.'.

82 *Claim against the Empire of Iran Case*, BVerfG 16, 27; 45 ILR 57.

83 It should be noted here that Art. 100 (2) Basic Law grants to the Constitutional Court the competence to decide questions about the existence or interpretation of rules of customary international law that have arisen in lower courts (the so-called norm-verification procedure, similar to the preliminary rulings of the European Court of Justice in matters of European Law).

court drew was not to let the old rule – absolute immunity – stand, but to decide, in the absence of a clear consensus to the contrary, in favour of Germany's (territorial) jurisdiction. Thus, despite the long and tedious inductive survey conducted by the court, the ultimate conclusion was reached by way of deduction from a rather abstract principle of international law.

2. The United Kingdom: The Trendtex Case

Similar in result, but even more daring in its approach was the decision of the UK Court of Appeal in the *Trendtex* case of 1977, whose reasoning was later substantially affirmed by the House of Lords in the case *I Congreso del* Partido.[84] Lord Denning, writing for the court, began by noting that the

> ... notion of consensus [on the rules of state immunity] is a fiction. The nations are not in the least agreed upon a doctrine of sovereign immunity. The courts of every country differ in their application of it. Some grant absolute immunity. Others grant limited immunity, with each defining the limits differently.... It is, I think, for the courts of this country to define the rule as best they can, seeking guidance from the decisions of the courts of other countries, from the jurists who have studied the problem, from treaties and conventions and, above all, defining the rule in terms which are consonant with justice rather than adverse to it.[85]

Interestingly, Lord Denning did not draw the conclusion that, in the absence of a consensus on a new rule, the classical rule – absolute immunity – had to be applied; nor did he fall back on the principle of territorial sovereignty, as the German Federal Constitutional Court had done. Rather, he recalled the increasing engagement of states in economic activities that had – allegedly – given rise to the trend to restrict immunity to official acts:

> In the last 50 years there has been a complete transformation in the functions of a sovereign state. Nearly every country now engages in commercial activities. It has its departments of state – or creates its own legal entities – which go into the market places of the world. They charter ships. They issue letters of credit. This transformation has changed the rules of international law relating to sovereign immunity.[86]

The *Trendtex* case presents us with an example of a court perceiving it as its duty to ground its reasoning in a sociological analysis of the changing conditions in the international community, and, if necessary, to adjust the law accordingly. The citation of foreign case law in this judgment does not serve

84 *I Congreso del Partido* [1981] 2 All ER 1064.
85 *Trendtex Trading Corp v Central Bank of Nigeria* [1977] QB 529 (CA), 364.
86 Ibid, 550.

the purpose of ascertaining the existence of a consensus, but rather to inform the court of the approaches followed elsewhere, among which it then could choose and adopt the one it considered to be most convincing.

3. *Colombia: García de Borrisow v Embassy of Lebanon*

As of today, it is safe to say that the doctrine of restrictive immunity is supported by a vast majority of states. It received a major support by being implemented in Part III (Articles 10–17) of the 2004 *UN Convention on the Jurisdictional Immunities of States and their Property*, which has so far been signed by 28 and already ratified by 16 states, thus falling short, however, of the tally of 30 ratifications required for its entry into force. Nevertheless, some domestic courts refer to this convention as an expression of customary international law. A good example in this respect is the case of *García de Borrisow v Embassy of Lebanon*,[87] decided by the Columbian Supreme Court of Justice in 2007. In this case, the court had to decide whether diplomatic missions of foreign states could claim state immunity in labour disputes before domestic courts. Holding that Art 31 of the *Vienna Convention on Diplomatic Relations* did not cover labour disputes, the court went on to ascertain the customary international law rules on this question. Recalling that it had hitherto rejected labour lawsuits against foreign embassies, based on the principle of sovereign equality enshrined in the maxim '*par in parem non habet imperium*', it now found that this traditional rule had changed. It based this assertion on three independent arguments:

First, a fundamental right to work had been recognised, not only in the Colombian constitution, but also in international law, such as in Art 6 of the International Covenant on Economic, Social and Cultural Rights (ICESCR). As a corollary of this right, the court held, certain basic guarantees, such as the right to obtain legal redress, had to be made available to the employees. Therefore, the principle of immunity of foreign states with respect to labour disputes had to be reconsidered.[88]

Secondly, the court relied on communications submitted to the Colombian foreign ministry by 25 foreign states, covering a wide geographical and political range (including the US, the Islamic Republic of Iran, Russia and India), each of which had stated that it followed the doctrine of restrictive immunity with respect to labour disputes.[89]

Finally, the court referred to the exception for labour contracts in the 2004 *UN Convention on Jurisdictional Immunities*, which, according to the court, could be regarded as codifying established customary international law on this matter.[90]

87 *García de Borrisow v Embassy of Lebanon*, Supreme Court of Justice, Decision on Admissibility of 13 December 2007, Case No 32096, ILDC 1009 (CO 2007).
88 Ibid, para 11 et seq.
89 Ibid, para 23.
90 Ibid, para 25.

In this Colombian case, we see a court relying heavily on what is frequently referred to as a 'modern'[91] conception of customary international law, stressing the importance of *opinio juris* at the expense of actual state practice. In particular, the court relied heavily on the deductive argument based on Art 6 ICESCR, as well as on the UN Convention as an expression of customary international law, but did not discuss actual cases where foreign courts had denied immunity in labour disputes, relying in this respect exclusively on the assertions made by foreign governments. Nevertheless, given the fact that the court supported its reasoning by three independent lines of argumentation, it is fair to say that this judgment belongs to the more carefully reasoned decisions rendered by domestic courts in the field of state immunity. Thus, although the court was not particularly receptive towards the judgments rendered by other courts abroad, and although its reasoning concerning Art 6 ICESCR may well be questioned, the decision nevertheless has the potential to further the international judicial dialogue on the subject-matter of immunity in labour disputes, as it is framed in a methodological 'language' that is internationally comprehensible.

4. PR China (Hong Kong): The Case of DR Congo v FG Hemisphere Associates

The decisions summarised above, despite differing considerably in their approaches, all have one trait in common: The desire of the courts who rendered them to scrutinise the substance of the matter, that is to objectively discern the current state of customary international law, and to do so by looking beyond their borders, at the practice and opinions of other states. However, there are also courts who, by virtue of their domestic legal environment or due to considerations of judicial restraint, are not free to determine the law for themselves but who, in one way or another, follow the opinions of the other domestic branches of government, be it the legislatives (in countries where conflicting domestic statutes take precedence over customary international law) or the executives. A poignant example of deference to the executive branch in the ascertainment of customary international law is the case of *DR Congo v FG Hemisphere Associates LLC*,[92] decided by the Hong Kong Court of Final Appeals in 2011. Hong Kong, by tradition a common law jurisdiction, had hitherto applied the doctrine of restrictive immunity, as it was interpreted in British courts since the mid-1970s. However, after UK's transferal of sovereignty over Hong Kong to the PR China in 1997, this jurisprudence led to a conflict with the doctrine of absolute immunity still adhered to by the latter. As the determination of the Chinese practice on state immunity is regarded as

91 See eg AE Roberts, 'Traditional and Modern Approaches to Customary International Law: A Reconciliation' (2001) 95 *American Journal of International Law* 757.

92 *Democratic Republic of the Congo and ors v FG Hemisphere Associates LLC* (Judgement on Final Appeal) [2011] 150 ILR 684.

being covered by the State Council's foreign policy prerogative under Art 89 (9) of the Chinese constitution, the question arose whether Hong Kong courts could still adhere to their established doctrine, thus having two different approaches to state immunity applicable in China. Asked by the Court of Final Appeals to decide this matter, the Standing Committee of the National People's Congress in Beijing answered in the negative, relying purely on the internal relationship between mainland China and Hong Kong under the PR China's constitution. The Court of Final Appeals dutifully obeyed, deciding that the doctrine of absolute immunity had to be applied again in Hong Kong henceforth.

This decision is remarkable for the conspicuous absence of any substantive considerations on how customary international law is ascertained, owing to the court's complete deference to the State Council's authority in this respect. Thus, it again demonstrates the pivotal importance of domestic law for the domestic court's competence with respect to customary international law. It is, however, just one extreme example of a wider tendency of courts to leave the determination of rules of customary international law to the executive branch of government, in particular to foreign policy bureaucracies. More often than being explicitly prescribed by law, this deference is exercised by the courts in the greater context of an ethos of judicial self-restraint in foreign affairs. As such, it can be another significant challenge to judicial dialogue on customary international law, and especially to the court's ability to partake in the progressive development of its rules.

F. Time's Arrow: Judicial Activism or Self-Restraint?

To note the increasingly active role of domestic courts in the application of international law has recently become a truism of sorts.[93] While their traditional attitude towards the engagement in substantive issues of international law has often been one of considerable reluctance, as demonstrated by their use of a number of techniques aptly described as 'avoidance canons'[94] (such as the 'act of state-doctrine'[95] or rigid interpretations of standing requirements),

93 To name but a few representative contributions: E Benvenisti, 'Reclaiming Democracy: The Strategic Use of Foreign and International Law by Domestic Courts' (2008) 102 *American Journal of International Law* 241; id/GW Downs, 'National Courts, Domestic Democracy, and the Evolution of International Law' (2009) 20 *European Journal of International Law* 59; A Roberts (n 52); F Francioni, 'International Law as a Common Language for National Courts' (2001) 36 *Texas International Law Journal* 587; K Knop, 'Here and There: International Law in Domestic Courts' (2000) 32 *New York University Journal of International Law and Politics* 501; A Nollkaemper, *National Courts and the International Rule of Law* (Oxford, Oxford University Press 2011).

94 This illustrative term was coined by E Benvenisti, 'Judicial Misgivings Regarding the Application of International Law: An Analysis of Attitudes of National Courts' (1993) 4 *European Journal of International Law* 159 (esp 169).

95 On the Anglo-American act of state-doctrine, see eg M Zander, 'The Act of State Doctrine' (1959) 53 *American Journal of International Law* 826; M Singer, 'The

it has widely been argued that this reserve is gradually disappearing, making room for bolder, more confident approaches.[96] This apparent waning of self-restraint of domestic courts in the application of rules of international law is often interpreted as an auspicious sign for the international rule of law, heralding an age in which the deficient state of enforcement of international law is improved by the intervention of independent judicial bodies which, despite being organs of their states, perceive themselves as agents of the international legal order, and are willing and able to protect the integrity of international law against encroachments and assaults by the 'political' branches of domestic government. It is in this context that Georges Scelle's optimistic notion of a '*dédoublement fonctionelle*', the idea that state organs can play a double role as organs of both their state and of the international legal order, seems to exert renewed attraction.[97]

However, even scholars who are generally optimistic about the possible role of domestic courts as impartial enforcers of international law acknowledge that the alleged trend towards greater activity is observable only in a fraction of the more than 190 sovereign states belonging to the ever-growing international community today.[98] The reluctance of the rest to engage consistently and forcefully in the enforcement of rules of international law, and in their further development, stems not only from the differences in the domestic legal environment already described above; nor does it result from sheer ignorance or incompetence, although the lack of information and expertise in many domestic courts with respect to theoretical and practical issues of ascertaining rules of international law is an important and well-documented aspect. Rather, the reluctance on the part of some domestic courts and the assertiveness and activism displayed by others seem to express fundamentally different self-perceptions of judges, and their legitimate role in the international legal order. Among progressively minded international law scholars, there seems to be a certain tendency to scorn those courts which adopt a rather restrictive, cautious approach to the application of international law, and to praise those which are more forthcoming.[99] And, to be sure, the motives for courts to

Act of State Doctrine of the United Kingdom: An Analysis, With Comparisons to United States Practice' (1981) 75 *American Journal of International Law* 283. Generally on the justiciability of so-called 'political questions' with respect to foreign relations, see T Franck, *Political Questions Judicial Answers* (Princeton, Princeton University Press 1992); for Germany see eg HD Treviranus, *Außenpolitik im Demokratischen Rechtsstaat* (Tübingen, Mohr Siebeck 1966) 22–6.

96 See eg Benvenisti (n 94); Roberts (n 52); Nollkaemper (n 94) 6 et seq and passim.

97 See Y Shany, 'Dédoublement fonctionelle and the Mixed Loyalties of National and International Judges' in F Fonatnelli (ed), *Shaping Rule of Law Through Dialogue: International and Supranational Experiences* (Maastricht, Europa Law Publishing 2009) 27.

98 Cf Nollkaemper (n 94) 6 et seq.

99 A poignant example is the dismissive treatment by scholars of the following public statement by a US District Court judge engaged in a lawsuit under the *Alien Tort Statute* (ATS): 'I'm nothing but a trial judge in one federal court … I do not rule

exercise self-restraint have been, and still are, at times less than praiseworthy. It is true that the traditional 'avoidance doctrines', such as the act of state-doctrine, have been adopted at least partly out of 'judicial timidity',[100], or as a result of the parochial desire to give their domestic executives 'a free hand' in the conduct of foreign relations. However, it seems that the cautious approach traditionally prevailing, and still practised by perhaps the 'silent majority' of domestic courts in the world, can claim certain legitimacy, especially where rules of customary international law are concerned. There are, as the present author believes, two principal lines of argument which justify a certain degree of judicial self-restraint in the application of international law, and both are of particular relevance to the application of customary international law.

1. Customary International Law and the Separation of Powers

The first pertains to the domestic separation of powers. For the purposes of international law, the state is in many respects treated as a unitary actor,[101] and domestic distributions of power between the different branches of government, as well as rules of competence, are, apart from some exceptions, irrelevant. In particular, the non-compliance with internal limitations on the competence of a state organ cannot generally be invoked to invalidate international commitments made by it on behalf of the state. However, there is a marked difference here between written and unwritten international law: Whereas in the case of treaties, international law recognises a functional differentiation among domestic state organs, granting the unconditional power to conclude binding agreements only to specifically enumerated high-ranking state officials (of Art 7 (2) (a) VCLT), such a limitation is absent in the case of customary international law, where it is widely acknowledged today that for the purposes of international law, all state organs are capable of producing acts of state practice.[102] As the processes of ascertainment, interpretation and

the universe. I have nothing to do with international affairs.' For an academic criticism of this statement see eg Kedian (n 57).

100 See Benvenisti (n 95) 173.

101 See eg M Herdegen, 'Das "konstruktive" Völkerrecht und seine Grenzen' in PM Dupuy et al (eds), *Völkerrecht als Wertordnung: Festschrift für Christian Tomuschat* (Kehl, Engel 2006) 899 (904 et seq).

102 This is at least the position of the majority of modern scholars; for a good restatement of the contemporary doctrine, see the Final Report of the International Law Association's Committee on Formation of Customary (General) International Law, *Statement of Principles Applicable to the Formation of General Customary International Law* (as amended at the ILA's London Conference in 2000) Principle 9: 'The practice of the executive, legislative and judicial organs of the State is to be considered, according to the circumstances, as State practice.' This modern position is a departure from views held by a significant number of positivist international law scholars, who regarded customary international law as a form of 'pactum tacitum' and therefore counted as state practice only the acts of those organs of the state capable under international law of concluding binding

progressive development of rules of unwritten international law are hardly separable, it is generally acknowledged that their application necessarily involves an even greater element of law-creation than the application of treaties.[103] And whereas the 'political' branches of government, the executive and the legislative, can be held (and hold each other) democratically accountable, the same is not usually the case when it comes to courts, as judicial independence from political influence is seen as a core postulate of the rule of law, be it in domestic or international affairs. This independence is especially crucial in the application of international law, where, due to international law's external view on the state, 'these courts are organs of the very entities they are to control'.[104] Thus, while the principle of judicial independence is an indispensable condition for the proper fulfilment of the function of domestic courts as promoters of the international rule of law, the same independence, and lack of democratic accountability, causes a certain tension with the very rule of law itself, which 'does not involve or require unlimited control by the courts over political branches, but likewise will require limitations of powers of courts'.[105] Especially in the application of the notoriously elusive[106] rules of customary international law, a mutual interdependence between the different branches of government can exert a stabilising effect, as does the concentration of competence to ascertain customary international law in certain – usually highest – courts and the involvement of the foreign offices as *amici curiae* in disputes involving its interpretation. Nevertheless, formal procedures such as these, especially when the executive branch is involved, pose the risk of undue influence of purely political reasons, perhaps leading to inconsistencies in the guidance given to the courts by the foreign departments; as Richard Falk aptly put it, 'judicial review of the validity of foreign expropriations of territorial property should not depend upon whether the executive seeks to harass or appease a particular state'.[107] Given the fact, then, that the application of customary international law comprises a potentially significant element of law-creation, and that formal procedural checks and balances, as well as general rules of deference to the executive, are somewhat clumsy means of control, which are also not provided for in many legal systems, a substantial amount of judicial self-restraint seems advisable in the application of rules of customary international law. This was recently acknowledged in a decision of the German Federal Constitutional

agreements; see eg D Anzilotti, *Corso di Diritto Internazionale: Vol I* (Padova, Athenaeum, 3rd ed 1928) 68 et seq.

103 See on this eg KF Gärditz, 'Die Legitimation der Justiz zur Völkerrechtsfortbildung' (2008) 47 *Der Staat* 381, passim, in particular 384–6.

104 Nollkaemper (n 94) 47.

105 Ibid, 56.

106 See eg S Sur, *L'interprétation en droit international public* (n 11) 286. On this problem see also P Staubach, 'The Interpretation of Unwritten International Law by Domestic Judges', in G Nolte/HP Aust (eds), *The Interpretation of International Law by Domestic Courts: Uniformity, Diversity, Coherence* (Oxford, Oxford University Press 2016) 113.

107 Falk (n 53) 11.

Court in a case concerning the NATO bombardment of the bridge of Varvarin in 1999; in this decision, the court rejected the argument that an individual right of compensation for victims of military operations existed under customary international law, explicitly stating that it was 'not called upon to progressively develop international law'.[108]

The present author's endorsement of a cautious approach should not be interpreted to imply, however, that courts should bow in unreflected deference to the whims of the executive; on the contrary, judicial self-restraint can provide an argument by which the courts can defend themselves against political encroachments.[109] Unfortunately, however, courts tend to mistake self-restraint for – more problematic – unbridled deference to the executive. Thus, instead of merely giving consideration to the view of the executive (and perhaps also the legislative) branch of government, they accept the executive views on customary international law without questioning. The matter is further complicated by the fact that even in countries where courts do not acknowledge a general doctrine of deference to the executive or legislative branches in the application of international law, deference to the legislative branch is paid when rules of customary international law are codified in statutes.[110] Deference to the executive, on the other hand, plays an important role in many countries when it comes to determining the extent of the privileges of a high-ranking foreign government official[111] or the recognition of governments or states.

2. *Judicial Self-Restraint and the International Legal Order*

Distinguishing between deference and judicial self-restraint is crucial, because a certain degree of self-restraint seems advisable not only from the perspective of

108 See the case of the *Bridge of Varvarin* [2013] 2 BvR 2660/06, para 51; for a discussion of this case see KF Gärditz, 'Bridge of Varvarin' (2014) 108 *American Journal of International Law* 86.

109 See generally E Franßen, 'Positivismus als juristische Strategie' (1969) 24 *Juristenzeitung* 766.

110 An example is the practice of Canadian courts on the *State Immunity Act* of 1985, see S Beaulac/JH Currie, 'Canada' in Shelton (n 67) 116 (142 et seq).

111 A good example is the determination of the reach of the privileges of acting heads of states, governments or foreign ministers: In the case of *Wei Ye v Jiang Zemin* [2004] 383 F3d 620, the question arose whether head of state-immunity protected Jiang Zemin against a service of process in a suit directed against a non-immune third party. Whereas the district court had dismissed the US governement's argument that a service of process violated the privileges of a head of state, the appeals court reversed the decision, stating that the question pertained to the conduct of foreign affairs and a court had to defer to the government's position on it. Whereas the result may well be correct under international law, what seems problematic is that it was reached by deferring to the government's position instead of by an independent evaluation of the applicable rules of international law; for a critical review of US practice in this respect see eg LS Yelin, 'Head of State Immunity as Sole Executive Lawmaking' (2011) 44 *Vanderbilt Journal of Transnational Law* 911.

domestic democratic legitimacy and the separation of powers, but also from the perspective of the international legal order. Although scholars of international law are understandably pleased with courts who abandon traditional 'avoidance doctrines' and decide matters of international law on the merits, thereby implementing notions of substantive justice, it should not be forgotten that one of the central social functions of international law in the world order is still – in a manner of speaking – a formal one: To determine the limits within which states, constantly increasing in number, in an international community that is constantly becoming more interconnected, can legitimately exercise their powers. It is a kind of paradox that despite all predictions about the inevitable decline of the state as the central actor in international law,[112] national independence is still a goal that people (and peoples) all over the world consider worth fighting and dying for, and that the failing of states is one of the most common causes of international conflict and disorder. After the end of the heyday of liberal universalism in international law, which enjoyed such a great popularity in the aftermath of the world-historical events of 1989/90, we are more and more faced with a situation of 'universal exceptionalism'[113] in which again fundamentally different value systems and ideologies coexist.[114] In such a legal order, it is not only expedient, but indeed a necessity to have formal criteria by which the legitimate sphere of actions is determined.

These criteria, which international law provides and which are supplemented by rules of domestic law,[115] are customarily summarised under the broad concept of 'jurisdiction'.[116] The international rules on jurisdiction, governing the distribution of authority in the international community, are historically among the most significant parts of customary international law which have been applied by domestic courts.[117] These rules are shaped to a particularly high degree by the structural propensities of the international order, especially its traditionally highly decentralised nature and its horizontal character.[118] The

112 See for a discussion of these predictions eg O Schachter, 'The Decline of the Nation-State and its Implication for International Law' (1998) 36 *Columbia Journal of Transnational Law* 7.

113 See eg EA Posner/A Bradford, 'Universal Exceptionalism' (2011) 52 *Harvard International Law Journal* 3;

114 For a general analysis and historical contextualisation of the present situation see M Mazower, *Governing the World: The History of an Idea* (New York and London, Penguin 2012); see also I Bremmer, *Every Nation for Itself: Winners and Losers in the G-Zero World* (New York, Portfolio/Penguin 2012).

115 See on the supplementary function of domestic legal rules eg the classical exposition by H Kelsen, *Principles of International Law* (New York, Rinehart & Co 1952) 192 et seq; see also id, *General Theory of Law and State* (Harvard University Press 1945) 343.

116 See generally on the concept of jurisdiction as a condition of the application of international law by domestic courts Nollkaemper (n 94) 22–46.

117 Falk (n 53) Ch III.

118 See A Bleckmann, 'Zur Strukturanalyse im Völkerrecht' (1978) 9 *Rechtstheorie* 143 (151 et seq).

concept of jurisdiction is linked in two significant ways to the application of customary international law by domestic courts: First, the rules on jurisdiction themselves are, for the most part, customary international law; and second, an extensive interpretation of these rules enables the courts to apply a whole range of substantive rules of customary international law which would not have been of concern had a claim been rejected for lack of jurisdiction. One of the most controversial as well as illustrative examples in this respect is perhaps the practice of courts under the United States 'Alien Tort Statute' (ATS, also known as the 'Alien Tort Claims Act' or ATCA), a law originally enacted in 1789, which grants US District Courts '... original jurisdiction of any civil action by an alien for a tort only, committed in violation of the law of nations or a treaty of the United States'.[119] Originally intended to convince the European governments that the US took the protection of foreign diplomats and merchants seriously (although the legislative history of the act is rather cryptic),[120] during the past 30 years or more[121] the provision has been repeatedly used by human rights activist groups to file lawsuits for alleged violations of customary international human rights law committed around the world without any significant link to the US.[122] Then in 2013, in the much-anticipated decision *Kiobel v Royal Dutch Petroleum Co.*,[123] the US Supreme Court finally declared the inapplicability to such cases of the grant of jurisdiction under the ATS, relying on a 'presumption against extraterritoriality', the 'perception that Congress ordinarily legislates with respect to domestic, not foreign matters'.[124] Although the decision to restrict the application of the ATS was thus based substantially on domestic law, it is full of language indicating that the court was motivated by concerns about the possible negative effects on international relations of US arrogation of jurisdiction over conduct on foreign territory.[125]

The decision in *Kiobel* may be seen as a backlash against efforts to enable the victims of terrible human rights abuses to obtain legal redress. However, from the systemic point of view of the sources of international law, it is certainly an anomaly when courts in a tiny number of particularly powerful Western states single-handedly adopt 'progressive' interpretations of customary international

119 See 28 USC § 1350 (2006).

120 See eg WR Castro, 'The Federal Courts' Protective Jurisdiction Over Torts Committed in Violation of the Law of Nations' (1985–86) 18 *Connecticut Law Review* 467 (468–9).

121 Since the momentous (and much criticised) decision of the US Court of Appeal for the Second Circuit in the case *Filartiga v Pena-Irala*, 630 F2d 876 (2d Cir 1980).

122 For an overview of the litigation under the ATS see eg C Vázquez, 'Alien Tort Claims and the Status of Customary International Law' (2012) 106 *American Journal of International Law* 531.

123 *Kiobel v Royal Dutch Petroleum Co* [2013] 133 S Ct 1659.

124 Ibid, 1672 (Breyer, J, concurring).

125 For an analysis see eg DP Stewart/I Wuerth, 'Kiobel v Royal Dutch Petroleum Co.: The Supreme Court and the Alien Tort Statute' (2013) 107 *American Journal of International Law* 601.

law, which they then enforce, using their countries' political and economic leverage. Such practice, instead of serving the promotion and enforcement of universal human rights, is rather prone to evoke scorn and resentment. As MO Chibundu aptly remarked fifteen years ago:

> Self-restraint in taking on cases should be seen as a greater virtue than the self-congratulation of functionally ineffective high-minded pronouncements on international human rights norms. If the international community of jurists is to create an enduring jurisprudence of international human rights law, it will be because those norms converge from adjudications in multiple jurisdictions each reflecting the socio-political structures of its constitution, while seeking to conform local practices to evolving international standards.[126]

Unfortunately, the so-called 'modern' conception of customary international law deceptivly suggests that the tedious dialectical process between local practices and international standards, between high-minded aspirations and harsh realities might be unnecessary, letting suffice some lofty statements in an international declaration or the like. It is true that especially in human rights law, the proof of practice in the classical sense, ie 'constant and uniform usage', might often be difficult if not impossible to obtain.[127] But it should be noted that especially when applying the modern conception of customary international law, domestic courts run a high risk of merely restating parochialist sentiments, ultimately obstructing judicial dialogue instead of promoting it. It is a trivial fact that a dialogue requires listening as well as speaking. In the context of customary international law, it is particularly important that courts with louder voices be quiet at times and listen carefully for new voices to emerge.

G. The Centrality and Elusiveness of the Concept of 'Purpose' in Unwritten International Law

The preceding sections of this chapter have illustrated some of the practical difficulties and theoretical controversies surrounding the judicial application of customary international law.

Especially the activities of domestic courts, which operate at the particularly sensitive point where domestic and international authorities intersect, may give rise to concern, as there is among them neither an agreement on the proper methodology to discern rules of customary international law, nor a common view on the question of whether they should act as agents of progress or

126 See MO Chibundu, 'Making Customary International Law Through Municipal Adjudication: A Structural Inquiry' (1999) 39 *Virginia Journal of International Law* 1069.

127 See C Tomuschat, *Human Rights – Between Idealism and Realism* (Oxford University Press, Oxford, 2nd ed 2008) 39.

self-restraint. How can these difficulties be reconciled with the picture of unwritten international law as a complex, emerging system of self-organisation that has been painted in the earlier chapters of this study? And, assuming it could, how could and should this understanding influence the work of domestic and international judges in the application of rules of customary international law?

Although Hayek ascribed to the judges a vital role in articulating and concretising the rules underlying a spontaneous order of actions, he did not deal with questions of legal methodology and the rules of interpretation in any detail, nor did he even mention the implications that his concept might have for the theory of ***international*** law. Thus, the value of his theory with respect to specific aspects of the application of unwritten international law is limited, and one can only guess from the trajectory of his theoretical approach what he might have had to say in this respect. Yet one aspect extensively dealt with by Hayek is of eminent importance to the interpretation of unwritten international law: The role played by the concept of the 'purpose' of a certain rule. In this context, Hayek asserted that the term 'purpose' with respect to law could be understood in two fundamentally different ways, namely to refer to either the 'concrete foreseeable results of particular actions', or to 'the aiming at conditions which will assist the formation of an abstract order, the particular contents of which are unpredictable'.[128] Only in the latter sense, Hayek argued, could the concept of 'purpose' be meaningfully used in the context of rules that emerged without central planning or design, but rather by societal self-organisation. This distinction, he insisted, had to be kept in mind whenever an interpreter used the concept of 'purpose' to discern the precise meaning and scope of such rule.

In the application of unwritten rules of international law, purposive interpretation and teleological arguments are among the dominant means of interpretation applied by domestic courts and the ICJ alike, especially in case where the precise scope of application of a given rule has to be discerned. Yet courts do not always make clear which kind of purpose they refer to: The motivation of individual actors to follow a certain rule, or rather the function it fulfils in the international community.

Good examples reflecting this ambiguity can be found, again, in the case law of domestic courts, especially in the field of state immunity. Here, purposive or teleological arguments are often used by the courts to solidify the results they have reached based on only a small number of instances of state practice.[129] However, similar arguments are also applied in order to discern the intention

128 See FA Hayek, *Law, Legislation and Liberty* (London, Routledge, reissue 2013).

129 A fine example is presented by the approach of the Federal Constitutional Court of Germany in the *Philippine Embassy Bank Account Case* (1977) BVerfGE 46, 342; 65 ILR 146. There, the court relied upon a mere five foreign precedents to support its conclusion that the bank account held by an embassy was absolutely immune from measures of enforcement; a conclusion that was reached mainly by relying upon the purpose of diplomatic privileges and immunities, namely 'to

behind a certain act of a state in this field, ie in a more subjective sense. Although these two forms of teleology, which one could refer to as the *functionalist* and the *intentionalist* approach, are theoretically distinct from one another, in practice the differences between them often appear blurred. One reason for this imprecision seems to be the vagueness of the concept of *opinio juris*, also referred to as the 'subjective' or 'psychological' element in the formation of a rule of customary international law: The belief that certain behaviour is warranted by a legal duty. The elusiveness of this criterion has given ground to various interpretations of *opinio juris*, not to mention those authors[130] who attempted to dispose with it altogether. To take a few examples only from more recent scholarship, the approaches to the problem of *opinio juris* differ fundamentally:[131] some explain it as the requirement of consent of states to be bound by a certain rule,[132] a sort of revival of Anzilotti's classical *pactum tacitum* theory; others apply rational choice analyses to reshape *opinio juris* as the expectation that other states will react to a certain behaviour with cooperation or confrontation;[133] yet another recent author attempts to free customary law entirely from the state practice requirement and ground the *opinio juris* criterion on the belief of states in 'ethics'.[134] In terms of the history of ideas, these different approaches to the concept of purpose or intent in the formation and observance of law can each be traced to venerable historical antecedents, whether to Machiavellian realism, to the social contract doctrines of the Enlightenment, to Benthamite utilitarianism or to the Kantian concept of the 'purposeless' character of the rules of just action. Unfortunately, these theories, dealing extensively with the philosophical underpinnings of the

ensure the unimpeded functioning of the diplomatic mission … in the fulfilment of its duties' (BVerfGE 46, 342 at 397).

130 Such as Kelsen, who famously claimed that *opinio juris* is in fact only used as a disguise of the freedom of judges to decide which practices they select to formulate a rule of customary international law; see H Kelsen, 'Théorie du droit international coutumier' (1939) *Revue internationale de la théorie du droit* 253 (265): '[I]l faut renoncer à la preuve de l'existence de cet élément psychique parce que le preuve en est pratiquement irréalisable. Cela signifie que l'organe compétent à appliquer une règle du droit international coutumier est absolument *libre* de considérer le fait de la répétition prolongée et constante des mêmes actes extérieurs comme suffisant ou non pour constituer une coutume créatrice de droit.' (Emphasis original).

131 For a brief discussion of some recently published works on customary international law see A D'Amato, 'Review Essay: New Approaches to Customary International Law' (2011) 105 *American Journal of International Law* 163.

132 See eg Bradley & Gulati (n 3).

133 Most notably A Guzman, 'Saving Customary International Law' (2005) 27 *Michigan International Law Journal* 115; a more radical rational choice analysis of customary international law was undertaken by Goldsmith and Posner in *The Limits of International Law* (Oxford, Oxford University Press 2006) 23–43, who argued that states follow customary international 'law' merely when and where it serves their immediate (short-term) interests.

134 B Lepard, *Customary International Law. A New Theory with Practical Applications* (Cambridge, Cambridge University Press 2010).

concept of customary international law, each provide relatively little guidance for the work of the practitioner (especially the judge) trying to establish, in a concrete case, whether a certain rule covers a specific behaviour.[135]

This difficulty is felt particularly acutely by domestic judges: not only are they often less acquainted with the methodology of international law (to the extent one is of the opinion that such distinct international methodology exists) than their colleagues on international courts and tribunals; also, the nature of the disputes they have to decide and the domestic legal environment they operate in leaves them considerably less leeway to avoid pronouncing on contentious or unclear matters of law or to declare a *non liquet*. This latter problem is reflected in cases where domestic judges have to apply a rule that has been pronounced in rather abstract, general terms by an international court, whose ruling leaves – intentionally or not – the particular rule either narrowly limited or impractically ambiguous and vague.[136] Faced with such difficulty, the judges sometimes tend to equate the purpose of a rule of unwritten international law with the subjective intention of governments to follow it, and to discern this intention primarily from the utterances of their respective national government in this respect. This attitude, it seems, is not necessarily due to the courts' nationalism, but rather due to the profound confusion of the concept of 'purpose' with respect to rules of customary international law. In the following chapter, it is attempted to look more closely on the approaches of domestic and international courts with respect to this problem. Thereby it is hoped to delineate more clearly the role of purposive and teleological arguments in the concretisation and interpretation of unwritten international law.

Moreover, the present author believes that the concept of 'purpose' has even more far-reaching implications: it is, as shall be argued in Chapter VI, the inevitable precondition for any jurisprudence that transcends the narrow limits of a purely inductive approach. This will be demonstrated by reference to two additional concepts or steps in the development of legal reasoning, which, as shall be shown, each builds upon the basic concept of 'purpose': Analogical reasoning and the evolution of 'general principles of law'.

135 For this argument, and its demonstration by practical examples, see SD Walt, 'Why Jurisprudence doesn't matter for Customary International Law' *University of Virginia School of Law Public Law and Legal Theory Research Paper* 2012/36.

136 A good example in this respect is the ICJ's advisory opinion on the *Legality of the Threat or Use of Nuclear Weapons* (Advisory Opinion) [1996] ICJ Rep 226, that left domestic courts without clear guidance (at least in the perception of some national judges); cf eg the British case of *Hutchinson v Newbury Magistrates' Court* (2000) ILR 499 para 23.

V The Riddle of Purposive Interpretation

A. Conceptual and Terminological Issues

When speaking of 'purposive interpretation' or 'teleological construction', what one usually has in mind are constitutions, statutes, contracts, wills or international treaties – in short, *written* legal instruments. The reason for this intuitive connection seems to be twofold: First, there is a general uncertainty as to whether one can use the term 'interpretation' in any meaningful sense with respect to unwritten law. This question is of terminological rather than substantive significance, and there does not seem to be a compelling reason *not* to use this word to denote the intellectual process by which a solution for a particular case is derived from a pre-existing norm of international custom.[1] Indeed, as one of the few authors who explicitly deal with the interpretability of customary international law aptly puts it, 'the interpretation of customary rules [is] a logical corollary of their status *qua* rules'.[2]

The second reason, however, is more specific to *purposive* interpretation; more precisely, to the problem of the ambiguity that is inherent in the concept of 'purpose' with respect to legal rules. It stems from the fact that the 'purpose' or '*télos*' of legal rules is frequently equated with a similar, yet narrower concept, namely the concept of 'intent'.[3] And, as 'intent' is a subjective notion that refers to a psychological will or motivation, it can be applied to law only where the rule in question was *consciously* created by human beings (leaving aside the idea of divinely sanctioned or inspired rules), either by one single author (as in the case of a will or of a statute promulgated by an absolute monarch or dictator), or by a specific number of individuals who have coordinated their wills at a certain moment of time. A rule which possesses a

1 See eg C de Visscher, *Problèmes d'Interprétation Judiciaire en Droit International Public* (Paris, Pedone 1963) 1, who is strongly in favour of using the term 'interpretation', also with respect to customary international law; more sceptical in this respect is W Wengler, *Völkerrecht: Band I* (Berlin, Springer 1964) 360–1, who prefers the umbrella term 'Feststellung' (ascertainment).

2 P Merkouris, *Article 31(3)(c) VCLT and the Principle of Systemic Integration* (Leiden, Brill 2015) 289.

3 See on this confusion eg A Barak, *Purposive Interpretation in Law* (Princeton, Princeton University Press 2005) 86–7 with ample references.

'purpose' in that sense (of a subjective 'intent' behind it) is thus a tool to achieve a certain factual state of affairs at which its creator(s) aimed, and thus a *means* to an *end.* Obviously, rules which gradually emerged from practice – such as those of customary international law – cannot be said to have a purpose in that sense (of a subjective intent), any more than they have a discernible author.

Even in written law, it has been questioned whether it is at all possible to prove the subjective intent behind a statute made by a legislative assembly, and thus by a plurality of individuals, and it is still more doubtful whether there is anything like a common subjective intent or purpose behind a contract.[4] In international law, this problem is well-known in the context of the law of treaties. It presents itself as the need to discern the 'object and purpose' of a treaty, a concept to which the rule of interpretation codified in Art 31 (1) of the Vienna Convention on the Law of Treaties (VCLT) refers.[5] Apart from its prominent place in the general rule of interpretation, the term 'object and purpose' appears in seven other provisions of the Vienna Convention.[6] Given this huge significance of the concept in the law of treaties, it is not surprising that it has been extensively analysed and interpreted in scholarly literature.[7] Although the topic at hand is the role that purposive interpretation plays in the context of *unwritten* international law, it seems that some aspects of the debate about the parallel concept in the law of treaties might be helpful to understand the more general problem of how rules emanating from the collaboration of a

4 See for an overview of the discussion eg Barak (n 3) 129 et seq; specifically with respect to legislation: K Shepsle, 'Congress Is a "They", not an "It": Legislative Intent as Oxymoron' (1992) 12 *International Review of Law & Economics* 239; F Easterbrook, 'Statute's Domain' (1983) 50 *University of Chicago Law Review* 533 (547). With respect to contracts, see eg SC Damren, 'A "Meeting of the Minds" – The Greater Illusion' (1996) 15 *Law and Philosophy* 271.

5 See generally RK Gardiner, *Treaty Interpretation* (Oxford, OUP 2008) 189 et seq; R Kolb, *Interprétation et Création du Droit International* (Bruxelles, Bruylant 2006) 531 et seq.

6 Art 18 states that after having signed a treaty not yet in force, a state 'is obliged to refrain from acts which would defeat the object and purpose of the treaty.'; Articles 19 (c) and 20 (2) deal with the conditions of admissibility of certain reservations, depending on the respective treaty's 'object and purpose'; Articles 41 and 58 (1) contain similar provisions with respect to 'change' and 'suspension' of treaties; Art 33 (4) is a specific rule of interpretation, demanding that uncertainties arising from the use of more than one authentic language shall be resolved through recourse to a treaty's 'object and purpose'; finally, Art 60 (3) (b) defines the concept of 'material breach' as the 'violation of a provision essential for the accomplishment of the object or purpose of the treaty.'

7 See eg Kolb (n 5), Ch III and IV; Gardiner (n 5) 189–202; I Buffard/K Zemanek, 'The "Object and Purpose" of a Treaty: An Enigma?' (1998) 3 *Austrian Review of International and European Law* 311; V Crnić-Grotić, 'Object and Purpose of Treaties in the Vienna Convention on the Law of Treaties' (1997) 7 *Asian Yearbook of International Law* 141; J Klabbers, 'How to Defeat a Treaty's Object and Purpose Pending Entry into Force: Toward Manifest Intent' (2001) 34 *Vanderbilt Journal of Transnational Law* 283.

plurality of actors with potentially hugely divergent individual goals can be said to have a common 'purpose'.

Therefore, as a point of departure some of the most widely accepted characteristics of purposive interpretation with respect to treaties shall be briefly summarised. After that, it will become easier to delineate the aspects of the problem which relate specifically to unwritten international law, and it will be attempted to solve them by way of contrasting them with the law of treaties.

B. Purposive Interpretation of Treaties – General Aspects

In the interpretation of treaties, as well as in the general theory of interpretation with respect to *written* law, notions of a purposive or teleological method have long occupied a dominant position.[8] However, *teleology* is a rather broad umbrella term for a variety of concepts and arguments, and legal scholars have historically differed remarkably on its meaning (whereas practitioners have frequently confounded the various notions, and still occasionally use them indifferently and without further specification).

The most fundamental distinction to be observed in this respect is that between *subjective* and *objective* teleology, ie between the *historical, subjective will* of a legislator, drafter etc (*authorial intent*) and the *objective, dynamical 'will' or purpose* of the law itself. The first alternative is easier to comprehend, and comes closer to the natural understanding one has in mind when speaking about the *purpose* of a given text: When we receive an invoice letter, for example, its purpose is usually to inform us about the fact that the author expects us to pay a certain amount of money. More precisely, the subjective purpose or authorial intent is to motivate us to pay the sum that allegedly is due. This understanding of purpose is easily applicable to a statutory provision as well: Its author says 'you shall …' or 'you must not' and thereby intends to motivate us to do (or abstain from doing) something.

The conception of a subjective teleology or intent lying behind empirically observable phenomena is apparently a primordial component of human consciousness, as indicated by the prevalence of animistic thought in early societies, where even natural phenomena were regarded as emanations of personal wills.[9] Thus, it is not surprising that the interpretation of legal texts by

8 For a discussion of the development of these concepts in general legal theory see eg K Larenz, *Methodenlehre der Rechtswissenschaft* (Heidelberg, Springer, 6th ed 1991) 315 et seq.

9 On this anthropological fact and its significance for the development of legal thought see eg H Kelsen, *Society and Nature: A Sociological Inquiry* (Chicago, University of Chicago Press 1943) passim, in particular 21 et seq:

> 'One is in the habit of characterizing the animistic view as anthropomorphic; and one sees in this belief the tendency to personify, which is rightly considered one of the oldest elements of the human mind. It is not quite correct, however, to speak of "personification" in connection with primitive man, for the personification of an object presupposes that the object is first perceived as such, i.e., as a thing and not as a person, and that the thing is only later personified. Primitive

reference to the (alleged) intention or will of a – real or mythical – historical lawgiver is one of the oldest procedures of legal methodology.[10] As jurisprudence became more sophisticated, however, and as the understanding of mental processes grew from an early uncritical stage to a more reflected level of comprehension, it was increasingly realised that 'intent' or 'will' are by no means basic, monolithic concepts whose meaning is self-evident, but rather complex notions comprising a variety of connotations. Therefore, even if the goal of interpretation is described as discerning the subjective purpose of one single author only, it is by no means clear to what is actually referred: To the real, psychological will the author had in mind when drafting the text, to the will as it can be discerned from the outward expression given to it (ie the text), or to a reconstruction of the former from the latter, supplemented by imputations about what the author had actually in mind, but failed to express clearly.[11] In other words, even within the field of subjective interpretations (in the sense of interpretations the goal of which is the discovery of the subjective intent of the legislator) there exist several possible approaches, which differ with respect to the level of objectivity they admit.

In the field of treaty interpretation, historical development shows a certain move from a more subjectivist towards a more objectivist approach,[12] albeit the basic goal, the discovery of the parties' shared intentions, has remained unchanged.[13] The tendency towards a rather objectivist approach is apparent in the wording of Art 31 (1) VCLT, stating that '[a] treaty shall be interpreted in good faith in accordance with the ordinary meaning to be given to the terms of the treaty … in the light of its object and purpose'. Thus, 'object and purpose' are not to be considered as a separate, distinct means of interpretation, but rather as part of a comprehensive textual analysis.[14] This approach is consistent with the relegation of some extra-textual indications of the parties' intentions, most notably the *travaux préparatoires*, to the rank of supplementary means of interpretation under Art 32 VCLT.

It is not necessary in the context of this inquiry to delve deeply into the technicalities of treaty interpretation, and to reflect on the precise interrelation of the twin concepts of 'object and purpose' in Art 31 (1) VCLT, an issue that

man, it should be noted, comprehends reality immediately in the personal category.' (Ibid, at 23).

10 See Kolb (n 5) 606, who also provides extensive bibliographical references on that matter.

11 Ibid, 626–8, where Kolb discusses these and many other possible understandings of 'will' as an interpretative concept.

12 See ibid, 533 et seq, where Kolb compares the jurisprudence of the International Court of Justice with that of its predecessor, the Permanent Court of International Justice.

13 See U Linderfalk, *On the Interpretation of Treaties: The Modern International Law as Expressed in the 1969 Vienna Convention on the Law of Treaties* (Heidelberg, Springer 2007) 205.

14 Ibid, 203.

is still subject to considerable debate,[15] and has even been described as 'an enigma'.[16] It suffices to note that in the field of treaties, the underlying goal of interpretation is the discernment of the parties' shared intentions, and that the most reliable source for it is the text of the instrument itself, as it is supposed that the contracting parties carefully deliberated on their choice of words and intended them to be an authentic expression of the substantive compromise they have ultimately agreed upon, a common standard by which they intended to measure each other's actions in the case of future controversies arising on issues pertaining to the subject-matter regulated by the treaty. In the classical words of Charles de Visscher:

> Dans le traité, la sécurité garantie par la fidélité à la parole donnée est l'objectif des contractants. La fonction de l'interprétation est de donner pleine effectivité à cette exigence fondamentale, particulièrement impérieuse dans les rapports entre Etats. … La méthode dérive directement de la fonction ainsi comprise. C'est parce que les termes choisis par les Parties sont presque toujours l'expression la plus certaine de leur intention commune que l'interprétation par le texte a les pas sur toute autre méthode. Mieux que toute autre, elle incarne cette extériorité qui est la marque la plus tangible de l'élaboration juridique et qui, par ailleurs, reste la meilleure défense du traité contre les pressions qui, au cours du temps et à la faveur de transformations survenues dans le rapport des intérêts et des forces, viennent à s'exercer sur lui.[17]

These two main axioms, that the discovery of the parties' common intentions is the goal of treaty interpretation, and that the analysis of the text is the primary means to achieve it, were shared by a majority both in the International Law Commission, as reflected in Art 27 of its 1966 Draft Articles,[18], and on the subsequent diplomatic conference at Vienna in 1969, where the text of Art 31 (1) VCLT was finally adopted. The diverging views in legal literature and practice were concisely summarised in the commentary on Art 27–28 of the ILC's 1966 Final Draft:

15 Cf for a general overview Gardiner (n 5) 190 et seq; unsurprisingly, it seems that especially French scholars maintain that a distinction has to be made between the two concepts, in a manner analogous to the well-known distinction in French public law between '*but*' and '*acte*', cf eg A Favre, 'L'interprétation objectiviste des traités internationaux' (1960) 17 *Schweizerisches Jahrbuch für Internationales Recht* 75.
16 Buffard/Zemanek (n 7).
17 De Visscher (n 1) 10.
18 See (1966) ILC Yearbook vol 2, 177 (181): 'Article 27. General rule of interpretation (1.) A treaty shall be interpreted in good faith in accordance with the ordinary meaning to be given to the terms of the treaty in their context and in the light of its object and purpose.' The formulation of Art. 27 (1) of the 1966 ILC Draft was adopted without modification by the Diplomatic Conference at Vienna as Art 31 (1) VCLT.

> Some [jurists] place the main emphasis on the intentions of the parties and in consequence admit a liberal recourse to the *travaux préparatoires* and to other evidence of the intentions of the contracting States as means of interpretation. Some give great weight to the object and purpose of the treaty and are in consequence more ready, especially in the case of general multilateral treaties, to admit teleological interpretations of the text which go beyond, or even diverge from, the original intentions of the parties as expressed in the text. The majority, however, emphasizes the primacy of the text as the basis for the interpretation of a treaty, while at the same time giving a certain place to extrinsic evidence of the intentions of the parties and to the objects and purposes of the treaty as means of interpretation.[19]

The Commission further stated in its commentary on the Draft Articles that the text of a treaty 'must be presumed to be an authentic expression of the intentions of the parties'.[20] Following up on this basic premise, it later concluded that 'the starting point of interpretation is the elucidation of the meaning of the text, not an investigation *ab initio* into the intention of the parties',[21] an idea that was endorsed by a number of states in their comments on the draft, most notably Czechoslovakia, which even suggested an amendment to the proposed general rule of interpretation which would make it explicit that the text of a treaty is 'presumed to be the authentic expression of the intentions of the parties'.[22]

The formulation suggested by Czechoslovakia, even though it was not adopted, aptly (though perhaps inadvertently) describes the nature of the idea that the parties' intentions are reflected in the text of a treaty: In stating that 'it must be presumed', it becomes obvious that what is relevant is not the actual, psychological will of any party, but the parties' shared intentions as a fictional, or rather a *normative* concept, established by means of a legal presumption.[23] This is only the beginning of the problem, however, and the question remains how to fill this concept with meaning in a particular case. While the purely or predominantly subjectivist school of interpretation can at least attempt to come as closely to the actual, psychological intent of the parties concerned, in the case of treaties by ample reference to the preparatory work and other statements, the 'objectivised' approach described here sets the interpreter a more difficult task: To reconstruct[24] the goal of the contracting parties primarily

19 Ibid, 218 para 2.
20 Ibid, 40 para 11.
21 Ibid, 220 para 11.
22 For the comments made by the governments see D Rauschning (ed), *The Vienna Convention on the Law of Treaties: Travaux Préparatoires* (Frankfurt, Metzler 1978) 239 et seq.
23 For the centrality of presumptions to the concept of purposive interpretation see esp Barak (n 3) 90–1.
24 For a similar method in the field of statutory and constitutional interpretation, Richard Posner uses the apt term 'imaginative reconstruction'; see RA Posner, *The*

through recourse to the words in which they chose to lay it down. This is precisely the task the fulfilment of which Art 31 (1) VCLT demands when it speaks of the 'object and purpose' of a treaty, in the light of which its provisions have to be interpreted.

In practice, interpreters use a variety of approaches to ascertain the object and purpose of a treaty. Frequently, the preamble of a treaty contains hints of what the parties had in mind, although usually stated in a rather general and abstract manner. Also the ILC apparently assumed the preamble to be among the best indicators of a treaty's object and purpose.[25] Besides, a systematic view of several substantive provisions can be revealing as to an instrument's underlying purpose.

C. The Problem of Multiple Purposes

Large multilateral agreements, especially those establishing international organisations, frequently serve a number of different purposes, which are often expressly proclaimed at the inception of the treaty, such as in Art 2 UN Charter or in the first clause of the preamble to the WTO Agreement. As these multiple purposes can contradict each other facially, the interpreter who uses them as an argument to construe a certain provision of the treaty in question must carefully balance them, avoiding to overemphasise one at the expense of the others.[26] In fact, given that the reason why a treaty contains more than one purpose often may result from its nature as a compromise between two or more parties with interests that do not necessarily coincide, the process of balancing among different purposes can also imply the harmonisation of a plurality of potentially opposed interests, in which case this balancing is far more than a mere technical side-aspect of the process of interpretation, but rather the core issue of the controversy at hand.

In recent years the harmonisation of a plurality of purposes of a treaty has become an increasingly acute topic in the law of international investment

Problems of Jurisprudence (Cambridge/MA, Harvard University Press 1990) 270–3; see also Barak (n 3) 150.

25 ILC Yearbook (n 18) 41; see on this question Gardiner (n 5) 194 et seq, esp 194 n 162.

26 This was stated clearly with respect to the WTO Agreement by the WTO Appellate Body in the case *US Import Prohibition of Certain Shrimp and Shrimp Products* [1998] WT/DS58/AB/R, para 17: '[M]ost treaties have no single, undiluted object and purpose but rather a variety of different, and possibly conflicting, objects and purposes. This is certainly true of the *WTO Agreement*. Thus, while the first clause of the preamble to the *WTO Agreement* calls for the expansion of trade in goods and services, this same clause also recognizes that international trade and economic relations under the *WTO Agreement* should allow for "optimal use of the world's resources in accordance with the objective of sustainable development", and should seek "to protect and preserve the environment". The Panel in effect took a one-sided view of the object and purpose of the WTO Agreement …'

protection.[27] This is because the preambles of bilateral investment treaties (BITs), besides stating the treaty's goal as 'the protection of foreign investments', commonly mention a plurality of other objectives, which are either expected to result as a consequence of investment protection (such as 'to maximise the effective use of economic resources' and thereby 'to improve living standards'), or which are regarded by the parties as a necessary condition of the agreement (such as 'the protection of health, safety, and the environment, and the promotion of internationally guaranteed labour rights').[28] In balancing these different objectives, arbitration tribunals differ as to the weight given to them respectively. Whereas some, as the tribunal in the case of *SGS v Republic of Philippines*,[29] saw fit to resolve interpretative ambiguities in favour of the investor, others, such as the tribunal in the case of *Renta v Russian Federation*,[30] took a more cautious approach, noting that '[t]he long-term promotion of investment is likely to be better ensured by a well-balanced regime rather than by one which goes so far that it provokes a swing of the pendulum in the other direction'.[31]

D. The Method of 'Typical' (or Cross-Treaty) Interpretation

Another interpretative technique used not infrequently by arbitral tribunals to elucidate the parties' shared intentions is the so-called 'cross-treaty interpretation', ie the attempt to discern a 'typical' interpretation of certain phrases that are commonly used in BITs, or to draw inferences from the conspicuous absence in the treaty to be interpreted of provisions usually found in other comparable BITs.[32] This cross-treaty interpretation can appear in two forms:

The first is the use of BITs concluded by the contracting parties with other states in order to clarify the meaning of terms in the BIT under consideration. This approach operates under the assumption that when states use similar terms in different treaties, they intend them to have a similar meaning; in a

27 See eg AR Sureda, *Investment Treaty Arbitration: Judging under Uncertainty – Hersch Lauterpacht Memorial Lecture* (Cambridge, Cambridge University Press 2012) 26.

28 The examples are taken from the preamble to the *2004 Model BIT* of the United States Department of State, which serves (as the title indicates) as a 'model' for negotiating the Bilateral Investment Treaties of the US; document available at: <http://www.state.gov/documents/organization/117601.pdf> accessed 20 August 2017. Most BITs contain similar clauses, whether in their preambles or in their substantive provisions; cf Sureda (n 27) 26–7.

29 *Société Générale de Surveillance SA v Republic of the Philippines*, ICSID Case No ARB/02/6 (Decision on Objections to Jurisdiction) 29 January 2004, 8 ICSID Reports 518, para 116.

30 *Renta 4 S.VS.A et al v The Russian Federation*, SCC Case No Arb V079/2005 (Award on Preliminary Objections) 20 March 2009.

31 Ibid, para 55.

32 See generally on this technique in the practice of investment arbitration tribunals eg SW Schill, *The Multilateralization of International Investment Law* (Cambridge, Cambridge University Press 2009) 305–8.

manner of speaking, this method supplements the notion of the 'context' to be taken account of under Art 31 (1) VCLT to construe the terms of a treaty by including unrelated third-party agreements. As the tribunal in the case of *Plama v Bulgaria* put it, 'treaties between one of the Contracting Parties and third States may be taken into account for the purpose of clarifying the meaning of a treaty's text at the time it was entered into'.[33] This practice is not uncontroversial, for, as another tribunal in the *Aguas del Tunari* case explicitly noted, '[t]he practice of a state as regards the conclusion of BITs other than the particular BIT involved in a dispute is not of direct value to the task of interpretation under Article 31 of the Vienna Convention'.[34]

Despite these misgivings, some tribunals even use a second, more far-reaching approach, namely the recourse to wholly unrelated third-party treaties (sometimes not even BITs) as interpretative guidance. Thus, in the *Tokios Tokelés v Ukraine* case, the tribunal referred both to provisions of the US–Argentine BIT and the Energy Charter Treaty (ECT) in support of its interpretation of a Ukrainian–Lithuanian BIT.[35] Cross-treaty and the use of third-party agreements interpretation is not only seen in the construction of BITs, but also of multilateral treaties. Thus, in the case of *International Thunderbird Gaming v México*, a tribunal interpreted a provision of the North Atlantic Free Trade Agreement (NAFTA) through comparison with a more specific parallel provision of the ECT, of which neither of the NAFTA states was a member.[36]

In international investment law, the inclination of tribunals to engage in cross-treaty interpretation has been described as being part of a relatively novel tendency, as a deliberate attempt to turn a field which has hitherto been largely regulated by bilateral instruments (and for the most part still is), into a more coherent, quasi-multilateral system.[37] While this may very well be the intent of arbitral tribunals in the field of foreign investment protection, the technique of cross-treaty interpretation itself is neither novel, nor limited to international courts or tribunals. In fact, domestic courts in several subject areas have long used a method that could be described as 'typical' interpretation of international treaties.[38]

33 *Plama v Bulgaria* (Decision on Jurisdiction) 8 February 2005, para 195.

34 *Aguas del Tunari v Bolivia* (Decision on Jurisdiction) 21 October 2005, para 206; even in this case, however, the tribunal went on to state that '[t]he practice of a state as regards the negotiation of BITs may be helpful … in testing the assertions of parties as to the general policies of either Bolivia or the Netherlands [the contracting states of the treaty at hand] concerning BITs, and in testing assumptions a tribunal may make regarding BITs.'

35 *Tokios Tokelés v Ukraine* (Decision on Jurisdiction) 29 April 2009, paras 21 et seq.

36 *International Thunderbird Gaming v México* (Arbitral Award) 26 January 2006, paras 96 et seq.

37 This is the main argument of Schill (n 32) passim; cf, esp with respect to interpretation, ibid ch VII.

38 On this apt term and examples of its application, see A Bleckmann 'Zur Feststellung und Auslegung von Völkergewohnheitsrecht' (1977) 37 *Zeitschrift für ausländisches Öffenliches Recht und Völkerrecht* 504 (517).

Although this concept of 'typical' interpretation bears a certain resemblance to the process of ascertaining a rule of customary international law from concurring provisions in a plurality of treaties, and especially from large multilateral agreements, these two concepts should be kept apart analytically. For example, although there are numerous bilateral extradition treaties, often with similarly worded provisions, there is no general legal concept of extradition under customary international law,[39] and domestic legislative enactments do not recognise a general duty to extradite in the absence of reciprocal treaty obligations.[40] Nevertheless, domestic courts do use the method of 'typical' or cross-treaty interpretation, drawing on a comparative analysis of various other extradition treaties, eg to ascertain the meaning of commonly used concepts and provisions, such as 'specialty clauses',[41], the concept of 'political offences', or the meaning of the legal term 'prosecution'.[42]

A similar approach can be found in domestic case law regarding the type of bilateral agreements falling under the broad traditional category of 'Treaties of Friendship, Commerce and Establishment'.[43] A recent interesting example in this regard is the International Court of Justice's decision in the *Case Concerning Certain Questions of Mutual Assistance in Criminal Matters* of 2008,[44] in which the court, among other issues, was asked to interpret the 1977 'Treaty of Friendship and Cooperation' between Djibouti and France. Here, Djibouti had relied on a strongly teleological interpretation of the treaty in the light of the (alleged) overarching goal of the parties, stated in its Art 1 as 'to

39 See generally eg A Verdross/B Simma, *Universelles Völkerrecht* (Berlin, Duncker & Humblot 1982) paras 1230–32; the right of a state to decide on the extradition of individuals is, however, subject to the prohibition under general international human rights law against the extradition of individuals to states where they may face torture or other inhuman treatment. Another qualification derives from the developing rules on the obligation '*aut dedere aut judicare*', imposing a duty on states to either prosecute perpetrators of certain international crimes, or to extradite them for prosecution to another state upon the latter's request; the obligation '*aut dedere aut judicare*' is under consideration by the ILC since 2004; in 2012, the commission decided to establish an open-ended Working Group to further study this topic, see UN Doc A/68/10 (2013), paras 145–9.

40 See eg JF Rezek, 'Reciprocity as a Basis of Extradition' (1981) 52 *British Yearbook of International Law* 171.

41 See for example the decision of the German Federal Court of Appeals in Criminal Matters of 16 October 1971, reprinted in (1970) *Neue Juristische Wochenschrift* 335 (esp 336), where the court had to interpret the specialty clause in Art 18 of the Austro-German extradition treaty of 22 September 1958.

42 See eg the *British case of R v Governor of Pentonville Prison, Ex parte Sinclair* [1991] 64 (HL) 92; for several other examples taken from the case law of (primarily) British courts see S Fatima, *Using International Law in Domestic Courts* (Oxford, Hart 2005) 159 ff.

43 For several examples see A Bleckmann, 'Deutsche Rechtsprechung in völkerrechtlichen Fragen' (1972) 32 *Zeitschrift für ausländisches öffentliches Recht und Völkerrecht* 127 (127 et seqq).

44 *Case Concerning Certain Questions of Mutual Assistance in Criminal Matters (Djibouti v France)* [2008] ICJ Rep 177.

found the relations between their two countries on equality, mutual respect and peace'; a duty which, Djibouti asserted, France had violated, inter alia by 'attacking the dignity and honour of the Djiboutian Head of State'.[45] The court, citing its decisions in the *Nicaragua* and *Oil Platform* cases, rejected the assertion that legal duties extending beyond the subject-matter envisaged by that treaty could be derived from the general purpose of a treaty of friendship.[46] Older examples of 'typical interpretation of treaties' from the case law of the ICJ and its predecessor include the *Genocide* and *Wimbledon* cases.[47]

In the context of the inquiry undertaken here, which attempts to draw lessons from the concept of purposive interpretation in the context of treaties that are relevant to the parallel process in the field of unwritten international law, this method of 'typical interpretation of treaties', as it has just been described, is of great importance. In a manner of speaking, it provides a hinge connecting the two concepts. This is so because in 'typical interpretation', it becomes practically quite relevant what has above been stated in a more theoretical way: That even in the field of treaties, which are usually regarded as pure emanations of their contracting parties' shared *wills* or *intentions*, the concept of will or intent is a normative, not an actual psychological one.[48] Behind this seemingly commonplace insight – as seen above, the fictional character of the idea of a treaty or contract as a genuine 'meeting of minds' has long been recognised in legal theory[49] – lies a deeper and very important truth: The essentially dialectical nature of the 'will' of states in international law. This dialectic appears on every level or stage of the negotiation, drafting, conclusion and ratification of a treaty.

The dialectical process starts at the very outset of treaty negotiations, when governments 'make up their mind' as to the goals or aims that should be pursued by way of an international agreement; even these aims or motivations are not (purely) individual, psychological and arbitrary ones, but influenced by (and, in turn, themselves influencing) the factual and normative environment

45 Ibid, para 96.
46 Ibid, paras 104 et seq; the court held, however, that the treaty of friendship could be used as a general means aiding the interpretation of a later, more specific convention on cooperation in criminal matters.
47 See Bleckmann (n 38) 517.
48 This point was clearly seen by Erich Kaufmann in his treatise on the *clausula rebus sic stantibus*; see E Kaufmann, *Das Wesen des Völkerrechts und die Clausula Rebus Sic Stantibus: Studie zum Rechts-, Staats- und Vertragsbegriffe* (Tübingen, Mohr 1911) 85–6: 'Darum erhält auch jeder sogen. "Erfahrungsbegriff" durch seine Hineinstellung in den Zusammenhang einer Rechtsnorm einen rechtsnormativen Charakter, der freilich bei den typischen Fällen, an die der Normsetzer gedacht hat, latent bleiben wird, aber sofort in die Erscheinung treten muss, sobald der zu beurteilende Fall auch nur in etwas von diesem Typus abweicht. Alle Auslegung besteht in der sinngemäßen Ausgleichung dieser Diskrepanzen. Sie wird dadurch möglich, dass jedes tatsächlich Gewollte aus bestimmten normativen Gründen und Motiven gewollt ist. Das tatsächlich Gewollte "verstehen" wir daher erst, wenn wir wissen, aus welchen allgemeineren normativen Gesichtspunkten es gewollt ist …'
49 See the references provided above (n 4).

in which the state – itself a concoction of normative and factual elements[50] – is situated and operates within the web of its international relations. In other words, the – individual and collective – will of states is both formed by and forming the sociological substratum of the international society, and is shaped by the objectively existing (or subjectively perceived) necessities and exigencies of a particular situation.[51]

This dialectical interplay between will and objective factors continues during the negotiations, especially in the case of multilateral agreements, when groups of like-minded states (or those sharing common interests) form alliances and when the general and well-known rules of international conferences are to be observed.[52] The formulation of a treaty's text, then, also follows along the lines of rather traditional forms and usages of language ('treaty language'[53]), a process in which the motives and intentions of the parties are often specified and sometimes reconsidered. After a document has been agreed upon, the text is, especially in democratic countries where a treaty has to be submitted to the domestic legislature for ratification, subject to extensive public scrutiny.[54] The dialectic between will and objective factors is again visible where reservations to provisions of a treaty are stipulated during ratification, as those are subject to normative restrictions under international law, as well as being dependent on explicit acceptance or implicit tolerance by the other contracting parties.

But even after a treaty's entry into force, this continuous interplay between subjective and objective elements, between will and necessity, remains, as Art 31 (3) VCLT mentions among the factors to be taken into account in the process of treaty interpretation 'any subsequent agreement between the parties

50 At least under the traditional doctrine, which is restated, inter alia, in Art I of the Montevideo Convention (Convention on Rights and Duties of States adopted by the Seventh International Conference of American States, 26 December 1933, 165 LNTS 19): 'The State as a person of international law should possess the following qualifications: (a) a permanent population; (b) a defined territory; (c) government; and (d) capacity to enter into relations with the other States.' Although each of these elements contains a strong factual, i.e. empirically observable component in itself, it is their interconnectedness by which the state as a unified *legal* entity becomes conceivable; this connection, however, can only be conceptualised as a normative bound. For a different, purely normative view of a state as being the embodiment of its legal order see eg H Kelsen, *General Theory of Law and State* (Cambridge/MA, Harvard University Press) passim, esp 181 et seq.

51 For the argument that the concept of 'national interests' of a state is a social construct which can develop over time through a learning process in the interactions with other states, see M Finnemore, *National Interests in International Society* (Ithaca, Cornell University Press 1996).

52 On the formal and informal rules of international conference diplomacy, see eg J Kaufmann, *Conference Diplomacy: An Introductory Analysis* (Leiden, Martinus Nijhoff 1988).

53 For an analysis of this concept and its impact on the process of treaty interpretation, see eg KJ Vandevelde, 'Treaty Interpretation: A Negotiator's Perspective' (1988) 21 *Vanderbilt Journal of Transnational Law* 281 (esp 307–10).

54 See RD Putnam, 'Diplomacy and Domestic Politics: The Logic of Two-Level Games' (1988) 42 *International Organization* 427.

regarding the interpretation of the treaty or the application of its provisions', and 'any subsequent practice in the application of the treaty which establishes the agreement of the parties regarding its interpretation'.

These complex, intricately connected yet distinct twin concepts of 'subsequent agreement' and 'subsequent practice' are being studied in a thorough, comprehensive manner in the framework of a project conducted by the ILC.[55] The present inquiry is not the appropriate place to portray in any detail the convoluted work carried out in this context, which has culminated in four reports by the Special Rapporteur, Georg Nolte, as well as in a set of Draft Conclusions with commentary; nor can the concurring academic controversies, eg about the degree of unanimity of practice required to be taken into account under Article 31 (3) VCLT, be discussed here.[56] In the context of the present brief analysis, whose principal goal is to determine which lessons can be drawn from purposive interpretation in the law of treaties for unwritten international law, it may suffice to note that, according to the Special Rapporteur's First Report of 2013, '[s]ubsequent agreements and subsequent practice, on the one hand, and the object and purpose of a treaty, on the other, can be closely interrelated'.[57] Citing several international cases as well as scholarly literature, he goes on to note that '… subsequent conduct of the parties is sometimes used for specifying the object and purpose of the treaty in the first place'.[58] In other words, the object and purpose of a treaty is not necessarily a static one, but can also evolve, dynamically adapting to the needs and experiences of the parties during their mutual relationship governed by the treaty.

E. The Principle of Systemic Integration or the 'Concentric Encirclement' of Purpose

One other concept pertaining to treaty interpretation also merits at least a brief mention, before the insights gained in the course of the preceding inquiry can be tested as to their applicability and usefulness to the interpretation of unwritten rules of international law. This concept is the so-called principle of 'systemic integration',[59] enshrined in Art 31 (3) (c) VCLT. Under this provision, 'there shall be taken into account, together with the context … any

55 The 'Study Group on Treaties over time' was established by the ILC in its 2009 session and is chaired by Georg Nolte as Special Rapporteur. For a (preliminary) overview of the work conducted in this context see G Nolte, 'Introduction' in id (ed), *Treaties and Subsequent Practice* (Oxford, Oxford University Press 2013) 1.

56 For some of these controversies see the contributions to the edited volume cited above (n 55); on the debate about consensualism compare esp the contributions by Luigi Crema (ibid, 13) and James Crawford (ibid, 29).

57 ILC, 'First Report on Subsequent Agreement and Subsequent Practice in Relation to Treaty Interpretation by Georg Nolte' (19 March 2013) UN Doc A/CN.4/660, para 51.

58 Ibid.

59 For a good general overview see eg C McLachlan, 'The Principle of Systemic Integration and Article 31(3)(c) of the Vienna Convention' (2005) 54

relevant rules of international law applicable in the relations between the parties'. While the method of 'typical' interpretation described above asks what the usual, characteristic intention of the parties with respect to a specific kind of agreement is, 'systemic integration' broadens the scope of inquiry, taking into account other treaties of a different nature and subject-matter, rules of customary international law and general principles. The idea behind it is, simply enough, that the international legal order is not an incoherent muddle of unrelated obligations, but a seamless web in which the content of bilateral and multilateral treaties is harmonised with obligations whose observance the parties owe to each other under general international law.

In fact, this underlying idea is already implied in the definition of 'treaty' in Art 2 (1) (a) VCLT as 'an international agreement … *governed by international law* … [italics added]'. As such it must, in the words of Arnold McNair, be 'applied and interpreted against the background of the general principles of international law'.[60] The aim of this process is to achieve what could be described as 'normative harmony'[61] within a legal system. With respect to the interpretation of domestic law, this concept was aptly characterised in a decision by the High Court of Israel:

> A piece of legislation does not stand alone. It constitutes part of the legislative alignment. It integrates into it, aspiring to legislative harmony. … He who interprets one statute interprets all statutes. The lone statute integrates as a tool into the legislative alignment. The legislative alignment as a whole influences the legislative purpose of a single statute. A prior statute influences the purpose of a later statute. A later statute influences the purpose of a prior statute.[62]

One might think that such a sweeping plea for normative harmonisation may be justified only (if at all) in the context of national legal systems, which possess a central legislative authority, and not in international law, where rule-creation, -application and -enforcement are exercised by the very subjects of the legal order, ie the states, individually or collectively.[63] However, it should not be forgotten that even in domestic legal systems, the idea of a uniform, 'quasi-immortal' legislator, whose will is ever-consistent and manifests itself in even

International and Comparative Law Quarterly 279; perhaps the most thorough study on the subject is that by Merkouris (n 2).

60 See A McNair, *The Law of Treaties* (Oxford, Oxford University Press 1961) 466.

61 For this apt term see Barak (n 3) 160.

62 *Efrat v Director of Population Registration at the Interior Ministry*, HC 693/91, 47(1) PD 749,765; cited in Barak (n 3) 160.

63 For a moderately sceptical account of the use of systemic integration in the application of international law by domestic courts see J d'Aspremont, 'The Systemic Integration of International Law by Domestic Courts: Domestic Judges as Architects of the Consistency of the International Legal Order' in OK Fauchald/A Nollkaemper (eds), *The Practice of International and National Courts and the (De-)Fragmentation of International Law* (Oxford, Hart 2012) 141 (esp 164–5).

the most insignificant legislative utterance, is evidently a fiction. Thus, the idea that every piece of legislation is thought to be consistent and in harmony with every other, despite the time that has intervened and the personal changes in the legislative body, is but a normative presumption with no necessary correlation to any psychological fact.

It is true that in the international legal order it is much more difficult to discern in the diversity of positive norms anything like a single, unified 'will of the law', even as a hypothetical construct. However, since we saw above that the process in which a treaty is designed is a dialectical one, in which the intentions of the negotiating parties are constantly subjected to mutual realignment and modification, and as the very instrument of treaty as a source of law is 'governed by international law', it is reasonable to impute the contracting states' intentions as being not only consistent, but in harmony with their obligations under other rules of (general or specific) international law. This point was aptly formulated by Max Huber in his response to Hersch Lauterpacht's report to the Institut de Droit International on treaty interpretation. After having said that '[o]n ne peut pas, sauf en vertu d'une clause spécifique, leur [the states] imposer une volonté fictive', he stated:

> Il faut donc chercher la volonté des parties dans le texte conventionnel, d'abord dans les clauses relatives à la contestation, ensuite dans l'ensemble de la convention, ensuite dans le droit international général, et enfin dans les principes généraux de droit reconnus par les nations civilisées. C'est par cet encerclement concentrique que le juge arrivera dans beaucoup de cas à établir la volonté présomptive des parties 'conformément aux exigences fondamentales de la plénitude du droit et la justice internationale', ainsi que le rapporteur formule admirablement la tâche du juge.[64]

This method of 'concentric encirclement' to which Huber alludes, without explicitly justifying it doctrinally, can derive its legitimacy from an idea that was developed above in theory: That the 'will' or 'intent' of the states is not something static and isolated, but a dialectical unity of subjective and objective elements, of psychological facts and normative precepts, of limited original foresight that is supplemented by subsequent practical experience.

F. Barak's Theory of Purposive Interpretation as a Bridge from Written to Unwritten Law

A similar concept of purposive interpretation was described, albeit in the context of domestic law, by the former Chief Justice of Israel, Aharon Barak, in his illuminating study on *Purposive Interpretation in Law*.[65] In this work, Barak

64 The statement, made on the 1952 session of the IDI in Siena, is reported in (1952-I) 44 *Annuaire de l'Institut de Droit International* 200–1.

65 See Barak (n 3).

advocates the use of a concept he refers to as 'ultimate purpose',[66] a notion that transcends and supersedes the unmitigated antagonism between subjective and objective purpose, as the guiding principle of interpretation.

Barak calls this quest for the ultimate purpose 'the decisive stage of the interpretative process' and claims it to be 'the stage that distinguishes purposive interpretation from other systems of interpretation'.[67] The process to be carried out, he says, is one of integration: The interpreter takes into account, on the one hand, all the information he or she can possibly obtain concerning the subjective intention(s) of the author(s), and considers, on the other hand, various elements pertaining to the objective purpose, eg the general social goal the statute in question serves (especially if that is not discernible from the elements of subjective purpose, such as legislative history, etc), how a 'reasonable' author would have attempted to reach this goal, or, most importantly, how the purpose of the statute to be interpreted fits within the context of the general purposes and values of the legal system in which it is designed to operate.

Having thus assembled all (or as much as possible) of the relevant 'data constituting the ultimate purpose',[68] the most difficult part of the process ensues, the 'synthesis and integration'. Here, the different presumptions concerning both subjective and objective purpose(s) are weighed, balanced and (if possible) reconciled, such as the presumption that the text is the authentic expression of subjective intent, or that the legislator's intent was to formulate a statute in harmony with other rules and principles of the legal system. It is also on the level of ultimate purpose that, according to Barak, a plurality of subjective and objective purposes can be reconciled, as the interpreter seeks to discern underlying, more general purposes, often not even mentioned in the text, but derived from the basic values of the system. The presumption here is that the text's authors sought to realise their goals in a manner consistent with these values, or even that their implicit motive for creating the text in question was to concretise these values in a specific field.[69]

Interestingly for the topic at hand, Barak stresses the need to be aware of the specific nature and the particular features of different kinds of legal texts when determining their ultimate purpose. Thus, he notes that

> [e]very kind of text has its own character and role; every kind of text creates its own expectations … Purposive interpretation applies to the interpretation of all legal texts, but it treats each type of text specifically, according to its nature, allowing texts to develop and express themselves. It is the concept of purpose that facilitates this development and expression. Purpose is a normative concept, shaped by the given legal system, and it extends to both subjective and objective purpose. In the ultimate

66 Ibid, 182 et seq.
67 Ibid, 182.
68 See ibid, 182–3.
69 Ibid, 183.

> formulation of this concept ('ultimate purpose'), an interpreter takes the kind of text into account, ensuring the consistent application of the system of interpretation and the interpretive viewpoint to all texts, while expressing the individuality of each kind of text and any special problems it may pose.[70]

Specifically, Barak discusses four different types of legal texts: Wills, contracts, statutes and constitutions.[71] Although the ultimate purposes of all these instruments comprise the same two components, namely a subjective and an objective element, the proportion in which the two elements are mixed varies: In the interpretation of a will, the subjective intent – the author's plan for the division of his or her property – is the 'north star' of interpretation, being supplemented by objective factors only if it is unclear or if circumstances arise which the author had not foreseen.

Contracts are positioned on the next higher level of objectivity: The subjective element, the shared intentions of the parties, still dominates, but, as their agreement may not always extend to a specific question, and as contracts are more likely than wills to affect the expectations of third parties worthy of protection, objective elements play a more significant role here, for example considerations of what the intentions of 'reasonable' parties would have been and how the contracting parties' intentions fit within the general social values of the legal system, in which the contract is embedded.

In the case of a statute, the interplay between subjective and objective elements of purpose (or interpretative 'presumptions', as Barak calls them) is more complex, as it requires the interpreter to balance the competing aspects of the democratic principle of legislative supremacy on the one hand, and the need to preserve the integrity of 'the system's fundamental values, including human rights' on the other.

Finally, in the ultimate purpose of a constitution, the objective component dominates: Although the intentions of the 'founding fathers', the 'original intent', plays a significant part in providing historical context to the document's provisions, the decisive consideration is that it is meant to provide a permanent foundation for the life of a society, a principal cornerstone based on fundamental values and principles, shaped by the experience of generations, uniting the individuals living in it and transcending the currents of contemporary political struggles. According to Barak, this nature of a constitution as a permanent, vital basis of community life requires it to let the objective elements prevail in its interpretation, ensuring the continued effectivity of its functioning.

To be sure, Barak's highly original and elaborate theory of purposive interpretation, which cannot possibly be presented here in adequate detail, is not on its face applicable to international law, as it does not address the question of

70 Ibid, 185.
71 On this and the following ibid, 185 et seq.

purposive interpretation of treaties, let alone unwritten rules of international law. However, there are some very interesting aspects in it which provide a theoretical background to the practices described above with respect to treaty interpretation, and may provide a bridge to understanding the possible meaning of the concept of purposive interpretation with respect to unwritten rules of international law. Of particular importance in this regard seems to be the insight that purposive interpretation can neither be conceptualised as purely subjective, nor purely objective, but comprises a dialectical interplay between subjective and objective factors. It is this insight that provides the theoretical justification for some of the phenomena described above, like typical interpretation or the principle of systemic integration. Also of high significance is Barak's insistence on the difference among various types of legal rules in the degree of objective influence on the process of purposive interpretation. Having this admonition in mind, it now becomes possible to analyse the meaning of the concept of purposive interpretation with respect to rules of customary international law.

G. The Concept of 'Purpose' in Customary International Law

In the preceding chapters, the use of the term 'customary international law' has frequently been supplanted by the broader umbrella term of 'unwritten international law'. This term seemed more appropriate, given the phenomenological nature of the inquiry undertaken here and the fact that one of the aims of the present study is to contribute to overcoming the 'pigeonholing' of traditional sources doctrine,[72] and to show that from the practical point of view of rule-application and -interpretation, the most important divide is that between 'written' and 'unwritten' rules of international law. This is so not only because of the obvious practical difference between applying textual and non-textual rules (in fact, the concept of 'unwritten international law', as described above, comprises rules that have been or could be put in writing as well), but because of the fundamental difference between rules that have been deliberately planned and those that have arisen spontaneously, as a 'product of human action, but not of human design'.

However, these statements should not be misunderstood as denigrating the established doctrine of the sources of international law in general, or the limited consensus that exists among academics and practitioners on the definition of customary international law, represented more or less accurately in the

72 For a similar point see A Bleckmann, *Die Funktionen der Lehre im Völkerrecht: Materialien zu einer Allgemeinen Methoden- und Völkerrechtslehre* (Heidelberg, CF Müller 1981), who demands 'Überwindung des "Kästchendenkens" in der völkerrechtlichen Rechtsquellenlehre' in the interest of creating a more viable methodology of international law; see also M Bos, *Methodology of International Law* (Amsterdam, North-Holland 1984), who altogether avoids the term 'sources' of international law, preferring to speak of 'recognized manifestations of international law'.

formulation laid down in Art 38 (1) (b) of the Statute of the International Court of Justice: '[I]nternational custom, as evidence of a general practice accepted as law'. Although this definition has been rightfully criticised as being somewhat unclear – it would perhaps be more accurate to say that a general practice is evidence of an international custom than the other way around[73] – it is not in any significant way inconsistent with or even contradictory to the view that has been advocated above in the more theoretically oriented chapters of this study, namely that many rules of customary international law are not the product of the will of states or even of their deliberate planning, but that they are rather forming part of a spontaneous order of human action, an order that developed and constantly develops further through a process of social evolution; an order, in short, that is not *made* but *grown*. This understanding is also fundamental to the practical question of how purposive interpretation with respect to customary international law can be conceptualised; therefore, it seems merited to add a few qualifying remarks on its practical implications and its relation to traditional sources doctrine before continuing with the analysis of the concept of purposive interpretation.

The aspect in which the view presented here deviates from the 'mainstream' conception of customary international law pertains to the fundamental question of its nature, not necessarily to the elements required for its proof.[74] It appears, however, that many authors writing on customary international law do not clearly separate conceptually the questions of *what it is* and *how it is discerned*. This imprecision is often disguised terminologically, as the two elements of practice (or 'usage', 'consuetudo'…) and *opinio juris* are referred to somewhat apodictically as 'constitutive' elements of customary international law, so that the problem is reduced to determining their proportional weight and their mutual interrelation.[75]

73 This point of criticism has been stated by a large number of authors; see eg J Makowski, *Podrecznik prawa miedzynarodowego* (Warszaw, Ksiazka 1948) 12; M Sørensen, *Les sources du droit international* (Copenhagen, Einar Munksgaard 1946) 84; C Rousseau, *Principes généraux du droit international public I* (Paris, Sirey 1944) 825; K Wolfke, *Custom in Present International Law* (Dordrecht, Martinus Nijhoff, 2nd ed 1993) 5–7.

74 It should be noted, however, that present international law scholarship often declines to answer the basic question of whether or not customary international law is a deliberate product of the states' shared wills. The theory that customary international law derives its obligatory nature from some sort of 'pactum tacitum', though apparently still held by not an inconsiderable number of scholars, is hardly advocated today as clearly as it was by Anzilotti; see eg D Anzilotti, *Völkerrecht, Bd I: Allgemeine Lehren* (Berlin/Leipzig, de Gruyter 1929) 53 et seq; a similar view was also held in the socialist doctrine of the sources of international law; see the representative example of GM Danilenko, 'The Theory of International Customary Law' (1988) 31 *German Yearbook of International Law* 14.

75 See out of many other examples eg A Roberts, 'Traditional and Modern Approaches to Customary International Law: A Reconciliation' (2001) 95 *American Journal of International Law* 757.

The distinction between 'modern' custom, derived predominantly if not exclusively from *opinio juris*, and 'traditional' custom, requiring the proof of a significant amount of actual state practice, is situated in this context.[76] The problem with these attempts to frame the jurisprudential issues pertaining to customary international law in terms of the proper relationship between practice and *opinio* is that they often operate under the assumption that it is possible to develop a method of ascertaining customary international law without engaging in the controversial and seemingly rather unproductive discussion of what actually is customary international law, and especially which role (if any) the consent of states to be bound by it plays in its formation. In the words of Gerald Postema, 'the additive conception [of customary international law, ie the view that it consists of practice and *opinio juris*] increasingly appears to be a practical test for international custom without any theoretical foundation'.[77] He added that the 'modern' conception of customary international law 'is no more firmly rooted theoretically than the additive analysis'.[78]

This is not the appropriate place to evaluate all the theoretical approaches to customary international law in current scholarship, or to criticise their shortcomings. Rather, it shall be pointed out that the notion of customary international law as the rules formative of a spontaneous order of human actions is not only compatible with, but that it also provides a more solid theoretical background to the well-established doctrine of the two basic elements of international custom, which were paradigmatically expressed in the ICJ's decision in the *Continental Shelf (Libya v Malta)* case as follows: 'It is of course axiomatic that the material of customary international law is to be looked for primarily in the actual practice and *opinio juris* of States ....'[79] In fact, as an expression of the method by which to discover the rules guiding the states' behaviour within the complex web of international relations, conceived of as a spontaneous order, this statement, if understood correctly, seems quite appropriate. To justify this assertion, and to explore its practical consequences, it is required now to apply the theoretical understanding of unwritten international law developed in the first chapters of the present study to the problem of ascertaining and interpreting customary international law, and in particular to the method of purposive interpretation.

Although Hayek did not spell out the implications of his theory of law as a spontaneous order for the understanding of international law, there are other, and for most practical purposes similar, approaches which provide further guidance. In particular the so-called *institutional* theories of law, such as those

76 See ibid.

77 GJ Postema, 'Custom in International Law as Normative Practice' in A Perreau-Saussine/JB Murphy (eds), *The Nature of Customary Law: Legal, Historical and Philosophical Perspectives* (Cambridge, Cambridge University Press 2007) 279 (280).

78 Ibid, 281.

79 [1985] ICJ Rep 13, para 27.

developed by Maurice Hauriou[80] in France and Santi Romano[81] in Italy, and such as the 'concrete-order thinking' in the later works of Carl Schmitt[82] come to mind here. Despite their subtle – and not so subtle – differences in detail, what all these theories have in common is their intention to transcend the seemingly irreconcilable positivist antinomies between fact and norm, between subjective will and objective law. They attempt to solve this self-imposed task by formulating a redefinition of the very concept of *law*: Not a mere collection of norms or of subjective rights and corresponding duties was what they understood to be the essence of law, but first and foremost an *institution*, or an *order*, in other words: the sum of interpersonal relationships, the way in which society as a whole is ordered and organised. In the words of Carl Schmitt:

> For concrete-order thinking, 'order' is also juristically not primarily 'rule' or a summation of rules, but conversely, rule is only a component and a medium of order. Norm or rule thinking is accordingly a more limited and indeed a more derivative part of the whole and complete jurisprudential purpose and application.[83]

The institutional or concrete-order based theories of law of the early 20th century, like those of Hauriou, Romano or Schmitt, are not as sophisticated or comprehensive as Hayek's theory of law as a spontaneous order. In particular, they do not address in detail the fundamental point of how the orders or institutions that they base their legal theories on came into being, or what the precise functional relationship between law as an order or institution and particular legal rules is. It should also not be forgotten that Carl Schmitt's institutional or concrete-order thinking was designed to support the National-Socialist deconstruction of the Weimar *Rechtsstaat* with its liberal legalism.[84] However, as far as the general insight that a legal order is not equivalent to a

80 See esp his two main works on public law: M Hauriou, *Principes de droit public* (Paris, Sirey 1910); id, *Précis élémentaire de droit constitutionnel* (Paris, Sirey 1925). In an article published in English in the *Harvard Law Review*, Hauriou summarised the main point of his theory thus: 'The fundamental basis of public law is not contract nor the rule of law nor statute; it is not even directly the state. The real basis is the institution, and the state attains its real form only on becoming a corporate institution.... It is within the institution by the phenomenon of custom that new governmental law is transformed into an established law imposed upon government as a constitutional statute, but to a statute to the formation of which it has itself contributed. We thus obtain our fundamental equation. A constitution involves an institution, and an institution involves the submission of sovereignty to law by objective means.' Quoted from M Hauriou, 'An Interpretation of the Principles of Public Law' (1918) 31 *Harvard Law Review* 813 (813–14).

81 See esp his *L'ordinamento giuridico* (Pisa, Mariotti 1918).

82 C Schmitt, *Über die drei Arten des rechtswissenschaftlichen Denkens* (Berlin, Duncker & Humblot 1935); English translation by JW Bendersky, *On the Three Types of Juristic Thought* (Westport/CT, Praeger 2004).

83 Ibid, 48.

84 See the introduction by JW Bendersky to his translation of Schmitt's work (n 82).

more or less arbitrarily formulated collection of positive norms, in the sense of legislative enactments, is concerned, the institutional legal theorists laid a very important intellectual foundation on which later thinkers, like Hayek, could build.[85]

Of particular interest in the context of customary international law is the work of Santi Romano, as he was the only of the three legal institutionalists mentioned above to apply his legal theory to the doctrine of the sources of international law. According to the view developed by Romano in his *L'ordinamento giuridico*, the international legal order is an institution in the sense of being 'the immanent order of the community of states'.[86] Although he admitted that the international community as such has no legal personality, he rejected the view that international law is but the sum of the positive rules agreed upon by the states, or, as he polemically described it, 'the view that regards international law as a shroud of Penelope that is woven anew with every new agreement'.[87] In language that seems to anticipate Hayek's legal theory, he notes that 'the existence of a community of states necessarily presupposes a legal order by which it is constituted', and argues that even the alleged principle – whose existence he disputes – 'according to which individual rules of international law … can be created only by the will of the members of the community of states and are binding only on those members who have agreed upon them is a *legal* principle'.[88] Thus, he concluded that there must necessarily be a legal order that predates particular agreements between particular states. This order, the community of states, he referred to as an 'institution' (*istituzione*).

In his later work *Corso di Diritto Internazionale*,[89] Romano developed the consequences of his theory of international law for the doctrine of sources. Concerning customary international law, he began by acknowledging the correctness of the traditional view according to which its recognition requires the proof of two elements, namely practice and *opinio*.[90] He stressed, however, the need for a correct understanding of these two concepts, and of the way in which they are embedded in the context of international relations. In

85 Hayek himself, however, did not acknowledge any intellectual debt to the 'institutionalists'; he did not cite Hauriou and Romano and dismissed the Schmittian 'concrete-order thinking' for its anti-liberal bias, without recognising that Schmitt's approach was in many respects fundamentally similar to his own; see eg FA Hayek, *Law, Legislation and Liberty* (London, Routledge, reissue 2013) 68. Other scholars, however, did notice these similarities, see esp FR Christi, 'Hayek and Schmitt on the Rule of Law' (1984) 17 *Canadian Journal of Political Science* 521; see generally also the very critical account by WE Scheuermann, 'The Unholy Alliance of Carl Schmitt and Friedrich A. Hayek' (1997) 4 *Constellations* 172.

86 See on this and the following Romano (n 81) § 17.

87 Ibid.

88 Romano (n 81), § 17 (emphasis original).

89 S Romano, *Corso di Diritto Internazionale* (Padova, Milani 1926).

90 Ibid, 28 et seq.

particular, he emphasised that the element of *opinio juris* could not be conceived of as being an emanation of the states' will:

> Le consuetudini non sono mai un vero e proprio 'ius voluntarium', e se implicano un accordo – si direbbe meno equivocamente una concordanza o coincidenza – ciò non vuol dire che siano un accordo di volontà. Esse hanno sovente un'origine quasi incosciente e quindi involontaria, e il loro valore deriva non dal fatto che si è avuta l'intenzione di costituirle, ma dalla convenzione che sia obbligatorio osservarle, e la convinzione non è atto di volontà ma qualche cosa che domina e vincola la volontà.[91]

This statement relates to what is perhaps *the* most fundamental question pertaining to the rules of customary international law, namely whether there is a requirement of consent by the states to be bound in order for them to arise. This question is relevant not only to determine whether a rule of customary international law has emerged, but also for the purposive interpretation of a rule already recognised: If one regards customary international law as a form of 'ius voluntarium', be it in the traditional sense of a genuine 'pactum tacitum' or in the more modern form of a requirement of 'inferred consent',[92], one would logically tend towards a more subjective approach to its purposive interpretation, similar to that described above for treaties; whereas, if one believes that customary international law is an objective form of law that develops through the states' actions, but is not the product of their deliberate design, one would consequently tend towards a more objective notion of purposive interpretation with respect to it. The problem here is, however, that this distinction is not always clearly observed either by theorists or practitioners, and that even authors who declare consent to be the basis of international law[93] do not follow up on this premise with the same consistency as, for example, Anzilotti with his theory of the 'pactum tacitum'.[94]. Thus, while they generally acknowledge the

91 Ibid, 29; in the present author's English translation: 'The customs are no true and proper "ius voluntarium", and if they imply an agreement – or, to say it less equivocally, a correspondence or coincidence – one cannot say that it is an agreement of will[s]. They rather have developed from a quasi-unconscious and therefore involuntary origin, and their value derives not from the intention to create them, but from the conviction that it is obligatory to observe them, and this conviction is not an act of will, but something that dominates and compels the will.'

92 See eg M Byers, *Custom, Power and the Power of Rules: International Relations and Customary International Law* (Cambridge, Cambridge University Press 1999) 142–6; ME Villiger, *Customary International Law and Treaties* (Leiden, Martinus Nijhoff 1985) 18–22, who also speaks of a requirement of 'qualified silence' in this respect (ibid, 19).

93 See eg A Aust, *Handbook of International Law* (Cambridge, Cambridge University Press 2005) 4; I Brownlie, *Principles of Public International Law* (Oxford, Oxford University Press, 6th ed 1995) 4.

94 This theory was later adopted in the official international law doctrine of the Soviet Union and other Socialist states; see eg Danilenko (n 74).

existence of the legal concept of a 'persistent objector', meaning that a state which protests against a growing custom during the process of its emergence and is consequently believed not to be bound by it, for the most part they do not draw the logical conclusion of this contractual or consent-based framework, namely that states can also withdraw their consent to be bound by a rule of customary international law once established, just as they can, under certain circumstances, terminate their written international agreements.[95] Also, the generally held view rejects the idea that objections against rules of customary international law can be successfully raised after their emergence is completed, and denies the so called 'subsequent objector'[96] doctrine, even in the case of new states which had no chance to object in due time during the formation of the rule.[97] If one follows a contractual or consent-based approach to international custom, it is indeed 'not obvious why it should be easier to exit from treaties than from customary international law', as Curtis Bradley and Mitu Gulati aptly pointed out.[98] But, as Hugh Thirlway recently observed, 'there is little state practice to support it [the theory of persistent objector], and if it exists, it is itself a rule of customary law established by practice …'.[99] Perhaps, as has been suggested by some, the – relatively rare – instances where a so-called 'persistent objector' protested successfully against the emergence of a rule may better be explained as processes of the development of a regional custom[100], a 'community of practice' in which the objecting state chose not to partake.

95 For a recent criticism of the perceived inconsistency of the predominant view in this respect see eg CA Bradley/M Gulati, 'Withdrawing from International Custom' (2010) 120 *Yale Law Journal* 202; for a general critique of the 'persistent objector doctrine', based on a thorough review of international case law, see RF Unger, *Völkergewohnheitsrecht – objektives Recht oder Geflecht bilateraler Beziehungen. Seine Bedeutung für einen 'persistent objector'* (München, tuduv Verlagsgesellschaft 1978) passim, in particular 66 et seq.

96 On this concept see eg Villiger (n 92) 19 et seq, who denies the possibility of subsequent objection as a means by which a state could get rid of an obligation under customary international law.

97 For a clear statement of what is perhaps the currently 'orthodox' view among international lawyers see eg the ILA's 'Statement of Principles Applicable to the Formation of General Customary International Law', Report of the ILA's 2000 (London) Conference, Commentary on Principle No 15 (b): 'There is fairly widespread agreement that, even if there is a persistent objector rule in international law, it applies only when the customary rule is in the process of emerging. It does not, therefore, benefit States which came into existence only after the rule matured, or which became involved in the activity in question only at a later stage.… In other words, there is no "subsequent objector" rule.'

98 Bradley/Gulati (n 95) 202.

99 H Thirlway, *The Sources of International Law* (Oxford, Oxford University Press 2014) 87.

100 See A d'Amato, *The Concept of Custom in International Law* (Ithaca, Cornell University Press 1971) 261; see also J Charney, 'The Persistent Objector Rule and the Development of Customary International Law' (1985) 56 *British Yearbook of International Law* 1 (24), who argues that 'the persistent objector rule is, at best,

The contradictory nature of the currently dominant view of customary international law becomes exacerbated by the tendency to ascertain rules of customary international law from multilateral treaties, and even more by the perceived trend towards an allegedly 'modern' conception of international custom that reduces the importance of 'deeds' (state practice) and enhances that of 'words' (declarations, resolutions and other utterances).[101] It has correctly been argued that the process of selection of materials used to support the claim that a rule of this 'modern' custom has arisen, especially human rights law are concerned, is liable to the charge of arbitrariness: As Simma and Alston noted in a classic article in 1988, adherents of a 'progressive, streamlined theory of customary international law, more or less stripped of the traditional practice requirement' tend to 'find customary international law wherever it is needed'.[102] A similar criticism has been raised against Anthea Robert's attempt[103] to 'reconcile' the traditional and modern approaches to customary international law by balancing what she refers to as the 'dimension of fit' (ie, what the practice has been hitherto) against the 'dimension of substance' (statements on what the law should be): As Thirlway aptly noted, such an approach of balancing facts against values facilitates the 'discovery of the solution that most appeals to the moral conceptions, or – dare one say it? – the prejudices of the observer'.[104]

Indeed, given the subjectivist tendency of the 'modern' approaches to customary international law, the question seems legitimate why states should be bound by its rules with more force (namely, without the possibility of quitting) than they are bound to treaties, which are at least the result of a process of formal negotiation and subject to ratification by the democratically legitimised organs of the state. Nevertheless, it is an important insight of Robert's approach that a reconciliation of subjective and objective elements, of deduction and induction, is possible and necessary. In the view of the present author, such reconciliation is the essence of the concept of purposive interpretation with respect to customary international law.

In the preceding chapters, the unwritten rules of international law, of which the rules of customary international law form an important part, have been described as an *objective* order of law. This does not mean, however, that they are devoid of any subjective elements, and that states have to accept them as they 'accept' the laws of nature, in the sense of being subjected to them irrespective of their actions and beliefs. Neither a purely voluntarist nor a purely objectivist interpretation of customary international law seems appropriate.

only of temporary or strategic value in the evolution of customary international law. It cannot serve a permanent role …'.

101 See generally Roberts (n 75).

102 See B Simma/P Alston, 'The Sources of International Human Rights Law: Custom, *Ius Cogens*, and General Principles' (1988) 5 *Australian Yearbook of International Law* 82.

103 See Roberts (n 75).

104 Thirlway (n 99) 229.

Rules of customary international law, conceived of as belonging to a spontaneous order, are based on human action, human volition, and human expectations, and are shaped by the behaviour of states in their interactions with one another. This behaviour is not, however, free of external constraint, carried out pursuant only to the actor's own pure will, as if written on blank sheets. Rather, it is shaped by experiences, expectations and externalities; it is through a dialectical process by which each actor is both influenced by the accepted rules and in turn influencing them, equally learning from the experiences of others and contributing from its own perspective to the preserving of order and stability in the international society.

It has been stated above that such dialectic is in fact not unique to unwritten international law, but that the processes of treaty-making, -application and -interpretation are shaped by it as well.[105] However, in unwritten international law, the objective element is stronger, the influence of subjective, conscious, volitional factors plays a weaker role, and, unlike the process of drafting of a treaty, the actors do not usually have a common design to create a rule; rather, the rule emerges through an evolutionary process and stands the test of time. In the words of Philip Allott, '[c]ustomary international law is the product of a dialectic of practice, as opposed to legislation, including international treaty-law, which is the product of a dialectic of ideas. Society-members produce the conditions of their orderly social co-existence through the practice of orderly co-existence.'[106] And this is the deeper meaning of the two elements, practice and *opinio juris*: A rule is stipulated, is tested in practice, the result is evaluated, eventually modified and again tested; all, however, without anyone having a comprehensive plan at the outset. On the contrary, as the actors involved pursue their individual goals, it is almost by a 'Cunning of Reason' that order and stability result. Yet the process is of such a complexity, and subject to so many volatile and unforeseeable contingencies, that no 'rational choice' analysis could have predicted its result at the outset; the inherent 'reasonableness' becomes apparent only as the rules produced have stood the test of time.

With these theoretical insights, the problem of the meaning of the concept of purposive interpretation with respect to customary international law becomes finally resolvable. It appears that Aharon Barak's theory of purposive interpretation[107] provides valuable guidance here: First, because it demonstrates that the 'ultimate purpose' of law, the kind of purpose Barak describes as the decisive one in the context of legal interpretation, comprises both subjective and objective elements. And second, because it explains how the composition of this 'ultimate purpose', ie the degree to which it is shaped by subjective or objective elements respectively, varies among the different sources of law, being lowest in a will, higher in contracts, still higher in statutes and highest in

105 Above, V, D–E.

106 P Allott, 'The Concept of International Law' (1999) 10 *European Journal of International Law* 31 (39).

107 See above, V, F.

a constitution.[108] In the sources of international law, there seems to be a similar distribution: The subjective element is greatest in unilateral acts of states;[109] treaties of different kinds, as has been argued above, comprise a greater element of objectivity, depending on their subject;[110] still greater is the objective element in rules of customary international law, while the general principles of international law reign paramount in both abstractness and objectivity. In customary international law, the two elements of 'practice' and '*opinio*' reflect the objective and subjective components of the rules' ultimate purpose.

However, the usual identification[111] of practice with the objective and *opinio* with the subjective component of international custom is misleading, as both elements contain objective and subjective aspects:[112] A 'practice' for the purposes of international law is not merely a neutral, objective fact, but a social action, and thus, in Max Weber's famous words, 'meaningfully related to the behaviour of other people'.[113] Practice in this sense is what Stephen Turner refers to in his *Social Theory of Practice* as a 'telic notion' of practice, an activity 'which is conceived as the result of following certain general principles of procedure'. Therefore, it necessarily involves the psychological processes of communication and understanding. *Opinio juris*, on the other hand, is but the outward expression of the interpretation which the individual subject ascribes to the rules it intends to follow, an interpretation which is not necessarily correct, but which should be taken seriously, especially when it is reciprocated and confirmed by similar statements of the other parties.[114] The reactions of the other parties then influence the future behaviour of the actor, depending on whether they are affirmative or critical. This dialectical nature of the process

108 See Barak (n 3) 185–91.

109 On the interpretation of unilateral acts, and the differences that exist in comparison to treaty interpretation, see the International Law Commission's 2006 'Guiding Principles applicable to unilateral acts of States capable of creating legal obligations, with commentaries thereto', esp Principle No 7; see (2006) ILC Yearbook vol 2, part 2, 369 (377).

110 It is in this context that the traditional distinction between '*traité-lois*' und '*traité-contrats*' may also become relevant.

111 As reflected, for example, in the ILA Draft (n 97), where the terms 'objective element' and 'subjective element' are used as synonyms of 'state practice' and '*opinio juris*'.

112 Cf on this also ILC, 'Second Report on Identification of Customary International Law' (22 May 2014) UN Doc A/CN.672, para 29: 'In any case … it is often difficult to consider the two elements separately.'

113 M Weber, *The Theory of Social and Economic Organization* (New York, Free Press 1968) 88.

114 Cf C de Visscher, *Théories et Réalités en Droit International Public* (Paris, Pedone, 4th ed 1970) 172: 'Le facteur psychologique implique un jugement tant moral que politique qui, s'attachant à des critères de raison, de justice et d'utilité commune, fait le départ entre ce qui dans une pratique donnée paraît dicté par une certaine conformité à l'intérêt général et ce qui ne paraît motivé que par des circonstances plus ou moins accidentelles ou par des mobiles particuliers.'

in which customary international law emerges and evolves implies that in order to ascertain its rules, one must not analyse each of the various pieces of evidence in isolation. It seems therefore particularly adequate that the ILC's Special Rapporteur on *Identification of Customary Law* stresses the contextual nature of the analysis in his 'Draft Conclusion 3':

> In assessing evidence for the purpose of ascertaining whether there is a general practice and whether that practice is accepted as law (*opinio juris*), regard must be had to the overall context, the nature of the rule, and the particular circumstances in which the evidence in question is to be found.[115]

Yet the interactions through which rules of customary international law emerge and change are not mere bargaining processes, as the 'mutual claims and tolerances'[116] approach of the New Haven school seems to suggest. Rather, they are based on a fundamental – though not necessarily conscious – shared conception about the way in which the international society is ordered, a conception that is based on experience, and the belief that, all differences in interests and political goals notwithstanding, certain general rules of behaviour have to be observed to maintain order and justice. These rules were aptly described by Robert Jackson as 'the constitutional framework of international relations'.[117]

It should be noted that this concept of a 'constitutional framework', used by Jackson and other theorists of the so-called 'English school'[118] of international relations, is different from, and in part even opposed to, the ideas and concepts that are frequently discussed under the catchphrase of a so-called 'constitutionalisation of international law':[119] Whereas for many proponents of the latter approach, the term 'constitutionalisation' connotes a tendency to overcome the traditional state system in international law and to move toward a new form of international community, based on shared values, goals and objectives,[120] and supplemented by forceful international institutions, the

115 See the 'Text of the draft conclusions provisionally adopted by the Drafting Committee', UN Doc. A/CN.4/L.872 (30 May 2016).

116 A paradigmatic example is the paper by MS McDougal, 'The Hydrogen Bomb Tests and the International Law of the Sea' (1955) 49 *American Journal of International Law* 356; for a more differentiated adaption of this approach to customary international law see B Simma, *Das Reziprozitätselement in der Entstehung des Völkergewohnheitsrechts* (München, Fink 1970).

117 See R Jackson, *The Global Covenant* (Oxford, Oxford University Press 2003) 102 et seq.

118 On the English school see eg T Dunne, 'The English School' in id/M Kurki/S Smith (eds), *International Relations Theories: Discipline and Diversity* (Oxford, Oxford University Press, 2nd ed 2010) 135.

119 For a thorough overview see eg T Kleinlein, *Konstitutionalisierung im Völkerrecht* (Heidelberg, Springer 2012); see also the essays in J Klabbers/A Peters/G Ulfstein, *The Constitutionalization of International Law* (Oxford, Oxford University Press 2009).

120 One of the most outspoken proponents of this cosmopolitan understanding of the concept of 'constitutionalisation of international law' is Jürgen Habermas; see eg

English school stresses the outcome-neutrality and procedurality of the rules governing international relations: '[T]hey are standards of conduct: that is, norms by reference to which international activity can be assessed.'[121] As such, they are 'purposive' in the same sense as rules of a game have a 'purpose', in that they enable the actors concerned (whether they are called members of the international 'community', 'society', or parts of an 'institution' in the sense of Romano and Hauriou) to maintain their relations in good order while pursuing their individual – and potentially conflicting – aims.

In the following section of this chapter, it is attempted to demonstrate how this understanding of 'purpose' is reflected in the jurisprudence of different international and domestic courts with respect to rules of customary international law.

H. Purposive Interpretation of Customary International Law by International and Domestic Courts

1. The International Court of Justice

The International Court of Justice, to begin with, has repeatedly used purposive arguments in the application and interpretation of customary international law; often, however, the recourse to teleological arguments was rather implicit, and the court did not provide a doctrinal justification for their use. Explicit references to purposive arguments by the ICJ can be found in a number of cases pertaining to the law of territory, especially in those concerning questions of border delimitation.

A good example in this respect is the court's jurisprudence on the rule (often also called a 'principle' or a 'doctrine') of *uti possidetis*, according to which internal administrative boundaries drawn by colonial powers shall become – in the absence of a specific agreement to the contrary – the borders of the newly independent states emerged from a process of decolonialisation.[122] The rule, most recently referred to by the Court in a 2013 decision,[123] was applied by a chamber of the ICJ in the 1986 case of the *Frontier Dispute (Burkina Faso/Mali)*,[124] where it was said to have developed into a rule of general customary international law. Interestingly, although the parties to the dispute had already acknowledged the existence of that rule and its applicability

his 'The Constitutionalization of International Law and the Legitimation Problems of a Constitution for World Society' (2008) 15 *Constellations* 444.

121 Jackson (n 117) 116.

122 On the doctrine in the context of decolonialisation see eg MN Shaw, 'The Heritage of States: The Principle of *Uti Possidetis Juris* Today' (1997) 67 *British Yearbook of International Law* 75; on the application of the doctrine by the ICJ, see id, 'The International Court of Justice and the Law of Territory' in C Tams/J Sloan (eds), *The Development of International Law by the International Court of Justice* (Oxford, Oxford University Press 2013) 151 (162–6).

123 *Frontier Dispute (Burkina Faso/Niger)* (Merits) para 63, available at <http://www.icj-cij.org/docket/files/149/17306.pdf> accessed 20 August 2017.

124 *Frontier Dispute (Burkina Faso/Mali)* [1986] ICJ Rep 554.

to the case at hand, the chamber found it necessary to underline the general importance of the rule, stating that '[i]ts obvious purpose is to prevent the independence and stability of new states being endangered by fratricidal struggles provoked by the challenging of frontiers following the withdrawal of the administrating power'.[125]

The chamber then went on to note that the rule of *uti possidetis* had emerged during the 19th century in Latin America, when the former Spanish colonies became independent; in this context, however, the apparent purpose of the rule – that is, the reason why it was invoked – was different, namely 'to scotch any design which non-American colonizing powers might have on regions which had been assigned by the former metropolitan State to one division or another, but which were still uninhabited and unexplored'.[126] In other words, it was used as a shield against possible claims made by European states to the effect that unsettled land had become *terra nullius* after the Spanish departure, and thus was up for grabs. However, the chamber found that 'there is more to the principle of *uti possidetis* than this particular aspect. The essence of the principle lies in its primary aim of securing respect for the territorial boundaries at the moment when independence is achieved.'[127] This 'essence' was also applicable to the process of decolonialisation in Africa. The chamber finally addressed the problem of the compatibility of *uti possidetis* with the right of peoples to self-determination of peoples, with which it 'at first sight conflicts outright'. However, the chamber resolved this apparent conflict by recourse to the purpose of the *uti possidetis* rule it had identified before, stating that

> the maintenance of the territorial status quo in Africa is often seen as the wisest course, to preserve what has been achieved by peoples who have struggled for their independence, and to avoid a disruption which would deprive the continent of the gains achieved by much sacrifice.... Thus, the principle of *uti possidetis* has kept its place among the most important legal principles, despite the apparent contradiction which explained [sic] its coexistence alongside the new norms implied [apparently a mistaken translation; in the French version: ... nonobstant l'apparente contradiction qu'impliquait sa coexistence avec les nouvelles normes.][128]

The approach of the chamber to the *uti possidetis* rule in this case provides an interesting example of the blending of subjective and objective elements in purposive interpretation, in a manner matching Barak's description of the process through which 'ultimate purpose' is discovered. Thus, the chamber referred to the 'numerous and solemn affirmations of the intangibility of the

125 Ibid, para 20.
126 Ibid, para 21.
127 Ibid.
128 Ibid, para 26.

frontiers existing at the time of the independence of African states, whether made by statesmen or by organs of the Organization of African Unity itself'.[129] These were said to be, however, 'evidently declaratory, not constitutive'. The core of the reasoning of the chamber appears to revolve around an analysis of the rule's objective purpose, that is, its desirability and even necessity as a stabilising factor in post-colonial situations, a fact that becomes evident as the changing subjective, historically contingent motivations to invoke the rule are distinguished from its fundamental rationale. In its decisions on questions of border disputes, the court has repeatedly and consistently stressed the stabilising function of the law of territory.[130]

An interesting, but somewhat opaque statement which provides an additional clue as to the court's conception of the purpose of rules of customary international law can be found in its decision in the *Gulf of Maine* case.[131] Rejecting the arguments of both Canada and the United States that certain 'principles ... constituting well-established rules of law' existed with respect to the question of the precise delimitation of the maritime boundary in the disputed area, the chamber noted that '[e]ach party's reasoning is in fact based on a false premise. The error lies precisely in searching general international law for, as it were, a set of rules that were not there.'[132] Then, the chamber went on to note that

> [a] body of detailed rules is not to be looked for in customary international law which in fact comprises a limited set of norms for ensuring the co-existence and vital co-operation of the members of the international community, together with a set of customary rules whose presence in the *opinio juris* of the States can be tested by induction based on the analysis of a sufficiently extensive and convincing practice, and not by deduction from preconceived ideas. It is therefore unrewarding, especially in a new and unconsolidated field like that involving the claims of States to areas which were until yesterday zones of the high seas, to look to general international law to provide a readymade set of rules that can be used for solving any delimitation problems that arise.[133]

What is striking in this statement is, on the one hand, that the chamber seems to distinguish two different classes or 'sets' of rules of customary international law: The rules belonging to the first, limited in number, are necessary for the preserving the stability and functioning of the international order, and

129 Ibid, para 24.
130 See eg the case *Temple of Preah Vihear (Cambodia v Thailand)* (Merits) [1962] ICJ Rep 6, 34; see further the *Tunisia/Libya Continental Shelf Case* [1982] ICJ Rep 18, 66.
131 *Case Concerning Delimitation of the Maritime Boundary in the Gulf of Maine Area* [1984] ICJ Rep 246.
132 Ibid, para 110.
133 Ibid, 111.

apparently can be recognised without extensive evidence of actual practice. Those belonging to the second class, which are not of the same high significance, require inductive proof. This interpretation of the chamber's *dictum* is somewhat difficult to reconcile with traditional sources doctrine, and the court has in fact 'not referred to such distinguishable categories of customary international law in later jurisprudence'.[134] Yet there is another possible interpretation of these rather opaque sentences, one that is indeed consistent with the court's practice in the application of customary international law: That in the interpretation of those rules the court deems essential to international stability and the pursuit of international relations, objective considerations dominate.

It should be noted here that the present use of the term 'objective' does not refer to the traditional distinction between practice as the 'objective' and *opinio juris* as the 'subjective' element of customary international law. In fact, in the *Nicaragua* case the court relied heavily on the so-called 'subjective' element of *opinio*, as it assigned considerable weight to the prohibition of the use of force in Art. 2(4) of the Charter of the United Nations, and the principles of non-use of force and non-intervention laid down in the UN General Assembly's 'Friendly Relations Declaration' of 1970.[135] Therefore, the *Nicaragua* case is frequently treated as a paradigmatic example of the so-called 'modern' approach to customary international law, which emphasises the importance of 'values', a trend that is described as a shift from traditional 'facilitative' to modern 'moral' customs.[136] Yet this interpretation implies that it is possible to distinguish customs according to their 'moral' content, so that the granting of diplomatic immunity is seen as a neutral, 'facilitative' custom, whereas the prohibition of the use of force is regarded as a more 'normative', value-laden one.[137] However, in the view of the present author, such a differentiation according to the 'moral' content of rules of customary international law is difficult, necessarily subjective, and not part of the intention of the court in *Nicaragua* and other cases. Rather, the court's concern seems to have been the acknowledgement of rules which allow for the peaceful coexistence in a divided world, rules whose expression it found, among other sources, in the 'Friendly Relations Declaration'. This resolution was not used by the court as an expression of policy goals for the future, but as the recognition of principles necessary for the preserving of order and stability in the world – a consensus of *views*, rather than an agreement of *wills*, similar to the court's interpretation of the statements by African political leaders endorsing the *uti possidetis* rule. Despite the court's recourse to sources traditionally described as being

134 See ILC, 'First Report on Formation and Evidence of Customary International Law by Michael Wood' (17 May 2013) UN Doc A/CN.4/663, para 59 note 112.

135 See *Case Concerning Certain Military and Paramilitary Activities in and Against Nicaragua (Nicaragua v United States)* (Merits) [1986] ICJ Rep 14, paras 187 et seq.

136 See eg Roberts (n 75) 764.

137 Ibid.

formative of the '*subjective*' element of *opinio juris*, such as statements or resolutions, the rules thus discerned are interpreted by the court with an emphasis on their *objective* purpose.

This is particularly relevant for the court's treatment of contradictory practices, in that it affects the degree of density and unanimity that it required for a practice to become law. Thus, where essential concerns of the international order were concerned, the court tended to interpret deviant practices as violations of a rule rather than obstacles to its formation: For example, in the *Nicaragua* case the court stated, referring to the principle of non-intervention, that it did 'not consider that, for a rule to be established as customary, the corresponding practice must be in absolutely rigorous conformity with the rule'.[138] It was sufficient, the court went on, that 'instances of State conduct inconsistent with a given rule should generally have been treated as breaches of that rule, not as indications of the recognition of a new rule'.[139] A similar reasoning can be found in the *Arrest Warrant* case of 2002,[140] which has already been briefly discussed above.[141] There, the court applied a purposive analysis of the immunity of high-ranking government officials: Arguing that acting foreign ministers had a similar need to travel abroad unimpededly as did heads of state, it decided that they were to be accorded the same absolute immunity under customary international law, the relative lack of unanimous state practice notwithstanding.

In the *Jurisdictional Immunities* case of 2012, purposive considerations concerning the law of state immunity do appear as well, although the court relied heavily on inductive arguments, analysing evidence of state practice and *opinio juris* contained primarily in the jurisprudence of domestic courts. However, to bolster these arguments, it was explicitly stated that '[t]he court considers that the rule of State immunity occupies an important place in international law and international relations'.[142] Of particular interest here is the court's description of the procedural nature of state immunity: While Italy claimed the existence of a conflict between the rules of state immunity and the norms of humanitarian law – allegedly of *jus cogens* character – which forbade the conduct for which compensation was sought, the court saw no such conflict:

> The two sets of rules address different matters. The rules of State immunity are procedural in character and are confined to determine whether or not the courts of one State may exercise jurisdiction in respect of another State … The application of the rules of State immunity to determine whether or not the Italian courts have jurisdiction to hear claims arising

138 *Nicaragua* case (n 135) para 186.

139 Ibid.

140 *Case Concerning the Arrest Warrant of 11 April 2000 (Democratic Republic of the Congo v Belgium)* [2002] ICJ Rep 3.

141 Above, Ch IV, C.

142 *Jurisdictional Immunities of the State (Germany v Italy, Greece Intervening)* [2012] ICJ Rep 99, para 57.

> out of those violations cannot involve any conflict with the rules which were violated. Nor is the argument strengthened by focusing upon the duty of the wrongdoing State to make reparation, rather than upon the original wrongful act. The duty to make reparations is a rule which exists independently of those rules which concern the means by which it is to be affected.[143]

This reasoning of the court has been criticised as formalistic, and it has been argued that in domestic legal systems, the substance/procedure distinction has 'long been the subject of critique which recognises that "procedural" rules may go to the heart of substantive justice, in facilitating or denying a remedy to a claimant'.[144] It is certainly correct that procedural rules have the capacity to severely impede the effectiveness of substantive norms. However, the court is correct to stress the fundamental difference in the purposes of procedural and substantive rules of international law, a difference that makes it impossible simply to weigh rules of one category against those of the other. It is not the function of the law of state immunity to let a state 'get away' with violations of substantive rules, but to ensure, through the recognition of abstract, outcome-neutral rules of general application, that the peaceful and stable coexistence of states with a variety of social, political and ideological systems is not disturbed by the possible abuse of domestic courts as a means to achieve political goals. Therefore, the substance/procedure distinction in international law has a fundamentally different function in international law than in domestic legal systems, where it has a mere formal character, and where conflicts of values and competences can be addressed through appeal to a central legislator, who ultimately can resolve them by modifying the laws or even amending the constitution.

The tendency of the International Court of Justice to be rather forthcoming in the recognition of abstract, outcome-neutral rules of behaviour as customary international law, and its reluctance to do so where rules pertaining to specific goals and outcomes were concerned is also visible in its jurisprudence in the field of customary international humanitarian law. Thus, the court had no difficulty in the *Nicaragua* case to hold that 'the general principles of international humanitarian law', especially those enshrined in the Common Articles 1 and 3 to the Geneva Conventions of 1949, were declaratory of rules of customary international law,[145] without explicitly discussing the fulfilment of the traditional requirements of practice and *opinio*. In its advisory opinion on the *Legality of the Threat or Use of Nuclear Weapons*,[146] on the other hand,

143 Ibid, paras 93–4.

144 See KN Trapp/A Mills, 'Smooth Runs the Water Where the Brook is Deep: The Obscured Complexities of Germany v Italy' (2012) 1 *Cambridge Journal of International and Comparative Law* 153 (160).

145 *Nicaragua* case (n 135), para 218.

146 *Legality of the Threat or Use of Nuclear Weapons* (Advisory Opinion) [1996] ICJ Rep 226.

the court held that it could not 'conclude definitely whether the threat or use of nuclear weapons would be lawful or unlawful in an extreme circumstance of self-defence, in which the very survival of a State would be at stake',[147] despite, as Judge Koroma put it in his dissenting opinion, 'the weight and abundance of material presented to the Court'[148] to support the allegation of an absolute prohibition of the use of nuclear weapons under any circumstances whatsoever. Indeed, although the court acknowledged that 'in view of the unique characteristics of nuclear weapons', their use 'seems scarcely reconcilable' with the requirements of international humanitarian law, it was unable to conclude that their use was absolutely illegal, noting 'the continuing tensions between the nascent *opinio juris* on the one hand, and the still strong adherence to the practice of deterrence on the other'.[149] The reasoning of the court's majority in this advisory opinion has been aptly described by Richard Falk as a 'soft *Lotus* approach',

> namely the view that limitations on a state's freedom of action cannot be presumed or deduced from world order values, but must rest on the consent of the state or the application of legal rules and principles to the context of actual use. The majority did not favour a 'hard *Lotus* approach', namely, that whatever is not explicitly forbidden to a state is permitted.[150]

The approach of the International Court of Justice in the *Nuclear Weapons* advisory opinion reflects a certain compromise between subjective and objective considerations in the process of interpretation, perhaps a result of the 'titanic tension between State practice and legal principle'[151] with which the court was faced. Although the court clearly stated the arguments for the general incompatibility of the use of nuclear weapons with international law, especially with the humanitarian law principles of proportionality and distinction between combatants and civilians, its majority took into account the divergences that existed among states on the issue and decided to leave the decision on a future unconditional prohibition of nuclear weapons to them, refusing to decide the – hypothetical – conflict between fundamental humanitarian principles and the right of a state to preserve its existence under conditions of extreme necessity.

2. International Criminal Tribunals

Interesting statements related to the purposive interpretation of rules of customary international humanitarian law can also be found in the case law of international criminal tribunals. In particular the International Criminal

147 Ibid, para 97.
148 Ibid, *Dissenting Opinion of Judge Koroma*, 556.
149 Ibid, para 73.
150 R Falk, 'Nuclear Weapons, International Law and the World Court: A Historic Encounter' (1997) 91 *American Journal of International Law* 64 (66).
151 *Nuclear Weapons* (n 146), *Dissenting Opinion of Vice-President Schwebel*, 311.

Tribunal for the Former Yugoslavia (ICTY) was faced, in a number of cases, with the need to determine the scope of application of specific rules, and also with more fundamental questions about the correct methodological approach to the ascertainment of customary international law.[152] In international criminal law, there exists a specific tension between the rather fluid nature of customary international law and the fundamental principle of legality underlying criminal law,[153] a tension that, it was argued, 'may have contributed to the rather rigorous practice of the tribunal'[154] in this respect.

However, especially for the ad-hoc international criminal tribunals, the ICTY and the Rwanda tribunal, both of which had been established by UN Security Council resolutions *post facto*[155] at a time when the acts to be judged upon had already been or were about to be committed, there existed an urgent need to resort to rules of customary international law, as the provisions of substantive law codified in the tribunals' statutes were not sufficiently differentiated and precise to meet the requirements of a criminal conviction consonant with the exacting standards of the rule of law.[156] The ascertainment of these customary rules was by no means an easy task. As the ICTY famously observed in the *Tadić* case:

> Before pointing to some principles and rules of customary law that have emerged in the international community for the purpose of regulating civil strife, a word of caution on the law-making process in the law of armed conflict is necessary. When attempting to ascertain State practice with a view to establishing the existence of a customary rule or a general principle, it is difficult, if not impossible, to pinpoint the actual behaviour of the troops in the field for the purpose of establishing whether they in fact

152 One of the clearest pronouncements by the ICTY pertaining to the elements necessary to prove the existence of a rule of customary international law can be found in the case *Prosecutor v Hadihasanović*, Decision on Interlocutary Appeal Challenging Jurisdiction in Relation to Command Responsibility (16 July 2003) IT-01–47-AR72, para 12, where the tribunal stated that 'to hold that a principle was part of customary international law, it has to be satisfied that State practice recognized the principle on the basis of supporting *opinio juris.*'.

153 See on the principle of legality in international criminal law eg S Dana, 'Beyond Retroactivity to Realizing Justice: A Theory on the Principle of Legality in International Criminal Law' (2009) 99 *The Journal of Criminal Law and Criminology* 857; see also N Arajärvi, *The Changing Nature of Customary International Law: Methods of Interpreting the Concept of Custom in International Criminal Tribunals* (London, Routledge 2014) Ch 4.

154 See T Treves, 'Customary International Law' in R Wolfrum (ed), *Max Planck Encyclopedia of Public International Law* (Oxford, Oxford University Press 2012) para 22.

155 See the resolutions S/RES/827 (1993) and S/RES/955 (1994).

156 See A Cassese, *International Criminal Law* (Oxford, Oxford University Press 2003) 28 et seq, who argues that the need to resort to unwritten rules of international criminal law will resort even under the Rome Statute of the International Criminal Court.

> comply with, or disregard, certain standards of behaviour. This examination is rendered extremely difficult by the fact that not only is access to the theatre of military operations normally refused to independent observers (often even to the ICRC) but information on the actual conduct of hostilities is withheld by the parties to the conflict; what is worse, often recourse is had to misinformation with a view to misleading the enemy as well as public opinion and foreign Governments. In appraising the formation of customary rules or general principles one should therefore be aware that, on account of the inherent nature of this subject-matter, reliance must primarily be placed on such elements as official pronouncements of States, military manuals and judicial decisions.[157]

Because of this lack of access to state practice in the classical sense, that is, the actual behaviour of the actors on the battlefield, but even more because of the peculiar character of international criminal law as a body of rules which directly regulate the behaviour of individuals rather than that of states,[158] questions of methodology with respect to the ascertainment and interpretation of rules of customary international law have occupied an important place in the jurisprudence of the ICTY. One of the most interesting examples in this respect is the *Erdemović* case, especially the decision of the Appeals Chamber of 1997.[159]

The defendant in this case, Dražen Erdemović, an ethnic Bosnian Croat fighting in the Bosnian Serb army, was accused of having participated in the massacre of Srebrenica. Appealing against his original conviction in the ICTY's Trial Chamber, Erdemović claimed to have acted under duress, arguing that he 'would have been killed together with the victims' had he refused to partake in the massacre.[160] In the view of the chamber's majority, reflected in the Joint Separate Opinion by Judges McDonald and Vohrah,[161] the plea of duress provided no absolute defence under international criminal law to a charge of

157 *Prosecutor v Duško Tadić*, Decision on Defence Motion for Interlocutory Appeal on Jurisdiction (2 October 1995) IT-94–1-A, para 99.
158 On the peculiar nature of international criminal law in this respect see generally LC Green, 'Criminal Responsibility of Individuals in Non-international Conflicts' (2002) 45 *German Yearbook of International Law* 82; F Harhoff, 'Legal and Practical Problems in the International Prosecution of Individuals' (2000) 69 *Nordic Journal of International Law* 53; J Vogel, 'Individuelle Verantwortlichkeit im Völkerstrafrecht' (2002) 114 *Zeitschrift für die gesamte Strafrechtswissenschaft* 403; however, this structural difference between 'traditional' international law and international criminal law should not be overstated, since rules applying to states also regulate the behaviour of individual human beings; see eg H Kelsen, *Das Problem der Souveränität und die Theorie des Völkerrechts* (Tübingen, Mohr, 2nd ed 1928) 163 et seq.
159 *Prosecutor v Dražen Erdemović*, Judgment on Appeal (7 October 1997) IT-96–22-A.
160 Ibid, para 4.
161 Judge Li, concurring with the majority on the issue of duress, wrote a brief separate opinion as well; Judges Cassese and Stephen wrote separate and partly dissenting opinions.

killing innocent civilians. In the absence of an explicit rule in the tribunal's statute, the judges looked to the unwritten rules of international law, customary international law and the general principles. Discussing – and distinguishing – a number of judicial precedents, mostly dealing with the prosecution of Nazi war criminals, the majority found that state practice and *opinio juris* did not provide a clear rule applicable to the case at hand.[162] Going on to compare the rules of duress in various domestic jurisdictions, the judges found significant disagreement on whether or not duress was applicable in cases of murder, concluding that no 'general principle of law' under Art 38 (1) (c) ICJ Statute in this respect existed either.[163] Having thus failed to discern an existing rule of international law pertaining to the defence of duress, it went on to develop one through what could be described as a teleological analysis of international criminal law, and of the underlying rules of international humanitarian law whose violations were the subject of the prosecution:

> If national law denies recognition of duress as a defence in respect of the killing of innocent persons, international criminal law can do no less than match that policy since it deals with murders often of far greater magnitude. If national law denies duress as a defence even in a case in which a single innocent life is extinguished due to action under duress, international law, in our view, cannot admit duress in cases which involve the slaughter of innocent human beings on a large scale. It must be our concern to facilitate the development and effectiveness of international humanitarian law and to promote its aims and application by recognising the normative effect which criminal law should have upon those subject to them.[164]

This *a fortiori* argumentation, based on the scale of the crimes which usually come under the purview of international criminal tribunals, is certainly questionable. Underlying the judges' reasoning, however, seems to be the more specific concern that the acceptance of the plea of duress in situations as that of Erdemović in Srebrenica would severely hamper the effectiveness of international criminal law in armed conflicts, as war crimes are often committed by soldiers in situations of structural duress. As the judges McDonald and Vohrah asserted, their approach 'is based on the proposition that it is unacceptable to allow a trained fighter, whose job necessarily entails the occupational hazard of

162 *Prosecutor v Erdemović* (n 159), Joint Separate Opinion of Judge McDonald and Judge Vohrah, para 55: 'In the light of the above decision, it is our view that no rule may be found in customary international law regarding the availability or the non-availability of duress as a defence to the charge of killing innocent human beings.'

163 Ibid, para 72: 'It is clear from the differing positions of the principal legal systems of the world that there is no consistent concrete rule which answers the question whether or not duress to the killing of innocent persons.'

164 Ibid, para 75.

dying, to avail himself of a complete defence to a crime in which he killed one or more innocent persons'.[165] The specific circumstances under which Erdemović had acted were to be taken into account, the judges argued, as mitigating factors in the context of sentencing. Deflecting possible criticism that they had ventured too far into the field of policy considerations, they approvingly quoted Rosalyn Higgin's assertion that in making a choice between different possible interpretations of a rule of international law, 'one must inevitably have consideration for the humanitarian, moral and social purpose of the law'.[166]

The decision of the Appeals Chamber's majority can be – and has been[167] – criticised as going too far in taking policy considerations into account, given the fact that an international criminal tribunal is charged with applying the law as it is rather developing it into what one might (or might not) wish it to be. From a more systemic perspective, the example of the *Erdemović* case shows that in international criminal law, the traditional methodology of ascertaining rules of customary international law sometimes comes into a structural conflict with the – understandable – desire not to let perpetrators of gross atrocities go unpunished, a situation in which the use of purposive arguments is regarded as a convenient way to complement an inductive approach based on the analysis of actual state behaviour.[168]

3. Domestic Courts

In the case law of domestic courts, purposive or teleological considerations with respect to the application of rules of customary international law play a significant role as well. This is unsurprising, given the fact that purposive interpretation often is of central importance in the context of domestic legal systems[169] and thus has become deeply ingrained in the methodological conceptions of many domestic judges.[170] Yet this familiarity also involves an

165 Ibid, para 84.
166 Quoted ibid, at para 78.
167 See eg the Dissenting Opinion of Judge Cassese; see also SC Newman, 'Duress as a Defence to War Crimes and Crimes Against Humanity' (2000) 166 *Military Law Review* 158, criticising the influence of policy considerations.
168 For a similar argument see eg KF Gärditz, 'Ungeschriebenes Völkerrecht durch Systembildung' (2007) 45 *Archiv des Völkerrechts* 1 (11): 'Eine teleologisch nicht gerüstete völkerrechtliche Systembildung konnte also mit nicht zuletzt auch emotional begründeten Sanktionsbedürfnissen nicht Schritt halten.'; for a more critical conclusion, see Arajärvi (n 153) 165: 'Especially in trials that touch upon morally conspicuous areas – international criminal trials being the prime example – courts have fused legal and extra-legal normative considerations in the attempt to identify CIL in a manner that supports delivering justice – sometimes at the cost of deteriorating the very essence of CIL.'
169 See A Barak, *The Judge in a Democracy* (Princeton, Princeton University Press 2006) 125.
170 See eg the classical essay by F Frankfurter, 'Some Reflections on the Reading of Statutes' (1947) 47 *Columbia Law Review* 527.

obvious peril, since domestic judges can be inclined to make use of purposive arguments in a rash, unreflecting manner, ascribing to a rule of international law a certain purpose without duly reflecting on the – potentially multifaceted – function that the rule actually fulfils within the context of international relations.[171]

These difficulties notwithstanding, purposive arguments serve as a guide through the abundance of sometimes contradictory practices and precedents of which customary international law ultimately consists. Even the most scrupulous analysis of international practice – which especially domestic courts often do not have the capacity, means or expertise to perform[172] – is not always sufficient to provide a rule clear or precise enough to determine the result of a particular case. In such a situation, domestic courts tend to combine an inductive analysis of practice accompanied by *opinio juris* with teleological considerations. More precisely, they often undertake a two-step inquiry: In a first step, they attempt to discern a rule whose existence is well-reflected in state practice and supported by *opinio juris.* As this rule will, however, frequently be too general and abstract to provide a definitive answer to the question posed by a particular case, courts then use teleological arguments to establish its meaning in relation to the specificities of that case.

A relatively elaborate example of such a combined approach in which an inductive analysis of state practice and teleological arguments are interwoven can be found in the decision of the German Federal Constitutional Court in a case where the question arose whether Argentina's general consent to measures of enforcement with respect to claims arising from sovereign bonds extended to bank accounts used by its embassy in Germany.[173] Here, the court began by recounting the development of the general rules of immunity from enforcement, and the distinction that had been recognised in state practice between property which did and that which did not serve official purposes. It went on to note that the possibility that a state consents to measures of enforcement was recognised as an exception to the general rule of state immunity from enforcement, in which case the – sometimes difficult – distinction between commercially and officially used property was irrelevant. Having thus established the possibility of consent as an exception to enforcement immunity even with respect to property that served official purposes, it now addressed the question whether this rule was applicable to diplomatic bank accounts as well, given the special status of diplomatic missions under international law, a status 'that goes beyond the rules of the Vienna Conventions [on Diplomatic

171 For the problem of bias in the teleological interpretation of international treaty law and the risk of 'judicial legislation' in this context, see generally Kolb (n 5) 548–54.

172 See eg M Mandelson, 'The Effects of Customary International Law on Domestic Law: An Overview' (2004) 4 *Non-State Actors and International Law* 75 (79): 'Quite often, national judges even at the highest level evidently find the process of the formation and ascertainment of customary international law hard to understand.'

173 [2006] BVerfGE 117, 141.

and Consular Relations]'.[174] The ability of diplomatic missions to fulfil their duties, the court argued, constitutes an interest of paramount importance under international law, an aspect that weighed in against an interpretation to the effect of applying a general waiver of immunity from enforcement measures to diplomatic property.[175] Having thus erected a precise framework of inquiry, the court now looked again to state practice, this time to decide whether a specific rule existed that allowed it to include diplomatic property in the scope of a blanket waiver of immunity. As the decisions of national courts dealing with this precise question were few and their results contradictory, the court concluded that no such rule existed. Although the court's decision in this case relies heavily on state practice, it is interesting to see the extent to which the result depended on purposive arguments:[176] Because the court had strongly emphasised the distinction between diplomatic property and property used for other official purposes, it had to look for the existence of a specific permissory rule in order to extend the scope of a general consent to enforcement accordingly.

Viewed in a historical perspective, the law of diplomatic and consular relations is generally an interesting field for studying the use of teleological arguments by domestic courts. Traditionally, there have been three main different theories used to explain the *raison d'être* of the privileges granted to diplomatic missions: The 'theory of extraterritoriality', which assumed that the premises of a mission were an extension of the territory of the sending state; the 'theory of representation', which was based on the notion that a diplomatic mission personified the sending state; and the 'theory of functional necessity', which justified the granting of diplomatic privileges as being necessary to enable the mission to perform its functions.[177] Prior to the entry into force of the 1961 Vienna Convention on Diplomatic Relations, the courts of various countries, which had to decide questions of diplomatic privileges on the basis of rules of customary international law, differed in their approaches to this fundamental question, with the consequence that the extent to which privileges and immunities were granted varied,[178] although there always has been a core consensus on the inviolability of the person of the diplomat and of the premises of the mission. The drafters of the 1961 Vienna Convention did not only codify many of the specific tenets of diplomatic law (although there

174 Ibid, para 47.
175 Ibid, para 45 et seq.
176 For a similar interpretation of this decision, positioning it in the context of the general approach of the Federal Constitutional Court to the ascertainment of customary international law, see R Geiger, *Grundgesetz und Völkerrecht* (München, Beck, 4th ed 2009) 149 et seq. Geiger describes the approach of the court thus: 'Bedarf es einer Norm spezielleren Inhalts (etwa über den Umfang der Immunität), so wird diese durch *teleologische Auslegung* des allgemeinen, fraglos geltenden Satzes im Hinblick auf den konkreten Fall gewonnen.' (Ibid, 149).
177 For a discussion of these theories, see (1958) ILC Yearbook, vol 2, 94–5.
178 See generally I Roberts (ed), *Satow's Diplomatic Practice* (Oxford, Oxford University Press, 6th ed 2009) 97–101.

remain issues still governed by customary international law alone), but also stated in the convention's preamble 'that the purpose of such privileges and immunities is not to benefit individuals but to ensure the efficient performance of the functions of diplomatic missions as representing States', thus expressing a certain preference for the 'theory of functional necessity'.[179] This statement of purpose now provides guidance to domestic courts, both in the application of the rules codified in the Vienna Convention, and in the interpretation of the supplementary rules of customary international law, being in the latter case a significant statement of *opinio juris*, given the great number[180] of state parties to the 1961 Vienna Convention on Diplomatic Relations.

A classical, illustrative example of the practice to concretise rules of customary international law through recourse to teleological arguments is provided by the decision of the US Court of Appeals for the Second Circuit in the 1964 case of *Victory Transport v Comisaría General de Abastecimientos y Transportes.*[181] Here, the court had to decide whether Spain's sovereign immunity protected it against claims arising out of a dispute concerning a voyage-charter agreement concluded between the Spanish Ministry of Commerce and a private American shipping company to transport food aid provided by the American government. More specifically, it had to construe the distinction between *acta jure imperii* and *acta jure gestionis* under the theory of restrictive immunity, which had already been adopted by US courts at that time. The Court of Appeals began by noting that '[i]n delineating the scope of a doctrine [ie state immunity] designed to avert possible embarrassment to the conduct of our foreign relations, the courts have quite naturally deferred to the policy pronouncements of the State Department'.[182] As the State Department had been silent in this case, however, the court was left to its own devices. Interestingly, it explicitly formulated the purpose of the doctrine of restrictive immunity as follows:

> The purpose of the restrictive theory of sovereign immunity is to try to accommodate the interest of individuals doing business with foreign governments in having their legal rights determined by the courts, with the interest of foreign governments in being free to perform certain political acts without undergoing the embarrassment or hindrance of defending the propriety of such acts before foreign courts. Sovereign immunity is a derogation from the normal exercise of jurisdiction by the courts and should be accorded only in clear cases.[183]

179 Cf on the preamble and the *travaux préparatoires* thereto E Denza, *Diplomatic Law: A Commentary on the 1961 Vienna Convention on Diplomatic Relations* (Oxford, Oxford University Press, 3rd ed 2008) 13–15.

180 As of October 2014, a total of 190 states are party to the 1961 Vienna Convention on Diplomatic Relations.

181 *Victory Transport Inc v Comisaria General de Abastecimientos y Transportes* [1964] 336 F2d 354.

182 Ibid, 358.

183 Ibid, 360.

The process was thus one of balancing of interests. The court went on to enumerate certain classes of acts of foreign states for which the interest of the foreign state would tend to prevail: 'Such acts are generally limited to the following categories: (1) internal administrative acts, such as expulsion of an alien. (2) Legislative acts, such as nationalisation. (3) Acts concerning the armed forces. (4) Acts concerning diplomatic activity. (5) Public loans.'[184] As the conduct in question, the chartering of a cargo ship did not constitute a 'strictly public or political act', but it had 'the earmarks of a typical commercial transaction'. The court went on:

> Even if we take a broader view of the transaction to encompass the purchase of wheat pursuant to the Surplus Agricultural Commodities Agreement to help feed the people of Spain, the activity of the Comisaría General remains more in the commercial than political realm. Appellant does not claim that the wheat will be used for the public services of Spain; presumptively the wheat will be resold to Spanish nationals. Whether the Comisaría General loses money or makes a profit on the sale, this purchasing activity has been conducted through private channels of trade.[185]

The Court of Appeals did not end its analysis there, but checked its result against the practice of courts in other states which had adopted the doctrine of restrictive immunity, finding support for its conclusion that maritime transport generally constituted *acta jure gestionis.*[186]

From the perspective of the development of the law of state immunity, the decision in the *Victory Transport* case is interesting because it is one of the early examples in which a court explicitly discussed the difficulty of distinguishing between public acts and commercial transactions, and decided that the nature of the act in question, and not the purpose for which it was undertaken, was decisive (although the question could ultimately be left open by the court, as Spain had not claimed that its purchase of wheat was done for public purposes). From a methodological perspective, it is remarkable how the Court of Appeals combined teleological reasoning with an analysis of the practice of other courts, an approach similar to that of the German Federal Constitutional Court in many cases where it applied rules of customary international law.[187]

In several of the cases described in the preceding pages, courts have used purposive arguments in a rather specific, limited fashion to interpret rules of customary international law in order to ascertain their meaning for concrete

184 Ibid.
185 Ibid, 361.
186 Ibid, 361–2.
187 See on the combined approach of the German Federal Constitutional Court eg R Geiger, 'Zur Lehre vom Völkergewohnheitsrecht in der Rechtsprechung des Bundesverfassungsgerichts' (1978) 103 *Archiv des Öffentlichen Rechts* 382 (esp 401–7).

cases. However, one could also see that teleological reasoning can have a broader scope of application, guiding courts in the balancing of competing principles (as in the cases concerning the *uti possidetis* principle), in the assessment of contradictory state practice, or in the framing of a new field of law where state practice is relatively scarce, as in international criminal law. In the *Arrest Warrant* case, the International Court of Justice has used a primarily teleological analysis to conclude that head of state-immunity also covers foreign ministers. The approach of the court in this case could be described as a form of analogical reasoning, an argument 'that cites accepted similarities between two systems [here: heads of state and foreign ministers] to support the conclusion that some further similarity [absolute immunity while in office] exists'.[188]

Up to this point, we have seen that purposive interpretation fulfils a vital role in the attempts of judges to discern the meaning of legal rules, be they written (such as treaty provisions) or unwritten (such as rules of international custom). In the following chapter, analogical reasoning and other more elaborate uses of teleological arguments in unwritten international law shall be discussed.

188 See P Bartha, 'Analogy and Analogical Reasoning' in EN Zalta (ed.), *The Stanford Encyclopedia of Philosophy* (Fall 2013 Edition).

VI Analogical Reasoning and the Recognition of General Principles of Law

A. Purposive Interpretation and Systematic Jurisprudence

The examples discussed in the previous chapter, which were taken from the case law of international and domestic courts, are illustrative of the significant role that purposive interpretation plays in the application of rules of customary international law. Yet it should be noted that teleological arguments can do more than just help to concretise a legal norm and narrow its meaning so that it can provide a solution for a specific case. They also constitute important methodological tools that can be used to generalise specific rules and legal concepts, to harmonise seemingly contradictory rules by laying bare their intrinsic rationale, to formulate general principles, and ultimately to restate the totality of rules belonging to a normative order in a more systematic, coherent fashion.[1] This inherent connection between the concept of 'purpose' and the rationality of a social system or order has been discussed extensively by Niklas Luhmann in his influential 1968 study *Zweckbegriff und Systemrationalität.*[2]

Processes of generalisation and systematisation are well-known in the domestic legal doctrine of many nations. Especially in civil law jurisdictions, major codifications of private law were undertaken towards the end of the 19th century in order to render the rules of the *jus commune*, which were based on the reception of Roman civil law, more accessible and easier to apply.[3] In line with the rationalistic spirit of the era, it was regarded as a desirable goal to lay down the totality of existing rules in a written code that was as brief,

1 For a theoretical discussion of the process of systematisation in domestic law see eg the classical study by C Alchourrón and E Bulygin, *Normative Systems* (Wien, Springer 1971).

2 See N Luhmann, *Zweckbegriff und Systemrationalität: Über die Funktion von Zwecken in sozialen Systemen* (Frankfurt, Suhrkamp, 6th ed 1999) passim; to Luhmann, the main functions of the concept of purpose in social systems are the reduction of complexity and the coordination of expectations.

3 On the history of codification in civil law jurisdictions see eg ML Murillo, 'The Evolution of Codification in the Civil Law Legal Systems: Towards Decodification and Recodification' (2001) 11 *Journal of Transnational Law & Policy* 163; J Dainow, 'The Civil Law and the Common Law: Some Points of Comparison' (1966–67) 15 *American Journal of Comparative Law* 419.

comprehensive and non-repetitive as possible. This jurisprudential 'principle of economy', which was already stipulated by Rudolf von Jhering in 1865,[4] has been aptly described by Carlos Alchourrón and Eugenio Bulygin as the requirement that

> … the basis of a legal system should be as small as possible, i.e. should contain the smallest possible number of sentences. This implies that the sentences of the basis, and in particular its norms, must be as *general* as possible. A norm is general – in the relevant sense of the term – when it solves a plurality of cases.… The reduction in the number of the paragraphs of a code is usually regarded as a progressive measure.… Generally speaking, the reformulation of a system consists in the replacement of the basis by a new one that is less extensive, more general and normatively equivalent.[5]

Codification of a certain field of law is the most comprehensive, but by no means the only way in which systematisation can occur. In fact, the application of legal rules to particular situations, as typically done by judges, often requires a significant amount of systematic reasoning as well. For example, the principle of systemic integration in treaty interpretation, which has been discussed above,[6] is based on the idea that legal rules do not stand alone, but are deeply embedded in the legal order as a whole, of which they form a substantial part, and by which their interpretation is influenced in turn. Where the unwritten rules of international law are concerned, which are structurally case law arising spontaneously from the interactions of states (and occasionally certain other actors)[7] with one another, the need for systematisation, be it in the form of codification, judicial interpretation or scholarly analysis, is acutely felt.[8] However, the conceptualisation of international law as a unified, systematic legal order is not unproblematic:[9] First, international law is increasingly described as being fragmented into several functionally and institutionally separated

4 See R Jhering, *Der Geist des Römischen Rechts auf verschiedenen Stufen seiner Entwicklung, Vol. III, Erste Abteilung* (Leipzig, Breitkopf & Härtel 1865).
5 Alchourrón/Bulygin (n 1) 78–9.
6 See above Ch V, E.
7 For the impact of non-state actors in the development of international humanitarian law see eg A Roberts/S Sivakumaran, 'Lawmaking by Nonstate Actors: Engaging Armed Groups in the Creation of International Humanitarian Law' (2012) 37 *Yale Journal of International Law* 108; for the example of international environmental law see D Tarlock, 'Non-Governmental Organizations in the Development of International Environmental Law' (1992–3) 68 *Chicago-Kent Law Review* 61; see also K Raustiala, 'The "Participatory Revolution" in International Environmental Law' (1997) 21 *Harvard Environmental Law Review* 537.
8 See eg KF Gärditz, 'Ungeschriebenes Völkerrecht durch Systembildung' (2007) 45 *Archiv des Völkerrechts* 1.
9 See for generally M Prost, *The Concept of Unity in Public International Law* (Oxford, Hart 2012) passim, in particular 1–30.

subsystems with relatively few unifying features.[10] Second, and more fundamentally, the material incompleteness of international law, the fact that many important problems of international concern are not regulated comprehensively by international legal rules, appears to be an inevitable consequence of the absence of a central legislative authority in the international community, and of a lack of consensus among its members, even as issues of vital importance are concerned.[11]

It is certainly correct to say that nothing is gained by depicting international law as being more coherent, systematic and complete than it actually is.[12] But it is equally correct to note that the postulation of a simple 'closing rule' – the rather tautological statement that everything which is not explicitly prohibited is implicitly allowed[13] – does not preclude the necessity of determining whether a certain act is prohibited, that is, to discern the scope of application of a prohibitory rule. In customary international law, there is a specific difficulty involved in this respect: When a state claims that a certain act is performed in pursuance of a rule of customary international law, it essentially makes two distinct, yet closely linked, assertions: First, the *existence* of a general rule; and second, the fact that the act in question falls *within the ambit* of this rule.[14] Thus, whereas the assertion of legality (the *opinio juris*) exists on two different levels of abstraction, on the level of the individual case and on that of the general rule, each individual act of state practice, the objective element in the

10 For an informative overview of the fragmentation debate and the International Law Commission's study group on fragmentation, see M Koskenniemi/P Leino, Fragmentation of International Law? Postmodern Anxieties (2002) 15 *Leiden Journal of International Law* 553.

11 See eg H Kelsen *Principles of International Law* (New York, Rinehart & Co 1952) 305: 'If there is no norm of conventional or customary international law imposing upon the state (or another subject of international law) the obligation to behave in a certain way, the subject is under international law free to behave as it pleases; … But this decision, though logically possible, may be morally or politically not satisfactory. Only in this sense are there "gaps" in the international as in any legal order.'

12 See J d'Aspremont, 'The Systemic Integration of International Law by Domestic Courts: Domestic Courts as Architects of the Consistency of the International Legal Order', in A Nollkaemper/OK Fauchald (eds), *The Practice of International and National Courts and the (De-)Fragmentation of International Law* (Oxford, Hart 2012) 141 (164–5), who concludes that 'judges should not delude themselves as to the existence of a sweeping substantive and procedural harmony of the international legal order and should instead remain amenable to the realities of international law. International law-making procedures remain fragmented and decentralized.'

13 An excellent analysis of the meaning and the implications of the existence of such a rule can be found in GH von Wright, *Norm and Action: A Logical Enquiry* (London, Routledge 1963) 86 et seq, who speaks in this context of 'strong' and 'weak permissions'; see also I Tammelo, 'On the Logical Openness of Legal Orders' (1959) 8 *American Journal of Comparative Law* 91.

14 See A Bleckmann, *Grundprobleme und Methoden des Völkerrechts* (Freiburg, Alber 1982) 133–4.

formation of a rule of customary international law, is tied to the factual circumstances of each particular case. In applying a rule of customary international law to a new situation, a process which inevitably involves a myriad of – major or minor – deviations from the instances in which the rule has hitherto been invoked, one necessarily has to resort to a basic form of analogical reasoning, namely a comparison of the normatively relevant aspects of the present case with the prior situations in which the rule in question had been invoked and accepted by the parties concerned.

B. Analogical Reasoning and its Critics

As far as the application of well-established rules of customary international law is concerned, the analogical nature of the process is usually not recognised, as the amount of precedents and of the accompanying *opinio juris* is sufficiently great and as their inductive analysis has already been undertaken many times before, resulting in a rule specific enough to determine the solution of the case at hand without requiring a *de novo* analysis of the presence of the constitutive elements of a rule of customary international law. Indeed, it seems advisable to distinguish 'the method of investigation as to whether the elements of international custom are fulfilled' from 'the method of application of customary rules which have already been established previously'.[15] Nevertheless, it is very important to be aware of the essentially analogical nature of rules of international custom, because by demonstrating the fundamental role that reasoning *per analogiam* plays in the practice of international law, the most common objections against the use of analogies can be refuted, or at least be put into perspective.[16]

It should be noted, however, that authors who raise objections against the use of analogy as a means of legal reasoning in international law usually do not refer to this rather simple kind of analogical reasoning, but to full-grown analogies, which are discussed in the context of domestic legal orders as a means to fill so-called 'gaps' in the law. From this point of view, the legitimacy of analogical arguments depends on the question whether or not international law contains such gaps or *lacunae* at all, or whether it is to be regarded as a complete legal order, where the very existence of *lacunae* is excluded by some 'closing rule',[17]

15 See K. Wolfke, *Custom in Present International Law* (Dordrecht, Martinus Nijhoff, 2nd ed 1993) 137, discussing the practice of the ICJ in this respect.

16 For a similar argumentation see S Vöneky, 'Analogy in International Law' in R Bernhardt (ed), *Max Planck Encyclopedia of Public International Law* (Oxford, Oxford University Press 2012) para 17, 23–4.

17 On the use of this term with respect to the international legal system see eg IF Dekker/WG Werner, 'The Completeness of International Law and Hamlet's Dilemma: Non Liquet, the Nuclear Weapons Case, and Legal Theory' in IF Dekker/HG Post (eds), *On the Foundations and Sources of International Law* (The Hague, TMC Asser Press 2003) 5 (7).

such as the principle that everything which is not explicitly prohibited to the states is consequently allowed.[18]

Such 'closing rule' is often inferred from the Permanent Court of International Justice's famous assertion in the *Lotus* case that '[r]estrictions upon the independence of States cannot … be presumed'.[19] The *Lotus* dictum has frequently been invoked to support a voluntarist conception of international law, the view that 'where there is State will, there is international law: no will, no law'.[20] As such, it has long been subjected to severe criticism: to James L Brierly, the court's opinion 'was based on the highly contentious metaphysical proposition of the extreme positivist school that the law emanates from the free will of sovereign independent States'.[21]

Whether the *Lotus* principle[22] necessarily implies such a sweeping statement of the rule '*in dubio pro libertate*', granting to states absolute freedom to do whatever is not prohibited by a rule to which they have consented, or whether it should better be interpreted as giving freedom to act only within the limits of the rights and competencies of other states,[23] is a question that has been controversially discussed ever since the *Lotus* decision was rendered in 1927.[24]

18 This question, which belongs to the most famous problems of international legal theory, has attracted widespread scholarly attention; to note but a few important contributions: H Lauterpacht, 'Some Observations on the Prohibition of "Non Liquet" and the Completeness of the Law' in FM van Asbeck (ed), *Symbolae Verzijl* (The Hague, Martinus Nijhoff 1958) 196; see also the response to Lauterpacht by J Stone, '*Non-Liquet* and the Function of Law in the International Community' (1959) 35 *British Yearbook of International Law* 124. See also L Siorat, 'Le problème des lacunes en droit international public' (1967) 3 *Revue Belge de droit international* 440; for an extensive general overview see also U Fastenrath, *Lücken im Völkerrecht* (Berlin, Duncker & Humblot 1991).

19 See the *Case of the SS Lotus (France v Turkey)* [1927] PCIJ Series A, No 10, para 44.

20 See A Pellet, 'The Normative Dilemma: Will and Consent in International Law', (1988–9) 12 *Australian Yearbook of International Law* 22 (26).

21 JL Brierly, 'The *Lotus* Case' (1928) 44 *Law Quarterly Review* 154 (155).

22 The *Lotus* statement is sometimes referred to as a rule, sometimes as a principle. Hersch Lauterpacht even called it an 'obiter dictum', arguing that it was irrelevant to the court's decision in the particular case; see H Lauterpacht, *The Development of International Law by the International Court* (Cambridge, Cambridge University Press, 2nd ed 1958) 361.

23 For such an alternative interpretation of the decision see eg M Huber, 'Observation' (1931) 36-I *Annuaire de l'Institut de Droit International* 77 (79): 'Je continue de penser que le principe proclamé par la Cour Permanente de Justice internationale dans l'affaire "*Lotus*" est exact; mail il a été quelquefois mal interprété par les critiques du dit ârret. L'absence d'une règle qui départagerait les droit des Etats et la liberté qui en résulte pour chaque Etat de faire ce qui n'est pas défendu ne signifie pas un état d'anarchie où chacun aurait le droit de passer outre à la situation créée par un autre Etat.'.

24 For a more recent overview of the discussion, viewed in the light of case law of the International Court of Justice, see eg H Handeyside, 'The Lotus Principle in ICJ Jurisprudence: Was the Ship Ever Afloat?' (2007–8) 29 *Michigan Journal of International Law* 71; see furthermore O Spiermann, '*Lotus* and the Double Structure of International Legal Argument' in LB de Chazournes/P Sands (eds),

One of the most notable instances in which the ICJ seemingly deviated from the *Lotus* principle was its 1996 advisory opinion on the *Legality of the Threat or Use of Nuclear Weapons*,[25] which has already been discussed above[26] in the context of purposive interpretation of rules of customary international law. Here it was discussed whether the court's majority, by stating that it 'could not definitely conclude' whether the use of nuclear weapons would be contrary to international law under any circumstances whatsoever, had acknowledged the possibility of the existence of a situation of *non liquet*, and thus rejected the view that existing international law provides definite answers to all possible questions about the legality or illegality of any given act.[27]

More recently, it has been argued that the *Lotus* principle was 'resuscitated'[28] by the International Court of Justice in its 2010 advisory opinion on the *Accordance with International Law of the Unilateral Declaration of Independence in respect of Kosovo*.[29] It was asserted that by concluding 'that general international law contains no applicable prohibition of declarations of independence',[30] the court's majority has adopted 'a quasi-binary stance on permissibility and prohibition',[31] a criticism that also permeates the declaration by Judge Simma that was attached to the advisory opinion:

> I find this approach [of the majority] disquieting in the light of the Court's general conclusion, in paragraph 3 of the operative clause, that the declaration of independence 'did not violate international law'. The underlying rationale of the Court's approach reflects an old, tired view of international law, which takes the adage, famously expressed in the 'Lotus' Judgment, according to which restrictions on the independence of States cannot be presumed because of the consensual nature of the international legal order.[32]

International Law, the International Court of Justice and Nuclear Weapons (Cambridge, Cambridge University Press 1999) 131.

25 *Legality of the Threat or Use of Nuclear Weapons* (Advisory Opinion) [1996] ICJ Rep 226.

26 See above, Ch V, H.

27 It is questionable, however, whether this *non liquet* stemmed from the uncertainty of the substantive rules on the issue or from the uncertainty regarding possible future situations in which they would apply, as the question was posed to the court in such an abstract way; whether, in other words, the result was due to the nature of the advisory proceeding before the court. Alchourrón and Bulygin (n 1) draw in this respect a very significant distinction between 'gaps of knowledge', which are positioned on the level of factual knowledge, and 'gaps of recognition', which are uncertainties related to the determination of the applicable legal rules.

28 GI Hernández, *The International Court of Justice and the Judicial Function* (Oxford, Oxford University Press 2014) 264.

29 *Accordance with International Law of the Unilateral Declaration of Independence in respect of Kosovo* (Advisory Opinion) [2010] ICJ Rep 40.

30 Ibid, para 84.

31 Hernández (n 28) 265.

32 *Kosovo opinion* (n 29), Declaration of Judge Simma, para 2 (references ommitted).

Instead of 'upholding the *Lotus* principle', the court, in Judge Simma's view, should have 'seize[d] a chance to move beyond this anachronistic, extremely consensualist vision of international law', and should have considered 'the possibility that international law can be neutral or deliberately silent on the international lawfulness of certain acts'.[33]

It is not necessary and not even possible in the context of the present inquiry to analyse exhaustively the reasoning of the court's majority in the *Kosovo* advisory opinion, or to discuss in detail Judge Simma's elegantly and forcefully argued declaration. However, the charge that the majority's reasoning is 'redolent of nineteenth-century positivism',[34] because it had answered the General Assembly's question whether Kosovo's declaration of independence was 'in accordance with international law' by simply noting the inexistence of a prohibitory rule, seems to the present author to be an overstatement: It has rightfully been noted that 'the narrow focus of the opinion was preordained by the [General Assembly's] question as it was posed'.[35] Indeed, the court 'would not ordinarily be expected to raise on its own issues that need not necessarily be considered when answering the question put',[36] such as the question whether and, if so, under which circumstances a positive right of secession (as the 'remedial secession' suggested by Judge Simma) might exist under international law.

It seems that the methodological approach of the court's majority in the *Kosovo* opinion, which was significantly affected by the already narrow design of the General Assembly's question, by the political sensitivity of the issues involved and by a certain element of caution that is characteristic of the court's *modus operandi* in the exercise of its advisory function,[37] should not be over-generalised to imply a return to the extremes of consensualist positivism in international law, nor as a sweeping assertion of the absolute logical impossibility of the existence of *lacunae* in international law. This insight is of particular importance in the context of the inquiry into the nature and the possibilities of using analogies in the application of the unwritten rules of international law undertaken here, as some of the strongest arguments against the admissibility of analogical reasoning in international law have been derived from the alleged 'closure', that is, the material completeness of the international legal order. The completeness of the international legal order, as that of any legal order, can be understood in two distinct, yet related ways: First, completeness can be

33 Ibid, para 3.
34 Ibid, para 8.
35 M Weller, 'Modesty Can Be a Virtue: Judicial Economy in the *Kosovo* Opinion?' (2011) 24 *Leiden Journal of International Law* 127 (147).
36 Ibid.
37 For a recent analysis of the nature and effectiveness of advisory proceedings in international courts and tribunals see R Wolfrum, 'Advisory Opinions: Are they a Suitable Alternative for the Settlement of International Disputes?' in id/I Gätzschmann (eds), *International Dispute Settlement: Room for Innovations?* (Berlin/Heidelberg, Springer 2013) 239.

understood as a *logical* property of a legal order, based on the interdefinability of permission and prohibition:[38] In the terminology of the legal theoretician Georg H von Wright, everything that is not *strongly* (explicitly) prohibited, is *weakly* (implicitly) permitted.[39] In this sense, the argument is necessarily true as a matter of logic, but it is also tautological. Without anything being lost, it could just as well be expressed as follows: Everything that is not explicitly prohibited is not explicitly prohibited.[40]

However, completeness (or 'closure') of a legal order can also be conceived in a different way, namely as a normative postulate, and this is the way in which it is apparently understood by the majority of scholars who argue in favour of the completeness of the international legal order: Because they perceive freedom of states to act as the default position in international law, and because they argue that limitations on the freedom of states can derive only from their own will, these authors assert that under international law, analogical reasoning is inadmissible.[41]

These authors, who regard as part of international law only the rules derived from the common consent of states, sometimes even explicitly acknowledge the existence of 'gaps' in the international legal order thus conceived, in the sense that not everything which requires international regulation is covered by them; they refuse, however, to acknowledge analogies as a proper means to fill those gaps. A typical example of this approach can be found in Karl Strupp's

38 As said above, this is the way in which Kelsen conceived the completeness of the international legal order, see Kelsen (n 11) 304 et seq; on Kelsen's theory with respect to the so-called 'gaps' in international law, see J Kammerhofer, 'Gaps, the Nuclear Weapons Opinion, and the Structure of International Legal Argument between Theory and Practice' (2009) 80 *British Yearbook of International Law* 333, who analyses the debate between Julius Stone and Hersch Lauterpacht about the possibility of a *non liquet* against the background of Kelsenian legal theory.

39 Cf von Wright (n 13) 86 et seq.

40 See Alchourrón/Bulygin (n 1); for a more detailed analysis of the interdefinability thesis, see also F Poggi, *Norme permissive* (Torino, Giappichelli 2004) 29–45.

41 A classical restatement of this position can be found in D Anzilotti, *Corso di diritto internazionale, Vol I* (Padova, CEDAM, 4th ed 1955) 106: 'La questione se il ricorso all'analogia debba considerarsi come un principio generale implicito dell'ordinamento giuridico internazionale, va risolta esclusivamente in base al senso e allo spirito dell'ordinamento stesso. Da questo punto di vista, non sembra azzardato dire che il diritto internazionale ripugna a qualsiasi estensione degli obblighi assunti, oltre i casi contemplati. Gli Stati sono ancora cosi gelosi della loro autonomia, che non si può certamente presumere che essi intendano di limitarla oltre quanto risulta dalle norme che adottano. La tesi, ad ogni memento e con tanta insistenza ripetuta, che no è lecito estendere per via d'interpretazione le limitazioni della sovranità, potrebbe meglio e più esattamente esprimersi dicendo che nel diritto internazionale non è ammisibile l'estensione analogica delle norme quando non risulti espressamente o tacitamente voluta dalle parti.' In other words, Anzilotti derives the normative argument against the admissibility of analogical arguments from the sociological observations that states are unwilling to accept any extension of the obligations they have explicitly accepted.

lecture on *Les Règles Générales du Droit de la Paix*,[42] delivered at the Hague Academy of International Law in 1934: 'Nous sommes fidèles à notre point de vue strictement positif sur la nature entièrement contractuelle de tout le droit des gens, *en refusant* catégoriquement, sauf disposition expresse en sens contraire, d'admettre *l'analogie* comme moyen de remédier aux vaste lacunes existant dans ce domaine du droit.'[43] However, despite his emphatic embracement of voluntarist positivism, he qualified this categorical rejection of analogical reasoning, noting that 'l'acceptation d'une norme [by the states] renferme ses présuppositions et les consequénces (immédiates) qui en découlent'.[44] Thus, Strupp intended to draw a distinction between analogy as a (legitimate) means of interpretation and analogy as an (illegitimate) way of imposing on the states more extensive obligations than they have consented to.

This suggestion, which was based on the assumption that it is possible to recognise a clear demarcation line between the use of analogies as a means of interpretation and as one of norm-creation (and thus, to discern a distinction between interpretation and norm-creation in general), had already been called into question by legal theorists at Strupp's time, in particular as far as rules of international law were concerned.[45] With the rise of the 'critical legal studies'[46] movement, the use of conventional methods of legal reasoning and the belief in methodology as a means of achieving objectivity were subjected to a far more formidable challenge, because proponents of the 'critical approach' are regarding legal methodology as yet another way to cloak the exercise of political power in the guise of objectivity and respectability.[47]

42 K Strupp, 'Les règles générales du droit de la paix' (1934) 47-I *Recueil des Cours* 263.

43 Ibid, 337 (emphasis original).

44 Ibid.

45 See eg P Fedozzi, *Introduzione al Diritto Internazionale e Parte Generale* (Padova, CEDAM, 2nd ed 1933) 54, arguing that analogical reasoning inevitably involves norm-creation: 'La teoria generale del diritto classifica l'analogia come una forma d'interpretazione. Non siamo di quest'avviso, che forse nel campo internazionale è ancor meno giustificabile che nel campo interno. È stato giustamente rilevato che se interpretazione de diritto è, come generalmente s'intende, accertamento della volontà del legislatore, l'analogia non è interpretazione.' (footnote omitted).

46 For a description and analysis of the 'critical approach' to international law see eg O De Schutter, 'Les Critical Legal Studies aux pays de droit international' (1992) *Droit et Societé* 585; for a recent textbook on international law, as viewed from the perspective of the 'critical legal studies' movement, see W Mansell/K Openshaw, *International Law: A Critical Introduction* (Oxford, Hart 2013); perhaps the two most influential contributions in the field of international law from a critical point of view are M Koskenniemi, *From Apology to Utopia: The Structure of International Legal Argument* (Cambridge, Cambridge University Press, reissue 2005), and D Kennedy, *International Legal Structures* (Baden-Baden, Nomos 1987).

47 For a review of various applications of this paradigm to international legal theory, see eg A Carty, 'Critical International Law: Recent Trends in International Legal Theory' (1991) 2 *European Journal of International Law* 1. For an analysis and a

Today, the use of analogical reasoning in international law is therefore liable to attacks from two directions: From one direction, proponents of voluntarist positivism still challenge its legitimacy on the grounds that it might give rise to rules to which the states have not explicitly consented.[48] Arguing from another direction, critical legal scholars reject categorically the supposition that there is anything like an 'objective' legal methodology, in the sense that it could be evaluated from a neutral standpoint unbiased by the observer's own particular worldview;[49] if one accepts this latter notion, it is a logical consequence to dismiss the relevance of analogical reasoning, or to portrait it as the rather sinister attempt to justify a result reached by other means.

The validity of the voluntarist line of criticism depends on the concept of analogy or analogical reasoning one has in mind: Thus, even a proponent of consensualist positivism can accept the validity of reasoning by analogy in the sense of a method of interpretation that is based on the assumption that a legislator, for example the contracting parties of a treaty, intended to regulate a broader range of circumstances than those explicitly covered by the language chosen.[50] For a proponent of the critical approach, on the other hand, it seems difficult to see any virtue in analogy as a means of legal reasoning: If one follows Koskenniemi in regarding international legal argument as shaped by two irreconcilably opposed patterns of argumentation,[51] one *utopian* that is deductive, starting with normative principles, and one *apologetic* that is inductive, limited to the analysis of actual state behaviour, a technique such as analogical reasoning that combines the normative with the empirical must *prima facie* appear to be self-contradictory – at best evidently impossible to apply, at worst an insidious tool of deception.[52]

Where Koskenniemi construes international legal argument (or in fact all legal argument) as being fraught with irreconcilable antinomies – of subjectivity vs

critique of these critical attitude see LB Solum, 'The Indeterminacy Crisis: Critiquing Critical Dogma' (1987) 54 *University of Chicago Law Review* 462.

48 For a more recent restatement of this old argument see eg W Heintschel von Heinegg, 'Die weiteren Quellen des Völkerrechts' in K Ipsen (ed), *Völkerrecht* (München, CH Beck, 5th ed 2004) 210 (245).

49 This point of view was concisely stated by Martti Koskenniemi in a letter in which he explained his reasons for declining their invitation to participate in a symposium on 'The Methods of International Law'. See M Koskenniemi, 'Letter to the Editors of the Symposion' (1999) 93 *American Journal of International Law* 351.

50 See eg G Herczegh, *General Principles of Law and the International Legal Order* (Budapest, Akadémiai kiadó 1969) 110 et seq: 'A condition of the application of analogy in municipal and in international law is the presumption that if the legislator has brought under regulation certain living conditions it is his intention to extend the regulation to all kindred relations and it is merely due to the deficiencies of formulation that the wording of the legal rule does not embrace them all.'

51 See Koskenniemi (n 46) 58–67; see also Kennedy (n 46), to whom Koskenniemi acknowledges his indebtedness in this respect.

52 For the argument that legal methodology, as taught in law schools, is merely tool for the promotion of political interests, see eg D Kennedy, 'Legal Education and the Reproduction of Hierarchy' (1982) 32 *Journal of Legal Education* 591.

objectivity, stability vs change, empiricism vs normativism, is vs ought, or generally apologism vs utopianism, he seems to base his theory on a rather simplistic conception of the nature of the human mind, and consequently of all social phenomena and interpersonal relations. However, Koskenniemi is hardly alone in misconstruing customary international law in terms of simplistic antagonisms: Indeed, it has recently been argued that one of the main flaws of many contemporary theories of customary international law is their exclusionism, the fact that they portray it in an 'either-or' fashion, and thus artificially split up reality into irreconcilable dichotomies.[53]

C. The Ubiquity of Analogical Reasoning in International Law

If there is one insight of Hegelian philosophy of mind that resonates well with modern conceptions of social and psychological phenomena, it is that of the sublation of the antagonism between universality and particularity, between subjectivity and objectivity, the understanding that the universal manifests itself in the particular, the objective in the subjective.[54] Recently, analogical reasoning as an essential mode in which the human mind proceeds in dealing with new and unfamiliar situations by combining elements of inductive or bottom up- and deductive or top down-approaches[55] has attracted renewed attention: Thus, the cognitive scientist Douglas Hofstadter and the developmental psychologist Emmanuel Sander have described analogies as 'the fire and fuel of thinking'.[56] In the field of legal theory, Cass Sunstein has argued that

53 See L Blutman, 'Conceptual Confusion and Methodological Deficiencies: Some Ways that Theories on Customary International Law Fail' (2014) 25 *European Journal of International Law* 529 (546): 'It must be recalled that setting up such dichotomies entails considerable simplification. Despite the theoretical elegance that these constructions display, dichotomies often collapse in practice or even in theory.'

54 See GF Hegel, *Science of Logic* (AV Miller transl, London, Allen & Unwin 1969) esp § 1779: 'In this process the general presupposition is sublated, namely the determination of the good as a merely subjective end limited in respect of content, the necessity of realising it by subjective activity, and this activity itself. In the result the mediation sublates itself; the result is an *immediacy* that is not the restoration of the presupposition, but rather its accomplished sublation. With this, the Idea of the Notion that is determined in and for itself is posited as being no longer merely in the active subject but as equally an immediate actuality; and conversely, this actuality is posited, as it is in cognition, as an objectivity possessing a true being.' See on the Hegelian philosophy of mind and its contemporary relevance RD Winfield, *Hegel and Mind. Rethinking Philosophical Psychology* (Basingstoke, Palgrave Macmillan 2010).

55 For a discussion of legal methodology in the framework of these two alternative approaches (bottom up vs. top down) see RA Posner, 'Legal Reasoning from the Top Down and From the Bottom Up' (1992) 59 *University of Chicago Law Review* 433.

56 See D Hofstadter/E Sander, *Surfaces and Essences: Analogy as the Fire and Fuel of Thinking* (New York, Basic Books 2013); their approach is aptly characterised in

analogical reasoning is the most fundamental tool in legal methodology.[57] Sunstein identifies four major features which characterise this form of legal reasoning: The achievement of 'principled consistency', a 'focus on particulars', and its allowing for 'incompletely theorized judgments' and 'principles operating at a low or intermediate level of abstraction'.[58] These four features combined, Sunstein claims, make analogical reasoning so attractive to the legal practitioner, as they enable him or her to analyse or decide cases in a consistent manner without having to develop a full-fledged, comprehensive theory of the respective field of the law beforehand.

Although these features appear to be of particular relevance to case law systems like the common law, the interest in analogical reasoning is not limited to Anglo-American legal scholarship. The Austro-Hungarian legal scholar Eugen Ehrlich, one of the founding fathers of sociology of law as an academic discipline, wrote in his 1918 study *Die Juristische Logik* ('The Juridical Logic') that the technique of analogy ranks among 'the highest intellectual achievements human minds are capable of', as it is 'creative, not just in its psychological foundations, but also in its results'.[59] In Germany, the legal philosopher and criminal law scholar Arthur Kaufmann has developed a forceful theory of law as being grounded substantially in analogical thought, based on the argument that '... every legal analysis, every so-called "subsumption" displays the structural propensities of an analogy'.[60] This is so, Kaufmann asserts, because law itself is the expression of a *correspondence* between norm and fact, a correspondence that, to him, is analogical in nature.[61] Legal reasoning is thus described as 'the mutual assimilation of facts of life and norms'.[62]

In a similar vein, and with a focus on the specificities of case law systems like the common law, Sunstein maintains that '[b]y themselves, factual situations tell us little until we impose some sort of pattern on them. We say that something is like something else only because we have a principle that tells us so ...'[63] The establishment of a relevant similarity is, to be sure, an indispensable precondition of analogical reasoning, and that similarity can only be determined by reference to a preconceived 'pattern' or 'principle' – two cases may be

their programmatic opening statement: '[W]ithout concepts, there can be no thoughts; and without analogies, there can be no concepts.' (Ibid, 3).

57 C Sunstein, 'On Analogical Reasoning' (1993) 106 *Harvard Law Review* 741.

58 Ibid, 764 (emphasis original).

59 E Ehrlich, *Die Juristische Logik* (Tübingen, Mohr 1918) 227 (English translation of the quote by the present author).

60 A Kaufmann, *Analogie und Natur der Sache: Zugleich ein Beitrag zur Lehre vom Typus* (Heidelberg, CF Müller, 2nd ed 1982) 37; in the German original: 'Von hier aus wird deutlich, dass jede Rechtserkenntnis, jede Rechtsfindung, jede sog. "Subsumtion" die Struktur einer Analogie aufweist.' (English translation of the quote by the present author).

61 Ibid, 19: 'Das Recht ist ursprünglich analog.'

62 Ibid, 37.

63 Sunstein (n 57) 774.

similar or alike with respect to an almost infinite number of contingencies, but only few of them are relevant for the purposes of *legal* reasoning.

But if we need principles anyway, why should we engage in the seemingly tedious and awkward process of analogical reasoning, instead of basing the decision of a case immediately on fundamental principles, as Ronald Dworkin famously suggested with respect to the 'one right answer' to be given in 'hard cases' by the allegorical figure of 'Judge Hercules'?[64] Because, Sunstein argues, 'relevant principles often cannot be described in advance except at an uninformatively high and crude level of generality'.[65] Moreover, in many situations it is unrealistic to assume that agreement on principles can easily be reached. But in the absence of such agreement, nothing could ever be decided under a genuine top down-approach to legal reasoning. Analogical reasoning, on the other hand, 'allows people who diverge on abstract principle to converge on particular outcomes'.[66] The analogical thinker, 'unequipped with (or unburdened by) a unitary theory of the good or the right, … is in a position to see clearly … the diverse and plural goods that are at stake and to make choices among them'.[67] Thus, people engaged in analogical reasoning 'are peculiarly alert to the inconsistent or abhorrent result, and they take strong convictions about particular cases to provide reasons for re-evaluating their views about particular cases or even about apparently guiding principles'.[68]

It is easy to see that the benefits of analogical reasoning so eloquently described by Cass Sunstein are of high relevance to unwritten international law as well.[69] There, perhaps more than in any domestic legal system, it is difficult (if not indeed virtually impossible) to achieve agreement on a 'unitary theory of the good or the right'. Agreement in international law often exists – if indeed it exists at all – only about either principles on the highest level of abstraction, such as sovereignty and non-intervention,[70], which are frequently incapable of yielding sufficiently precise rules of decision, or about the evaluation of a highly specific precedent, for example a consensus that a specific form of mistreatment (such as 'waterboarding')[71] violates the prohibition of torture.

64 See R Dworkin, *Taking Rights Seriously* (Cambridge, Harvard University Press 1977); for a criticism of Dworkin's top down-approach of legal reasoning, see Posner (n 55).
65 Sunstein (n 57) 775.
66 Ibid, 791.
67 Ibid, 789.
68 Ibid, 791.
69 However, it is attempted with surprising frequency to apply Dworkin's theory of principles to the field of international law; for an application of Dworkin's approach to the ICJ's jurisprudence on self-defence, see JA Green, *The International Court of Justice and Self-Defence in International Law* (Oxford, Hart 2009) 182–88.
70 One may think of Charles-Maurice de Talleyrand's cynical remark about the meaning of the term 'intervention': 'C'est un mot métaphysique et politique, qui signifie à peu près la même chose qu'intervention.'
71 A remarkable admission with respect to the existence of a consensus on the assessment of waterboarding as torture was recently made by US President Barack

But in the vast areas of customary international law where neither a generally recognised principle provides adequate guidance, nor a well-known precedent immediately calls for application, analogical reasoning recommends itself as a modestly ambitious means of legal analysis and systematisation. It is therefore most unfortunate that the reputation of this mode of reasoning in international law, as has already been described above, is tarnished not only by doubts about its legitimacy in a system based on state consent, but also by the suspicions that are constantly being raised against its logical validity.

Only few scholars have taken notice of the fact that analogical reasoning in international law *already* fulfils a much more substantial function than that of occasionally filling alleged 'gaps': Thus, Albert Bleckmann has rightly emphasised the analogical nature of the logical inferences *a maiore ad minus* and *a fortiori*,[72] which are used not infrequently[73] in international law. The same is also true for the opposite argument, the *argumentum e contrario*,[74] as well as the closely related interpretative precept *expressio unius est exclusio alterius*.[75] For example, the Permanent Court of International Justice, in the *Wimbledon* case, applied the *argumentum e contrario* in its construction of Article 380 of the Treaty of Versailles, deciding that the specific treaty provisions about the Kiel Canal could not be abrogated by an analogical application of the provisions regulating the use of Germany's other navigable waterways.[76] Interestingly, in that same case the dissenting judges Anzilotti and Huber suggested to base the decision on a very different analogical argument, namely an inference *a fortiori*: They argued that the admissibility of certain security measures even in times of

Obama, who stated at a White House press conference on August 1, 2014, that the US administration had been 'engaged in some of these enhanced interrogation techniques, techniques that I believe and I think any fair-minded person would believe were torture ...' a transcript of this press conference is available at <http://www.whitehouse.gov/the-press-office/2014/08/01/press-conference-president>accessed 20 August 2017.

72 See Bleckmann (n 14) 221.

73 For an overview of the practice of international courts in this respect, see generally R Kolb *Interprétation et Création du Droit International* (Bruxelles, Bruylant 2006) 737–48; Kolb aptly subsumed the arguments *a fortiori* and *a maiore ad minus* under a category he refers to as 'l'analogie renforcée' (ibid, 737).

74 Ibid, 748–56; again, Kolb coined an appropriate term, referring to the argument *e contrario* as 'l'analogie inversée'.

75 On this rule in the context of treaty interpretation see eg U Linderfalk, *On the Interpretation of Treaties: The Modern International Law as Expressed in the 1969 Vienna Convention on the Law of Treaties* (Dordrecht et al, Springer 2007) 299–303; Linderfalk, however, disagrees with those authors who regard the argument *e contrario* as a form of analogical reasoning. This terminological question depends, of course, on whether one conceives of such 'negative' or 'inverted' forms of analogical reasoning as being analogies at all.

76 See the *Case Concerning the SS Wimbledon* [1923] PCIJ Series A, No 1, 24: 'The idea which underlies Article 380 and the following articles of the Treaty is not to be sought by drawing an analogy, but rather by arguing *a contrario*, a method of argument which excludes them.' In this passage, the nature of the argument e contrario as a form of 'negative' or 'inverted analogy' becomes quite apparent.

peace meant they could be applied *a fortiori* in times of war.[77] This example is perhaps illustrative of both the richness and the – occasional – ambivalence of analogical reasoning.

To be sure, analogical arguments such as *a maiore ad minus, e contrario* and *a fortiori* feature more prominently and explicitly in the interpretation of treaty law than in the application of unwritten rules of international law. This does not imply, however, that analogical reasoning is less relevant in the area of customary international law. Quite the contrary: If Sunstein and others are correct in asserting that the peculiar nature of the common law – the fact that it is structurally case law – means that the judge administering it must rely to a significant degree on (positive or negative) analogies to achieve the predictability and coherence that are indispensable attributes of any legal system conforming to the requirements of the rule of law,[78] this applies – *a fortiori*, as it were – to customary international law, which lacks a central legislative authority capable of correcting the inconsistencies and contradictions which inevitably ensue from the processual nature[79] of a case law system.[80]

In a preceding chapter,[81] a number of cases in which the International Court of Justice has used analogical reasoning with respect to rules of customary international law have already been discussed. One of the most interesting of those was the *Arrest Warrant* case, where the ICJ had decided that the *ratio legis* behind the rule providing absolute immunity *ratione personae* from foreign criminal proceedings to acting Heads of States was applicable to incumbent Foreign Ministers as well. In the aftermath of the decision, it has been questioned how far the 'functional rationale'[82] of the ICJ in the *Arrest Warrant* case could be extended beyond the so-called 'troika'[83] consisting of

77 Ibid, Dissenting Opinion of Judges Anzilotti and Huber, 39.

78 See on the advantages of analogical reasoning from a common law perspective E Sherwin, 'A Defense of Analogical Reasoning in Law' (1999) 66 *University of Chicago Law Review* 1179; on the importance of achieving coherence through legal reasoning, see also J Raz, 'The Relevance of Coherence' in S Brewer (ed), *Moral Theory and Legal Reasoning* (New York and London, Garland 1998) 303.

79 On this aspect of customary international law, see A Bleckmann, 'Die Praxis des Völkergewohnheitsrecht als konsekutive Rechtssetzung' in R Bernhardt/WK Geck/G Jaennicke/H Steinberger (eds), *Völkerrecht als Rechtsordnung: Festschrift für Hermann Mosler* (Heidelberg/Berlin, Springer 1983) 89.

80 For a similar argument about the necessity of achieving some sort of systematization with respect to unwritten international law, see Gärditz (n 8).

81 Above, Ch IV, C.

82 For this apt term see J Foakes, *The Position of Heads of States and Senior Officials under International Law* (Oxford, Oxford University Press 2014) 125.

83 The term was coined by the first Special Rapporteur of the International Law Commission on the issue of 'Immunity of State officials from Foreign Criminal Jurisdiction', Roman Kolodkin; see his Preliminary Report, UN DOC A/CN.4/601 (29 May 2008), para 111. In the Russian version, the term 'коренную тройку' is used; in the official English translation, the phrase reads 'basic threesome'. However, in academic discourse, the more catchy word 'troika' has often been used in English as well, see eg Foakes (n 82) 5.

Head of State, Head of Government and Foreign Minister, which were explicitly referred to in the judgment. The International Law Commission, discussing the issue in the context of its project on 'Immunity of State officials from Foreign Criminal Jurisdiction', seems inclined to keep the granting of immunity *ratione personae* limited to this 'basic troika',[84] although the commission apparently remains divided on the issue.[85]

It is not feasible, and indeed not necessary in the context of the present inquiry, to restate the arguments for a more or less expansive or restrictive position in this respect. What is interesting about the discussions on the scope of immunities is that they essentially proceed along the lines of basic analogical reasoning, whether in the form of positive or negative analogies. Thus, the principal question is whether state official X discharges a function sufficiently akin to that of state official Y to be accorded the same legal position. This is not to say, however, that the determination of immunities by courts or by the International Law Commission is an exercise in – as it were – reasoning *more geometrico*, which starts from some 'first principles', such as abstract considerations of utility, and thence deduces the most minute legal details. To the contrary, both the case law of domestic and international courts and the reports of the International Law Commission on the issue of immunities of state officials abound with examples of the actual behaviour of states. Yet the ascertainment of a rule of customary international law is not confined merely to the rather mechanical assembly of the greatest possible amount of practices and precedents. If it were, the process would indeed be liable to the criticism of being arbitrary: Not only is it often impossible for a court (and sometimes difficult even for the ILC) to obtain virtually *all* information about possibly relevant state behaviour, but it is also impossible to determine which behaviour could be regarded as *legally relevant*.[86] The question is, however, which consequence is to be drawn from this insight.

84 See the text of Draft article 3, as provisionally adopted by the Drafting Committee at the ILC's 65th session in 2013, UN Doc A/CN.4/L.814: 'Heads of State, Heads of Government and Ministers for Foreign Affairs enjoy immunity ratione personae from the exercise of foreign criminal jurisdiction.'

85 On the discussions on this point within the ILC, see Foakes (n 82) 132–3.

86 The criterion of *relevance* of practice occupies a prominent place in the theories of customary international law. The problem of such theories often consists in their attempt to define this criterion in general terms, as an abstract standard that applies always. A good example is the approach of M Byers, *Custom, Power and the Power of Rules: International Relations and Customary International Law* (Cambridge, Cambridge University Press 1999), who argues that the most important criterion of distinguishing legally relevant state practice from other forms of state behaviour is 'the *cost* that is entailed by the instance of State practice in question…' (ibid, 156, emphasis added); while this criterion is consistent with Byer's self-styled 'non-normative' (ibid, 15–18, 147) theory of customary international law, the present author has doubts whether this criterion is generalisable even as a purely descriptive theory: For example, how can the 'cost' of inaction or acquiescence in the emergence of a new rule be determined? And does the fact that a

One of the arguments repeatedly put forward in the context of the debate about the ascent of purportedly 'modern' approaches to customary international law has been that in a community of states that is constantly expanding in numbers and becoming both more interconnected and more asymmetric in terms of power, the 'less-than-helpful abstractions' of traditional sources doctrine, with their emphasis on sovereign equality and quasi-universal or at least widespread participation in the creation of new rules of customary international law, have to be abandoned in favour of a conception of 'deductive' or 'constructive international law'.[87] The proponents of this 'constructive' approach to international law are partly correct insofar as they claim that the impossibility of a purely inductive approach to international law, in the sense of a method that starts and ends with the collection of instances of state practice unguided by any directing principle, has become more apparent today than it might have been some decades ago. Yet it would be a fundamental error to play out 'inductive' and 'deductive' reasoning against each other, and to conceive of them as being opposed or even mutually exclusive.[88] Rather, one should regard them as components of a blend, the particular composition of which depends on the individual question for which an answer is sought, and on the nature of the relevant field of law.[89] Analogical reasoning, it seems, is essentially the method by which this joinder is effected. As de Visscher argued, '[o]n s'accorde à voir dans le droit coutumier le terrain d'élection de l'extension analogique'.[90] The usefulness of analogical reasoning in customary international law analysis consists of the fact that it allows to base legal argument on the gradual expansion to new phenomena of a limited consensus already existing about the legal evaluation of particular acts and circumstances. Wherever a new field of law emerges, such as environmental law,[91] air and space law

protest may be particularly costly in political terms make it automatically legally relevant for the purpose of determining customary international law?

87 See eg M Herdegen, 'Asymmetrien in der Staatenwelt und die Herausforderungen des "konstruktiven Völkerrechts"' (2004) 64 *Zeitschrift für ausländisches öffentliches Recht und Völkerrecht* 571; see also id, 'Das "konstruktive Völkerrecht" und seine Grenzen: die Dynamik des Völkerrechts als Methodenfrage' in PM Dupuy (ed), *Völkerrecht als Wertordnung: Festschrift für Christian Tomuschat* (Kehl, Engel 2006) 899.

88 For a similar argument, see the recent contribution by WT Worster, 'The Inductive and Deductive Methods in Customary International Law Analysis: Traditional and Modern Approaches' (2014) 45 *Georgetown Journal of International Law* 445.

89 See ibid, 521: '[E]ach act of customary international legal analysis employs a blend of approaches across a handful of questions. In doing so, it balances the tension between apology and utopia, and realizes the benefit of the differing approaches.'

90 C de Visscher, *Théories et Réalités en Droit International Public* (Paris, Pedone, 4th ed 1970) 41.

91 On the methodological difficulties involved in the process of establishing customary international law as a source of international environmental law, see A Bodansky, 'Customary (and Not So Customary) International Environmental Law' (1995) 3 *Global Legal Studies Journal* 105.

or the international law of cyberspace,[92], analogical reasoning allows the participants in the process to base their arguments on something more acceptable than unsubstantiated suggestions of utility or fairness.

D. The Virtues of Analogical Argument

Especially in an environment as diverse and ideologically and politically divided as the present international community, the advantage of this mode of argument is by no means negligible. Analogical reasoning is thus a method that conforms to Amartya Sen's description of a 'comparative', as opposed to a 'transcendental', approach to justice.[93] According to Sen, the purpose of a theory of justice cannot be to devise 'a perfectly just social arrangement', or to harmonise competing values by subordinating them to some paramount principle identified *in abstracto*, as the transcendental approach attempts; rather, one should make decisions based on the comparative assessment of the advantages and disadvantages of the competing alternatives. In other words, in order to agree on making a choice between two competing values, one does not need to agree on the essence of the ultimate good.[94] Although Sen did not explicitly refer to this mode of reasoning as 'analogical', but used the term 'social choice' (as opposed to 'rational choice') instead, others have expressed the connection between analogies and social choice more clearly.

Thus, Bruce Chapman applied social choice theory, as developed by Sen and other economists such as Kenneth Arrow, to judicial decision-making.[95] In an influential paper, entitled 'The Rational and the Reasonable: Social Choice Theory and Adjudication', Chapman argues that legal reasoning – at least in

92 One of the hotly debated issues in this respect concerns the question of whether – and, if so, under which conditions – computer network attacks can be classified as an illicit 'use of force' under the Charter of the United Nations as well as under customary international law, or even as an 'armed attack', triggering the right of self-defence under the *jus ad bellum*; on these problems, see eg H Harrison Dinnis, *Cyber Warfare and the Laws of War* (Cambridge, Cambridge University Press 2012) 37–116.

93 On the conceptual distinction between 'comparative' and 'transcendental' frameworks for the assessment of justice, see A Sen, *The Idea of Justice* (London, Penguin 2010) 15–18 and passim.

94 Sen (ibid, at 16) gives an illustrative example of the difference between the transcendental and the comparative approach: '[I]f we are trying to choose between a Picasso and a Dali, it is of no help to invoke a diagnosis (even if such a transcendental diagnosis could be made) that the ideal picture in the world is the *Mona Lisa*. That may be interesting to hear, but it is neither here nor there in the choice between Picasso and Dali. Indeed, it is not at all necessary to talk about what may be the greatest or most perfect picture in the world, to choose between the two alternatives that we are facing. Nor is it sufficient, or indeed of any particular help, to know that the *Mona Lisa* is the most perfect picture in the world when the choice is actually between a Dali and a Picasso.'

95 B Chapman, 'The Rational and the Reasonable: Social Choice Theory and Adjudication' (1994) 61 *University of Chicago Law Review* 41.

common law legal systems – aspires to an ideal of rationality which is fundamentally different from that pursued in (economic) rational choice analysis. Whereas rational choice analysis is forward-looking in that it makes decisions based on the individual desirability of the foreseeable consequences of certain actions in the future, legal reasoning looks to the past in that it seeks to achieve consistency by comparing new situations with precedents. The benefit of the latter approach, Chapman asserts, consists in the fact that it ultimately yields more *efficient* results:

> This is because a conscious pursuit of the goal opens up for individuals (or coalitions of individuals) too many possibilities of reconsidering past choices and, therefore, insufficiently anchors the different choosers, whose choices have to be coordinated after all, in some common convention or past history. Better is the process of common law adjudication that (within limits, of course) reinforces rather than constantly reconsiders our past precedents or conventions, even if to do so is to miss, from time to time, some obvious possibility of social improvement.[96]

For Chapman, legal reasoning of an analogical kind is the answer to the problem of coordinating human actions, an approach that is very close to Hayek's view of law as a 'spontaneous order': As it is impossible in an extended social order to achieve coordination by reference to a transcendental optimum state, a common ultimate goal, it is better to 'get on with *some* minimally acceptable convention for coordinating human action [than] always to seek out some uniquely "best" one'.[97]

This is a point that seems to be a valid argument not only against rational choice approaches centred around the *homo oeconomicus*, the self-interested individual, but also against attempts to construe law in accordance with a transcendental theory of justice. Thus, one might argue with respect to international law that abstract concepts such as 'moral truth' and 'justice' are goals that are inadequate to achieve coordination among the members of the international community, as such concepts are both too abstract and too controversial.[98] This does not mean that the idea of justice is not one that is of central importance in international law, but it is an idea of 'comparative' justice, in Sen's terminology, not dependent on a theory of ultimate, transcendental values. Analogical reasoning plays a vitally important part here, not only as a means of social coordination: After all, the maxim that 'like cases should be treated alike' is one of the most fundamental precepts associated with the idea of justice.[99]

96 Ibid, 110.
97 Ibid, 111.
98 For a similar argument with respect to law in general, see NB Reynolds, 'Law as Convention' (1989) 2 *Ratio Juris* 105 (108–9).
99 See eg J Waldron, *"Partly Laws Common to All Mankind": Foreign Law in American Courts* (New Haven, Yale University Press 2012) 109–41, making this

An illustrative example of the intricate connection between analogical reasoning and the values of both efficiency and justice can be found in the law of state responsibility, especially where the rules governing the liability of states for transboundary damage are concerned.[100] It goes without saying that this field of international law is regarded by the states as particularly sensitive, which makes it difficult if not impossible to reach an agreement on a multilateral treaty regulating all of its aspects comprehensively. On the one hand, regulation of hazardous activities with potentially disastrous transboundary effects is one of the major challenges with which international law has to cope in an age when the rapid industrialisation of former developing countries leads to a significant increase of activities that, whether accidentally (such as in the case of nuclear disasters or oil spills in the oceans) or as an inevitable consequence of regular behaviour (such as the emission of carbon dioxide into the atmosphere by industrialised nations) affect people and peoples living far beyond their borders, and perhaps even on other continents.[101] On the other hand, states are reluctant to submit to any overarching regulatory principle of compensation whose implications and consequences in future cases they cannot foresee, and whose potential costs they cannot reliably calculate.

This is so in particular since more and more states have liberalised their economies over the course of the past two decades, which means that hazardous activities are frequently undertaken not by the territorial state itself or by an entity under its immediate control, but by private companies whose behaviour a state can only indirectly influence through domestic regulation, and whose financial resources may often not be sufficient to compensate for the destruction caused by certain ultra-hazardous activities.[102]

Looking at the development over the course of time of the international rules pertaining to the compensation for transboundary damage, especially in the environmental field, one might be tempted to expect a linear development

argument in the context of the use of comparative constitutional law in deciding human and civil rights cases; see also HLA Hart, *The Concept of Law* (Oxford, Oxford University Press, 2nd ed 1994) ch VIII. The maxim originates in Aristotle's 'Nicomachean Ethics', 1131a10–b15.

100 For a thorough analysis of the theoretical as well as practical aspects of this complex subfield of the law of state responsibility, see H Xue, *Transboundary Damage in International Law* (Cambridge, Cambridge University Press 2003).

101 The disastrous accident that occurred in the nuclear power plant of Fukushima Daichii on March 11, 2011, is but one recent example. For a discussion of the international liability issues in this respect, see eg H Cook, 'International Nuclear Law: Nuclear Safety, Emergency Response and Nuclear Liability' in S Butt/H Nasu/L Nottage (eds), *Asia-Pacific Disaster Management Comparative and Socio-Legal Perspectives* (Heidelberg, Springer 2014) 279; for a discussion of the liability issues involved in the 2010 spill caused by the BP-operated oil platform Deepwater Horizon in the Gulf of Mexico, see TJ Schoenenbaum, 'Liability for Damages in Oil Spill Accidents: Evaluating the USA and International Law Regimes in the Light of Deepwater Horizon' (2012) 24 *Journal of Environmental Law* 395.

102 See Xue (n 100)

in the sense that an increase of the quantity and quality of hazardous activities conducted by states would have been reflected in a parallel increase of the strictness of rules of compensation.[103] This expectation is supported by another consideration: Since the process of globalisation has made available sophisticated facilities of chemical and even nuclear industry to a great number of formerly underdeveloped countries, the risk of being disastrously affected by the consequences of an accident in such facilities is no longer limited to the immediate neighbours of a relatively small number of powerful industrial nations, which, through their great economic and political leverage, might hitherto have been successful in impeding the development of stricter rules of international liability in this particular field. Thus, it should theoretically be in every state's well-conceived self-interest to insist on the implementation of rather rigid, general rules.

Such expectations, which would be consistent with the kind of 'rational choice' approaches prevalent in the scholarly analysis (much less in the practice) of domestic tort law,[104] are bound to be disappointed when it comes to the international legal order. Here, the factors to be taken into account in the attribution of liability and the interests at stake are considerably more diverse, and often hardly quantifiable at all.[105] Unlike in domestic contexts, the question of attribution with respect to the damage caused by hazardous activities cannot simply be analysed under a 'free rider' paradigm, which asserts that tort law has to prevent participants in the market from shifting the cost incurred by their – profitable but dangerous – business to the public, while keeping the gains for themselves. Thus, the principle of strict liability (liability without fault), which many domestic legislations adopt as a standard rule of compensation for damages caused by certain ultra-hazardous activities, cannot simply be imported 'lock, stock and barrel' into international law. There, the 'balance of needs to develop industry and the interests to be protected from the possible harm caused by the activity has to be weighed on a concrete basis.'[106]

103 For some rather optimistic expectations in this respect, see eg O Schachter, 'The Environment, Community, and International Law' (1989) 30 *Harvard International Law Journal* 393; id, 'The Emergence of International Environmental Law' (1991) 44 *Journal of International Affairs* 157.

104 For a classical example of this approach, see W Landes/RA Posner, *The Economic Structure of Tort Law* (Cambridge/MA, Harvard University Press 1987).

105 But see EA Posner/AO Sykes, 'An Economic Analysis of State and Individual Responsibility Under International Law' (2007) 9 *American Law and Economics Review* 72, finding substantial similarities between state responsibility in international law and the doctrine of vicarious liability in domestic tort law. However, Posner and Sykes themselves admit that they 'do not mean to suggest that efficiency is the sole objective or rationale for international law. Our claim is much more modest, and amounts simply to the suggestion that economic efficiency is relevant in thinking about international law …' (ibid, 76). In such a moderate way, the recourse to efficiency arguments in international law seems hardly objectionable.

106 Xue (n 100).

This cannot and does not mean, however, that there should be no general legal rules and principles applicable in this field, and that decisions have to be made purely on the basis of ad-hoc considerations of what is subjectively perceived as a 'fair' division of loss in a particular case. Rather, it means that these rules derive from a comparative analysis of several prior instances in which such losses have been apportioned, whether in judicial or arbitral decisions or in diplomatic negotiations. In other words, the rules in this field emerge through *analogical* reasoning. A famous example in this respect is provided by the 1941 award in the *Trail Smelter* arbitration.[107] By way of a double analogy – in a manner of speaking – the tribunal applied principles of *domestic*[108] law governing compensation for the pollution of *rivers* to establish the *international* liability for transboundary harm caused by pollution of the *air*.[109] The rationale of this precedent, however significant it may be, should perhaps not be overstretched, and it is correct that '[t]o this day, cases where transboundary damage is settled by the application of general principles of international law are few and far between.'[110]

Nevertheless, whenever there are no applicable treaty rules on the matter, conclusions have to be drawn by way of analogy: Only by comparing a particular case with the rationale of 'precedents' (in the widest sense of the word), and by sorting out common features that are normatively relevant, it becomes possible to achieve a solution that blends individual fairness with principled consistency and that thus, if anything in international law, can plausibly claim to aspire to 'justice'.[111]

E. General Principles: Their Nature and Place

Over the course of the present chapter, the concepts of 'purpose' in general, and the technique of 'purposive interpretation' in particular, have been used to illustrate both the unity and the distinctiveness of the different sources of international law. From this perspective, the sources are distinguished by the relative weight attached to the subjective and objective component of their purpose. They are united, however, by the fact that all of them can be analysed with recourse to the 'purpose' which they respectively serve: In Rudolf von

107 *Trail Smelter Arbitration (USA v Canada)* (1938, 1941) 3 RIAA 1905.

108 The application of domestic sources of law was expressly authorised by the parties in the *Trail Smelter* case, which had called upon the tribunal to apply 'law and practice followed in dealing with cognate question in the United States of America as well as principles of international law'. See Art IV of the arbitral agreement between the United States and Canada of 1935, quoted after V Lowe, *International Law* (Oxford, Oxford University Press 2007) 240.

109 See for a (critical) reappraisal of this case, AP Rubin, 'Pollution by Analogy: The Trail Smelter Arbitration' (1970) 50 *Oregon Law Review* 259.

110 Xue (n 100) 269.

111 For the need to constantly balance the relationship between the safety and stability provided by hard rules and considerations of adequacy with respect to individual circumstances, see Xue (n 100) 279, citing Aristotle's notion of the 'equitable'.

Jhering's famous words, 'purpose is the creator of all law'.[112] And yet, depending on their degree of objectivity, the 'purpose' of the rules emanating from the different sources is a somewhat variable concept, as it resembles at times the notion of a subjective, authorial intent, while at others it rather refers to the objective task or function which the respective rule accomplishes as part of the framework of legal relations within the international community of states.

There are, to be sure, many other aspects in respect of which the different sources mentioned in Article 38 (1) of the Statute of the International Court of Justice can be distinguished from – or likened to – one another: for example, their form (written or unwritten), the procedure by which they come into existence (formal or informal), or the role that the consent of states to be bound by them plays in their formation.[113] With respect to the practical aspects of their ascertainment and interpretation, however, the concept of 'purpose', in its respective meaning, seems to be a particularly adequate criterion by recourse to which the sources of international law can be analysed. In the preceding chapter, such analysis has been attempted, using the basic structure provided by Aharon Barak's theory of purposive interpretation. In this respect it has been argued that the 'purpose' relevant in the context of purposive interpretation has the strongest subjective connotation with respect to unilateral acts of states, although even here considerations of good faith and reasonable expectations play an important role.[114] In treaties, the subjective component, ie the intent of the contracting parties, is still a dominant consideration, but its impact is mediated by several objective elements, most notably the fact that Article 31 (1) VCLT stresses the importance of the text as the authentic expression of the shared intentions of the contracting parties. Still greater is the objective element in the 'purpose' of customary international law, where even the subjective component, the *opinio juris*, does not denote a will or intent, but the belief or conviction that a legal obligation exists.

112 R v Jhering, *Der Zweck im Recht, vol I* (Leipzig, Breitkopf und Härtel, 3rd ed 1893) iii.

113 For such an analysis of the sources of international law under the broad categories of 'consensual' and 'non-consensual law', see A D'Amato, 'International Law as a Unitary System' in D Armstrong (ed), *Routledge Handbook of International Law* (London and New York, Routledge 2010) 101. According to D'Amato, 'consensual [international] law' is characterised by being 'conventional', 'written', 'specific' and by the fact that it 'applies only to the parties'; contrariwise, typical attributes of 'non-consensual [international] law' are its being 'customary', 'unwritten', 'general', and its 'appl[icability] to all states equally'.

114 Cf de Visscher (n 90) 163, who notes, however, the 'extreme diversity' among the various types of unilateral acts. For a discussion of the role of 'intent' in the interpretation of unilateral acts, see eg Kennedy (n 46) 54–66. See also Principle 1 of the ILC's 'Guiding Principles applicable to unilateral acts of States' of 2006: 'Declarations publicly made and manifesting the will to be bound may have the effect of creating legal obligations. When the conditions for this are met, the binding character of such declarations is based on good faith'.

From individual rules of customary international law, then, certain patterns may be derived by way of analogical reasoning. This not only makes it possible to apply rules of customary international law to situations not specifically covered by earlier precedents, but it also provides a certain degree of consistency, predictability and coherence, in that it allows for principled reasoning on a low or intermediate level of abstraction. Thus, it is consistent with Amartya Sen's concept of a 'comparative' idea of justice, an approach that, as has been argued above, fits well with the decentralised nature of the international community, the continued existence of which depends on the constant maintenance of a delicate balance between its centrifugal and centripetal forces.[115]

One source of international law has so far been mentioned only by way of passing reference: The 'general principles of law recognised by civilised nations', as is the formulation of Article 38 (1) (c) ICJ Statute. It is no exaggeration to say that the general principles are still, as Bin Cheng put it in his ground-breaking 1953 study on the issue, 'the most controversial of the various sources of international law enumerated in Article 38 of the Statute, and thus of international law in general',[116] although customary international law has lately attracted more than its fair share of doctrinal controversies[117] as well. The task which this section of the present chapter is designed to fulfil does not include affording a complete exposition of the various, and often widely divergent, doctrinal positions that have been adopted by many scholars of international law with respect to the meaning of the term 'general principles of law'.[118] And yet, in a study entitled *The Rule of Unwritten International Law* it is impossible not to discuss the role that this controversial, yet (as the present author

115 For an analysis of the difficulty of maintaining that balance, see eg R Buchan, *International Law and the Construction of Liberal Peace* (Oxford, Hart 2013) 44–9; Buchan uses the example of the 2003 US-led invasion of Iraq to discuss the disruptive influence of a unilateral military intervention not backed by a general 'consensus' of the international community. He concludes, however, that international cooperation in the reconstruction of Iraq, and especially the shared aspiration to build up a liberal democracy in that country, has had a 'cathartic' influence, 'rehabilitating' relations within the community after the fierce disagreement over the legality of the invasion. The currently imminent danger of a collapse of the state of Iraq due to the rise of the militias of the 'Islamic State', and the threat to the region as a whole posed by this development, makes his assessment in this respect appear rather too optimistic in hindsight.

116 B Cheng, *General Principles of Law as Applied by International Courts and Tribunals* (London, Stevens 1953) xv.

117 For a critical commentary on this trend, see eg J d'Aspremont, 'Guest Post: Amidst the Academic Mania for the Identification of Customary International Law: The ILC and the Operative Value of Distinctions' <http://opiniojuris.org/2014/11/12/guest-post-amidst-academic-mania-identification-customary-international-law-ilc-operative-value-distinctions/>accessed 20 August 2017.

118 For a recent concise overview of many of the doctrinal controversies surrounding this source, see eg G Gaja, 'General Principles of Law' in R Wolfrum (ed), *The Max Planck Encyclopedia of Public International Law* (Oxford, Oxford University Press 2012).

believes) highly significant source of international law plays, and the 'purpose' which it serves. The line of argumentation which has been pursued so far would be incomplete, and perhaps even self-contradictory, if it were not able to accommodate the general principles of law. Two things are therefore necessary in the following pages: First, to analyse the meaning of the concept of the 'general principles of law', and its potential place in the theory of unwritten international law that has been developed so far. And second, pertaining more specifically to the topic of the present chapter, how the concept of 'purpose' can be defined with respect to these general principles; in other words, whether they, as the working hypothesis in the heading of the present section suggests, are positioned on the 'supreme level of objectivity' in terms of the proportion of subjective and objective elements in their 'purpose'.

Concerning the first part of the analysis, it seems convenient to start with the wording of Article 38 (1) (c) ICJ Statute. It is widely known that the phrase 'the general principles of law recognized by civilized nations' has been copied verbatim from the parallel provision, Article 38 (1) (c) of the 1920 Statute of the Permanent Court of International Justice. It is almost universally agreed today that the term 'civilized nations' has no restrictive effect anymore (if indeed it was ever really intended to have one),[119] and that all members of the international community are to be considered as 'civilized nations'.[120] It is considerably more difficult to figure out the meaning of the word 'principles' and its qualifying adjective, 'general'. In their attempts to discern the meaning of these terms, authors frequently begin by looking at the drafting history of Article 38 of the PCIJ Statute.[121] There are two problems with this approach: First, it seems rather questionable from a methodological point of view to look at the *travaux préparatoires* of a treaty provision before even having made a serious attempt to discern its meaning from its text and context. Second, and more fundamentally, the preparatory works, ie the deliberations of the 'Advisory Committee of Jurists',[122] whose task was to 'prepar[e] plans for the establishment of the Permanent Court of International Justice provided for in Article 14 of the Covenant [of the League of Nations]',[123] disclose a great

119 The appropriateness of the insertion of the epithet 'civilized' had been questioned even before the adoption of the Statute of the PCIJ; see on the *travaux préparatoires* in this respect Herczegh (n 50) 11.

120 For a recent proposal to delete this controversial phrase from Article 38 ICJ Statute, see S Yee, 'Arguments for Cleaning Up Article 38 (1) (b) and (1) (c) of the ICJ Statute' (2007) 4 *Romanian Journal of International Law* 34; for a general overview of the historical context of the use of the term 'civilized nations' in international law, see J Sloan, 'Civilized Nations' in R Wolfrum (ed) *The Max Planck Encyclopedia of Public International Law* (Oxford, Oxford University Press 2012).

121 See Herczegh (n 50) 12–20; Gaja (n 118).

122 See Permanent Court of International Justice (ed), *Proceedings of the Advisory Committee of Jurists: Procès-verbaux of the Proceedings of the Committee* (The Hague, Van Langenhuysen Brothers 1920).

123 See ibid, iii; the Committee held its first public meeting on 16 June 1920 at the Peace Palace at the Hague.

amount of divergence of opinion on the question of whether, and to what extent, the Court should be permitted to apply sources of international law other than treaties and custom. It has been asserted that the conflict was mainly one 'between positivists and all those who, starting either from the natural-law approach or other views, were opposed to positivism. The wording adopted as a result of these discussions reflected an endeavour to reconcile these two ... antagonistic tendencies then current in the discipline of international law'.[124]

On a more practical level, the goals that the members of the Committee intended to achieve by adopting what was to become Article 38 (1) (c) were hard to reconcile: On the one hand, they were worried that a narrow delimitation of the applicable sources of law would severely hamper the effectiveness of the Court in providing legal solutions to international conflicts, as the state of treaty and customary international law was seen as insufficiently developed.[125] On the other hand, they feared that to give the Court too great a freedom in the selection of the rules it applied would discourage states from submitting to its compulsory jurisdiction, which made some Committee members reluctant to accept principles originating from domestic legal systems.[126]

The compromise they finally agreed upon was to insert 'the general principles of law recognized by civilized nations', without, as Committee member Albert de Lapradelle observed, 'indicating exactly the sources from which the principles should be derived'.[127] In other words, 'the compromise text adopted by the Committee covered a division of opinions, especially on the question whether a general principle was to be regarded as part of international law only because it was already present in municipal systems'.[128] Along this dividing line, the controversy over the nature of the 'general principles of law' continued to be fought over for decades to come. The view that these 'general principles' were to be understood as 'principles of international law', ie abstractions from the specific rules of treaties and international custom, rather than principles discerned through a comparative analysis of domestic legal systems, was strongly held by socialist scholars of international law. They claimed that an important clarification in this respect had been the amendment

124 Herczegh (n 50) 13.

125 This concern was voiced especially by Francis Hagerup, the Norwegian representative, who stated that 'there might be cases in which no rule of conventional or general law was applicable. A rule must be established to meet this eventuality, to avoid the possibility of the Court declaring itself incompetent (*non liquet*) through lack of applicable rules.' See the *Proceedings of the Advisory Committee of Jurists* (n 122) 296.

126 This objection was raised notably by Elihu Root, who feared that even states which were generally willing to submit to the Court's compulsory jurisdiction might be reluctant if the Court 'would apply principles, differently understood in different countries'. See the *Proceedings of the Advisory Committee of Jurists* (n 122) 308.

127 Ibid, 335–6.

128 Gaja (n 118) 371.

made to the *chapeau* of Article 38 when the provision was transplanted into the ICJ Statute in 1945, the only major change made in the wording of this article in comparison to the Statute of the PCIJ. Instead of the old wording 'The Court shall apply…', the phrase read now: 'The Court, whose function it is to decide *in accordance with international law* such disputes as are submitted to it, shall apply … [italics added]'.[129] However, it is questionable whether the insertion really was intended 'to affect the meaning of any of the references to the various sources listed in Art 38 ICJ Statute'.[130] And behind the apparently textualist argument brought forward by Tunkin and other scholars from the socialist bloc, there was the ideological belief that capitalist and socialist legal systems (which were believed to be but superstructures of the respective economic systems) could not possibly share common 'principles'.[131]

After the end of the Cold War, the ideological disagreement on the meaning of the general principles may have shifted away from the economic field, although fundamental divergences about questions of economic policy have by no means disappeared,[132] a fact that is illustrated by both the reactions to the global financial crisis and the controversy over the planned 'Transatlantic Trade and Investment Partnership'. In other fields, such as those of cultural and religious values, the conflicts between fundamentally different worldviews have significantly increased.[133] As a substantial number of countries in the Middle East, but also in South-East Asia,[134] recently have adopted legislation to

129 This argument was stressed by G Tunkin, 'General Principles of Law in International Law' in M René et al (eds), *International Festschrift für Alfred Verdross zum 80. Geburtstag* (München, Fink 1971) 523 (525): 'The amendment invalidates the understanding of Article 38 (1) (c) that was prevailing in the Commission of Jurists in 1920. It makes impossible the interpretation of Article 38 (1) (c) according to which "general principles of law" are simply principles "common to all civilised nations". It clearly defines that "general principles of law" are principles of international law.'

130 Gaja (n 118) 372.

131 See for an elaboration of this argument, supported by ample references to Soviet, Hungarian and Czechoslovakian literature Herczegh (n 50).

132 For examples of recent areas of disagreement, see eg T Cottier, 'International Economic Law in Transition from Liberalism to Trade Regulation' (2014) 17 *Journal of International Economic Law* 671.

133 As famously predicted by S Huntington, 'The Clash of Civilizations?' (1992) 71 (3) *Foreign Affairs* 22: 'It is my hypothesis that the fundamental source of conflict in this new [post-Cold War] world will not be primarily ideological or primarily economic. The great divisions among humankind and the dominating source of conflict will be cultural… Nation states will remain the most powerful actors in world affairs, but the principal conflicts of global politics will occur between nations and groups of different civilizations.'

134 Among the most recent examples of this trend is the Sultanate of Brunei, which announced in April 2014 to base its penal law system on the *sharia*; see L Hunt, 'Brunei Imposes Sharia Law' *The Diplomat* (Tokyo, 1 May 2014) <http://thediplomat.com/2014/05/brunei-imposes-sharia-law/>accessed 20 August 2017.

make their legal systems compatible with the precepts of *shariah* law,[135] and as 'Asian Values'[136] are regarded as an important conceptual alternative to the Western focus on the legal protection of individual liberty, the chances of discovering legal principles of universal validity through a comparative study of domestic legal systems can hardly be said to have improved. These difficulties notwithstanding, the view that general principles in the sense of Article 38 (1) (c) ICJ Statute can be derived through a comparative analysis of domestic legal systems is no longer opposed as vehemently as it was during the Cold War.

F. General Principles in Practice

On the other hand, it has rightly been pointed out that 'principles drawn from municipal law [are] applied only with caution by the ICJ'.[137] In fact, in recent years principles derived from comparative domestic law have at most been referred to by individual judges in their dissenting or concurring opinions, rather than by the Court's majority.[138] Other international tribunals, however, have been more eager in the application of general principles drawn from domestic law; as Giorgio Gaja puts it, '[a]rbitration tribunals have shown little hesitation in referring to municipal systems even when they arguably offer a variety of solutions and the adoption of one or the other solution necessarily implies a considerable discretion'.[139] The International Criminal Court, on the other hand, is explicitly authorised by Article 21 (1) (c) of the Rome Statue to draw on comparative municipal law, albeit as a subsidiary source of law, to be applied when neither the Statute itself nor 'rules and principles of international law' provide sufficient guidance.[140] It should be noted that the application of

135 For a detailed comparative study of the influence of the *sharia* on various national legal systems, see JM Otto (ed), *Sharia Incorporated: A Comparative Overview of the Legal Systems of Twelve Muslim Countries in Past and Present* (Leiden, Leiden University Press 2005).

136 For a critical overview of the debate, see A Sen, *Human Rights and Asian Values* (New York, Carnegie Council 1997).

137 See Gaja (n 118) 376.

138 For a recent example, see the Separate Opinion of Judge Simma in the case concerning the *Application of the Interim Accord of 13 September 1995 (Former Yugoslav Republic of Macedonia v Greece)* [2011] ICJ Rep 695, where Simma suggested that the Court should have considered the *exeptio non adimpleti contractus* as a possible justification for the non-performance of a treaty obligation. Simma explicitly acknowledged the domestic pedigree of the principle: 'The question is, of course, the transferability of such a concept developed in foro domestico to the international legal plane, respectively the amendments that it will have to undergo in order for such a general principle to be able to play a constructive role also at the international level.' (ibid, para 13).

139 Gaja (n 118) 376.

140 Cf the Rome Statute of the International Criminal Court (adopted 17 July 1998, entered into force 1 July 2002) 2187 UNTS 3 art 21 (1): 'The Court shall apply: (a) In the first place, this Statute, Elements of Crimes and its Rules of Procedure and Evidence; (b) In the second place, where appropriate, applicable treaties and

principles of domestic law is arguably more justified in international criminal law than in other branches of international law, especially when essential procedural guarantees and fundamental rights of the accused are concerned. While it is rather doubtful in many areas of international law whether rules of domestic law, regulating the conduct of individual human beings, are applicable to the structurally very different relations among states,[141] there exists no such fundamental difference in international criminal law: A defendant is a defendant, whether he or she stands before a national court or an international criminal tribunal.[142] The problem in international criminal law consists therefore less in the difficulty of adapting principles of domestic origin to the international sphere, but rather in assuring that the law thus discerned fairly reflects the various different legal traditions of the world.[143]

The procedural law of international courts and tribunals is generally a rich source of examples of so-called 'general principles' originating from domestic legal orders.[144] However, some of them – such as the maxim *audiatur et altera pars* or the principle of equality of the parties – are based on such fundamental considerations of procedural fairness and equity that one may well ask whether they are recognised on the international plane because of their being common to the great legal traditions of the world, or because they

the principles and rules of international law, including the established principles of the international law of armed conflict; (c) Failing that, *general principles of law derived by the Court from national laws of legal systems of the world* including, as appropriate, the national laws of States that would normally exercise jurisdiction over the crime, provided that those principles are not inconsistent with this Statute and with international law and internationally recognized norms and standards.' (italics added).

141 See on this problem Bleckmann (n 14) 145: 'Die Annahme einer Übernahme eines gemeinsamen nationalen Rechtssatzes in das Völkerrecht ist nur möglich, wenn der gemeinsame Rechtssatz in die Strukturen des Völkerrechts passt.'

142 See eg O Corten, *Méthodologie du Droit International Public* (Bruxelles, Editions de l'Université de Bruxelles 2006) 187: '[C]e principe doit, par définition, être transposable en droit international, ce qui fait notamment de la procédure (pénale notamment) un champ privilégié d'application.'

143 For a quantitative analysis of the influence of different legal traditions on the shaping of the Rome Statute, see eg S Mitchell/EJ Powell, *Domestic Law Goes Global: Legal Traditions and International Courts* (Cambridge, Cambridge University Press 2011) ch 4. Mitchell and Powell conclude that '[t]he ICC emerged as an interesting amalgamation of civil and common law principles.' (ibid, 127); for the application of general principles by international criminal courts and tribunals, see F Raimondo, *General Principles of Law in the Decisions of International Criminal Court and Tribunals* (Leiden, Martinus Nijhoff 2008).

144 For a more recent study of these procedural principles and their application by the International Court of Justice, see eg S Negri, *I principi generali del processo internazionale nella giurisprudenza della Corte internazionale di Giustizia* (Naples, Edizione Scientifiche Italiane 2002); R Kolb, 'General Principles of Procedural Law' in A Zimmermann/C Tomuschat/K Oellers-Frahm/CJ Tams (eds), *The Statute of the International Court of Justice: A Commentary* (Oxford, Oxford University Press, 2nd ed 2012) 870–908.

belong to some sort of 'natural law of judicial proceedings'.[145] Moreover, some of these procedural maxims are rather specific in their content, so that it has been disputed whether it is fit to refer to them as 'principles' at all – let alone 'general principles.'[146]

An example in this respect would be the 'attorney–client privilege', a rule originating in common law jurisdictions which affords far-reaching protection of the confidentiality of communication between clients and legal counsel. It is interesting to note, however, that when the International Court of Justice recently applied this rule in its order of provisional measures in the case *Timor-Leste v Australia*,[147] it did not draw on a comparative analysis of domestic rules in this respect. Rather, it suggested that the attorney–client privilege in inter-state arbitration could be derived by way of deduction from the principle of *international law* of sovereign equality of states: 'The Court notes that this claimed right might be derived from the principle of the sovereign equality of States, which is one of the fundamental principles of the international legal order and is reflected in Article 2, paragraph 1, of the Charter of the United Nations.'[148] Perhaps this approach can be interpreted as another example of the hesitation of the International Court of Justice to apply principles derived from comparative domestic law. To deduce the attorney–client privilege in international law from the principle of sovereign equality of states, rather than acknowledge its independent existence as a general principle of law under Article 38 (1) (c) ICJ Statute, led the court to ignore, at least in the context of its order of provisional measures, the argument made on behalf of Australia, namely that the attorney-client privilege under common law was inapplicable in cases where the possibility of confidential communication with an attorney had been abused for fraudulent or other criminal purposes.[149] Moreover, the ICJ's reasoning, basing the privilege on state sovereignty, would be

145 See Kolb (n 144) 877: 'The principle of equality *in judicio* is so evident and indispensable for modern legal thinking that it could well be termed a principle of "natural law of judicial proceedings".'

146 For an analysis of this question, see R Kolb, 'Les maximes juridiques en droit international public: Questions historiques et théoriques' (1999) 32 *Revue belge de droit international* 407 (412 ff).

147 *Questions Relating to the Seizure of Certain Documents (Timor-Leste v Australia)* (Request for the Indication of Provisional Measures: Order of 3 March 2014) <http://www.icj-cij.org/files/case-related/156/156-20140303-ORD-01-00-EN.pdf> accessed 20 August 2017.

148 Ibid, para 27.

149 See the statement of the Australian Solicitor-General Gleeson in *Questions Relating to the Seizure of Certain Documents* (Verbatim Record of the Public Sitting held on Tuesday 21 January 2014) available at <http://www.icj-cij.org/files/case-related/156/156-20140121-ORA-01-00-BI.pdf >accessed 20 August 2017, para 27: 'As a matter of Australian law, as is the case with the law of most countries, legal professional privilege does not exist where the communications are produced in pursuance of a criminal offence, fraud or other improper purpose… That is Australian law, that is English law and you will see from Tab 15 of your folder, from a brief survey of State practice: many States recognize either the

inapplicable to arbitrations between a state and a private party (such as in investment arbitrations). It should be noted, however, that arbitral tribunals, eg in the field of international investment law, have already recognised the applicability of the attorney–client privilege, even when the relevant rules of procedure did not explicitly provide for it.[150]

Authors who attempted to discern the meaning of the 'general principles of law' in Article 38 traditionally tended to focus their analysis on the concept of 'principle' of law, trying to find the criterion that distinguishes legal 'principles' from mere 'rules'. Gerald Fitzmaurice, in his 1957 course at the Hague Academy of International Law, proposed the following definition:

> By a principle, or general principle, as opposed to a rule, even a general rule, of law is meant chiefly something which is not itself a rule, but which underlies a rule, and explains or provides the reason for it. A rule answers the question "what": a principle in effect answers the question "why". In the event of a dispute as to what the correct rule is, the solution will often depend on what principle is regarded as underlying the rule.[151]

As this quote makes clear, Fitzmaurice regarded principles as the *raison d'être* of legal rules, or, in other words, as expressions of their underlying purpose. As such, they are not just academic speculations, or mere philosophical constructs, but are in fact of concrete relevance to the solution of specific cases. They incorporate and express what Ronald Dworkin has dubbed the 'background theory'[152] under which a judge or other law-applying agent operates.

In a similar fashion, Bin Cheng identified it as the 'first function of general principles' that they 'constitute the source of various rules of law, which are merely the expression of these principles'.[153] It seems that 'source' here is meant by Cheng not in the sense of 'source of law' – otherwise the general principles would be to him some sort of super- or meta-source of international law – but in the sense of a 'justification' or 'rationale' behind some of the more specific rules, similar to the function that Fitzmaurice had in mind when he stated that a general principle 'provides the reason for it [the rule]'.

A particularly interesting interpretation of the notion of principles of international law was rendered by the Hungarian scholar Géza Herczegh,[154] who,

crime/fraud exception, or other appropriate exceptions such as for national security.'

150 For examples in this respect, see eg J Rubinstein/B Guerrina, 'The Attorney-Client Privilege and International Arbitration' (2001) 18 *Journal of International Arbitration* 587.

151 G Fitzmaurice, 'The General Principles of International Law Considered from the Standpoint of the Rule of Law' (1957-II) 92 *Recueil des Cours* 1 (7).

152 See R Dworkin, *Taking Rights Seriously* (Cambridge/MA, Harvard University Press 1980) 123–30.

153 See Cheng (n 116) 85.

154 See Herczegh (n 50) passim.

while generally adhering to the consensus on a voluntarist understanding of international law prevalent in Socialist international legal theory, and thus ultimately rejecting the existence of principles of domestic pedigree as a genuine, *ipso facto* binding source of international rights and obligations,[155] nevertheless developed an original approach that to a certain extent set him apart from mainstream Socialist legal doctrine. Herczegh elaborated a functional theory of the general principles of international law, taking as a point of departure a conundrum that had bedevilled Cheng, namely the curious fact that general principles appear to be at the same time of greater and of lesser importance than specific rules of international law. According to Cheng,

> the problem [of the rank of general principles] has to be approached from two different angles. From the juridical point of view, the superior value of general principles of law over customs and treaties cannot be denied; for these principles furnish the juridical basis of treaties and customs and govern their interpretation and application. From the operative point of view, however, the hierarchical order is reversed. Rules of law, though in derogation of general principles of law, are binding. But the possibility of establishing rules in derogation of general principles of law must not be exaggerated.[156]

Herzcegh, while acknowledging that the problem of general principles comprised two different aspects, doubted the soundness of the distinction between a 'juridical' and an 'operative' point of view insisted on by Cheng: 'The "operative" view is as much a juridical one, as the one Bin Cheng calls juridical.'[157] Instead, he proposed a different distinction: According to Herczegh, principles of international law comprise a 'postulate' and a 'factual' aspect.

> Obviously it would be more convenient to stress the consequences forthcoming from the 'postulate' and 'fact' aspects of a legal principle, or from the dialectical unity of these two aspects. The principles of law formulate and embody the postulates the legal system as a whole has to satisfy. Their effects are therefore greater, their functions are more important, than those of specific legal rules in which only parts, atoms of social needs and requirements are manifested. As facta, the principles of law are equivalent

155 See ibid at 97: 'Since the notion of a technical or legal (formal) source of law has been defined in a sense that a source of law is the outward form of rules of a legal system, it is only evident that the principles of municipal law cannot be qualified as sources of international law, because international legal rules, [which] come into being as the result of the agreement of the wills of states, may in conformity with the explicit or tacit character of an agreement of will manifest themselves only in the form of international treaties or custom, but never in the form of principles of municipal law.'

156 Cheng (n 116) 393.

157 Herczegh (n 50) 69.

> to other rules of the legal system. The problem of the hierarchy of legal rules – as studied in the various branches of law – belongs to the factual aspect of the principles of law; and this is the reason why an answer in the negative has to be given to the question whether or not the principles of law have to be assigned a place on the higher ranks or summits of the hierarchy of legal rules.[158]

Although Herczegh's use of the term 'factual' seems a bit opaque – apparently he uses the word to refer to the function of principles as precepts of positive law – the basic argument he advances seems plausible: Principles or general principles of law obtain their particular significance not from their form, but from their content. It is hardly surprising, therefore, that general principles appear to be sort of an alien element in formalist theories of law-ascertainment.[159] This content-dependent nature of the general principles means, on the other hand, that their normative sway is not limited to the instances in which they immediately apply. Thus they may well be supplanted in a concrete case by a more specific rule of custom or treaty law; however, it is them that shape the legal system as a whole, and that influence the interpretation of more specific rules of treaty or customary international law.

It is interesting to see that as far as the concept of 'general principles of law' is concerned, scholars of international have been at the forefront of the development of legal theory, motivated by the challenge posed by the formulation of Article 38 (1) (c) ICJ Statute. The fundamental importance of the distinction between 'rules' and 'principles', which has been recognised by scholars of general legal theory only during the past few decades, is anticipated in the lively controversies on the role of principles in international law. Today, especially in the English-speaking world, the discovery of the significance of the distinction between 'rules' and 'principles', and the characterisation of both,[160] is attributed largely to the work of the late Ronald Dworkin. Curiously, even international lawyers nowadays tend to regard Dworkin as the intellectual father of the theory of legal principles; as Hugh Thirlway recently stated,[161] '[t]hat law consists of more than rules has been demonstrated by Dworkin, who has shown that not only must there also be principles, but that they are neither case-specific nor automatic in their operation, and may even conflict.'

158 Ibid, 69.

159 On this aspect, see eg J d'Aspremont, *Formalism and the Sources of International Law: A Theory of the Ascertainment of Legal Rules* (Oxford, Oxford University Press 2011) 171: 'It thus seems hardly disputable that the ascertainment of general principles of law is devoid of any formal character.'

160 Dworkin first developed his theory of the distinctive features of rules and principles in his article 'The Model of Rules' (1967–8) 35 *Yale Law Journal* 14; his explicit goal was, as he stated it, to 'make a general attack on positivism, and I shall use H. L.A. Hart's version as a target, when a particular target is needed.' (ibid at 22).

161 See H Thirlway, *The Sources of International Law* (Oxford, Oxford University Press 2014) 94.

To be sure, Dworkin deserves credit not only for having popularised the distinction between legal rules and principles in the English-speaking world,[162] but also for having developed a highly sophisticated theory of the function of legal principles in the context of adjudication.[163] Yet it seems that Dworkin's identification of the general principles with such abstract values as 'justice' and 'fairness', and his emphasis on adjudication – his particular focus lay on the judicial interpretation of constitutional rights – makes his theory rather difficult to apply to international law, where its claims seem to be even more controversial than in the context of domestic constitutional law.[164]

Yet international lawyers should not harbour any feelings of inferiority with respect to the philosophical sophistication of their theories of the general principles of law: First, because some of the theories on the general principles in international law, like those of Fitzmaurice, Cheng and Herczegh described above, go far beyond a mere exegesis of the wording of Article 38 (1) (c) ICJ Statute, and, despite considerable differences among them, each of these authors undertook to develop a conception of the function of principles in the international legal system, a conception they believed to be both theoretically defendable and practically feasible. And second, because the problem of general principles in international law is intrinsically more complex than the parallel question in domestic legal systems: Not only is the question as to the meaning of the term 'principle' as opposed to 'rule' particularly intricate here,[165] but also the issue of whether these principles are to be discerned exclusively through an inductive analysis of the more specific rules of international law, or through a comparative study of domestic legal systems, or – as seems to be an increasingly influential position – whether there are several distinct categories

162 It should be noted, however, that several other authors, in particular in Germany, but also in Scandinavia, have been developing theories of legal principles contemporaneously with Dworkin; cf, for example, A Ross, *Directives and Norms* (London, Routledge 1968); W Lorenz, 'General Principles of Law: Their Elaboration in the Jurisprudence of the Court of Justice of the European Communities' (1964) 13 *American Journal of Comparative Law* 1; W Fikentscher, *Methoden des Rechts in vergleichender Darstellung – Band 2: Der Anglo-Amerikanische Rechtskreis* (München, Beck 1975) 133 et seqq, 251 et seqq; R Alexy, 'Zum Begriff der Rechtsprinzipien' (1979) 1 *Rechtstheorie-Beiheft* 59.

163 See esp R Dworkin, *Law's Empire* (Cambridge/MA, Harvard University Press 1986) 239 et seqq, where Dworkin famously introduced the allegorical figure of a super-human judge he called 'Hercules', who was conceived to be able – by the application of 'principles' – to find the 'one right answer' in 'hard cases'.

164 See on this problem eg d'Aspremont (n 159) 90: '[I]t must be acknowledged that Dworkin's argument was premised on his ambition to construct a theory of adjudication which, if followed correctly, only yields answers to questions of American law.'; see also Prost (n 9) 80: 'Dworkin's theory of unity [of the legal order] is thus rooted in the *practice of adjudication* and lies in the hermeneutical act of tying explicit rules to underlying principles in search of the "right answer" to moral/legal dilemmas' (emphasis original).

165 See on these definitorial problems eg C Parry, *The Sources and Evidences of International Law* (Manchester, University of Manchester Press 1965) 90 et seq.

of 'general principles' in international law. Indeed, it has been argued that these different categories of general principles are functions of different meanings attributed to the term 'general': As Jean Combacau and Serge Sur aptly put it, 'elle [la généralité] renvoie, d'une part, au caractère abstrait de la règle, d'autre part, à l'universalité de sa portée.'[166] In this respect, Oscar Schachter even distinguished 'five categories of general principles', which he found to be referred to in international legal theory and practice, and each of which, he said, 'has a very different basis for its validity as law'.[167] The five categories Schachter thus identified were:

1 The principles of municipal law 'recognized by civilized nations'.
2 General principles of law 'derived from the specific nature of the international) community'.
3 Principles 'intrinsic to the idea of law and basic to all legal systems'.
4 Principles 'valid through all kinds of societies in relationships of hierarchy and co-ordination'.
5 Principles of justice founded on 'the very nature of man as a rational and social being'.[168]

The problem with this and similar classifications lies in the fact that their different categories are neither mutually exclusive, nor particularly helpful as a heuristic device. The assignment of principles to these categories does not depend, it seems, on their objective nature, but on the 'normative ideology'[169] of international law to which one subscribes.[170] For example, to which category would the principle *pacta sunt servanda* have to be assigned? Arguably, it could be counted under each and any of the above headings.[171] This does not mean, however, that it is irrelevant whether one regards it as 'derived from the specific nature of the international community', or as founded upon 'the very nature of man as a rational and social being': The specific nature of the

166 J Combacau/S Sur, *Droit international public* (Paris, Montchrestien, 10th ed 2012) 107; see also B Vitanyi, 'La signification de la "généralité" des principes de droit' (1976) 80 *Revue Générale de Droit International Public* 536.

167 O Schachter, *International Law in Theory and Practice* (Leiden, Martinus Nijhoff 1994) 50.

168 Ibid (footnotes omitted).

169 See on this expression A Ross, *On Law and Justice* (London, Stevens & Sons 1959) 73–5.

170 For a discussion of this phenomenon in the context of the general principles in international law, see M Koskenniemi, 'General Principles: Reflexions on Constructivist Thinking in International Law' (1985) 18 *Oikeustiede-Jurisprudentia* 120 (137, esp at n 75).

171 This possibility is explicitly acknowledged by Schachter (n 167) 50: 'Although these five categories are analytically distinct, it is not unusual for a particular general principle to fall into more than one of the categories.' Schachter illustrates this by the principle of *nemo judex in sua causa*, which, he says, is considered both 'part of most, if not all, systems of municipal law and as intrinsic to the basic idea of law'.

international community as a decentralised, even 'anarchical society' may well merit to apply *pacta sunt servanda* more strictly, and to construe its exceptions (such as the *clausula rebus sic stantibus*) more narrowly, than would seem appropriate under an abstract, philosophical speculation about what the social nature of human beings calls for.[172] Another example in this respect is the attorney-client privilege, which has already been discussed above in the context of the *Timor-Leste v Australia*[173] case: As far as the scope of exceptions to it are concerned, it is of considerable relevance whether one bases the privilege on the sovereign equality of states, or derives it from a comparative analysis of municipal law.

A similar question arises in the context of the principle *inadimpleti contractus non est adimplendum* (literally, 'an unfulfilled contract does not have to be fulfilled'), the exception of non-performance, a rule of Roman law origin[174] by use of which a party to a synallagmatic contract can defend itself against the accusation of breach of contract, provided the other party has also failed to perform the agreement properly.[175] This principle has recently been invoked by Greece in the context of the case concerning the *Application of the Interim Accord of 13 September 1995 (Former Yugoslav Republic of Macedonia v Greece)*.[176] While the Court's majority rejected Greece's argument on factual grounds, noting that it had not sufficiently proved any of the violations allegedly committed by the FYR of Macedonia, and consequently found it 'unnecessary … to determine whether that doctrine [of *inadimpleti contractus*] forms part of contemporary international law'[177], Judge Simma would have liked the International Court to look more closely at the substantive issue of whether this 'doctrine' was a principle of international law: In his Separate

172 Even the 'specific nature of the international community' is, of course, not a fixed, immutable quality, but changes over time; for an analysis of the effect of such changes on the construction of *pacta sunt servanda*, see C Binder, 'Stability and Change in the Time of Fragmentation: The Limits of *Pacta Sunt Servanda* Revisited' (2012) 25 *Leiden Journal of International Law* 909.

173 See above n 147.

174 For the origins of this rule, which has been formulated explicitly only by the glossators of the late Medieval period, see eg H Roland/L Boyer, *Locutions Latines du Droit Français* (Paris, Librairie de la Cour de Cassation, 3rd ed 1993) 119–20.

175 For a recent discussion of the international legal quality of its principle, its rationale, its conditions and its relations to more specific rules of the law of treaties and of state responsibility, see eg F Fontanelli, 'The Invocation of the Exception of Non-Performance: A Case-Study on the Role and Application of General Principles of International Law of Contractual Origin' (2012) 1 *Cambridge Journal of International and Comparative Law* 119.

176 *Application of the Interim Accord of 13 September 1995 (Former Yugoslav Republic of Macedonia v Greece)* (Merits) (n 138).

177 Ibid, para 161: 'The Respondent has thus failed to establish that the conditions which it has itself asserted would be necessary for the application of the *exceptio* have been satisfied in this case. It is, therefore, unnecessary for the Court to determine whether that doctrine forms part of contemporary international law.'

Opinion, Simma argued that the Court should have answered the question as to the relationship of the defence of *inadimpleti contractus* to the other two defences brought by Greece to justify its conduct, which were derived from the law of treaties (Art 60 VCLT, which is narrower than the exception of non-performance, allowing for suspension and termination only in case of a 'material breach' by the other party) and the law of state responsibility.[178]

In his analysis, an issue of particular concern to Simma was the applicability of the domestic contract law exception of *inadimpleti contractus* on the international plane: 'The question is, of course, the transferability of such a concept developed *in foro domestico* to the international legal plane, respectively the amendments that it will have to undergo in order for such a general principle to be able to play a constructive role also at the international level.'[179] He had already noted before that the exception of *inadimpleti contractus* was closely related to the more fundamental principle of reciprocity in contractual relations, a principle that he believed to be of even greater relevance in international law than in the more institutionalised national legal orders: 'The importance of this notion [of reciprocity] for the "health" of international law can hardly be overestimated.'[180] Nevertheless, he found a substantial difference between the invocation of the exception of non-performance in domestic law and in the international legal order. In the latter, the lack of obligatory adjudication could make 'our principle prone to abuse',[181] as states may invoke a – real or purported – minor violation by another party as a pretext for an abrogation of a treaty they deem no longer as advantageous to their interests; a tendency which could prove to be especially hazardous for the stability of large multilateral agreements. Therefore, the drafters of the VCLT had had good reason to incorporate the exception of non-performance only in a very restricted version, as expressed in its Art 60. Citing Art 42 VCLT, Simma concluded that '*extra conventionem nulla salus*': '... Article 60 regulates the legal consequences of treaty breach in an exhaustive way; thus no version of the *exceptio* has survived the codification of the law of treaties – may it rest in peace.'[182] From a doctrinal point of view, one might well question whether a treaty is capable of abrogating a general principle in its entirety. However, it has rightly been noted that Art 60 VCLT does not rescind the exception of *inadimpleti*

178 See his concluding statement in *Application of the Interim Accord of 13 September 1995 (Former Yugoslav Republic of Macedonia v Greece)* (Separate Opinion of Judge Simma) [2011] ICJ Rep 695, para 29: 'Let me summarize: in the present case, the Court would have had the opportunity to clarify a number of legal issues arising from the Respondent's "defences" against the Applicant's accusation of treaty breach, in particular, by giving an authoritative answer to the question whether Article 60 of the Vienna Convention on the Law of Treaties still leaves some place for the so-called exceptio non adimpleti contractus.'.

179 Ibid, para 13.

180 Ibid, para 10.

181 Ibid, para 13.

182 Ibid, para 29.

contractus, but 'in fact preserves and enacts the essence of this principle'.[183] The *essence* thus being preserved, the *form* in which the principle has been incorporated in international law has been adapted to the specific demands of the decentralised international legal order.

G. The Challenges of Functionalism

The incorporation of the principle *inadimpleti contractus non est adimplendum* in the VCLT is a typical example of the methodology that international lawyers traditionally used to determine general principles of law under Art 38 (1) (c) ICJ Statute. This classical methodology entails a three-step inquiry.[184] The first step consists of finding a rule which is present in similar form in the major legal systems of the world (in practice, mostly those based on common law and civil law are taken into account).[185] The second step, then, requires the international lawyer to discern what might be described as the 'common core' underlying the various domestic rules that are taken into consideration. The importance of this reduction of the various domestic rules to their common basis has been stressed by the ICJ in the *Barcelona Traction* case:[186]: 'It is to rules generally accepted by municipal legal systems … and not to the municipal law of a particular State, that international law refers.'[187] Depending on the nature of the principle in question, occasionally a third step then has to ensue: The 'transposition' or 'adaptation' to the international legal order of the principle thus emerged from a process of 'distillation' of rules of domestic origin.[188]

The direction of this traditional inquiry has recently been criticised as being misguided and founded on outdated concepts of comparative legal methodology.

183 See Thirlway (n 161) 101.
184 See, eg, Combacau/Sur (n 166) 109.
185 Legal systems based on Islamic law are, it seems, rarely considered in the context of this inquiry. While this reluctance may be understandable when it comes to some of the more controversial tenets of *sharia* law, especially in the field of criminal justice, there are also significant parts of the highly sophisticated Islamic theory of jurisprudence that could well be taken into consideration when it comes to the determination of principles underlying the major legal systems of the world. An example in this respect would be the theory of the defences of 'state of necessity' and 'duress'; see eg, M Muslehuddin, 'Islamic Jurisprudence and the Rule of Necessity and Need' (1973) 12 *Islamic Studies* 103.
186 *Case Concerning the Barcelona Traction, Light and Power Company (Belgium v Spain)* (Second Phase) [1970] ICJ Rep 3.
187 Ibid, para 50.
188 See Combacau/Sur (n 166) 110, describing the third step as a process of 'transmutation'; Bleckmann (n 14) 148: 'Bei der Anwendung der hier entwickelten Regeln ist zu beachten, dass man, bevor man die Übernahme des gemeinsamen nationalen Rechts etwa wegen der Strukturunterschiede zwischen dem nationalen Recht und dem Völkerrecht ausschließt, prüfen muss, ob das nationale Recht den Völkerrechtsstrukturen nicht angepasst werden kann.'.

According to Jayne Ellis,[189] the quest for principles common to the major families of legal systems of the world is not only 'futile' (she doubts that principles fitting this description actually exist), but the very requirement of 'commonality' or 'representativeness', she believes, is based on several dubious assumptions, be it the idea that the fact that a rule is common to several legal systems signifies (implicit) state consent to its eventual application in international relations, or the belief that such representativeness enhances democratic legitimacy, or even the – naturalistic – conviction that it implies a rule's belonging to the 'objective idea of law'.[190] Ellis also criticises the attempt to 'purge' rules of their municipal origins in a process of 'distillation' before transferring them to the international plane: This method, she claims, is 'leaving behind most of what is interesting and useful'[191] of the process of comparative law.

In the method that international lawyers traditionally use to discern general principles through a comparative analysis of domestic legal systems, Ellis sees the well-known comparative law approach of 'functionalism' at work. This approach, which has been described by the comparatist Ralf Michaels as being 'both the mantra and the *bête noire* of comparative law',[192] proceeds on the assumption that similar social functions can be fulfilled by very disparate rules or norms across the different legal systems of the world. Functionalism, at least in its traditional form, is based on the belief that human societies are generally confronted with similar social problems, but that they develop, over the course of time, a variety of different ways to address them.[193] The functionalist comparative lawyer attempts to classify rules with recourse to the purpose to which they serve, and thus ideally is able to discover substantive similarities in rules of very different outward form – in other words, to separate the essentials of legal rules (which are similar) from the accidentals (which are different due to the specificities of the legal culture and tradition in which a rule is embedded).

For a significant part of the past century, functionalism has almost completely dominated the methodology of comparative law scholars; as Konrad Zweigert and Hein Kötz put it in their influential textbook, '[t]he basic methodological principle of all comparative law is that of functionality.'[194] This great appeal of functionalism is easily explained: Boiling down rules of wildly different origin, form and content to one common denominator, their 'function', considerably reduces complexity, so that contingent generalisations

189 See J Ellis, 'General Principles and Comparative Law' (2011) 22 *European Journal of International Law* 949.
190 Ibid, 954 et seqq.
191 Ibid, 949.
192 See R Michaels, 'The Functional Method of Comparative Law' in M Reimann/R Zimmermann (eds), *Oxford Handbook of Comparative Law* (Oxford, Oxford University Press 2006) 340 (340).
193 For a recent overview of this approach and the arguments of its critics, see Michaels (n 192); see also M Siems, *Comparative Law* (Cambridge, Cambridge University Press 2014) 25–40.
194 K Zweigert/H Kötz, *An Introduction to Comparative Law* (T Weir tr, Oxford, Oxford University Press, 3rd ed 1998) 34.

become possible. Yet this tendency to oversimplify, which to a certain extent is inherent in the functional method, is also its Achilles' heel, as it constitutes an easy target for criticism.[195] Thus, the very notion that universally shared social problems exist is seen as an ethnocentric delusion, based on the allegedly obsolete Aristotelian conception of a universal human good or purpose.[196] More fundamentally, it is questioned whether law does have a discernible function or purpose with respect to the solution of societal problems at all, a function that can be analysed in abstraction from the culture in which the rule emerged, or whether the whole concept of law's function or purpose is itself a Western-centric, overly rationalistic idea.[197]

To be sure, some of the criticism that has been levelled against the functional method of comparative law – especially in its rather naïve, unreflected form – seems well merited. Indeed, it has been the gist of the argument brought forward in the present chapter that 'function' or 'purpose' should not hastily be equated with the narrower concepts of 'will' or 'intent'; in other words, that the purpose or function of a rule is not necessarily identical with the intent of its author, if there is a discernible author at all. In a similar vein, sociologist Robert Merton distinguished between 'manifest' and 'latent' functions of social norms and institutions: While the actors involved are often unaware of these latent functions, they are nevertheless important (sometimes decisive) for the success of a rule or institution, and thus for the society which adheres to it.[198] This concept of latent function(s) seems to be an adequate description of the way in which the rules of customary international law can be said to have a function, a purpose that transcends the intentions of the actors who participated in their emergence.

Concerning the other main line of criticism, the argument that the functional method of comparative law adheres to the antiquated illusion of a universal 'human nature' that transcends cultural boundaries, it can be admitted that there is some merit to this as well, but the strength of this reproach should not be overestimated.[199] Rather, it should be acknowledged that the

195 For a summary of several of the points of criticism levelled against the functional method, see Siems (n 193) 37–9, who concludes that though some of the lines of attack against functionalism 'raise important objections, but it is submitted that they do not discredit functionalism as a whole.' (ibid, 39).

196 For these and similar lines of criticism, see eg G Frankenberg, 'Critical Comparisons: Rethinking Comparative Law' (1985) 26 *Harvard International Law Journal* 411; P Legrand, 'On the Singularity of Law' (2006) 47 *Harvard International Law Journal* 517; E Örücü, 'Methodological Aspects of Comparative Law' (2006) 8 *European Journal of Law Reform* 29.

197 See eg W Twining, 'Globalisation and Comparative Law' in E Örücü/D Nelken (eds), *Comparative Law: A Handbook* (Oxford, Hart 2007) 69 (75–6).

198 See RK Merton, 'Manifest and Latent Functions' in id, *Social Theory and Social Structure* (New York, Free Press, enlarged ed 1968) 73.

199 For a critical review of this line of argumentation, see eg A Peters/H Schwenke, 'Comparative Law Beyond Post-Modernism' (2000) 49 *International and Comparative Law Quarterly* 800; Peters and Schwenke aptly summarise their refutation

functionalist approach to comparative law constitutes an attempt to overcome the legal parochialism attached to unreflected formalism, an attitude which devaluated foreign legal traditions and their institutions precisely because of their perceived 'strangeness'. Functionalism, by contrast, allows to value legal diversity as what it is: The result of a long evolutive process of conscious or unconscious responses to the challenges that have confronted a society, a process that was shaped partly by common social problems, partly by distinct cultural features, partly by contingencies of a given historic or economic situation.

As such, it allows analysing differences as well as commonalities. It must not be forgotten, of course, that functionalism always implies a reduction of complexity, and that 'function' is but a heuristic tool for classification, not an absolutely immutable property of a certain rule or institution. Nevertheless, the charge that functionalism involves an undue simplification seems unfair: By adding the functional perspective to the comparativist agenda, one is able to establish a more complete picture of reality than could be achieved by focusing exclusively on legal forms and institutions.[200] Moreover, it should be noted that the functionalist strand in comparative legal scholarship, with its oft-criticised and derided *praesumptio similitudinis*,[201] has evolved as a reaction of progressively minded scholars to the experience of two devastating World Wars, which they attributed at least in part to the belief in the inevitability of a conflict between fundamentally incompatible cultural values, political systems and legal institutions, a belief they felt had been prevalent in both 1914 and 1939.[202] In a time like ours, when a trend towards 'universal exceptionalism'[203] in international law appears to gain more and more ground,[204] and when even the

of the critics of (functionalist) comparative law thus: 'To scorn srupulous scholarship as "chastened search for true understanding" and to disparage "all this ego suppression and careful listening" is a good excuse for not even trying.' (ibid, 834).

200 See Michaels (n 192) 364: 'The great advantage of functionalism over substantivism … is precisely that it makes generalizations possible without loss of specificity.'

201 See on this term eg K Zweigert, 'Des solutions identiques par des voies différentes' (1966) 18 *Revue Internationale de Droit Comparé* 5.

202 This connection can be demonstrated both with respect to the origins of functionalism in the interwar period and to the revived interest in it as an approach to comparative law after WW II; for the interwar period, see eg S Marck, *Substanz- und Funktionsbegriff in der Rechtsphilosophie* (Tübingen, Mohr 1925), which was among the many works by liberal Jewish legal scholars put to the torch during the Nazi book burnings in 1933; see further M Rheinstein, 'Teaching Comparative Law' (1937–8) 5 *University of Chicago Law Review* 615. For the revival of functionalism in early post-WW II Europe, see esp J Esser, 'Universale Prinzipien als Basis der Funktionsvergleichung' in id, *Grundsatz und Norm in der richterlichen Fortbildung des Privatrechts* (Tübingen, Mohr 1956) 346.

203 A Bradford/E Posner, 'Universal Exceptionalism in International Law' (2011) 52 *Harvard International Law Journal* 1.

204 Although this debate is sometimes criticised as exaggerated; see eg the critical discussion of the use of the term 'European exceptionalism' in G Nolte and H Aust, 'European exceptionalism?' (2013) 2 *Global Constitutionalism* 407.

scholarly emphasis seems to be shifting from the universalist aspirations of the 1990s to a focus on diversity and legal pluralism,[205] it seems that the dose of optimism attached to the functionalist approach could provide an antidote to these disparate tendencies.

In any event, it should not be forgotten that the comparative analysis used to discern 'general principles of law accepted by civilized nations' is directed towards a more specific goal than the academic study of comparative law. Whereas comparative legal scholarship is done for various purposes – or for no extraneous purpose at all, as *la science pour la science* – the work of the international lawyer who compares domestic legal systems is not interested in their specificities, but in their commonalities. What he or she *should* be interested in, however, are the peculiarities of *international law* as a distinct legal order. This is so because the differences between domestic and international law are considerably greater than those between any two domestic legal orders, both due to the fundamentally different nature of international law's main subjects (ie, the states), and due its considerably lower state of integration and centralisation.[206]

With a grain of salt, one could therefore say that while on the comparative stage of the inquiry (ie, the ascertainment of a principle underlying various domestic rules), a *praesumptio similitudinis* applies, on the transformative stage (the adaptation of the basic principle thus discerned to the international plane), a *praesumptio dissimilitudinis* is more appropriate.[207] On both of these stages, however, the functional method can provide valuable guidance: On the comparative stage, it allows for the abstracting generalisation, and thus for the intellectual *assimilation*, of various domestic norms of very different form, origin and appearance; whereas, on the transformative stage, the recourse to the functional method yields vital information about the *dissimilarities* between any given municipal law system and international law, as it connects particular concepts and rules to the basic underlying functions of the system,

205 To name but three recent representative publications out of many, see N Krisch, *Beyond Constitutionalism: The Pluralist Structure of Postnational Law* (Oxford, Oxford University Press 2013); M Rosenfeld, *Law, Justice, Democracy, and the Clash of Cultures: A Pluralist Account* (Cambridge, Cambridge University Press 2011); J Klabbers/Touko Piiparinen (eds), *Normative Pluralism and International Law: Exploring Global Governance* (Cambridge, Cambridge University Press 2013); see esp the contribution by T Piiparinen, 'Exploring the Methodology of Normative Pluralism' (ibid, 35).

206 For an analysis of these differences from a structuralist perspective, see A Bleckmann, 'Zur Strukturanalyse im Völkerrecht' (1978) 9 *Rechtstheorie* 143.

207 For an analysis of some of these basic differences, see H Thirlway, 'Concepts, Principles, Rules and Analogies: International and Municipal Law Reasoning' (2002) 294 *Recueil de Cours* 267; Thirlway (ibid, 275) states his purpose thus: 'My intention in these lectures is to study the circumstances in which this process of argument by analogy from [domestic] private law cannot or should not be used, because of the special features of the relevant field of international law or international relations.'

demonstrating that apparent similarities between concepts in domestic and international legal systems can be quite deceiving. Thus, the value of the functional comparative approach for international law is not limited to determining whether explicit borrowing of rules and concepts from domestic law is possible: it also enhances the understanding of genuine concepts of international law by way of contradistinction to apparently similar concepts in municipal legal systems.[208]

In a manner of speaking, the functional approach thus links the two seemingly disparate interpretations of the term 'general principle' in international law, a term which is sometimes understood to refer to abstractions from specific rules and institutes of international law, sometimes to principles of municipal law: In the first instance, the specific properties of the international legal system are stressed, whereas, in the second, the commonalities prevail. In this sense, the reference to 'general principles of law' in Article 38 (1) (c) ICJ Statute does not only denote a distinct source of law, but also – and perhaps essentially – a *method* of legal reasoning, or of comprehension. More precisely, it refers to the practice of reconstructing and re-enacting intellectually the process in which the rules of law – whether domestic or international – have evolved, and by which common fundamental ideas, however unavowed, they have been motivated. After all, every international lawyer comes from a specific domestic legal background, and thus has a tendency to project – if only subconsciously – his or her particular domestic notions and concepts onto the international plane.[209] Often, the parochial legal concepts that we have grown used to are so deeply entrenched in our consciousness that we tend to identify them with notions of 'justice' and 'right'.[210] Especially those domestic legal rules grounded on close intra-group solidarity appeal to our basic social instincts, yet naïve attempts to transplant them into the international legal system have the potential to wreak havoc on the fragile fabric of world public order.[211]

208 A classic example in this respect are the differences between the seemingly analogous concepts of 'property' in domestic law and 'sovereignty' in international law; see in this respect eg the Dissenting Opinion of Judge ad hoc Fernandes in the *Case Concerning Rights of Passage over Indian Territory* [1960] ICJ Rep 123, esp at 134 et seqq.

209 For a thorough analysis of these cultural influences, see O Korhonen, *International Law Situated: An Analysis of the Lawyer's Stance Towards Culture, History and Community* (Hague, Kluwer Law 2000).

210 This is so because our instincts have evolved to be accustomed to those rules of behaviour that faciliate the living together in rather small groups or tribes; see eg FA Hayek, *The Fatal Conceit: The Errors of Socialism* (London, Routledge 1988) esp ch iv: 'The Revolt of Instinct and Reason'.

211 An example in this respect would be the attempt to justify unilateral humanitarian intervention through recourse to the right of 'defense of another person' as recognised in many domestic criminal law systems; for this argument, see eg K Doehring, 'Die Humanitäre Intervention – Überlegungen zu ihrer Rechtfertigung', in AA Cançado Trindade (ed) *The Modern World of Human Rights – El Mundo Moderno de Derechos Humanos: Essays in Honour of Thomas Buergenthal* (San José, Inter-American Institute of Human Rights 1996) 549.

Sometimes, domestic preconceptions deceivingly suggest the identity of a certain concept in domestic and international law, while the context in which the respective concepts operate, and the function they respectively fulfil, differs considerably. Thus, the prevalence of the concept of 'proportionality' in both domestic constitutional jurisprudence and in certain fields of international law (especially in the *ius ad bellum* and *ius in bello*, but also in the law of state responsibility) tempts one to construct an overarching general principle of proportionality, and to identify it with 'law's golden rule',[212] the essence of the 'rule of law'. The obvious danger of such an approach is that it renders the concept so vague that it becomes meaningless and trite, and thus does not serve to advance the international rule of law, but only to discredit it. This does not mean that a comparative analysis of the principle of proportionality in domestic and international law is not a highly valuable and informative exercise; it only means that the comparison has to be carried out with a watchful eye and an attentive mind, in full awareness of the structural differences that exist between international and domestic legal orders, and even between different sub-fields of international law.[213] It is through such a comparative process, both within and outside of the boundaries of international law proper, that we can (and should) try to discern general principles.

These principles may express distinct features of the international legal system – such as the notion of 'effectivity' as a fundamental principle of international law, a concept that one hardly finds in the more centralised domestic legal systems, where the monopoly of power usually resides with a – more or less – unified public authority. Or they may incorporate general legal concepts which are indeed shared by many systems of municipal law. The migration of these concepts to international law could be described in terms of the concept of 'legal memes', ie a form of 'cultural software' that is transmitted and adapted by way of cultural evolution.[214]

This way of describing the transmission and replication of legal ideas seems particularly adequate, as it goes beyond the rationalistic view that notions like 'legal transplants' and the practice of 'judicial borrowing' are part of a deliberate, instrumental activity that is carried out consciously in order to select the 'best' solutions for certain (perceived or real) social problems. In the process of

212 See D Beatty, 'Law's Golden Rule' in G Palombella/N Walker (eds), *Relocating the Rule of Law* (Oxford, Hart 2009) 99.

213 An excellent analysis in this spirit has recently been undertaken with respect to the principle of proportionality: See M Newton/L May, *Proportionality in International Law* (Oxford, Oxford University Press 2014).

214 The concept of 'legal memes' was developed by Jack Balkin in several publications; see eg his book *Cultural Software: A Theory of Ideology* (New Haven, Yale University Press 1998); Balkin himself adapted the idea of 'memes' as units of information transmitted by way cultural evolution (analogous to the 'genes' of biological evolution) from the works of Richard Dawkins; see esp R Dawkins, *The Selfish Gene* (Oxford, Oxford University Press 1976); on the concept of 'meme', see generally SJ Blackmore, *The Meme Machine* (Oxford, Oxford University Press 1999).

migration of ideas from domestic to international law, those specific elements of a principle which are inconsistent with the function that it has assumed in the international order are gradually abraded, while other features, which are adjusted to the new normative environment, emerge. This process is sometimes consciously directed, as the example of the codification of the principle *inadimpleti contractus* in Article 60 VCLT has demonstrated. Often, however, it progresses without such conscious direction. It is the essence – and often only it – of a normative concept that survives this process of adaption; and concepts whose basic idea is thus reducible to a very flexible yet poignant core have the best chances of replicating,[215] as the remarkable career of the principle of 'proportionality' demonstrates.

Such basic legal ideas, concepts, indeed – principles – form the defining structures of legal orders. In this sense, it is true that '[t]he law of general principles is constitutional law in the fullest sense of the word'.[216] The degree to which one legal order shares them with others is indicative of its autonomy and individuality. In this way, they can indeed be described as being positioned on the 'supreme level of objectivity' in any legal order. As the examples of this and the preceding sections of the present chapter have demonstrated, one should not underestimate the degree of international law's 'otherness', by the extent to which it is shaped by peculiar structural conditions that are manifested in principles not found in any domestic legal order. Any attempt to 'bridge' the gap between international and domestic law carefully has to take this fact into account.

215 See on this point Hayek (n 210) 151: 'The possibility of forming structures by a process of replication gives those elements that have the capacity for doing so better chances of multiplying.... In the structures of interaction, the patterns of activities of groups are determined by practices transmitted by individuals of one generation to those of the next; and these orders preserve their general character only by constant change (adaptation).'

216 See R Kolb, 'Principles as Sources of International Law: With Special Reference to Good Faith' (2006) 53 *Netherlands International Law Review* 1 (36).

VII Conclusion

The Dialectics of World Public Order

In 1957, the Slovenian legal philosopher and former diplomat[1] Leonidas Pitamic picked up his pen to compose a letter to his friend and erstwhile mentor Hans Kelsen, who served at that time as a Professor Emeritus of political science at the University of California, Berkeley.[2] After the usual polite phrases (both Kelsen and Pitamic had been socialised in the courteous world of late Austro-Hungarian academia), he addressed an aspect of Kelsen's theory that had for a long time troubled him: The concept of the *Grundnorm* ('basic norm') as a point of origin from which the validity of the whole legal order is derived. From Kelsen's neo-Kantian point of view, the existence of such a norm was a logical necessity, as the validity of a legal norm can only ever be derived from another legal norm, but never from a fact (such as the will of a legislator). The basic norm's content was conceived of as purely formal, not having any claim to substantive 'rightness' or 'justice': 'The basic norm of the Pure Theory of Law is the reason of the validity of a democratic as well as of an autocratic law, of a capitalistic as well as of a socialistic law, of any positive law, whether considered to be just or unjust.'[3]

However, as we have seen,[4] Kelsen made one significant concession that blurred his seemingly impeccable distinction between the 'Is' and the 'Ought': The validity of norms of a legal order, he admitted, depended not only on their consistency with a hypothetical basic norm, but also on the *general effectivity* of the legal order as a whole, ie the question whether the norms belonging to it were generally obeyed. At this point, Pitamic found himself both in agreement and disagreement with Kelsen: He agreed that the effectivity of a legal order is a condition of its validity, but disagreed with the representation of the

1 Pitamic had served as ambassador of the Kingdom of Yugoslavia to the United States from 1929–1934; for a brief biographical sketch, see I Tomišić, 'In Memoriam Leonidas Pitamic' (1972) 23 *Österreichische Zeitschrift für Öffentliches Recht* 201.

2 This letter has recently been published and commented upon; see M Pavčnik, 'Die Frage der rechtlichen Grundnorm (Pitamic' Brief and Kelsen)' (2010) 96 *Archiv für Rechts- und Sozialphilosophie* 86.

3 H Kelsen, 'On the Basic Norm' (1959) 47 *California Law Review* 107 (110).

4 On Kelsen's concept of the basic norm, see above Ch III B.

basic norm as a purely formal epistemological tool that could bear any possible content. For him, the normative character of the law can only be reconciled with its factual side, ie its effectivity, if law's effectivity is not portrayed as a *mere* 'Is', but as the realisation of an 'Ought'. A legal system is effective, therefore, if it responds to the needs of the members of the group whose behaviour it regulates. And a legal system that regulates the behaviour of human beings must address the basic needs of human nature. The content of Pitamic' basic norm thus comprises two necessary elements: The element of order, and the element of humanity. The legal order the validity of which it establishes must be effective in regulating behaviour, and its norms must not be grossly offensive to human nature.[5]

It is not known whether Kelsen has responded to Pitamic' letter; in any event, it seems unlikely that the argument made much impression on him. Probably he regarded it as another act of apostasy by one of his students, similar to Alfred Verdross' turn to natural law. However, the argument sketched in the letter is not so much a plea for natural law, but an attack on the Achilles' heel of legal positivism, its treatment of the criterion of 'effectivity'. Unless positivism is to degenerate into a crude doctrinal rationalisation of gunman's order (or, in the context of international relations, of power politics), it cannot give up the distinction between what is normatively demanded and what actually happens. In other words, it cannot maintain that everything that exists is normatively warranted. And yet, it has to explain why some legal orders are in force, while others are not – or no longer – observed; why, for example, the Code of Hammurabi is no longer the law of the land. On the other hand, it cannot give up its claim to define law without reference to a substantive criterion of validity, ie the attempt to define law by its form rather than its content. It is easy to see why positivism's complex relationship with effectivity is felt acutely in the field of unwritten international law, which by nature does not lend itself easily to formal criteria of law-ascertainment, and where the point at which a mere regularity of behaviour turns into a binding legal rule is often uncertain. It seems that both Kelsen's attempt to formulate the basic norm of customary international law ('States shall behave as they have customarily behaved') and Hart's characterisation of international law as a 'simple form of social structure, consisting only of primary rules of obligation' are capitulations of legal positivism before the complexities of (unwritten) international law.

On the other hand, the attempts to ground unwritten international law immediately on values did not fare much better, as notions of values are inherently subjective and culture-dependant and it is hardly possible to reach a consensus on them among the members of the international community. Moreover, as has been argued in the previous chapter, values and moral precepts are often attuned to our domestic environment and not transposable to the international plane. In other words, what we may regard instinctively as a

5 Pavčnik (n 2) 94–5.

fair and just rule of behaviour in our day-to-day life in domestic communities may involve serious challenges to the stability of the international system, the structural conditions of which are fundamentally dissimilar.

Much of the humanitarian activism which flourishes in Western societies, and which seeks to reform the way in which the traditional international system functions, takes its strength from its appeal to basic feelings of solidarity to which we have become accustomed through evolutionary processes as well as ethical education. Thus, it is certainly a highly recommendable impulse to intervene when we see a helpless person being attacked in the subway. Yet it is far from clear whether we can apply this reasoning to a military intervention in a foreign civil war, especially if this intervention means to take sides in a century-old sectarian struggle. As David Kennedy has argued in his book *The Dark Side of Virtue*:

> Aspiring to good, humanitarians too often mute awareness that their best ideas can have bad consequences. When things do go wrong, rather than facing the darker consequences of humanitarian work, we too often simply redouble our efforts and intensify our condemnation of whatever other forces we can find to hold responsible.[6]

This clearly does not mean that moral arguments should not have a place in our reasoning about international relations and, consequently, about international law. To be sure, even the most hard-nosed political realists do have to take into account values: Those values, when shared by a sufficient number of people, can become as much a part of the real world as tanks and aircraft carriers.[7] It is clear that much of the development of international law during the 20th century was owed to the fact that certain practices hitherto regarded as acceptable were increasingly considered to be morally repugnant.[8]

Yet – and there's the rub – rules and institutions that have evolved over time, the purpose of which we often do not fully appreciate, in fact often even profoundly misunderstand, can be of vital importance for the maintenance of the modicum of fragile stability that exists in international relations. Therefore, it is crucial to make every possible attempt to properly understand the function of certain rules and principles before dismissing them as antiquated, illiberal or morally reprehensible. In this context, we ought to be careful to separate the essence of rules from their time-bound rationalisations or justifications. The continued relevance of the rules of state immunity – at least in their core tenets – in the face of profoundly changing ideas about the nature of the

6 D Kennedy, *The Dark Side of Virtue: Reassessing International Humanitarianism* (Princeton, Princeton University Press 2004) 327.

7 This argument is stated forcefully by H Kissinger, *World Order: Reflections on the Character of Nations and the Course of History* (New York, Penguin 2014) esp 326 et seqq.

8 For an analysis, see eg M Barnett, *Empire of Humanity: A History of Humanitarianism* (Ithaca, Cornell University Press 2011).

international order testifies to that.[9] Lawyers have a conscious or intuitive tendency to resort to a rule's 'purpose' when they attempt to discern its meaning and implications for a particular case, as well as when they decide whether or not it prevails when it comes into a (real or purported) conflict with other norms. Yet frequently they fail to notice that the concept of 'purpose' is fundamentally problematic when it is applied to rules which did not emanate from the familiar domestic legislative process, but resulted from a long process of self-organisation of the international community of states. Rules and concepts can undergo an almost complete metamorphosis to meet the demands of entirely divergent environments. An example in this respect that has been discussed above is the *uti possidetis* doctrine, which originated in 19th-century Latin America: Originally intended to serve as a legal shield to prevent the ambitions of land-grabbing European powers from sweeping over to the South American continent, the doctrine has also played a crucial role in the prevention of territorial wars among the African nations that emerged through the process of decolonialisation since the middle of the 20th century.[10]

The great virtue of unwritten international law, as it has been portrayed in this study, is that it is able to combine the authority of tradition with a degree of flexibility and adaptability to the unpredictable exigencies of an ever-precarious world order. Some states may have played a greater or a lesser role in their formation, but it is precisely the fact that the unwritten rules and principles of the international legal system have not been *made* in the sense that laws or treaties are made which implies that they do not belong to anyone in particular – or, rather, that they belong to all. And the frequently lamented fact that rules of customary international law do not have a fixed beginning or end in time, and that it is often impossible to indicate the exact moment when a mere usage became a binding rule of law, or when such rule ceases to exist, also has a positive side, as it urges the states to exercise caution and constraint in the twilight zones of unsettled law.

One may of course be of the opinion that such a form of law-creation is hopelessly outdated, that it is anachronistic or even atavistic in a time when events and developments that threaten the stability of nations unfold at such a pace that politicians and diplomats hardly find the time to deliberate with their foreign colleagues on even a provisional crisis management agenda. As W Michael Reisman rhetorically asked in 1987: 'If purposive legislation is so important an instrument for clarifying and implementing policy in an industrial and science-based civilization such as ours, how can we dispense with it in the much more complicated and varied global civilization?'[11]

9 For the changing theoretical explanations of the law of state immunity, see H Fox, *The Law of State Immunity* (Oxford, Oxford University Press, 3rd ed 2013) 25 et seqq.

10 See above Ch V H.

11 WM Reisman, 'The Cult of Custom in the Late 20th Century' (1987) 17 *California Western International Law Journal* 133 (134).

The arguments presented in this book in favour of *The Rule of Unwritten International Law* as a suitable response to the challenges of contemporary international order are hardly going to convince a whole-hearted believer in the superiority of rationally designed legislation at the supra-national level. Nevertheless, today there seems to be a growing awareness that international institutions do not necessarily produce more desirable or agreeable results than their national counterparts, and that the transfer of competencies from the domestic to the international level is a two-edged sword that does not necessarily always cut in a – purportedly – 'progressive' direction.[12] Moreover, after several decades in which the multilateral treaty was regarded as *the* most important instrument for creating general international law, there is today a perceived 'stagnation'[13] in this source.

The arguments made in this book should not be understood to imply, however, that unwritten international law should *replace* multilateral treaty-making or law-creation by international institutions: The aim was rather to show that the unwritten sources of international law continue to fulfil a vital function in the international legal order, a function that is complementary to the role of allegedly more modern forms of law-creation. The way in which rules of customary international law were traditionally conceived to emerge, ie through repeated practice which is gradually complemented by belief in the existence of a legal obligation, resembles processes of self-organisation similar to the operation of complex adaptive systems studied in the emerging field of complexity theory. Moreover, there is also a profoundly moral element in such law-creation through practice: In a way, the emergence of rules of customary international law almost embodies the Kantian categorical imperative: 'Act only on that maxim whereby thou canst at the same time will that it should become a universal law.'

As the present study sought to demonstrate, the concept of law as a form of spontaneous societal self-organisation has been a recurrent theme in the history of political and legal thought, forming a distinct tradition that transcended the usual natural law-positivism dichotomy. It is precisely the open-texturedness of this tradition that allowed it to include pragmatic, moral and formalist strands of legal reasoning. As such, it may provide inspiration for a meaningful, comprehensive reunification of practical reasoning with legal theory in our post-Postmodernist world.

12 The debate on the UN Security Council's so-called 'targeted sanctions' is an apt example of this; see eg the arguments presented in A Tzanakopoulos, *Disobeying the Security Council: Countermeasures against Wrongful Sanctions* (Oxford, Oxford University Press 2011).

13 For the argument that there is such a 'stagnation' in formal international law-making, see eg the recent contribution by J Pauwelyn/R Wessels/J Wouters, 'When Structures become Shackles: Stagnation and Dynamics in International Lawmaking' (2014) 25 *European Journal of International Law* 733.

Bibliography

Aber, S, et al: 'Unintended Consequences: Refugee Victims of the War on Terror' (2006) 37 *Georgetown Journal of International Law* 759.

Abramson, JB: *Minerva's Owl: The Tradition of Western Political Thought* (Cambridge/MA, Harvard University Press 2009).

Alchuorron, C/Bulygin, E: *Normative Systems* (Wien/New York, Springer 1971).

Alexy, R: 'Zum Begriff der Rechtsprinzipien' (1979) 1 *Rechtstheorie-Beiheft* 59.

Allen, CK: *Law in the Making* (Oxford, Clarendon, 7th ed 1964).

Allott, P: 'Comment on Jean d'Aspremont, Formalism and the Sources of International Law' (EJIL Talk!, 12 December2012) <http://www.ejiltalk.org/comments-on-jean-daspremont-formalism-and-the-sources-of-international-law-a-theory-of-the-ascertainment-of-legal-rules/>accessed 12 February 2015.

Allott, P: 'The Concept of International Law' (1999) 110 *European Journal of International Law* 31.

Alvarez-Jimenez, A: 'Methods for the Identification of Customary International Law in the International Court of Justice's Jurisprudence 2000–2009' (2011) 60 *International and Comparative Law Quarterly* 681.

Anderson, K: 'The Rise of International Criminal Law: Intended and Unintended Consequences' (2009) 20 *European Journal of International Law* 331.

Anzilotti, D: *Corso di diritto internazionale, Vol I* (Padova, CEDAM, 4th ed 1955).

Anzilotti, D: *Il Diritto Internazionale Nei Giudizi Interni* (Bologna, Zanetti 1905).

Anzilotti, D: *Völkerrecht, Bd I: Allgemeine Lehren* (Berlin/Leipzig, de Gruyter 1929)

Arajärvi, N: *The Changing Nature of Customary International Law: Methods of Interpreting the Concept of Custom in International Criminal Tribunals* (London, Routledge 2014).

Arendt, H: *On Revolution* (London, Penguin, repr 1990).

Ashraf, A, et al: 'Adam Smith: Behavioural Economist' (2005) 19*Journal of Economic Perspectives* 131.

Aust, A: *Handbook of International Law* (Cambridge, Cambridge University Press 2005).

Bacqué, JA: 'Stufenbau der Rechtsordnung' in E Bulygin/EG Valdez (eds), *Argentinische Rechtstheorie und Rechtsphilosophie heute* (Berlin, Duncker und Humblot 1987) 111.

Balkin, J: *Cultural Software: A Theory of Ideology* (New Haven, Yale University Press 1998).

Balot, RK: *Greed and Injustice in Classical Athens* (Princeton, Princeton University Press 2001).

Barak, A: *Purposive Interpretation in Law* (Princeton, Princeton University Press 2005).

Barak, A: *The Judge in a Democracy* (Princeton, Princeton University Press 2007).

Barnett, J: 'Toward a Theory of Legal Naturalism' (1978) 2 *Journal of Libertarian Studies* 97.

Barnett, J: *Empire of Humanity: A History of Humanitarianism* (Ithaca, Cornell University Press 2011).

Bartha, P: 'Analogy and Analogical Reasoning' in EN Zalta (ed.), *The Stanford Encyclopedia of Philosophy* (Fall 2013 Edition).

Battifol, H: *Aspects Philosophiques du Droit International Privé* (Paris, Dalloz 1956).

Beatty, D: 'Law's Golden Rule' in G Palombella/N Walker (eds), *Relocating the Rule of Law* (Oxford, Hart 2009) 99.

Bederman, D: *Custom as a Source of Law* (Cambridge, Cambridge University Press 2010).

Beitz, C: *Political Theory and International Relations* (Princeton, Princeton University Press 1979).

Benvenisti, E: 'Judicial Misgivings Regarding the Application of International Law: An Analysis of Attitudes of National Courts' (1993) 4 *European Journal of International Law* 159.

Benvenisti, E: 'Reclaiming Democracy: The Strategic Uses of Foreign and International Law by Domestic Courts' (2008) 102 *American Journal of International Law* 241.

Benvenisti, E/Downs, GW: 'National Courts, Domestic Democracy, and the Evolution of International Law' (2009) 20 *European Journal of International Law* 59.

Berman, F: 'The ILC within the UN's Legal Framework: Its Relationship with the Sixth Committee' (2006) 49 *German Yearbook of International Law* 107.

Bernhardt, R: 'Ungeschriebenes Völkerrecht' (1976) 36 *Zeitschrift für ausländisches öffentliches Recht und Völkerrecht* 50.

Besson, S: 'Theorizing the Sources of International Law' in S Besson/J Tasioulas (eds), *The Philosophy of International Law* (Oxford, Oxford University Press 2010) 163.

Binder, C: 'Stability and Change in the Time of Fragmentation: The Limits of *Pacta Sunt Servanda* Revisited' (2012) 25 *Leiden Journal of International Law* 909.

Blackmore, SJ: *The Meme Machine* (Oxford, Oxford University Press 1999).

Blackstone, W: *Commentaries on the Laws of England* (Oxford, Clarendon, 8th ed 1768).

Bleckmann, A: 'Deutsche Rechtsprechung in völkerrechtlichen Fragen' (1972) 32 *Zeitschrift für ausländisches öffentliches Recht und Völkerrecht* 127.

Bleckmann, A: 'Die Praxis des Völkergewohnheitsrecht als konsekutive Rechtssetzung' in R Bernhardt/WK Geck/G Jaennicke/H Steinberger (eds), *Völkerrecht als Rechtsordnung: Festschrift für Hermann Mosler* (Heidelberg/Berlin, Springer 1983) 89.

Bleckmann, A: 'Völkergewohnheitsrecht trotz widersprüchlicher Praxis?' (1976) 36 *Zeitschrift für ausländisches öffentliches Recht und Völkerrecht* 374.

Bleckmann, A: 'Zur Feststellung und Auslegung von Völkergewohnheitsrecht' (1977) 37 *Zeitschrift für ausländisches Öffenliches Recht und Völkerrecht* 504.

Bleckmann, A: 'Zur Strukturanalyse im Völkerrecht' (1978) 9 *Rechtstheorie* 143.

Bleckmann, A: *Die Funktionen der Lehre im Völkerrecht: Materialien zu einer Allgemeinen Methoden- und Völkerrechtslehre* (Heidelberg, CF Müller 1981).

Bleckmann, A: *Grundprobleme und Methodenlehre des Völkerrechts* (Freiburg/München, Alber 1982).

Blutman, L: 'Conceptual Confusion and Methodological Deficiencies: Some Ways that Theories on Customary International Law Fail' (2014) 25 *European Journal of International Law* 529.

Bodansky, D: 'Customary (and Not So Customary) International Environmental Law' (1995) 3 *Global Legal Studies Journal* 105.

Bodansky, D: 'Prologue to a Theory of Non-Treaty Norms' in M Arsanjani et al (eds), *Looking to the Future: Essays on International Law in Honour of W Michael Reisman* (Leiden, Brill 2010) 119.

Bos, M: *Methodology of International Law* (Amsterdam, North-Holland 1984).

Bracton, H de: *De Legibus et Consuetudinibus Angliae* (G Woodbine ed, New Haven, Yale University Press 1922).

Bradford, A/Posner, EA: 'Universal Exceptionalism in International Law' (2011) 52 *Harvard International Law Journal* 3.

Bradley, CA: *International Law in the US Legal System* (Oxford and New York, Oxford University Press 2013).

Bradley, CA/Goldsmith, JL: 'Customary International Law as Law of the United States' (1989) 10 *Michigan Journal of International Law* 450.

Bradley, CA/Gulati, M: 'Withdrawing from International Custom' (2010) 120 *Yale Law Journal* 202.

Bremmer, I: *Every Nation for Itself: Winners and Losers in the G-Zero World* (London and New York, Penguin 2012).

Brierly, JL: 'The *Lotus* Case' (1928) 44 *Law Quarterly Review* 154.

Brierly, JL: 'Vital Interests and the Law' (1944) 21 *British Yearbook of International Law* 56.

Brock, G: *Global Justice: A Cosmopolitan Approach* (Oxford, Oxford University Press 2009).

Brölmann, CM/Vierdag, EW: 'Netherlands' in PM Eisemann (ed), *The Integration of International and European Community Law in the National Legal Order* (Alphen aan den Rijn, Kluwer Law 1996) 433.

Brownlie, I: *Principles of Public International Law* (Oxford, Oxford University Press, 6th ed 1995).

Bubner, R: *Welche Rationalität bekommt der Gesellschaft? Vier Kapitel aus dem Naturrecht* (Frankfurt am Main, Suhrkamp 1996).

Buchan, R: *International Law and the Construction of Liberal Peace* (Oxford, Hart 2013).

Buchanan, A: *Justice, Legitimacy and Self-Determination: Moral Foundations for International Law* (Oxford, Oxford University Press 2007).

Buchanan, J: *The Limits of Liberty: Between Anarchy and Leviathan* (Chicago, University of Chicago Press 1975).

Buffard, I/Zemanek, K: 'The "Object and Purpose" of a Treaty: An Enigma?' (1998) 3 *Austrian Review of International and European Law* 311.

Bull, H: *The Anarchical Society* (Basingstoke, Palgrave Macmillan, 4th ed 2012).

Byers, M: *Custom, Power and the Power of Rules: International Relations and Customary International Law* (Cambridge, Cambridge University Press 1999).

Cardozo, B: *The Growth of the Law* (New Haven, Yale University Press 1924).

Cardozo, B: *The Nature of the Judicial Process* (New Haven, Yale University Press 1921).

Cardozo, B: *The Paradoxes of Legal Science* (New York, Columbia University Press 1928).

Carty, A: 'Critical International Law: Recent Trends in International Legal Theory' (1991) 2 *European Journal of International Law* 1.

Carty, A: 'Scandinavian Realism and Phenomenological Approaches to Statehood and General Custom in International Law' (2003) 14 *European Journal of International Law* 817.

Carty, A: *The Decay of International Law? A Reappraisal of the Limits of Legal Imagination in International Affairs* (Manchester, Manchester University Press 1986).

Cassese, A: *International Criminal Law* (Oxford, Oxford University Press 2003).

Castberg, F: *Problems of Legal Philosophy* (London, Allen & Unwin 1957).

Castro, WR: 'The Federal Courts' Protective Jurisdiction Over Torts Committed in Violation of the Law of Nations' (1985–6) 18 *Connecticut Law Review* 467.

Chapman, B: 'The Rational and the Reasonable: Social Choice Theory and Adjucation' (1994) 61 *University of Chicago Law Review* 41.

Charney, J: 'The Persistent Objector Rule and the Development of Customary International Law' (1985) 56 *British Yearbook of International Law* 1.

Chavura, SA: *Tudor Protestant Political Thought 1547–1603* (Leiden, Brill 2011).

Chen, Y: 'Structural Limitations and Possible Future of the Work of the International Law Commission' (2010) 9 *Chinese Journal of International Law* 473.

Cheng, B: *General Principles of Law as Applied by International Courts and Tribunals* (London, Stevens 1953).

Chibundu, MO: 'Making Customary International Law Through Municipal Adjudication: A Structural Inquiry' (1999) 39 *Virginia Journal of International Law* 1069.

Christakis, T: 'Human Rights from a Neo-Voluntarist Perspective' in J Kammerhofer/J d'Aspremont (eds), *International Legal Positivism in a Post-Modern World* (Cambridge, Cambridge University Press 2014) 421.

Christi, FR: 'Hayek and Schmitt on the Rule of Law' (1984) 17 *Canadian Journal of Political Science* 521.

Clapham, A: *Brierly's Law of Nations* (Oxford, Oxford University Press, 7th ed 2012).

Combacau, J/Sur, S: *Droit international public* (Paris, Montchrestien, 10th ed 2012).

Conklin, W: *The Invisible Origins of Legal Positivism: A Re-Reading of a Tradition* (Dordrecht, Kluwer Law 2001).

Cook, H: 'International Nuclear Law: Nuclear Safety, Emergency Response and Nuclear Liability' in S Butt/H Nasu/L Nottage (eds), *Asia-Pacific Disaster Management Comparative and Socio-Legal Perspectives* (Heidelberg, Springer 2014) 279.

Corten, O: *Méthodologie du droit international public* (Bruxelles, Editions de l'Université de Bruxelles 2009).

Cotterell, R: *The Politics of Jurisprudence* (Oxford, Oxford University Press, 2nd ed 2003).

Cottier, T: 'International Economic Law in Transition from Liberalism to Trade Regulation' (2014) 17 *Journal of International Economic Law* 671.

Crnić-Grotić, V: 'Object and Purpose of Treaties in the Vienna Convention on the Law of Treaties' (1997) 7 *Asian Yearbook of International Law* 141.

Cross, FB: 'Paradoxical Perils of the Precautionary Principle' (1996) 53 *Washington & Lee Law Review* 851.

Cudworth, E/Hobden, S: *Posthuman International Relations: Complexity, Ecologism and Global Politics* (New York, Zed 2011).

D'Amato, A: 'International Law as a Unitary System' in D Armstrong (ed), *Routledge Handbook of International Law* (London and New York, Routledge 2010) 101.

D'Amato, A: 'International Law as an Autopoietic System' in R Wolfrum/V Röben (eds), *Developments of International Law in Treaty Making* (Heidelberg, Springer 2005) 335.

D'Amato, A: 'New Approaches to Customary International Law' (2011) 105 *American Journal of International Law* 163.

D'Amato, A: *The Concept of Custom in International Law* (Ithaca, Cornell University Press 1971).

d'Aspremont, J: 'The Systemic Integration of International Law by Domestic Courts' in A Nollkaemper/O Fauchald (eds), *The Practice of International and National Courts and the (De-)Fragmentation of International Law* (Oxford, Hart 2012) 141.

d'Aspremont, J: *Formalism and the Sources of International Law: A Theory of the Ascertainment of Legal Rules* (Oxford, Oxford University Press 2011).

Daase, C/Friesendorf, C: *Rethinking Security Governance: The Problem of Unintended Consequences* (Milton Park, Routledge 2010).

Dagan, H: 'The Realist Conception of Law' (2005) *Tel Aviv University Law School Paper* 21 available at <http://papers.ssrn.com/sol3/papers.cfm?abstract_id=608383> accessed 6 February 2015.

Dainow, J: 'The Civil Law and the Common Law: Some Points of Comparison' (1966–7) 15 *American Journal of Comparative Law* 419.

Damren, SC: 'A "Meeting of the Minds" – The Greater Illusion' (1996) 15 *Law and Philosophy* 271.

Dana, S: 'Beyond Retroactivity to Realizing Justice: A Theory on the Principle of Legality in International Criminal Law' (2009) 99 *The Journal of Criminal Law and Criminology* 857.

Danilenko, GM: 'The Theory of International Customary Law' (1988) 31 *German Yearbook of International Law* 14.

Dawkins, R: *The Selfish Gene* (Oxford, Oxford University Press 1976).

De Schutter, O: 'Les Critical Legal Studies aux pays de droit international' (1992) 22 *Droit et Société* 585.

De Visscher, C: 'La codification de droit international' (1925-I) *Recueil des Cours* 325.

De Visscher, C: *Problèmes d'Interprétation Judiciaire en Droit International Public* (Paris, Pedone 1963).

De Visscher, C: *Théories et Réalités en Droit International Public* (Paris, Pedone, 4th ed 1970).

Dekker, IF/Werner, WG: 'The Completeness of International Law and Hamlet's Dilemma: *Non Liquet*, the *Nuclear Weapons* Case, and Legal Theory' in IF Dekker/HG Post (eds), *On the Foundation and Sources of International Law: Dedicated to the Memory of Professor Herman Meijers* (The Hague, TMC Asser Press 2003) 3.

Denza, E: *Diplomatic Law: A Commentary on the 1961 Vienna Convention on Diplomatic Relations* (Oxford, Oxford University Press, 3rd ed 2008).

Diamond, S: 'The Rule of Law versus the Order of Custom' (1971) 38 *Social Research* 42.

Diels, H (ed): *Die Fragmente der Vorsokratiker, vol II* (Berlin, Weidmann, 3rd ed 1912).

Dimitrijevic, V: *Customary Law as an Instrument for the Protection of Human Rights*, Istituto per gli Studi di Politica Internazionale (ISPI) Milano, Working Paper 7 (2006).

Doehring, K: 'Die Humanitäre Intervention – Überlegungen zu ihrer Rechtfertigung' in AA Cançado Trindade (ed) *The Modern World of Human Rights – El Mundo Moderno de Derechos Humanos: Essays in Honour of Thomas Buergenthal* (San José, Inter-American Institute of Human Rights 1996) 549.

Dunne, T/Kurki, M/Smith, S (eds): *International Relations Theories: Discipline and Diversity* (Oxford, Oxford University Press, 2nd ed 2010).

Dworkin, R: 'The Model of Rules' (1967–8) 35 *Yale Law Journal* 14.

Dworkin, R: *Law's Empire* (Cambridge/MA, Belknap 1986).
Dworkin, R: *Taking Rights Seriously* (Cambridge/MA, Harvard University Press 1977).
Easterbrook, F: 'Statute's Domain' (1983) 50 *University of Chicago Law Review* 533.
Ehrlich, E: *Die Juristische Logik* (Tübingen, Mohr 1918).
Ehrlich, E: *Die Tatsachen des Gewohnheitsrechts: Inaugurationsrede, gehalten am 2. Dezember 1906* (Leipzig and Wien, Deuticke 1907).
Eisemann, PM (ed): *The Integration of International and European Community Law in the National Legal Order* (Alphen aan den Rijn, Kluwer Law 1996).
Elliott, ED: 'The Evolutionary Tradition in Jurisprudence' (1985) 85 *Columbia Law Review* 38.
Ellis, J: 'General Principles and Comparative Law' (2011) 22 *European Journal of International Law* 949.
Escorihuela, AL: 'Alf Ross: Towards a Realist Critique and Reconstruction of International Law' (2003) 14 *European Journal of International Law* 703.
Esser, J: 'Universale Prinzipien als Basis der Funktionsvergleichung' in J Esser, *Grundsatz und Norm in der richterlichen Fortbildung des Privatrechts* (Tübingen, Mohr 1956) 346.
Etzioni, A: 'The Domestic Sources of Global Adhocracy' (2012) 10 *Social Change Review* 99.
Falk, R: 'Nuclear Weapons, International Law and the World Court: A Historic Encounter' (1997) 91 *American Journal of International Law* 64.
Falk, R: *The Role of Domestic Courts in the International Legal Order* (Syracuse, Syracuse University Press 1964).
Fassbender, B: 'The United Nations Charter as the Constitution of the International Community' (1998) 36 *Columbia Journal of Transnational Law* 529.
Fastenrath, U: *Lücken im Völkerrecht* (Berlin, Duncker & Humblot 1991).
Fatima, S: *Using International Law in Domestic Courts* (Oxford, Hart 2005).
Favre, A: 'L'interprétation objectiviste des traités internationaux' (1960) 17 *Schweizerisches Jahrbuch für Internationales Recht* 75.
Fedozzi, P: *Introduzione al Diritto Internazionale e Parte Generale* (Padova, CEDAM, 2nd ed 1933).
Ferguson, A: *An Essay on the History of Civil Society* (Edinburgh, Millar and Caddel 1767).
Fikentscher, W: *Law and Anthropology* (München, Verlag der Bayerischen Akademie der Wissenschaften 2009).
Fikentscher, W: *Methoden des Rechts in vergleichender Darstellung – Band 2: Der Anglo-Amerikanische Rechtskreis* (München, Beck 1975).
Finnemore, M: *National Interests in International Society* (Ithaca, Cornell University Press 1996).
Fish, S: 'The Law Wishes to Have a Formal Existence' in S Fish, *There's No Such Thing As Free Speech (And It's a Good Thing, Too)* (Durham, Duke University Press 1993).
Fitzmaurice, G: 'The General Principles of International Law Considered from the Standpoint of the Rule of Law' (1957-II) 92 *Recueil des Cours* 1.
Foakes, J: *The Position of Heads of States and Senior Officials under International Law* (Oxford, Oxford University Press 2014).
Fontanelli, F: 'The Invocation of the Exception of Non-Performance: A Case-Study on the Role and Application of General Principles of International Law of Contractual Origin' (2012) 1 *Cambridge Journal of International and Comparative Law* 119.

Fortescue, J: *De Laudibus Legum Angliae* (A Amos tr, Cambridge, Cambridge University Press 1825).
Fox, H: *The Law of State Immunity* (Oxford, Oxford University Press, 3rd ed 2013).
Francioni, F: 'International Law as a Common Language for National Courts' (2001) 36 *Texas International Law Journal* 587.
Franck, T: 'The Emerging Right to Democratic Governance' (1992) 86 *American Journal of International Law* 46.
Franck, T: *Political Questions Judicial Answers* (Princeton, Princeton University Press 1992).
Franck, T: *The Structure of Impartiality* (New York, Macmillan 1968).
Frankenberg, G: 'Critical Comparisons: Rethinking Comparative Law' (1985) 26 *Harvard International Law Journal* 411.
Frankfurter, F: 'Some Reflections on the Reading of Statutes' (1947) 47 *Columbia Law Review* 527.
Franßen, E: 'Positivismus als juristische Strategie' (1969) 24 *Juristenzeitung* 766.
Gaja, G: 'General Principles of Law' in R Wolfrum (ed), *The Max Planck Encyclopedia of Public International Law* (Oxford, Oxford University Press 2012).
Galbraith, PW: *Unintended Consequences: How War in Iraq strengthened America's Enemies* (New York, Simon & Schuster 2008).
García-Salmones Rovira, M: *The Project of Positivism in International Law* (Oxford, Oxford University Press 2014).
Gardiner, R: *Treaty Interpretation* (Oxford, Oxford University Press 2008).
Gärditz, KF: 'Bridge of Varvarin' (2014) 108 *American Journal of International Law* 86.
Gärditz, KF: 'Die Legitimation der Justiz zur Völkerrechtsfortbildung' (2008) 47 *Der Staat* 381.
Gärditz, KF: 'Ungeschriebenes Völkerrecht durch Systembildung' (2007) 45 *Archiv des Völkerrechts* 1.
Geiger, R: 'Zur Lehre vom Völkergewohnheitsrecht in der Rechtsprechung des Bundesverfassungsgerichts' (1978) 103 *Archiv des Öffentlichen Rechts* 382.
Geiger, R: *Grundgesetz und Völkerrecht* (München, Beck, 4th ed 2009).
Genugten, W van/Bultermann, M: 'Chapter 1: Crises – Concern and Fuel for International Lawyers' (2013) 44 *Netherlands Yearbook of International Law* 3.
GoldsmithJL/Posner, EA: *The Limits of International Law* (New York, Oxford University Press 2006).
Goodrich, P: 'Ars Bablativa: Ramism, Rhetoric, and the Genealogy of English Jurisprudence' in G Leyh (ed), *Legal Hermeneutics: History, Theory and Practice* (Berkeley, University of California Press 1992).
Green, JA: *The International Court of Justice and Self-Defence in International Law* (Oxford, Hart 2009).
Green, LC: 'Criminal Responsibility of Individuals in Non-international Conflicts' (2002) 45 *German Yearbook of International Law* 82.
Greenawalt, K: *Law and Objectivity* (New York and Oxford, Oxford University Press 1992).
Grzybowski, K: 'Soviet Theory of International Law for the Seventies' (1983) 77 *American Journal of International Law* 862.
Guthrie, WKC: *A History of Greek Philosophy, vol III: The Fifth Century Enlightenment* (Cambridge, Cambridge University Press 1969, 13th printing 2003).
Guzman, AT: 'Saving Customary International Law' (2005) 27 *Michigan International Law Journal* 115.

Guzman, AT: *How International Law Works: A Rational Choice Theory* (New York, Oxford University Press 2008).

Haass, RN: 'The Unraveling: How to Respond to a Disordered World' (2014) 93(6) *Foreign Affairs* 70.

Habermas, J: 'The Constitutionalization of International Law and the Legitimation Problems of a Constitution for World Society' (2008) 15 *Constellations* 444.

Hägerström, A: *Die Philosophie der Gegenwart in Selbstdarstellungen, vol VII* (Leipzig, Felix Meiner 1929).

Handeyside, H: 'The Lotus Principle in ICJ Jurisprudence: Was the Ship Ever Afloat?' (2007–8) 29 *Michigan Journal of International Law* 71.

Harhoff, F: 'Legal and Practical Problems in the International Prosecution of Individuals' (2000) 69 *Nordic Journal of International Law* 53.

Harrison Dinnis, H: *Cyber Warfare and the Laws of War* (Cambridge, Cambridge University Press 2012).

Harrison, NE (ed): *Complexity in World Politics: Concepts and Methods of a New Paradigm* (New York, State University of New York Press 2006).

Hart, HLA: *The Concept of Law* (Oxford, Oxford University Press, 2nd ed 1994).

Hathaway, O/Lavinbuck, AN: 'Rationalism and Revisionism in International Law: Book Review of JL Goldsmith/EA Posner, The Limits of International Law' (2006) 119 *Harvard Law Review* 1404.

Hauriou, M: 'An Interpretation of the Principles of Public Law' (1918) 31 *Harvard Law Review* 813.

Hauriou, M: *Précis élémentaire de droit constitutionnel* (Paris, Sirey 1925).

Hauriou, M: *Principes de droit public* (Paris, Sirey 1910).

Hayek, FA: *Law, Legislation and Liberty* (London, Routledge, reissue 2013).

Hayek, FA: *The Fatal Conceit: The Errors of Socialism* (London, Routledge 1988).

Hayek, FA: *The Political Ideal of the Rule of Law* (Cairo, National Bank of Egypt 1955).

Hayek, FA: *The Road to Serfdom* (London, Routledge, reissue 2004).

Hegel, GF: *Science of Logic* (AV Miller transl, London, Allen & Unwin 1969).

Heidegger, M: *Sein und Zeit* (Tübingen, Mohr Siebeck, 10th ed 1963).

Heintschel von Heinegg, W: 'Die weiteren Quellen des Völkerrechts' in K Ipsen (ed), *Völkerrecht* (München, CH Beck, 5th ed 2004) 210.

Henkin, L: 'That "S-Word": Sovereignty, and Globalization, and Human Rights, et cetera…' (1999) 68 *Fordham Law Review* 1.

Herczegh, G: *General Principles of Law and the International Legal Order* (Budapest, Akadémiai kiadó 1969).

Herdegen, M: 'Asymmetrien in der Staatenwelt und die Herausforderungen des "konstruktiven Völkerrechts"' (2004) 64 *Zeitschrift für ausländisches öffentliches Recht und Völkerrecht* 571.

Herdegen, M: 'Das "konstruktive" Völkerrecht und seine Grenzen' in PM Dupuy et al (eds), *Völkerrecht als Wertordnung: Festschrift für Christian Tomuschat* (Kehl, Engel 2006) 899.

Hernández, GI: *The International Court of Justice and the Judicial Function* (Oxford, Oxford University Press 2014).

Hertogh, M (ed): *Living Law: Reconsidering Eugen Ehrlich* (Oxford, Hart 2009).

Hofstadter, D/Sander, E: *Surfaces and Essences: Analogy as the Fire and Fuel of Thinking* (New York, Basic Books 2013).

Holland, JH: *Complexity: A Very Short Introduction* (Oxford, Oxford University Press 2014).

Holland, JH: *Hidden Order: How Adaptation Builds Complexity* (New York, Perseus 1995).
Holmes, OW: 'Codes, and the Arrangement of the Law' (1870) 5 *American Law Review* 1.
Huber, M: 'Observation' (1931) 36-I*Annuaire de l'Institut de Droit International* 77.
Huntington, S: 'The Clash of Civilizations?' (1992) 71(3) *Foreign Affairs* 22.
Infantino, L: *Individualism in Modern Thought: From Adam Smith to Hayek* (London, Routledge 1998).
Jackson, R: *The Global Covenant* (Oxford, Oxford University Press 2003).
Jennings, RY: 'The Identification of International Law' in: B Cheng (ed), *International Law: Teaching and Practice* (London, Stevens & Sons 1982) 3.
Jennings, RY: 'The Judiciary, International and National, and the Development of International Law' (1996) 45 *International and Comparative Law Quarterly* 1.
Jessup, P: *A Modern Law of Nations* (Hamden/CT, Archon 1948, repr 1968).
Jhering, R v: *Der Zweck im Recht, vol I* (Leipzig, Breitkopf und Härtel, 3rd ed 1893).
Jhering, R: *Geist des römischen Rechts auf den verschiedenen Stufen seiner Entwicklung. Zweiter Theil, Zweite Abteilung* (Leipzig, Breitkopf & Härtel 1858).
Jolowicz, HF: *Lectures on Jurisprudence* (London, Athlone 1963).
Jung, HW: *Rechtserkenntnis und Rechtsfortbildung im Völkergewohnheitsrecht* (Göttingen, vr unipress 2012)
KaempferWH/LowenbergAD: 'The Theory of International Economic Sanctions: A Public Choice Approach' (1988) 78 *American Economic Review* 78.
Kammerhofer, J: 'Gaps, the Nuclear Weapons Opinion, and the Structure of International Legal Argument between Theory and Practice' (2009) 80 *British Yearbook of International Law* 333.
Kammerhofer, J: 'Hans Kelsen's Place in International Legal Theory' in A Orakhelashvili (ed), *Research Handbook on the Theory and History of International Law* (Cheltenham/Northampton, Edward Elgar 2011) 143.
Kammerhofer, J: 'Uncertainty in the Formal Sources of International Law: Customary International Law and Some of Its Problems' (2004) 15 *European Journal of International Law* 523.
Kant, I: *Akademie-Ausgabe, vol X: Briefwechsel aus den Jahren 1747–1787* (Berlin, Walter de Gruyter 1996).
Kant, I: *Perpetual Peace. A Philosophical Essay* (Campbell Smith tr, London, Swan Sunshine 1903).
Kantorowicz, H: *Der Kampf um die Rechtswissenschaft* (Heidelberg, Winter 1906).
Kauffman, SA: *Reinventing the Sacred* (New York, Basic Books 2008).
Kaufmann, A: *Analogie und Natur der Sache: Zugleich ein Beitrag zur Lehre vom Typus* (Heidelberg, CF Müller, 2nd ed 1982).
Kaufmann, E: *Das Wesen des Völkerrechts und die Clausula Rebus Sic Stantibus: Studie zum Rechts-, Staats- und Vertragsbegriffe* (Tübingen, Mohr 1911).
Kaufmann, J: *Conference Diplomacy: An Introductory Analysis* (Leiden, Martinus Nijhoff 1988).
Kedian, K: 'Customary International Law and International Human Rights Litigation in United States Courts: Revitalizing the Legacy of The Paquete Habana' (1995) 40 *William & Mary Law Review* 1395.
Kelsen, H: *Das Problem der Souveränität und die Theorie des Völkerrechts* (Tübingen, Mohr, 2nd ed 1928).

Kelsen, H: 'A "Dynamic" Theory of Natural Law' (1956) 16 *Louisiana Law Review* 597.

Kelsen, H: 'Die Einheit von Völkerrecht und staatlichem Recht' (1958) 19 *Zeitschrift für ausländisches öffentliches Recht und Völkerrecht* 234.

Kelsen, H: 'On the Basic Norm' (1959) 47 *California Law Review* 107.

Kelsen, H: 'The Natural Law Doctrine before the Tribunal of Science' (1949) 2 *The Western Political Quarterly* 481.

Kelsen, H: 'Théorie du droit international coutumier' (1939) *Revue internationale de la théorie du droit* 253.

Kelsen, H: *General Theory of Law and State* (Cambridge/MA, Harvard University Press 1945).

Kelsen, H: *Peace Through Law* (Chapel Hill, University of North Carolina Press 1944).

Kelsen, H: *Principles of International Law* (New York, Rinehart 1952).

Kelsen, H: *Society and Nature: A Sociological Inquiry* (Chicago, University of Chicago Press 1943).

Kelsen, H: *The Law of the United Nations* (London, Stevens & Sons 1950).

Kennedy, D: 'Kelsen als Pragmatist des Völkerrechts – Die Oliver Wendell Holmes Lectures des Jahres 1941' in A Carrino/G Winker, *Rechtserfahrung und Reine Rechtslehre* (Wien/New York, Springer 1995) 95.

Kennedy, D: 'Legal Education and the Reproduction of Hierarchy' (1982) 32 *Journal of Legal Education* 591.

Kennedy, D: *International Legal Structures* (Baden-Baden, Nomos 1987).

Kennedy, D: *The Dark Side of Virtue: Reassessing International Humanitarianism* (Princeton, Princeton University Press 2004).

Kim, RE/Mackey, B: 'International Environmental Law as a Complex Adaptive System' (2014) 14 *International Environmental Agreements* 5.

Kipp, H: *Völkerordnung und Völkerrecht im Mittelalter* (Cologne, Deutsche Glocke 1950).

Kissinger, H: *World Order: Reflections on the Character of Nations and the Course of History* (London, Allen Lane 2014).

Klabbers, J/Peters, A/Ulfstein, G: *The Constitutionalization of International Law* (Oxford, Oxford University Press 2009).

Klabbers, J/Piiparinen, T (eds): *Normative Pluralism in International Law: Exploring Global Governance* (Cambridge, Cambridge University Press 2013).

Klabbers, J: 'How to Defeat a Treaty's Object and Purpose Pending Entry into Force: Toward Manifest Intent' (2001) 34 *Vanderbilt Journal of Transnational Law* 283.

Kleinlein, T: *Konstitutionalisierung im Völkerrecht* (Heidelberg/New York, Springer 2011).

Knop, K: 'Here and There: International Law in Domestic Courts' (2000) 32 *New York University Journal of International Law and Politics* 501.

Koh, HH: 'Is there a "New" New Haven School of International Law?' (2007) 32 *Yale Journal of International Law* 559.

Kolb, R: 'General Principles of Procedural Law' in A Zimmermann/C Tomuschat/K Oellers-Frahm/CJ Tams (eds), *The Statute of the International Court of Justice: A Commentary* (Oxford, Oxford University Press, 2nd ed 2012).

Kolb, R: 'Les maximes juridiques en droit international public: Questions historiques et théoriques' (1999) 32 *Revue Belge de droit international* 407.

Kolb, R: 'Principles as Sources of International Law: With Special Reference to Good Faith' (2006) 53 *Netherlands International Law Review* 1.

Kolb, R: *Interprétation et Création du Droit International* (Bruxelles, Bruylant 2006).
Korhonen, O: *International Law Situated: An Analysis of the Lawyer's Stance Towards Culture, History and Community* (Hague, Kluwer Law 2000).
Korovin, E: *Mezhdunarodnoe pravo perekhodnogo vremeni* (Moscow/Petrograd, Gosudarstvennoe Izdatel'stvo 1923).
Koskenniemi, M/Leino, P: 'Fragmentation of International Law? Postmodern Anxieties' (2002) 15 *Leiden Journal of International Law* 553.
Koskenniemi, M: 'Alf Ross and Life Beyond Realism' (2003) 14 *European Journal of International Law* 653.
Koskenniemi, M: 'Declaratory Legislation: Towards a Genealogy of Neoliberal Legalism' in R Liivoja/J Petman (eds), *International Law-making: Essays in Honour of Jan Klabbers* (London, Routledge 2014) 17.
Koskenniemi, M: 'General Principles: Reflexions on Constructivist Thinking in International Law' (1985) 18 *Oikeustiede-Jurisprudentia* 120.
Koskenniemi, M: 'Letter to the Editors of the Symposion' (1999) 93 *American Journal of International Law* 351.
Koskenniemi, M: 'The Normative Force of Habit: International Custom and Social Theory' (1990) *1 Finnish Yearbook of International Law 77*.
Koskenniemi, M: *From Apology to Utopia: The Structure of International Legal Argument* (Cambridge, Cambridge University Press, reissue 2005).
Krabbe, H: *The Modern Idea of the State* (GH Sabine and WJ Shepard tr, Leiden, Martinus Nijhoff 1921).
Krisch, N: 'The Decay of Consent: International Law in an Age of Global Public Goods' (2014) 108 *American Journal of International Law* 1.
Krisch, N: *Beyond Constitutionalism: The Pluralist Structure of Postnational Law* (Oxford, Oxford University Press 2010).
Ku, J/Nzelibe, J: 'Do International Criminal Tribunals Deter or Exacerbate Humanitarian Atrocities?' (2006) 84 *Washington University Law Review* 776.
Kulski, WW: 'The Soviet Interpretation of International Law' (1955) 49 *American Journal of International Law* 518.
Landes, W/Posner, RA: *The Economic Structure of Tort Law* (Cambridge/MA, Harvard University Press 1987).
Lang, A: *The Politics of Aristotle: Introductory Essays* (London, Longmans 1886).
Langström, T: *Transformation in Russia and International Law* (Leiden, Martinus Nijhoff 2003).
Larenz, K: *Methodenlehre der Rechtswissenschaft* (Heidelberg, Springer, 6th ed 1991).
Lauterpacht, H: 'Codification and Development of International Law' (1955) 49 *American Journal of International Law* 16.
Lauterpacht, H: 'Decisions of Municipal Courts as a Source of International Law' (1929) 10 *British Yearbook of International Law* 65.
Lauterpacht, H: 'Some Observations on the Prohibition of "Non Liquet" and the Completeness of the Law' in FM van Asbeck (ed), *Symbolae Verzijl* (The Hague, Martinus Nijhoff 1958) 196.
Lauterpacht, H: *Private Law Sources and Analogies in Public International Law* (London, Longmans Green & Co 1927).
Lauterpacht, H: *The Development of International Law by the International Court* (London, Stevens and Sons 1958)
Lauterpacht, H: *The Function of Law in the International Community* (Oxford, Oxford University Press 1933).

Lebow, RN: *The Tragic Vision of Politics: Ethics, Interests and Orders* (Cambridge, Cambridge University Press 2003).
Legrand, P: 'On the Singularity of Law' (2006) 47 *Harvard International Law Journal* 517.
Lepard, BD: *Customary International Law: A New Theory With Practical Applications* (Cambridge, Cambridge University Press 2010).
Linderfalk, U: *On the Interpretation of Treaties: The Modern International Law as Expressed in the 1969 Vienna Convention on the Law of Treaties* (Heidelberg, Springer 2007).
Lorenz, W: 'General Principles of Law: Their Elaboration in the Jurisprudence of the Court of Justice of the European Communities' (1964) 13 *American Journal of Comparative Law* 1.
Lowe, V: *International Law* (Oxford, Oxford University Press 2007).
Luhmann, N: *Das Recht der Gesellschaft* (Frankfurt, Suhrkamp 1993).
Luhmann, N: *Zweckbegriff and Systemrationalität: Über die Funktion von Zwecken in sozialen Systemen* (Frankfurt, Suhrkamp, 6th ed 1999).
MacIntyre, A: *After Virtue* (South Bend/IL, University of Notre Dame Press, 2nd edn 1984).
Makarov, AN: 'Das Urteil des IGH im Fall Nottebohm' (1955) 16 *Zeitschrift für ausländisches öffentliches Recht und Völkerrecht* 407.
Makowski, J: *Podrecznik prawa miedzynarodowego* (Warszaw, Ksiazka 1948).
Malksöö, L: 'The History of International Legal Theory in Russia: a Civilizational Dialogue with Europe' (2008) 19 *European Journal of International Law* 211.
Mandelson, M: 'The Effects of Customary International Law on Domestic Law: An Overview' (2004) 4 *Non-State Actors and International Law* 75.
Mansell, W/Openshaw, K: *International Law: A Critical Introduction* (Oxford, Hart 2013).
Marck, S: *Substanz- und Funktionsbegriff in der Rechtsphilosophie* (Tübingen, Mohr 1925).
Mazower, M: *Governing the World: The History of an Idea* (New York and London, Penguin 2012).
McDougal, MS: 'International Law, Power, and Policy: A Contemporary Conception' (1954) 82 *Recueil des Cours* 137.
McDougal, MS: 'The Hydrogen Bomb Tests and the International Law of the Sea' (1955) 49 *American Journal of International Law* 356.
McGinnis, J/Somin, I: 'Should International Law Be Part of Our Law' (2007) 57 *Stanford Law Review* 1175.
McLachlan, C: 'The Principle of Systemic Integration and Article 31(3)(c) of the Vienna Convention' (2005) 54 *International and Comparative Law Quarterly* 279.
McNair, A: *The Law of Treaties* (Oxford, Oxford University Press 1961).
Meerning, J: 'Justice and Peace? How the International Criminal Tribunal Affects Societal Peace in Bosnia' (2005) 42 *Journal of Peace Research* 271.
Mendelson, M: 'The Effect of Customary International Law on Domestic Law: An Overview' (2004) 4 *Non-State Actors and International Law* 75.
Merkouris, P: *Article 31(3)(c) VCLT and the Principle of Systemic Integration* (Leiden, Brill 2015).
Merkouris, P: 'Interpreting the Customary Rules of Interpretation' (2017) 19 *International Community Law Review* 126.

Merton, RK: 'Manifest and Latent Functions' in RK Merton, *Social Theory and Social Structure* (New York, Free Press, enlarged ed 1968) 73.

Michaels, R: 'The Functional Method of Comparative Law' in M Reimann/R Zimmermann (eds), *Oxford Handbook of Comparative Law* (Oxford, Oxford University Press 2006) 340.

Mitchell, S/Powell, EJ: *Domestic Law Goes Global: Legal Traditions and International Courts* (Cambridge, Cambridge University Press 2011).

Moschtaghi, R: 'The Relation between International Law, Islamic Law and Constitutional Law of the Islamic Republic of Iran – A Multilayer System of Conflict?' (2009) 13 *Max Planck UN Yearbook* 376.

Murillo, ML: 'The Evolution of Codification in the Civil Law Legal Systems: Towards Decodification and Recodification' (2001) 11 *Journal of Transnational Law & Policy* 163.

Murphy, JB: *The Philosophy of Customary International Law* (Oxford, Oxford University Press 2014).

Murphy, SD: 'Codification, Progressive Development, or Scholarly Analysis? The Art of Packaging the ILC's Work Product' in M Ragazzi (ed), *The Responsibility of International Organizations: Essays in Memory of Sir Ian Brownlie* (Leiden, Martinus Nijhoff 2013) 29.

Muslehuddin, M: 'Islamic Jurisprudence and the Rule of Necessity and Need' (1973) 12 *Islamic Studies* 103.

Navari, C: 'The Concept of Practice in the English School' (2010) 17 *European Journal of International Relations* 611.

Negri, S: *I principi generali del processo internazionale nella giurisprudenza della Corte internazionale di Giustizia* (Naples, Edizione Scientifiche Italiane 2002).

Newman, SC: 'Duress as a Defence to War Crimes and Crimes Against Humanity' (2000) 166 *Military Law Review* 158.

Newton, M/May, L: *Proportionality in International Law* (Oxford, Oxford University Press 2014).

Nill, M : *Morality and Self-Interest in Protagoras Antiphon and Democritus* (Leiden, Brill 1985).

Nollkaemper, A: 'The Process of Legalisation After 1989 and its Contribution to the International Rule of Law' in J Crawford/S Nouwen (eds), *Select Proceedings of the European Society of International Law: Third Volume* (Oxford, Hart 2012) 89.

Nollkaemper, A: *National Courts and the International Rule of Law* (Oxford, Oxford University Press 2011).

Nolte, G: 'Between Informed Pragmatism, Morality and Form' in E Jouannet/H Ruiz-Fabri/JM Sorel (eds), *Regards d'une génération sur le droit international* (Paris, Pedone 2008) 277.

Nolte, G: 'Introduction' in G Nolte (ed), *Treaties and Subsequent Practice* (Oxford, Oxford University Press 2013) 1.

Nolte, G: 'Persisting and Developing between Hope and Threat: International Law during the Past Two Decades and Beyond' in J Crawford/S Nouwen (eds), *Select Proceedings of the European Society of International Law: Third Volume* (Oxford, Hart 2012) 74.

Nolte, G/Aust, H: 'European Exceptionalism?' (2013) 2 *Global Constitutionalism* 407.

Novak, MN et al: 'The Evolution of Eusociality' (2010) *Nature* 466, 1057.

Nozick, R: *Anarchy, State and Utopia* (Oxford, Blackwell 1974).

Oppenheim, L: *International Law: A Treatise* (London, Longmans Green & Co 1905).
Orakhelashvili, A: *The Interpretation of Acts and Rules in Public International Law* (Oxford, Oxford University Press 2008).
Örücü, E: 'Methodological Aspects of Comparative Law' (2006) 8 *European Journal of Law Reform* 29.
Oswald, M: 'Was There a Concept of "ágraphos nómos" in Classical Greece?' in EN Lee/APD Mourelatos/RM Rorty (eds), *Exegesis and Argument: Studies in Greek Philosophy Presented to Gregory Vlastos* (Assen, Humanities Press 1973).
Otto, JM (ed): *Sharia Incorporated: A Comparative Overview of the Legal Systems of Twelve Muslim Countries in Past and Present* (Leiden, Leiden University Press 2005).
Page, SE/Jones-Rooy, A: 'The Complexities of Global Systems History' (2010) 10 *Journal of the Historical Society* 345.
Parry, C: *The Sources and Evidences of International Law* (Manchester, University of Manchester Press 1965).
Pauwelyn, J/Wessels, R/Wouters, J: 'When Structures become Shackles: Stagnation and Dynamics in International Lawmaking' (2014) 25European Journal of International Law733.
Pauwelyn, J/Wouters, J (eds): *Informal International Lawmaking* (Oxford, Oxford University Press 2012).
Pauwelyn, J: 'At the Edge of Chaos? Foreign Investment Law as a Complex Adaptive System, How it Emerged and How it Can be Reformed' (2014) 29 *ICSID Review* 372.
Pavčnik, M: 'Die Frage der rechtlichen Grundnorm (Pitamic' Brief and Kelsen)' (2010) 96 *Archiv für Rechts- und Sozialphilosophie* 86.
Pawlik, M: *Die Reine Rechtslehre und die Rechtstheorie H.L.A. Hart: Ein kritischer Vergleich* (Berlin, Duncker & Humblot 1993).
Pellet, A: 'The Normative Dilemma: Will and Consent in International Law' (1988–9) 12 *Australian Yearbook of International Law* 22.
Peters, A/Schwenke, H: 'Comparative Law Beyond Post-Modernism' (2000) 49 *International and Comparative Law Quarterly* 800.
Petersen, J: *Adam Smith als Rechtstheoretiker* (Berlin, Walther de Gruyter 2012).
Petersen, J: *Freiheit unter dem Gesetz: Friedrich August von Hayeks Rechtsdenken* (Tübingen, Mohr Siebeck 2014).
Poggi, F: *Norme permissive* (Torino, Giapichelli 2004).
Pollock, F: *Oxford Lectures and Other Discourses* (London, Macmillan & Co 1890).
Posner, EA/Sykes, AO: 'An Economic Analysis of State and Individual Responsibility Under International Law' (2007) 9 *American Law and Economics Review* 72.
Posner, EA: *The Perils of Global Legalism* (Chicago, University of Chicago Press 2009).
Posner, RA: 'Hayek, Law and Cognition' (2005) 1 *New York University Journal of Law and Liberty* 147.
Posner, RA: 'Legal Reasoning from the Top Down and From the Bottom Up' (1992) 59 *University of Chicago Law Review* 433.
Posner, RA: *The Problems of Jurisprudence* (Cambridge/MA, Harvard University Press 1990).
Postema, GJ: 'Custom in International Law as Normative Practice' in A Perreau-Saussine/JB Murphy (eds), *The Nature of Customary Law: Legal, Historical and Philosophical Perspectives* (Cambridge, Cambridge University Press 2007) 279.

Pound, R: *Interpretations of Legal History* (New York, Macmillan 1923).

Pound, R: *The Spirit of the Common Law* (Boston, Marshall Jones 1921).

Prost, M: *The Concept of Unity in Public International Law* (Oxford, Hart 2012).

Putnam, H: *The Collapse of the Fact/Value Dichotomy and Other Essays* (Cambridge/MA, Harvard University Press 2008).

Putnam, RD: 'Diplomacy and Domestic Politics: The Logic of Two-Level Games' (1988) 42 *International Organization* 427.

Raimondo, F: *General Principles of Law in the Decisions of International Criminal Court and Tribunals* (Leiden, Martinus Nijhoff 2008).

Rauschning, D (ed): *The Vienna Convention on the Law of Treaties: Travaux Préparatoires* (Frankfurt, Metzler 1978).

Raustiala, K: 'The "Participatory Revolution" in International Environmental Law' (1997) 21 *Harvard Environmental Law Review* 537.

Ravier, AO: 'Globalization and Peace: A Hayekian Perspective' (2009) 1(10) *Libertarian Papers* 1.

Rawls, J: *A Theory of Justice* (Cambridge/MA, Harvard University Press 1971).

Rawls, J: *The Law of Peoples. With 'The Idea of Public Reason Revisited'* (Cambridge/MA, Harvard University Press 1999).

Raz, J: 'The Relevance of Coherence' in S Brewer (ed), *Moral Theory and Legal Reasoning* (New York and London, Garland 1998) 303.

Recaséns Siches, L: *Nueva Filosofía de la Interpretación del Derecho* (Mexico and Buenos Aires, Fondo de Cultura Economica 1958).

Reid, JP: 'The Jurisprudence of Liberty: The Ancient Constitution in the Legal Historiography of the Seventeenth and Eighteenth Centuries' in E Sandoz (ed), *The Roots of Liberty: Magna Charta, Ancient Constitution, and the Anglo-American Tradition of the Rule of Law* (Columbia/MO, University of Missouri Press 1993) 147.

Reid, JP: *Rule of Law: The Jurisprudence of Liberty in the Seventeenth and Eighteenth Century* (DeKalb, Northern Illinois University Press 2004).

Reisman, WM: 'The Cult of Custom in the Late 20th Century' (1987) 17 *California Western International Law Journal* 133.

Rentto, JP: '*Ius Gentium*: A Lesson from Aquinas' (1992) 3 *Finnish Yearbook of International Law* 103.

Rentto, JP: 'Postmodern Aquinas: A Fresh Start' in DW Hudson/D Moran (eds), *The Future of Thomism* (South Bend, University of Notre Dame Press 1992) 14.

Reynolds, NB: 'Law as Convention' (1989) 2 *Ratio Juris* 105.

Rezek, JF: 'Reciprocity as a Basis of Extradition' (1981) 52 *British Yearbook of International Law* 171.

Rheinstein, M: 'Teaching Comparative Law' (1937–8) 5 *University of Chicago Law Review* 615.

Ricoeur, P: 'The Teleological and Deontological Structures of Action: Aristotle and/or Kant?' (1987) 21 *Royal Institute of Philosophy Lecture Series* 99.

Riesbeck, D: 'Nature, Normativity, and Nomos in Antiphon, Fragment 44a' (2011) 65 *Phoenix* 268.

Roberts, A/Sivakumaran, S: 'Lawmaking by Nonstate Actors: Engaging Armed Groups in the Creation of International Humanitarian Law' (2012) 37 *Yale Journal of International Law* 108.

Roberts, A: 'Comparative International Law? The Role of National Courts in Creating and Enforcing International Law' (2011) 60 *International & Comparative Law Quarterly* 57.

Roberts, A: 'Traditional and Modern Approaches to Customary International Law: A Reconciliation' (2001) 95 *American Journal of International Law* 757.

Roberts, I/ Denza, E: 'Special Missions' in I Roberts (ed), *Satow's Diplomatic Practice* (Oxford, Oxford University Press, 6th ed 2009) 187.

Roberts, I (ed): *Satow's Diplomatic Practice* (Oxford, Oxford University Press, 6th ed 2009).

Rodiles Breton, A: 'Coalitions of the Willing: Coyuntura, Contexto y Propiedades. Un Primer Esbozo' (2007) 7 *Annuario Mexicano de Derecho International* 675.

Roland, H/Boyer, L: *Locutions Latines du Droit Français* (Paris, Librairie de la Cour de Cassation, 3rd ed 1993).

Romano, S: *Corso di Diritto Internazionale* (Padova, Milani 1926).

Romano, S: *L'ordinamento giuridico* (Pisa, Mariotti 1918).

Rosenfeld, M: *Law, Justice, Democracy, and the Clash of Cultures: A Pluralist Account* (Cambridge, Cambridge University Press 2011).

Ross, A: *Directives and Norms* (London, Routledge 1968).

Ross, A: *Kritik der sogenannten Praktischen Erkenntnis: Zugleich Prolegomena zu einer Kritik der Rechtswissenschaft* (Copenhagen, Munksgaard 1933).

Ross, A: *Lehrbuch des Völkerrechts* (M Brakas tr, Stuttgart, Kohlhammer 1951).

Ross, A: *On Law and Justice* (London, Stevens & Sons 1959).

Rousseau, C: *Principes généraux du droit international public I* (Paris, Sirey 1944).

Rubenfeld, J: 'Unilateralism and Constitutionalism' (2004) 79 *New York University Law Review*1971.

Rubin, AP: 'Pollution by Analogy: The Trail Smelter Arbitration' (1970) 50 *Oregon Law Review* 259.

Rubinstein, J/Guerrina, B: 'The Attorney-Client Privilege and International Arbitration' (2001) 18 *Journal of International Arbitration* 587.

Russell Mead, W: 'The Return of Geopolitics: The Revenge of the Revisionist Powers' (2014) 93(3) *Foreign Affairs* 69.

Russell, B: *The Problems of Philosophy* (Oxford, Oxford University Press, reissue 2001).

Sahni, IP: 'Max Weber's Sociology of Law: The Judge as Mediator' (2009) 9 *Journal of Classical Sociology* 209.

Sands, P: *Torture Team. Rumsfeld's Memo and the Betrayal of American Values* (New York, Palgrave Macmillan 2008).

Savigny, FC: *Of the Vocation of Our Time for Legislation and Jurisprudence* (Abraham Hayward tr, London, Littlewood & Co 1831).

Savigny, FC: *System des heutigen römischen Rechts, vol VIII* (Berlin, Veit u Co 1849).

Scalia, A: 'The Rule of Law as a Law of Rules' (1989) 56 *University of Chicago Law Review* 1175.

Scanlon, T: *What We Owe to Each Other* (Cambridge/MA, Belknap 1998).

Scelle, G: 'Le Droit constitutionnel international' in *Mélanges R. Carré de Malberg* (Paris, Recueil Sirey 1933).

Schachter, O: 'The Decline of the Nation-State and its Implication for International Law' (1998) 36 *Columbia Journal of Transnational Law* 7.

Schachter, O: 'The Emergence of International Environmental Law' (1991) 44 *Journal of International Affairs* 157.

Schachter, O: 'The Environment, Community, and International Law' (1989) 30 *Harvard International Law Journal* 393.

Schachter, O: *International Law in Theory and Practice* (Dordrecht, Martinus Nijhoff 1991).

Schaller, L: *Der Rechtsformalismus Kelsens und die thomistische Rechtsphilosophie: Vergleich zweier Systeme des Rechtsdenkens* (Fribourg, Kanisius 1949).

Scharf, MP/Centner, A/McClain, K: 'Foreword: Symposium International Law in Crisis' (2011) 44 *Case Western Reserve Journal of International Law* 1.

Scharf, MP: 'Seizing the Grotian Moment' (2010) 43 *Cornell International Law Journal* 440.

Schauer, F: 'Do Cases Make Bad Law?' (2006) 73 *University of Chicago Law Review* 882.

Scheuermann, WE: 'The Unholy Alliance of Carl Schmitt and Friedrich A. Hayek' (1997) 4 *Constellations* 172.

Schill, SW: *The Multilateralization of International Investment Law* (Cambridge, Cambridge University Press 2009).

Schmitt, C: 'Die Lage der europäischen Rechtswissenschaft' in C Schmitt, *Verfassungsrechtliche Aufsätze aus den Jahren 1924–1954* (Berlin, Duncker & Humblot, 4th ed 2003).

Schmitt, C: *Über die drei Arten des rechtswissenschaftlichen Denkens* (Berlin, Duncker & Humblot 1935) 386.

Schoenenbaum, TJ: 'Liability for Damages in Oil Spill Accidents: Evaluating the USA and International Law Regimes in the Light of Deepwater Horizon' (2012) 24 *Journal of Environmental Law* 395.

Schwarzenberger, G: *The Inductive Approach to International Law* (London, Stevens & Sons 1965).

Schweller, RL: 'Domestic Structure and Preventive War: Are Democracies more Pacific?' (1992) 44 *World Politics* 235.

Sen, A: 'Rational Fools: A Critique of the Behavioral Foundations of Economic Theory' (1977) 6 *Philosophy & Public Affairs* 317.

Sen, A: *Human Rights and Asian Values* (New York, Carnegie Council 1997).

Sen, A: *The Idea of Justice* (London, Penguin 2010).

Shany, Y: 'Dédoublement fonctionelle and the Mixed Loyalties of National and International Judges' in F Fontanelli (ed), *Shaping Rule of Law Through Dialogue: International and Supranational Experiences* (Maastricht, Europa Law Publishing 2009) 27.

Shaw, MN: 'The Heritage of States: The Principle of *Uti Possidetis Juris* Today' (1997) 67 *British Yearbook of International Law* 75.

Shaw, MN: 'The International Court of Justice and the Law of Territory' in C Tams/J Sloan (eds), *The Development of International Law by the International Court of Justice* (Oxford, Oxford University Press 2013) 151.

Shelton, D (ed): *International Law and Domestic Legal Systems* (Oxford, Oxford University Press 2011).

Shepsle, K: 'Congress Is a "They", not and "It": Legislative Intent as Oxymoron' (1992) 12 *International Review of Law & Economics* 239.

Sherwin, E: 'A Defense of Analogical Reasoning in Law' (1999) 66 *University of Chicago Law Review* 1179.

Sherwood Dunne, F: 'Book Review: *The Soviet Union and International Law*' (1936) 51 *Political Science Quarterly* 630.

Siems, M: *Comparative Law* (Cambridge, Cambridge University Press 2014).

Simma, B/Alston, P: 'The Sources of International Human Rights Law: Custom, *Ius Cogens*, and General Principles' (1988) 5 *Australian Yearbook of International Law* 82.

Simma, B: *Das Reziprozitätselement in der Entstehung des Völkergewohnheitsrechts* (München, Fink 1970).

Singer, M: 'The Act of State Doctrine of the United Kingdom: An Analysis, With Comparisons to United States Practice' (1981) 75 *American Journal of International Law* 283.

Siorat, L: 'Le problème des lacunes en droit international public' (1967) 3 *Revue Belge de droit international* 440.

Slaughter, AM: 'A Liberal Theory of International Law' (2000) 94 *Proceedings of the American Society of International Law* 240.

Slaughter, AM: 'A Typology of Transjudicial Communication' (1994) 29 *University of Richmond Law Review* 99.

Slaughter, AM: 'International Law in a World of Liberal States' (1995) 6 *European Journal of International Law* 503.

Slaughter, AM: *A New World Order* (Princeton, Princeton University Press 2004).

Sloan, J: 'Civilized Nations' in R Wolfrum (ed) *The Max Planck Encyclopedia of Public International Law* (Oxford, Oxford University Press 2012).

Smith, A: *Theory of Moral Sentiments* (London, A Millar, 6th ed 1790).

Smith, ML: 'The International Criminal Court: An Effective Means of Deterrence?' (2001) 167 *Military Law Review* 156.

Soler, S: *La Interpretación de la Ley* (Barcelona, Aries 1962).

Solum, LB: 'The Indeterminacy Crisis: Critiquing Critical Dogma' (1987) 54 *University of Chicago Law Review* 462.

Sørensen, M: *Les sources du droit international* (Copenhagen, Einar Munksgaard 1946).

Spiermann, O: '*Lotus* and the Double Structure of International Legal Argument' in LB de Chazournes/P Sands (eds), *International Law, the International Court of Justice and Nuclear Weapons* (Cambridge, Cambridge University Press 1999) 131.

Stahl, FJ: *Die Philosophie des Rechts* (Tübingen, Mohr, 5th ed 1878).

Staubach, P: 'The Interpretation of Unwritten International Law by Domestic Judges' in G Nolte/HP Aust (eds), *The Interpretation of International Law by Domestic Courts: Uniformity, Diversity, Coherence* (Oxford, Oxford University Press 2016) 113.

Stewart, DP/Wuerth, I: 'Kiobel v Royal Dutch Petroleum Co.: The Supreme Court and the Alien Tort Statute' (2013) 107 *American Journal of International Law* 601.

Stirling-Zanda, S: 'The Determination of Customary International Law in European Courts' (2004) 4 *Non-State Actors and International Law* 3.

Stone, J: '*Non-Liquet* and the Function of Law in the International Community' (1959) 35 *British Yearbook of International Law* 124.

Stone, J: 'On the Vocation of the International Law Commission' (1957) 57 *Columbia Law Review* 16.

Streck, W: 'Neo-Voluntarism: A New European Social Policy Regime?' (1995) 1 *European Law Journal* 31.

Strupp, K: 'Les règles générales du droit de la paix' (1934) 47-I*Recueil des Cours* 263.

Sunstein, C: 'On Analogical Reasoning' (1993) 106 *Harvard Law Review* 741.

Sur, S: *L'interprétation en droit international public* (Paris, Pichon 1974).

Sureda, AR: *Investment Treaty Arbitration: Judging under Uncertainty – Hersch Lauterpacht Memorial Lecture* (Cambridge, Cambridge University Press 2012).

Swift, J: *Gulliver's Travels into Several Remote Nations of the World* (London, A Moore 1726).

Szaif, J: '*Doxa* and *Episteme* as Modes of Acquaintance in *Republic* V' (2007) 4 *Les Études Platoniciennes* 253.

Talmon, S: 'Determining Customary International Law: Between Induction, Deduction and Assertion' (2014) 4 *Bonn Research Papers on Public International Law*.

Tammelo, I: 'On the Logical Openness of Legal Orders' (1959) 8 *American Journal of Comparative Law* 91.

Taracouzio, T: *The Soviet Union and International Law: A Study Based on the Legislation, Treaties and Foreign Relations of the Union of Socialist Soviet Republics* (New York, Macmillan & Co 1935).

Tarlock, D: 'Non-Governmental Organizations in the Development of International Environmental Law' (1992–3) 68 *Chicago-Kent Law Review* 61.

Taylor, C: *Philosophical Arguments* (Cambridge/MA, Harvard University Press 1995).

Telman, DAJ: 'International Legal Positivism and Legal Realism' in J Kammerhofer/J d'Aspremont (eds), *International Legal Positivism in a Post-Modern World* (Cambridge, Cambridge University Press 2014) 241.

Teubner, G: 'Global Bukowina: Legal Pluralism in the World Society' in G Teubner (ed), *Global Law Without a State* (Dartmouth, Aldershot 1997).

Teubner, G: *Recht als autopoietisches System* (Frankfurt, Suhrkamp 1989).

Thirlway, H: 'Concepts, Principles, Rules and Analogies: International and Municipal Law Reasoning' (2002) 294 *Recueil de Cours* 267.

Thirlway, H: *The Sources of International Law* (Oxford, Oxford University Press 2014).

Tomišić, I: 'In Memoriam Leonidas Pitamic' (1972) 23 *Österreichische Zeitschrift für Öffentliches Recht* 201.

Tomuschat, C: *Human Rights: Between Idealism and Realism* (Oxford, Oxford University Press, 2nd ed 2008).

Trachtman, JP: *The Future of International Law: Global Government* (New York, Cambridge University Press 2012).

Trapp, KN/Mills, A: 'Smooth Runs the Water Where the Brook is Deep: The Obscured Complexities of Germany v Italy' (2012) 1 *Cambridge Journal of International and Comparative Law* 153.

Treves, T: 'Customary International Law' in R Wolfrum (ed), *Max Planck Encyclopedia of Public International Law* (Oxford, Oxford University Press 2012).

Treviranus, HD: *Außenpolitik im demokratischen Rechtsstaat* (Tübingen, Mohr Siebeck 1966).

Triepel, H: *Völkerrecht und Landesrecht* (Leipzig, Hirschfeld 1899).

Tunkin, G: 'General Principles of Law in International Law' in M René et al (eds), *International Festschrift für Alfred Verdross zum 80. Geburtstag* (München, Fink 1971) 523.

Turner, S: *The Social Theory of Practices* (Chicago, University of Chicago Press 2000).

Twining, W: 'Globalisation and Comparative Law' in E Örücü/D Nelken (eds), *Comparative Law: A Handbook* (Oxford, Hart 2007) 69.

Tzanakopoulos, A: *Disobeying the Security Council: Countermeasures against Wrongful Sanctions* (Oxford, Oxford University Press 2011).

Unger, KF: *Völkergewohnheitsrecht – objektives Recht oder Geflecht bilateraler Beziehungen. Seine Bedeutung für einen 'persistent objector'* (München, tuduv Verlagsgesellschaft 1978).

van de Haar, E: 'Hayekian Spontaneous Orders and the International Balance of Power' (2011) 16 *The Independent Review* 101.

Vandevelde, KJ: 'Treaty Interpretation: A Negotiator's Perspective' (1988) 21 *Vanderbilt Journal of Transnational Law* 281.

Vázquez, C: 'Alien Tort Claims and the Status of Customary International Law' (2012) 106 *American Journal of International Law* 531.

Verdross, A/Simma, B: *Universelles Völkerrecht* (Berlin, Duncker & Humblot 1982).

Verdross, A: 'Entstehungsweisen und Geltungsgrund des universellen völkerrechtlichen Gewohnheitsrechts' (1969) 29 *Zeitschrift für ausländisches öffentliches Recht und Völkerrecht* 635

Verdross, A: *Die Verfassung der Völkerrechtsgemeinschaft* (Wien/Berlin, Springer 1926).

Villiger, ME: *Customary International Law and Treaties* (Leiden, Martinus Nijhoff 1985).

Virally, M: 'Contribution to the Discussion' in A Cassese/JHH Weiler (eds), *Change and Stability in International Lawmaking* (Berlin, Walter de Gruyter 1988) 110.

Vitanyi, B: 'La signification de la "généralité" des principes de droit' (1976) 80 *Revue Générale de Droit International Public* 536.

Vogel, J: 'Individuelle Verantwortlichkeit im Völkerstrafrecht' (2002) 114 *Zeitschrift für die gesamte Strafrechtswissenschaft* 403.

Vöneky, S: 'Analogy in International Law' in R Bernhardt (ed), *Max Planck Encyclopedia of Public International Law* (Oxford, Oxford University Press 2012).

Waldron, J: 'The Rule of International Law' (2006) 30 *Harvard Journal of Law & Public Policy* 15.

Waldron, J: *"Partly Laws Common To All Mankind": Foreign Law in American Courts* (New Haven, Yale University Press 2012).

Walt, SD: *Why Jurisprudence Doesn't Matter for Customary International Law*- University of Virginia School of Law Public Law and Legal Theory Research Paper2012/36.

Walzer, M: 'The Moral Standing of States: A Response to Four Critiques' (1980) 9 *Philosophy & Public Affairs* 209.

Weber, M: *The Theory of Social and Economic Organization* (New York, Free Press 1968).

Weeramantry, CG: 'Custom: The Growing Role of Customary International Law' in CG Weeramantry, *Universalising International Law* (Leiden, Martinus Nijhoff 2004) 219.

Weller, M: 'Modesty Can Be a Virtue: Judicial Economy in the *Kosovo* Opinion?' (2011) 24 *Leiden Journal of International Law* 127.

Wengler, W: *Völkerrecht: Band I* (Berlin, Springer 1964).

Wilson, EO: *The Social Conquest of Earth* (New York, Liveright 2012).

Wilson, P: 'The English School's Approach to International Law' in C Navari (ed), *Theorising International Society: English School Methods* (Basingstoke, Palgrave Macmillan 2008) 167.

Winfield, HD: *Hegel and Mind. Rethinking Philosophical Psychology* (Basingstoke, Palgrave Macmillan 2010).

Wolfke, K: *Custom in Present International Law* (Dordrecht, Martinus Nijhoff, 2nd ed 1993).

Wolfrum, R: 'Advisory Opinions: Are they a Suitable Alternative for the Settlement of International Disputes?' in R Wolfrum/I Gätzschmann (eds), *International Dispute Settlement: Room for Innovations?* (Berlin/Heidelberg, Springer 2013) 239.

Wood, M: 'Legal Advisers' in R Wolfrum (ed) *The Max Planck Encyclopedia of Public International Law* (Oxford, Oxford University Press 2012).

Worster, WT: 'The Inductive and the Deductive Approach to Customary International Law Analysis: Traditional and Modern Approaches' (2014) 45 *Georgetown International Law Journal* 445.

Wright, GH von: *Norm and Action: A Logical Enquiry* (London, Routledge 1963).

Xue, H: 'The Role of the ILC's Work in Promoting Peace and Security' in G Nolte (ed), *Peace through International Law: The Role of the International Law Commission* (Heidelberg, Springer 2009) 183.

Xue, H: *Transboundary Damage in International Law* (Cambridge, Cambridge University Press 2003).

Yang, X: *State Immunity in International Law* (Cambridge, Cambridge University Press 2012).

Yee, S: 'Arguments for Cleaning Up Article 38(1) (b) and (1) (c) of the ICJ Statute' (2007) 4 *Romanian Journal of International Law* 34.

Yelin, LS: 'Head of State Immunity as Sole Executive Lawmaking' (2011) 44 *Vanderbilt Journal of Transnational Law* 911.

Yoo, J/Ku, J: *Taming Globalization: International Law, the US Constitution, and New World Order* (Oxford and New York, Oxford University Press 2012).

Zakaria, F: *The Post-American World* (New York, Norton & Co 2009).

Zander, M: 'The Act of State Doctrine' (1959) 53 *American Journal of International Law* 826.

Zweigert, K/Kötz, H: *An Introduction to Comparative Law* (T Weir tr, Oxford, Oxford University Press, 3rd ed 1998).

Zweigert, K: 'Des solutions identiques par des voies différentes' (1966) 18 *Revue Internationale de Droit Comparé* 5.

Index

For Product Safety Concerns and Information please contact our EU
representative GPSR@taylorandfrancis.com
Taylor & Francis Verlag GmbH, Kaufingerstraße 24, 80331 München, Germany

www.ingramcontent.com/pod-product-compliance
Ingram Content Group UK Ltd.
Pitfield, Milton Keynes, MK11 3LW, UK
UKHW022118190926
475702UK00013B/1507